Readings in
BEHAVIOR MODIFICATION

Special Learning Corporation

42 Boston Post Rd. Guilford, Connecticut 06437

SPECIAL LEARNING CORPORATION

Publisher's Message:

The Special Education Series is the first comprehensive series designed for special education courses of study. It is also the first series to offer such a wide variety of high quality books. In addition, the series will be expanded and up-dated each year. No other publications in the area of special education can equal this. We stress high quality content, a superb advisory and consulting group, and special features that help in understanding the course of study. In addition we believe we must also publish in very small enrollment areas in order to establish the credibility and strength of our series. We realize the enrollments in courses of study such as Autism, Visually Handicapped Education, or Diagnosis and Placement are not large. Nevertheless, we believe there is a need for course books in these areas and books that are kept up-to-date on an annual basis! Special Learning Corporation's goal is to publish the highest quality materials for the college and university courses of study. With your comments and support we will continue to do this.

John P. Quirk

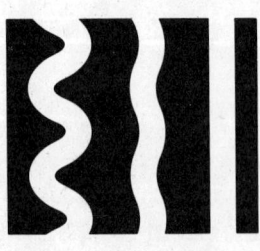

©1978 by Special Learning Corporation, Guilford, Connecticut 06437

All rights reserved. No part of this book may be reproduced, stored, or communicated by any means--without written permission from Special Learning Corporation.

First Edition
1 2 3 4 5

ISBN No. 0-89568-004-1

Manufactured by the Redson Rice Corporation, Chicago, Illinois

SPECIAL EDUCATION SERIES

- ● Autism
- ● Behavior Modification
- Biological Bases of Learning Disabilities
- Brain Impairments
- Career and Vocational Education
- Child Abuse
- Child Development
- Child Psychology
- Cognitive and Communication Skills
- Creative Arts
- Curriculum and Materials
- ● Deaf Education
- Developmental Disabilities
- ● Diagnosis and Placement
- Down's Syndrome
- ● Dyslexia
- Early Learning
- Educational Technology
- ● Emotional and Behavioral Disorders
- Exceptional Parents
- ● Gifted Education
- Hyperactivity
- ● Learning Disabilities
- Learning Theory
- ● Mainstreaming
- ● Mental Retardation
- Multiple Handicapped Education
- Occupational Therapy
- ● Physically Handicapped Education
- Pre-School and Day Care Education
- ● Psychology of Exceptional Children
- Reading Skill Development
- Research and Development
- Severe Mental Retardation
- Slow Learner Education
- Social Learning
- ● Special Education
- ● Speech and Hearing
- Testing and Diagnosis
- ● Visually Handicapped Education

● Published Titles • Major Course Areas

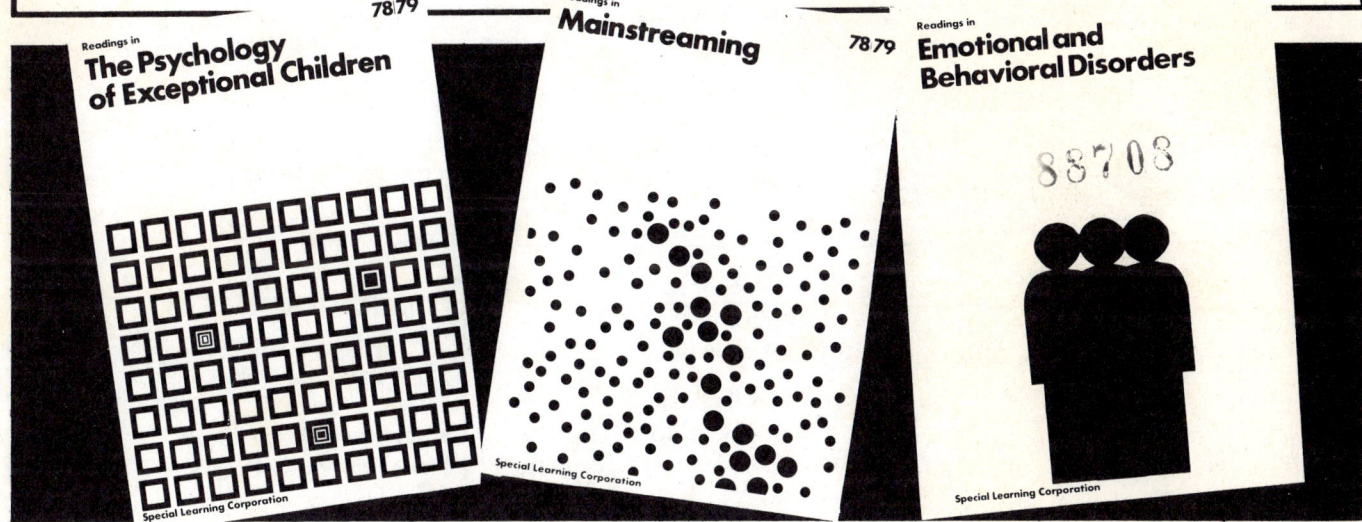

SENIOR AUTHOR

HERBERT GOLDSTEIN, currently at New York University and formerly of Yeshiva University, is a professor of Special Education and Director of the Curriculum Research and Development Center in Mental Retardation. He received his Ed.D from the University of Illinois and was a Fulbright Scholar and Lecturer in Mental Retardation at the University of Oslo. A coauthor of the Illinois Curriculum Guide for Mentally Handicapped Children, Professor Goldstein has written extensively about special education. He also has served as an editorial consultant for the American Association on Mental Deficiency and the Council for Exceptional Children.

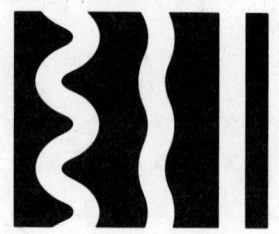

Special Education Series Content Specialists

Dr. Judy Smith
Director, Special Education
Teacher-Training Program
Alexandria, Virginia

Ms. Carlene Van Etten
Dept. of Special Education
University of New Mexico
Albuquerque, New Mexico

Dr. Gary Adamson
Dept. of Special Education
University of New Mexico
Albuquerque, New Mexico

Dr. Malcolm Norwood
Director of Dissemination
Bureau of Education for the
   Handicapped
Washington, D.C.

Advisory Board

Ann Fabe Isaacs
Chief Executive Officer
The National Association for
   Creative Children and Adults
Cincinnati, Ohio

Joseph Sullivan
Area Cooperative Educational
   Services
Director, Village School
North Haven, Connecticut

Judith Kaufman
Associate Professor
Ferkauf Graduate School of
   Humanities and Social Sciences
Yeshiva University, New York

Theodore Bergeron
Former Executive Director
Shoreline Association for the
   Retarded and Handicapped
Chapel Hill, North Carolina

Lorraine H. Marchi
Founder, National Association for
the Visually Handicapped
New York, N.Y.

E. Eugene Black
Division of Special Education,
State Department of Education
Sacramento, California

Cecil Bobo
Consultant
Exceptional Children and Youth
State Department of Education
Montgomery, Alabama

Conwell G. Strickland
Department of Special Education
Baylor University
Waco, Texas

Field-Testing and Reviewers

Ms. Eida Lynn Hinson
Infant Intervention Specialist,
Shoreline Association for Retarded
   and Handicapped,
Guilford, Connecticut

Ms. Dona Chiappe
Director, Shoreline Learning Center
Guilford, Connecticut

Ms. Mary Ellen Ryan
Early Education Instructor,
Department of Mental Retardation,
Waterford, Connecticut

International Advisory Board

Sweden
Karl Gustav Stukat
Goteborg, Sweden

Lars Alin
Professor, Psychological Institute
Göteburg University
Göteburg, Sweden

France
Madame Grandrut
Secretariat aux Handicap

United Kingdom
Christopher Jones
Professor of Special Education

Mexico
Jean de-Blumeville
Director of Special Projects
Mexico City, Mexico

Puerto Rico
Sra. Virguinia Stgo Udo Torres
Department of Health
Santurce, Puerto Rico

Norway
Karl Evang M.D.
Director of General Health Services
Oslo, Norway

Barbara Halstromm
De Blindas Forening
Enskede, Norway

Trygve Bore
Head of Division for Special Schools
Oslo, Norway

CONTENTS

Glossary of terms viii
Topic matrix ix

1. The Origins of Behavior Therapy

Preface 1

Overview 3

1. **"Therapy Between the Pages,"** Janet Barkas, *Human Behavior,* Vol. 4 No. 3, March 1975. 4
A deeply thought out analysis of bibliotherapy, taking into consideration the individual problems of success or failure which make a person seek help in solving human problems.

2. **"Ben Franklin's Pursuit of Perfection,"** John R. Snortum, *Psychology Today,* Vol. 9 No. 11, April 1976. 7
Benjamin Franklin applied the basic principles of behavior modification almost two hundred years before B.F. Skinner's birth, to manage his own personal faults.

3. **"Why You Do What You Do-Sociobiology: A New Theory of Behavior,"** *Time Magazine,* August 1, 1977. 9
With the concepts of social theory falling by the wayside with the 1970's, we find the emergence of a new doctrine of sociobiology which shows us that man is caught up in history and only able to exercise his free will within the limits of his genes.

4. **"Shapers At Work,"** Kenneth Goodall, *Psychology Today,* Vol. 6 No. 6, November 1972. 15
A far-reaching overview of the effective use of Skinnerian psychology as used in classrooms, kitchens, rehabilitation wards, prisons, hospitals, churches, reform schools, nursing homes, day-care centers, factories, movie theatres, community mental health centers, stores, recreation centers all over the world.

2. Behavior Modification in the Classroom

Overview 33

5. **"How Can This Child Be Helped?"** Hugh Carberry, *Instructor,* January 1976. 34
A step by step analysis of how to help four types of troubled learners attain more effective behavior patterns.

6. **"Your Praise Can Smother Learning,"** David L. Martin, *Learning,* Vol. 5 No. 6, February 1977. 36
A teacher's program of effective use of praise in the classroom to condition academic behavior toward specific tasks, not persons.

7. **"I'm Just Plain Dumb!"-how to change negative self-concepts in low ability children,** James R. Watson, *Today's Educatio,* Vol. 62 No. 3, March 1973. 41
An educational approach which is laid out by steps in order to counteract and contradict negative self-concepts in low-ability children.

8. **"Behavior Modification-an approach to education of young children with learning and behavior difficulties,"** William I. Gardner, Ph.D., The National Easter Seal Society for Crippled Children and Adults, 1975. 43
A humanizing behavior modification approach thoughtfully executed especially for those young children with learning problems with emphasis on acquisition of positive behavioral skills.

9. **"Punch Me, I Earned It,"** Frances Crow, Dede Johnston, Margery Meeks, Phillip Wilson, *Teaching Exceptional Children,* Vol. 8 No. 1, Fall 1975. 60
This modification program is designed around the use of a punch card to reward good behavior for children with social, emotional, intellectual, and/or learning difficulties which has proved successful for the students and staff.

10. **"Effects of Touch and Verbal Reinforcement on the Classroom Behavior of Emotionally Disturbed Boys,"** J. Eugene Clements, D.B. Tracy, *Exceptional Children.* 63
Potentialities of the use of touch and verbal reinforcement on classroom behavior of 10 emotionally disturbed boys is analyzed as to possible cumulative effects.

11. **"Pseudo-Retardation As A Form of Learning Disability: The Case of Jean,"** Denis H. Stott, Ph.D., *Journal Of Learning Disabilities,* Vol. 9 No. 6, June/July 1976. 64
Rehabilitation of a four-year-old girl suspected of playing the role of a low-grade retardate is highlighted through use of a behavior modification program.

12. **"Behavioral Disorders; Teachers Perceptions,"** *Exceptional Children,* February 1977. 69
The factors of how teachers perceive the behavior of their students is discussed along with the importance of determining the needs of both in the process.

13. **"Behavior Modification: Teacher Training and Attitudes,"** William A. Stewart, Gay Goodman, Brad Hammond, *Exceptional Children,* Vol. 42 No. 7, April 1976. 71
Viable alternatives for improving classroom behavior and increasing achievement levels

14. "Monkeying Around, or How To Make Mistakes Pay Off," Bill Harin, Bonnie Bernstein, *Teacher*, January 1977. ... 73
Strategies of supportive behavior which encourage children to "monkey around" with their language and capitalize on their mistakes are evaluated.

15. "In Praise of Praise," Regina Hackett, *American Education*, Vol. 11 No. 2, March 1975. ... 75
An Oregon based program devised for hyperactive children which accentuates their positive behavior through the use of praise.

16. "Altering Schedules of Reinforcement for Improved Classroom Behavior," Ronnie N. Alexander, Cathy H. Apfel, *Exceptional Children*, Vol. 43 No. 2, October 1976. ... 78
The use of classroom token reinforcement programs is discussed with resulting target behavior modification and its consequences.

17. "Classrooms for the Autistic Child," Wayne Sage, *Human Behavior*, Vol. 4 No. 3, March 1975. ... 81
A pioneering group of California educators have found that autistic children can achieve and learn in a classroom setting through behavior modification techniques, regardless of the fact that they were once considered uneducable.

18. "Helping Teachers Work With 'Unteachable' Children," W. Gregory Allard, John M. Dodd, Rowena B. Foos, *Children Today*, Vol. 4 No. 5, September/October 1975. ... 86
The results of a 4½ week workshop designed for teachers who work with children in special classes of severe problems of learning.

19. "Role Playing and Behavior Modification: A Demonstration With Mentally Retarded Children," L. Gerald Buchan, Sally Teed, Craig Peterson, *Clearing House*, Vol. 50 No. 2, October 1976. ... 88
A teaching tool of role playing and behavior modification programs is laid out for teaching curriculum so that students might help teach each other.

20. "Behavior Modification: Here, There and Everywhere," Robert J. Trotter, *Science News*, Vol. 103, April 21, 1973. ... 92
The widespread applicability of behavioral technology at work is examined through progress at Achievement Place where juvenile delinquents are treated for their behavioral problems with efficient results.

FOCUS ... 96

3. Methods of Behavior Modification

Overview ... 99

21. "Teaching Independence," Joanne Mitchell, *American Baby*, August 1977. ... 100
Distressed by her child's disruptive behavior, one woman relates her program for creating more independence, and therefore decreasing negative behavior.

22. "Days of Anguish, Moments of Hope for a Child Called Noah," Josh Greenfeld, *Today's Health*, Vol. 50 No. 6, June 1972. ... 102
Written one year after the classic study about the child called Noah, this follow up report traces his progress in a behavior modification setting at U.C.L.A.

23. "Does Your Quirk Irk You...and others too?" Neal Ashby, *Family Health*, Vol. 9 No. 3, March 1977. ... 112
The author looks at common idiosyncracies and suggests several ways of extinguishing or coping with them.

24. "The Torture Cure," Jessica Mitford, *Harper's*, Vol. 247 No. 1479, August 1973. ... 115
This well known author gives us a look at California prison treatment circles, which carry out secret "behavior modification" programs through drugs such as Prolixin, brainwashing techniques.

25. "Behavioral Training Strategies in Sheltered Workshops for the Severely Develomentally Disabled," Paul Weitman, Adelle Renzaglia, Richard Schutz, *Education and Training of the Mentally Retarded*. ... 122
A three section behavioral analysis of learning and behavior problems which provide a direction for treatment for the severely developmentally disabled.

26. "Stop Putting Up With Put-Downs," Neal Ashby, *Today's Health*, Vol. 53, No. 7, July/August 1975. ... 129
Assertive Training techniques are outlined and elaborated on through the premise that meek behavior is learned behavior.

27. "AUTISM: A Defeatable Horror: How Parents Can Treat Their Troubled Children," Laura Schreibman, Robert L. Koegel, *Psychology Today*, March 1975. ... 134
A significant step forward in the treatment of autism, which previously had been termed untreatable, is brought forward in a five point behavior modification program.

28. "How Never To Be Late Again," James Hailey, *The Saturday Evening Post*, Vol. 249 No. 1, January/February 1977. ... 139
The author plots a point by point program of how to break the bad habit of being late through the use of 60 minutes, which can result in fewer mental pressures.

29. "Employing Negative Reinforcement to Establish and Transfer Control of a Severely Retarded and Aggressive Nineteen Year Old," Dennis E. Mithaug, David A. Hanawalt, *AAESPH Review,* Vol. 2 No. 1, March 1977.   142
   The procedures involved in applying aversive stimulus to decrease negative behavior in a severely retarded girl is reviewed.

30. "The Fear of Open Space," *Human Behavior,* Vol. 6 No. 5, May 1977.   151
   Agoraphobia has been up to now only partially treatable, but a British group at Oxford have developed this home-based behavior program.

4. Ethical Issues in Behavior Modification

Overview   153

31. "Is the Pigeon Always Right?" Edgar Z. Friedenberg, *Ramparts,* Vol. 13 No. 5, December 1974/January 1975.   154
   Although the author finds behavior modification to be a highly effective technique, he also views it as an unauthentic substitute for love and will.

32. "Humanism vs. Behaviorism," Madeline Hunter, *Instructor,* Vol. LXXXVI No. 8, April 1977.   160
   An end to the battle between humanists and behaviorists is stressed, for without the tools of science.

33. "Behavioral Technology: A Negative Stand," James F. Day, *Intellect,* February 1974.   162
   The author takes B.F. Skinner, and behavioral technology to task with its controls and pressures, suggesting free and more flexible.

34. "Brain Surgery to Control Behavior," B.J. Mason, *Ebony,* Vol. XXVIII No. 4, February 1973.   165
   A controversial look at surgical procedures which are administered on the brain.

35. "The Complete Behavior Modifier: Confessions of an Overzealous Operant Conditioner," Roger MacNamara, *Mental Retardation,* Vol. 15 No. 1, February 1977.   173
   A pointed look at past and future impacts of behavior modification programs, its rights, its wrongs, along with proposals.

5. Self Behavior Modification Techniques

Overview   177

36. "Behavior Therapy: A Road to Self-control," G. Terrence Wilson, Gerald C. Davison, *Psychology Today,* Vol. 9 No. 5, October 1975.   178
   Strategies of behavioral treatment which allow the client, not the doctor, to pick goals.

37. "We're Gonna Tear You Down and Put You Back Together," Mark Brewer, *Psychology Today,* Vol. 9 No. 3, August 1975.   182
   Pop-psych is examined through Erhard Seminars Training, or EST which stresses systematic self-delusion being replaced with hope in finding personal fulfillment.

38. "The Discovery of Middle Age," William Bridges, *Human Behavior,* Vol. 6 No. 5, May 1977.   189
   A comprehensive look at midlife transitions with helpful suggestions for behavior modification.

39. "How to Overcome Shyness," Philip G. Zimbardo, *Ladies Home Journal,* Vol. XCIV No. 5, May 1977.   193
   The authors offer specific skills of behavior to overcome shyness through assertion techniques of self-initiation.

40. "The Liberated Grandmother," Dorothy C. Finkelhor, Ph.D., *Modern Maturity,* Vol. 19 No. 2, April/May 1976.   197
   This well-planned program is laid out for grandmothers who would like to "liberate" their behavior for an untypical slice of life.

41. "Psychotherapy After Forty," T.L. Brink, Ph.D., *Mental Hygiene,* Vol. 60 No. 2, Summer 1976.   200
   The aged and their families share case histories of how they changed their behavior in the second half of their lives.

42. "Mistakes That Can Ruin Your Life, and how to avoid them," Arnold Lazarus, Ph.D., Allen Fay, M.D., *Good Housekeeping,* October 1975.   203
   Two noted doctors show how one may cause his own emotional problems and what he can do to change his behavior with the goal being inner peace and balance.

Index   206
Appendix   208

GLOSSARY OF TERMS

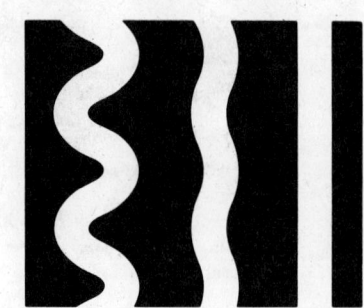

apprehensive child A child who approaches most learning tasks by being frightened of anything new, strange, or complex in nature, thus equating learning with anxiety which tends to further confuse and disorganize his thought processes.

assertive training Employment of basic role-playing activities which are designed to bring out more assertive behavior through practical application, perhaps in group therapy.

aversive conditioning Programmed events which are designed to reduce need through deprivation of reinforcement which will result in appropriate behavior due to the value of survival.

behavior modification A set of educational procedures designed to influence and develop the occurrence of a wide range of language, social, emotional, cognitive, motor, and perceptual behavioral patterns.

behavior therapy A mid 19th century outgrowth of classical conditioning experimentation and learning theories of psychological study based on scientific data.

chaining The connecting together in a sequence of two or more previously learned responses before reinforcement is presented.

compulsion The irresistable impulse to act, regardless of the rationality of the motivation or force of the act itself.

conditioned response Repeated actions of appropriate behavior in order to gain primary reinforcers.

contingencies Environmental conditions or factors which determine a response, be it conditioned or unconditioned.

deviant behavior Learned behaviors as a result of the failure of social and physical environmental factors which directly determine behavior patterns.

hypochondria Persistant neurotic feelings of conviction that one is going to be ill, often accompanied by real pain, when real illness is neither actually present nor likely.

impulsive children A child who cannot focus either his auditory or visual attention long enough to learn, and who displays disruptive behavior toward direction.

negative children A child who typically pouts and refuses to begin work, is antagonistic when he experiences failure or disappointment, thus often resulting in violence and general negativism.

negative reinforcement Behavior which results in the removal or termination of events that are unpleasant in consequence.

operant conditioning The use of primary reinforcers to obtain unconditioned responses or conditioned responses in relation to determined contingencies.

passive-dependent children A child who perceives the teacher as doing the work and presents himself the helpless receiver who never takes the initiative needed for the process of learning.

positive reinforcement Strengthened behavior through receipt of pleasurable consequences or the removal of unpleasant consequences.

primary reinforcers The use of food, praise, or other natural materials as reward for appropriate behavior.

psychotherapy Psychological treatment of mental, emotional, and nervous disorders.

role reversal A technique where an individual is allowed to reverse his role, such as interviewer becoming the interviewee, thus increasing the reality of the given situation to the individual.

role playing The planned process in which the person takes on the characteristics of another so as to discover appropriate behavioral alternatives to be employed in given situations.

scientific behaviorism Scientific experimentation and theory of behavior.

startle response Teacher behavior designed for use in the autistic classroom where loud shouts of "no!" are coupled with slaps on the table to gain desired behavioral attention.

target behavior Those behaviors which will directly benefit from treatment through modification, such as learning disabilities, physical handicaps, social and educational disturbances, mental health, and personal betterment.

TOPIC MATRIX

Readings in Behavior Modification provides the college student in special education a comprehensive overview of the subject. The book is designed to follow a basic course of study.

COURSE OUTLINE:

Behavior Modification Techniques for Exceptional Children

I. Identifying target behaviors
II. Collecting data
III. Designing objectives
IV. Planning and implementing interventions
V. Evaluating program components

Readings in Behavior Modification

I. The Origins of Behavior Therapy
II. Behavior Modification in the Classroom
III. Methods of Behavior Modification
IV. Ethical Issues in Behavior Modification
V. Self Behavior Modification Techniques

Related Special Learning Corporation Titles

I. Readings in Special Education
II. Readings in Psychology of Exceptional Children
III. Readings in Autism
IV. Readings in Emotional and Behavioral Disorders

PREFACE

Behavior modification first grew out of the American reaction to the growing philosophy among post World War Two scientists, that it was the environment that shaped mankind. Today it is challenging the more traditional psychological ideas of behaving man. In making this challenge, behavior modification has grown into a social and scientific phenomenon. In several diverse areas of study, it's philosophies and techniques are applied in the hope of altering man's behavior.

Although the basis of behavior modification is grounded in solid laboratory and actual-life experiments, there exists much skepticism on the part of experts in a variety of disciplines. Advocates of behavior modification attempt to alter these doubts by providing new explanations for past problems.

One of the most important opposers of behavior modification is Dr. Carl Rogers. He favors the "nondirective" approach, in which the therapist does not take an active role in the behavior change process. Instead he merely provides a comfortable setting and an interested ear for the patient. Using these factors, the patient, in essence changes his own behavior. the patient. Using these factors, the patient, in essence changes his own behavior.

Behaviorists feel that change may take place in such a situation, but the concept of behavior modification is the causative factor. As the therapist listens to the patient he responds to "healthy" speech with verbal reinforcement, therefore resulting in the extinction of the "unhealthy" speech, clearly a behavior modification based event.

In the final analysis, the controversy and debate surrounding behavior modification will rage on. Questions must be first answered such as why control mans behavior, and what in man makes this necessary? It was once pointed out by Aldous Huxley that "all of the political, social, and industrial revolutions through which man has passed are as nothing compared to the behavioral revolution now beginning."

Origins of Behavior Modification

Despite the fact that isolated instances of the application of behavior modification principles have been reported much earlier, research and training in the concept has taken place primarily in the past two decades. Development has been swift and the acceptance of behavior modification is taking place in a wide variety of disciplines.

The earliest application of conditioning principles to behavior problems dates back to the turn of the twentieth century when Pavlov and his co-workers in Russia and Watson in the United States began their work with classic conditioning. Both men attempted to account for complex human interaction by establishing conditioning as the basic model of learning. The well known experiment with dogs, in which the animals were trained to salivate at the sound of a tuning fork after the fork had repeatedly preceded the presentation of meat paste, illustrates the Pavlovian approach. In the United States, Watson began also with the basic conditioning concept and expanded it to encompass all human behavior. He found the basic stimulus-response concepts learned in early infancy to be the foundation for all units of behavior acquired later through life.

The early 1940's saw the emergence of a formulation which would eventually provide the foundation for many of the behavior modification techniques used today. This was accomplished through the work of B.F. Skinner. Skinner's approach differed from others at the time, in that he saw the behavioral response as more important, rather than the preceding stimuli.

In the United States, during the post war years, the climate for acceptance of new approaches to the treatment of undesirable behaviors was favorable, largely due to therapeutic approaches and a shortage of trained manpower in the field of psychiatric disorders.

Behavior modification projects originally were essentially experimental. Gradually the approaches involved were applied to populations for whom other approaches had been found inadequate. Therefore, the early reports of behavior modification projects were essentially derived from work with seriously disturbed psychotic patients, children displaying adverse behavior, and the mentally retarded. Here the factor of environmental control could be more easily carried out. In time, the approach of behavior modification spread to work with clients in psychiatric counseling centers, neurotic patients, and others. Concurrently, the educational system, in revision of traditional school curricula, found increasing application of behavior modification techniques, especially in the behavioral analysis of academic programs and the school population.

Any scientific theory is temporary, with constant evaluation, new research data and investigations essential for effectiveness. Thus, behavior modification should not be thought of as a complete and unchangeable approach. Continuing revision will be critical for development into a comprehensive theory.

Therapy Between the Pages

JANET BARKAS

There are plenty of books available to help solve human problems, and often they are a comfort and a help. But if you say, "I'm OK, you're OK" to a book, is the book going to say it back?

Janet Barkas teaches at The New School for Social Research and is the author of *The Vegetable Passion: A History of the Vegetarian State of Mind.*

If psychotherapy is "the method of curing psychological abnormalities or disorders by psychological techniques," what type of books fulfill that definition? A wide range of volumes that encourage self-analysis and introspection, leading theoretically to positive personal growth and actions —from *The Art of Loving* by psychoanalyst Erich Fromm to *I'm OK— You're OK* by transactional analyst Thomas A. Harris, to even a book by bestselling financial writer Harry Browne, *How I Found Freedom in an Unfree World.*

What is the reason for the upsurge of interest in books delving into the cause-and-effect relationships between personal psychological makeup and life problems? What is bibliotherapy? Aren't psychiatrists doing their jobs?

In the nonfiction sphere, one might say psychology, sex and food appear the most intriguing contemporary subjects to Americans. However, the popularity of psychology books is not a new development. Erik Erikson's *Childhood and Society*, first published in 1951, has been economically and critically advantageous for both lay analyst Erikson and his publisher, W. W. Norton. Prior to that, Sigmund Freud's *The Psychopathology of Everyday Life* was rather widely read and applied to daily habits, such as forgetting or substituting names for other names, or the so-called Freudian slip. The style was different in both of these earlier psychology books than the "cure yourself" approach of today's selection reflected even in the titles *How to Be Your Own Best Friend* and *Do-It-Yourself Psychotherapy.* Obviously, the emphasis in general trade books has changed from educating the therapist or student to "treating the layman."

The change in focus of such psychology books is a direct result of the success of Dr. Eric Berne's *Games People Play,* published in 1964—a book that became one of the all-time bestsellers. Since then, books are more often than not used as an end in themselves by persons who have no intention of pursuing a career in psychology or even going into therapy. Berne intended *Games People Play* as a sequel to his earlier book *Transactional Analysis in Psychotherapy* (1961). However, the earlier book never attracted one-tenth of the attention of *Games People Play;* few persons ever returned to the earlier segment.

Although *Games People Play* has been criticized for its "layman's" language, it is not an easy book to understand. It lacks the fast, pat answers of later books by other therapists who carry a similar theme. In fact, Berne makes no guarantees in his analysis of how human beings interact—he is merely expressing his observations, according to his theory of transac-

1. Therapy Between the Pages

tions or encounters between persons, termed *transactional analysis*.

What does a sample paragraph from *Games People Play* offer the self-analyst? Berne writes: "Pastimes are typically played at parties ('social gatherings') or during the waiting period before a formal group meeting begins.... In one corner of a room a few people are playing 'PTA,' another corner is the forum for 'Psychiatry,' a third is the theater for 'Ever Been' or 'What Became,' the fourth is engaged for 'General Motors' and the buffet is reserved for women who want to play 'Kitchen' or 'Wardrobe.'"

This is a succinctly stated truism of group relationships, but it is too easy for the reader to intellectualize an enactment of *Pastimes* in his own life; he tries to construct what roles his friends take at a similar function or what roles he *thinks* he takes. While reading *Games People Play*, there is no second person to utilize for feedback or to test out a hypothesis; no "objective and educated" bystander to interrupt rationalizations or projections of behavior.

Berne followed up his radical expositions in *What Do You Say After You Say Hello?*, a longer and more technical book published posthumously in 1972. Here Berne advocates the necessary tool of the therapist to be the life "script" of the patient, rather than the overwhelming historical documentation associated with the approach of the Freudian analyst. Of course, there are numerous basic truths buried in the endless examples in this 457-page book—for example, "To say hello rightly is to see the other person, to be aware of him as a phenomenon, to happen to him and to be ready for him to happen to you . . ." But does realization of how to say hello foster a change in technique?

I recently received a letter after a year of silence from John, a former companion. He stated simply that he had discovered a book, *On Caring*, and it had helped him in his "seeking and feeling." However, I always felt John *felt* too much and did not *act* enough. But the advantage of a so-called Do-It-Yourself Psychotherapy Book is that in the privacy of your home it can generate a sincere "aha!" response. The author's point can become clear without prodding or tension, as is common in the analyst's or psychotherapist's office. John was curing what *he* felt was a problem; I disagreed with his emphasis.

Then what? Obviously John felt a thrust toward "seeking and feeling"

"Whether it is from a book or from an in-the-flesh therapist, it all boils down to the same question – how much can a person change?"

but would it be more focused than that? In writing to me, he was trying to gain recognition for his "change"; he also demonstrated a need to intellectually verbalize his insight, of course he avoided a concrete declaration of *exactly* how it helped his "seeking and feeling" or what that change really amounted to in his everyday life.

A therapist, if it is an insightful and well-trained one, offers a constant feedback. He or she becomes a chronicle of growth for the patient. The time period may be months or years, but both share an insight into the direction that a patient's life has been able to take. The continuing relationship between a therapist and patient may be interrupted for several reasons: the patient decides he has reached a point in treatment where he wants to "try life on his own," or a defensive system interferes so that he refuses to give way to change, and so forth. But there is always the feeling for the former patient of someone to go back to if the going gets rough or if new unexpected situations exacerbate emotional problems in remission.

A book, such as *How to Be Your Own Best Friend* by analysts Mildred Newman and Bernard Berkowitz, does not offer such an individualized approach. The strongest selling point of the book is its saccharine philosophy and low cost—about five dollars for a "talk" that would cost $50 if it were face to face and not within two hardcovers.

This little book does reiterate what many patients hear endlessly in treatment: "The first thing is to realize that we've probably been looking in the wrong place. The source is not outside us; it is within. Most of us haven't begun to tap our own potential; we're operating way below capacity." The reader has to mentally fill in what aspects of *his* or *her* life this applies to—professionally—am I aiming too low in my career choice; socially—am I preventing myself from becoming successful with men or women; financially—am I being lazy and not having enough initiative; etc. If the reader has a clear background into his or her psyche because of extensive analysis, the book may serve to recapsulize what a therapist once described and to keep the former patient in touch with his primary goals or problems. Without that background, it sounds like advice from a kind and optimistic grandmother.

However, the success of *How to Be Your Own Best Friend* is also its failure—the simplicity of the answers in contrast to the dilemmas of life. What the book boils down to is "face the dragons in your life, and slay them." Most problems are caused because persons are either unable to face their dilemma, won't face it or if they see it, are paralyzed to evoke changes because of far deeper fears and anxieties.

"Do you want to lift yourself up or put yourself down? Are you for yourself or against yourself? That may seem like a strange question, but many people are literally their own

1. THE ORIGINS

worst enemy," continues this little bible of self-analysis. Of course, everyone consciously desires to be nice to himself and do only what is in one's best interest, but other unconscious motivations are at work. Those are the ones inhibiting major and constructive change. Perhaps it might be said it is the self-constructive self that would even buy a book that offers some help, but the stubborn, negative patterns that prohibit the changes that are made to seem so easy and achievable in that little book.

I spoke with a man who both read *How to Be Your Own Best Friend* and has been in treatment with the authors for several years. He explained that the book was helpful, but its effectiveness lay mainly in its ability to consolidate the philosophy already expressed during his treatment. "They've helped me a great deal," he says, "but it's impossible to guess how the book would have affected me if I wasn't their patient. I do feel that the more I am exposed to their particular form of therapy, the better off I am."

Should the 56-page book be a replacement for individual treatment? "No," he confirms. "It shouldn't be a substitute. But some people have no choice—those who live in out-of-the-way places, removed from practicing therapists, and those who do not have the financial means for psychotherapy. However, to take the book as an alternative is foolish."

The persons who gain the most from psychotherapy self-help books are often those who have been in treatment and are able to continue the techniques that they learned on their own. Pandora's box, already opened, can be faced and understood. Books often reconfirm those strides made and prevent a total backsliding. Other persons who are "healthy" but annoyed by some personality conflicts or life struggles also profit from bibliotherapy. Those persons, although they have adequate financial means for therapy, would never consider a therapeutic situation because they firmly believe "only sick people go to therapists," but of course "only healthy people read books."

Perhaps the strongest endorsement for psychotherapy self-help books is in the preface by Dr. Harris to *I'm OK—You're OK*: "One of the most significant contributions of Transactional Analysis is that it has given patients a tool they can use.... Anybody can use it. People do not have to be 'sick' to benefit from it...." In other words, the person paralyzed and driven desperately to pay $50 an hour to relieve an oozing sore of anxiety may not be the same person who is just bothered or annoyed and wants to glean some insights by reading a book such as *I'm OK—You're OK*." We are dealing with two substantially contrasting situations: a depressed or desperate person who is barely functioning as compared to a functioning, achieving person who may be a little unhappy.

A middle-aged teacher I know found it very helpful to read the *New York Post* excerpts from Dr. Martin Shepard's 1973 *The Do-It-Yourself Psychotherapy Book*. Dr. Shepard mouthed such truths as when you divorce you trade companionship for loneliness, but in the long run the loneliness will have its rewards. Or, that to face and understand death is to be able to live. She enjoyed Dr. Shepard's capsulization of her own thoughts but found the book rewarding only when it agreed with her previous beliefs.

But the mechanism operating here is quite similar to that in many of these psychotherapy self-help books: taking the generalization and extrapolating a particular. "Yes, I do that " is one response. Or you reach for the telephone to call up a friend and explain that you have read the solution to his problem in this book. "Doesn't that sound just like what you do?"

What is the reaction when a layman writes a book that appears to be psychotherapeutic? "Almost wholly negative" critical reviews, writes Harry Browne, author of *How I Found Freedom in an Unfree World,* which sold 45,000 hardcover copies. He received several hundred letters in response to the book, most indicated that it made a "significant difference in the reader's life and his ability to deal with other people." In our correspondence, Harry Browne indicated that he did not intend the book to replace pure psychotherapy; however, "it may have solved a few problems for individuals who would have otherwise turned to psychotherapy."

One of the main thrusts of Browne's book is that the intellect and the emotions are quite different aspects of a person's psyche. It is on the intellectual level that he sees his book as most helpful—solving problems by creating awareness of "additional alternatives or seeing the fallacies in previous 'truths.' " But if the problem is an emotional one of a deep basis, some type of psychotherapy is the answer.

That raises the general question of when is treatment imperative and bibliotherapy irrelevant?

— If a condition is so impaired that reading is not even possible, e.g., severe depression, intense lethargy, inability to concentrate.

— If someone tends to intellectualize all conflicts so that the points of the book will be merely words.

— A nonverbal person who needs music, art or dance therapy as a tool for communication.

We are surrounded by inexpensive or free psychotherapy. Our friends, rarely trained, throw out free interpretations or advice. Newspapers are filled with columns by analysts, often in answer to a particular question posed in a letter, that will be used as the source of a "from the particular to the general" type of analysis—for example, a 1967 issue of *The Long Island Press* newspaper contained a column by Dr. Joyce Brothers titled "To Love Others, Love Self First." It was the story of a 35-year-old woman who viewed the present by her hostile early years. From that story, anyone who does a similar juxtapositioning of responses is supposed to profit, from that singular situation to the seriously ill who are beyond the point of self-help. However, those individuals are usually compelled by themselves or friends and family to make the financial and emotional investment required in a traditional psychotherapeutic setting, whether the technique employed is pure Freudian analysis, or any of the numerous derivatives, such as primal therapy, transactional analysis, Adlerian and so forth.

Whether it is from a book or from an in-the-flesh therapist, it all boils down to the same question—how much can a person change? How much anxiety can he endure during that changing period? How much change remains permanent before he has to adjust to the next changes necessary because, as Erikson pointed out, life does not stand still. As you solve your childhood problems and reperceive your adulthood, you are thrust into middle age and the concurrent changes of that phase of your life. How much does bibliotherapy or psychotherapy help? The answer points out bibliotherapy's failure— each person poses an individual case or problem; success or failure.

BEN FRANKLIN'S PURSUIT OF PERFECTION

*Long before B.F. Skinner took behavior modification public,
our inquisitive founding father used be-mod principles to wrestle with his own faults.
By John R. Snortum*

BENJAMIN FRANKLIN applied the principles of behavior modification almost 200 years before B. F. Skinner was born.

While browsing through the Huntington Library in Pasadena, California, I spotted Franklin's handwritten autobiography. As I read the yellowed pages, I found our eminent forefather dealing with problems in much the same way that contemporary behaviorists might recommend. Franklin believed that judiciously applied reinforcers were more powerful than "mere exhortations to be good." And he recognized, as Skinner did decades later, that rewarding good acts works better than punishing bad ones. For example, when a military chaplain complained about poor church attendance by the soldiers, Franklin advised: "It is, perhaps, below the dignity of your profession to act as steward of the rum, but if you were to deal it out and only just after prayers, you would have them all about you." The experiment succeeded. ". . . never were prayers more generally and . . . more punctually attended," Franklin tells us, "so that I thought this method preferable to the punishment inflicted by some military laws for nonattendance on divine services."

Franklin's most ambitious behavior-modification project was aimed at changing his own behavior. "I wished to live," he wrote, "without committing any fault at any time . . . As I knew, or thought I knew, what was right and wrong, I did not see why I might not *always* do the one and avoid the other." He decided that to accomplish this noble end, "the contrary habits must be broken and good ones acquired and established before we can have any dependence on a steady, uniform rectitude of conduct." Applying the same ingenuity that he displayed in politics and the physical sciences, Franklin invented self-management procedures that clearly anticipated those developed by behaviorists within the past 10 years. Franklin began by specifying the behavior he wished to change. He compiled a list of 13 virtues, complete with descriptions of the conduct they designated. TEMPERANCE, for example, meant "Eat not to dullness. Drink not to elevation." Under CLEANLINESS he wrote, "Tolerate no uncleanliness in body, clothes or habitation."

Some of his goals were more abstract than modern behaviorists would like. HUMILITY, for instance, meant to "imitate Jesus and Socrates." Vague as this sounds, Franklin had a very clear idea of what he intended. For, in another passage, he tells us how he came to add HUMILITY to the list of virtues: "A Quaker friend . . . kindly informed me that I was generally thought proud, that my pride showed itself frequently in conversation, that I was not content with being in the right when discussing any point, but was overbearing and rather insolent—of which he convinced me by mentioning several instances . . . ." So Franklin tried to avoid words such as "certainly," "undoubtedly" and "obviously," and instead used phrases such as "I imagine," "I conceive," and "It so appears to me at present."

Franklin's next step was to devise a method to keep track of his transgressions, "self-monitoring" in behavior-mod jargon. "I made a little book in which I allotted a page for each of the virtues. I ruled each page with red ink so as to have seven columns, one for each day of the week, marking each column with a letter for the day." In turn, the rows were marked with the first letter of each of the virtues. At the end of each day, he made a mark for each misdeed.

Franklin began with TEMPERANCE, planning to focus his attention on that virtue for one week. He would tally his other frailties, but would make no special effort to change them. The following week would be devoted to developing the virtue of SILENCE; during the next week ORDER would be foremost, and so on. In 13 weeks he would go through the entire list of virtues and then start over again with TEMPERANCE. Over a period of months, he expected to see his sins diminish, and this would reward his good efforts: ". . . so I should

1. THE ORIGINS

FRANKLIN'S BE-MOD LOG

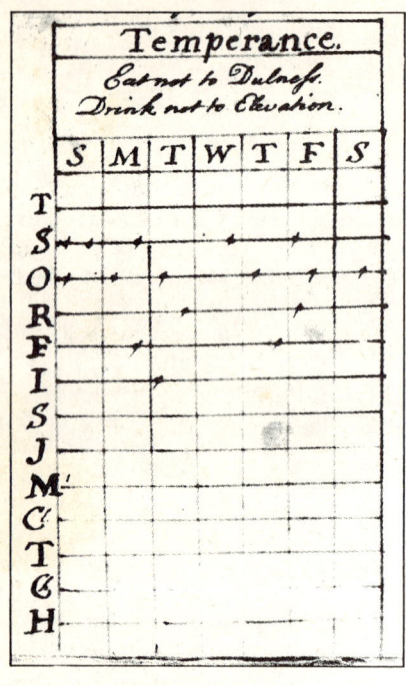

These names of virtues with their precepts were:

TEMPERANCE
Eat not to dullness. Drink not to elevation.

SILENCE
Speak not but what may benefit others or yourself. Avoid trifling conversation.

ORDER
Let all your things have their places. Let each part of your business have its time.

RESOLUTION
Resolve to perform what you ought. Perform without fail what you resolve.

FRUGALITY
Make no expence but to do good to others or yourself; i.e., waste nothing.

INDUSTRY
Lose no time. Be always employed in something useful. Cut off all unnecessary actions.

SINCERITY
Use no hurtful deceit. Think innocently and justly; and, if you speak, speak accordingly.

JUSTICE
Wrong none by doing injuries or omitting the benefits that are your duty.

MODERATION
Avoid extremes. Forbear resenting injuries so much as you think they deserve.

CLEANLINESS
Tolerate no uncleanness in body, clothes or habitation.

TRANQUILLITY
Be not disturbed at trifles or at accidents common or unavoidable.

CHASTITY
Rarely use venery but for health or offspring—never to dullness, weakness, or the injury of your own or another's peace or reputation.

HUMILITY
Imitate Jesus and Socrates.

have (I hoped) the encouraging pleasure of seeing on my pages the progress I made in virtue by clearing successively my lines of their spots...."

D.H. Lawrence's Quibble. Franklin apparently thought that after going through each virtue a few times, he would be very nearly perfect. But, as is often reported by people who monitor their own behavior, Franklin was surprised to find himself "so much fuller of faults" than he had expected. Over the years he gradually reduced the number of 13-week courses of self-monitoring. Eventually, "being employed ... with a multiplicity of affairs that interfered," he gave up the effort. "But," he said, "I always carried my little book with me."

Looking at Franklin's words through our 20th-century Cool-Ray glasses, it would be easy to quibble about the social utility of one or another of the virtues or to be put off by the moralistic tone to his writing. D. H. Lawrence, for one, was not impressed with Franklin's progress in developing humility: "Imitate Jesus and Socrates,"—to which Lawrence appended "and mind you don't outshine either of these two." In his scathing critique of Franklin's project, Lawrence feared that such a program of order and control could strangle the "dark forest of the soul" and yield "a virtuous little automaton." Lawrence showed what fun it could be to turn the 13 moral guidelines upside down and make each virtue a vice. While it is true that Franklin believed that the social benefits of his virtues could be objectively demonstrated, it is my reading that Franklin's primary purpose was to leave us a method rather than a list.

Franklin was the first to admit the uneven results of his project. "... I never arrived at the perfection I had been so ambitious of obtaining but fell far short of it, yet I was by the endeavor a better and a happier man...." He felt his greatest gains had come in the virtues of TEMPERANCE, INDUSTRY, FRUGALITY, SINCERITY and JUSTICE, but conceded almost complete failure in ORDER and HUMILITY. Like the man who grows weary of polishing a rusty ax to perfection, he found himself drawn to consider the merits of a "speckled ax." "A perfect character," he wrote, "might be attended with the inconvenience of being envied and hated; ... a benevolent man should allow a few faults in himself, to keep his friends in countenance." Not one for self-deception, he wryly acknowledged that this argument only "pretended to be reason."

For those, like Lawrence, who worry that Franklin's strict behavioral regimen might have spawned a rigid and sanctimonious old man, it is comforting to read the closing paragraph of his project, written in his 79th year:

"In reality there is perhaps no one of our natural passions so hard to subdue as *pride*; disguise it, struggle with it, beat it down, stifle it, mortify it as much as one pleases, it is still alive and will every now and then peep out and show itself. You will see it perhaps often in this history. For even if I could conceive that I had completely overcome it, I should probably be proud of my humility."

John R. Snortum is professor of psychology at Claremont's Men's College in California. His own efforts in behavior modification have included using self-management techniques, similar to those Franklin developed, in the treatment of female drug addicts. His other interests include the psychology of police/community relations and the criminal-justice system. While on a sabbatical to study Swedish prisons, he developed a fascination for Scandinavian archeology and now finds carving replicas of Viking artifacts very reinforcing.

Why You Do What You Do
SOCIOBIOLOGY: A New Theory of Behavior

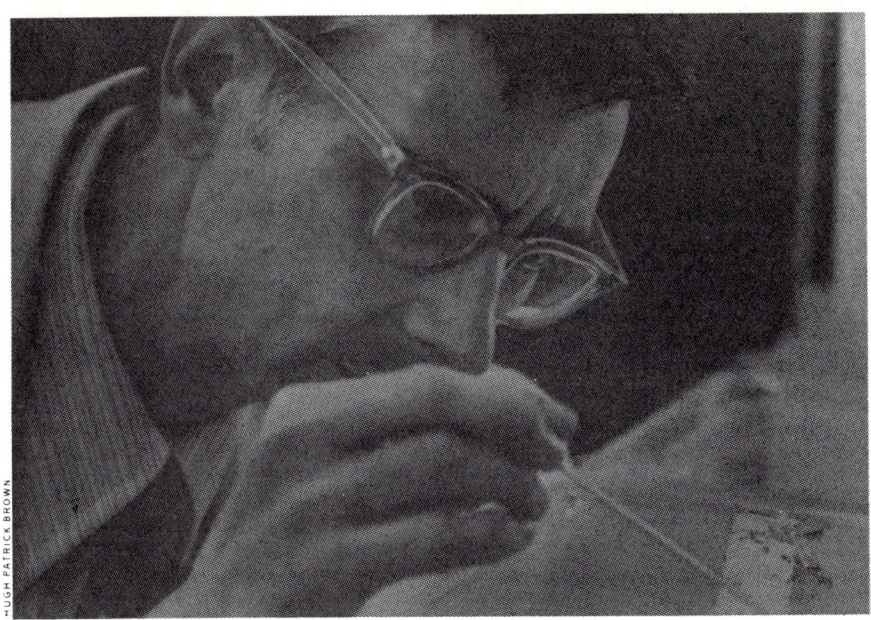
SOCIOBIOLOGIST EDWARD WILSON STUDYING COLONY OF ANTS IN HIS LABORATORY

ROBERT TRIVERS IN CAMBRIDGE
Inflammatory doctrine.

The concepts are startling—and disturbing. Conflict between parents and children is biologically inevitable. Children are born deceitful. All human acts—even saving a stranger from drowning or donating a million dollars to the poor—may be ultimately selfish. Morality and justice, far from being the triumphant product of human progress, evolved from man's animal past, and are securely rooted in the genes.

These are some of the teachings of sociobiology, a new and highly controversial scientific discipline that seeks to establish that social behavior—human as well as animal—has a biological basis. Its most striking tenet: human behavior is genetically based, the result of millions of years of evolution. Some sociobiologists go so far as to suggest that there may be human genes for such behavior as conformism, homosexuality and spite. Carried to an extreme, sociobiology holds that all forms of life exist solely to serve the purposes of DNA, the coded master molecule that determines the nature of all organisms and is the stuff of genes. As British Ethologist Richard Dawkins describes the role and drive of the genes, they "swarm in huge colonies, safe inside gigantic lumbering robots, sealed off from the outside world, manipulating it by remote control. They are in you and me; they created us body and mind; and their preservation is the ultimate rationale for our existence ... we are their survival machines."

Sociobiologists—whose growing ranks include some 250 biologists, zoologists and social scientists—argue that without consideration of biology, the study of human culture makes no sense. Indeed, sociobiology has significant implications for most areas of human concern—from education to relations between the sexes. Says Harvard Physicist Gerald Holton: "It's a breathtaking ambition ... as if Sigmund Freud had set out to subsume all of Darwin, Joyce, Einstein, Whitehead and Lenin." Robert Trivers, a Harvard biologist and leading sociobiology theorist, makes a bold prediction: "Sooner or later, political science, law, economics, psychology, psychiatry and anthropology will all be branches of sociobiology."

These and other claims by proponents of sociobiology have made it one of the most inflammatory doctrines to emerge from the campuses in decades. Since 1975, when Harvard Zoologist Edward Wilson's mammoth 700-page book *Sociobiology: The New Synthesis* brought the new science to public attention, the controversy has spread beyond Harvard—where it originated—dividing faculty departments and disrupting academic conventions. Angry opponents denounce "so-so biology" as reactionary political doctrine disguised as science. Their fear: it may be used to show that some races are inferior, that male dominance over women

1.

1. THE ORIGINS

is natural and that social progress is impossible because of the pull of the genes.

By far the most vocal critics have been Marxist and other scholars with political points to make. University of Chicago Anthropologist Marshall Sahlins dismisses sociobiology as "genetic capitalism"—an attempt to defend the current structures of Western society as natural and inevitable. Jerome Schneewind, a philosopher at Manhattan's Hunter College, calls it "mushy metaphor ... a souped-up version of Hobbes." Harvard Evolutionary Biologist Richard Lewontin is earthier; he thinks sociobiology is "bullshit."

Edward Wilson has been picketed, and at Harvard, the left-wing Committee Against Racism has called sociobiology "dangerously racist." The committee also charged that the new science would give comfort to the supporters of Psychologist Arthur Jensen, a leading proponent of another controversial theory: that racial differences in IQs have a genetic basis. Wilson angrily called that attack "slander," and even Lewontin came to his defense, conceding that "sociobiology is not a racist doctrine." But he added, "Any kind of genetic determinism can and does feed other kinds, including the belief that some races are superior to others."

Opponents of sociobiology were heartened this spring when Harvard failed to give tenure to Biologist Trivers, though denying that his work in sociobiology was the reason. It was a surprising move that Trivers interpreted as an invitation to leave the university —which he plans to do. Still he insists: "I don't think they will be successful in stopping me or slowing down the work. It has spread too far, to too many people, and to far too many studies." Indeed, sociobiology is establishing itself as part of the scientific spectrum. In June, for example, academics from around the nation gathered at San Francisco State University for a two-day meeting on the implications of sociobiology.

Sociobiologists call their doctrine "the completion of the Darwinian revolution"—the application of classic evolutionary theory and modern studies of genetics to animal behavior. Darwin's theory, now virtually unchallenged in the world of science, holds that all organisms evolve by natural selection —those that are better adapted to the environment survive and reproduce; the rest die out. Thus organisms are constantly perfected by the cruel competition to survive. Sociobiologists believe the behavior that promotes survival of the winners in the evolutionary game is passed on by their genes.

Many recent theorists—such as Nobel-prizewinning Ethologist Konrad Lorenz and Scots Biologist V.C. Wynne-Edwards—have focused on the group or species as the primary unit of selection. Darwin wrote that it was the individual organism. But sociobiologists believe it is the genes themselves that conduct the life-or-death evolutionary struggle. This gene-based view of life is compatible with a finding made independently by researchers in a widely divergent branch of science. Rutgers Biochemist George Pieczenik has discovered patterns in DNA coding that he sees as evidence of selection occurring at the molecular level (TIME, April 4). "What this means," he says, "is that the DNA sequences exist to protect themselves and their own information. It's not the organism that counts. The DNA sequences don't really care if they have to look like a lowly assistant professor or a giraffe."

Yet sociobiology did not arise from molecular studies but as an answer to a century-old gap in Darwinian theory: Darwin could not fully explain why some organisms help other members of their species. His theory held that every organism fights for its own survival and chance to reproduce, not that of others. Since altruistic behavior reduces an organism's chances to survive, evolution should be expected to breed it out of all species. Still, some birds risk their lives for the flock by crying out to warn of the presence of a predator—thus chancing attracting the attention of the enemy and being singled out for attack. Dolphins sometimes try to save injured dolphins from drowning. Social insects serve the entire community, some going so far as to give their lives to protect the colony from invaders.

Sociobiology tries to resolve the dilemma. Its solution: altruism is actually genetic selfishness. The bird that warns of an approaching hawk is protecting nearby relatives that have many of the same genes it has—thus increasing the chance that some of those genes will survive. Sterile female insects work and give their lives to promote the spread of genes they share with their sisters.

Some 20 years ago, British Biologist

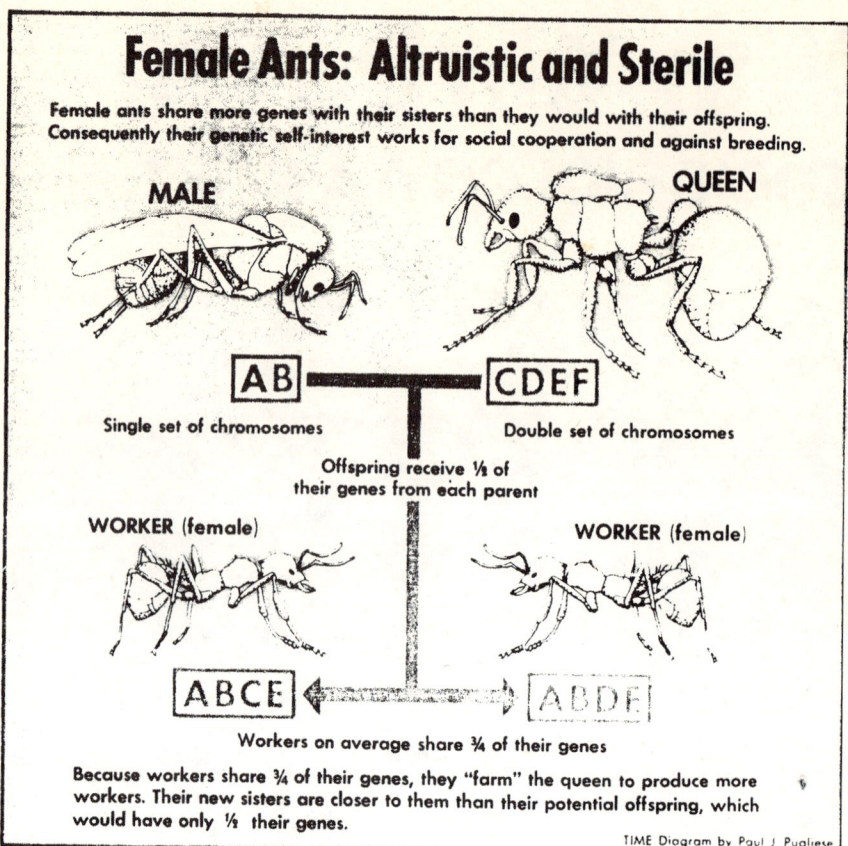

Female Ants: Altruistic and Sterile

Female ants share more genes with their sisters than they would with their offspring. Consequently their genetic self-interest works for social cooperation and against breeding.

MALE — Single set of chromosomes — AB
QUEEN — Double set of chromosomes — CDEF
Offspring receive ½ of their genes from each parent
WORKER (female) — ABCE
WORKER (female) — ABDE
Workers on average share ¾ of their genes

Because workers share ¾ of their genes, they "farm" the queen to produce more workers. Their new sisters are closer to them than their potential offspring, which would have only ½ their genes.

TIME Diagram by Paul J Pugliese

2.

FRIENDS SAVING HARPOONED DOLPHIN
Rooted in gene selfishness.

J.B.S. Haldane anticipated the gene-based view of sociobiology when, tongue in cheek, he announced that he would lay down his life for two brothers or eight cousins. His reasoning: the survival of two full siblings (each with about half of his genes identical to Haldane's) or the group of cousins (each with about one-eighth of his genes the same as Haldane's) made the decision genetically acceptable.

According to sociobiologists, evolution produces organisms that automatically follow this mathematical logic, as if they were computers, totting up the genetic costs or benefits of helping out relatives who bear many of the same genes. If aiding the relatives increases the chances that familial genes will prosper and propagate, the organism will act altruistically—even to the extent of giving up its life, as a parent may, for example, by rushing into a burning house to save a child. Yet in humans, this genetic push is less binding; sociobiologists believe that human social behavior is largely controlled by facultative genes—the ones that can be influenced by environment to change their effects. Thus there is room for cowardly and selfish—as well as unselfish—behavior.

British Biologist William Hamilton in 1964 explained how altruism could help an individual spread his genes; he argued that the principle explained the social life of insects. In all ants, bees and wasps, daughters of the queen share an average of three-quarters of their genes *(see diagram)*. Because the daughters are more related to each other than they would be to their own offspring, said Hamilton, it is in their genetic self-interest not to breed but to assist the queen in producing more daughters. Thus the females evolved as sterile workers who cooperate socially for genetically selfish reasons.

Some years later, Trivers reasoned that if Hamilton was right about the social insects, worker ants would spend three times the energy rearing sisters as rearing brothers, because the workers are three times more closely related to their sisters than to their brothers. Trivers and his associate, Hope Hare, then analyzed thousands of ants of 20 different species and confirmed the 3-to-1 female dominance—the strongest evidence so far that organisms act as if they understand the underlying genetics.

Still, there are problems in explaining all altruism as a direct investment in one's own genes. For example, some birds give warning cries for the flock even when their young and close relatives are absent. Trivers proposed a solution in a 1971 paper on reciprocal altruism that has become a central text for sociobiologists. "In other organisms," Trivers wrote, "the evidence that altruism is genetic is rather overwhelming. It is therefore irrational to argue that the first species in which altruism has no genetic contribution is human beings." Using game theory, he concluded that natural selection produces individuals that exchange favors—in effect saying, "You scratch my back; I'll scratch yours." In other words, the favor will eventually be returned, thus improving the outlook for the genes of the first altruist. According to the theory, human charitable acts are therefore rooted in biology and gene selfishness. This theory could explain human loyalty to nation, corporation or church; these institutions can provide benefits to members that increase the chances for them to survive and propagate.

Some philosophers and theologians have been dismayed by the theory. So was one young man who had won a Carnegie Gold Medal for saving a drowning victim; he wrote Wilson a troubled letter. Recalls Wilson: "He found it difficult to grasp the notion that somehow his act was preordained through genes. I convinced him that the impulse and emotion behind his rational choice, though genetically determined, in no way detracted from the rationality and value of his altruistic act."

For many, such explanations of noble deeds are cold comfort. But Harvard Anthropologist Melvin J. Konner sees a bright side to reciprocal altruism. Sociobiologists, he says, "have in fact uplifted [human nature] by showing that altruism, long thought to be a thin cultural veneer, belongs instead to the deepest part of our being, produced by countless aeons of consistent evolution."

In Trivers' model, non-backscratchers (who refuse to play the game) and overt cheaters (who accept favors but never return them) are long-term losers in the evolutionary game. Yet subtle cheaters who pretend to cooperate but do not are winners. As a result, Trivers believes, humans survived by evolving a complex psychology and set of emotions to keep the altruist from being exploited by cheaters: indignation, guilt, gratitude, sympathy and moralism.

Indeed, to sociobiologists deceit is a crucial factor in evolution. Some birds, like the nighthawk, can feign a broken wing to lure predators away from a nest. In some avian species, a female that has been inseminated by a departed male may try to hide the fact, thus tricking a new male into investing his time and resources in offspring—and genes—that are not his. In the long run, however, natural selection sharpens up both the ability to cheat and the ability to detect cheating. Trivers and Dawkins suggest that the need for deceit—and for its detection—may have been responsible for the rapid enlargement of the human brain during the Pleistocene era.

Sociobiologists believe that self-deception is also a product of evolution, simply because a cheater can give a more convincing display of honesty if he lies to himself as well as to his neighbor. Says Zoologist Richard Alexander of the University of Michigan: "Selection has probably worked against the understanding of such selfish motivation becoming a part of human consciousness." Adds Trivers: "The conventional view that natural selection favors nervous systems which produce ever more accurate images of the world must be a very naive view of mental evolution."

Of all sociobiologists, Trivers has been the boldest in applying the gene-based view to humans. In part, that accounts for his rise—in just ten years—from an author of children's texts to a biology guru at age 34. The son of a Foreign Service officer, Trivers entered Harvard on a scholarship in 1961 to study math and prepare for a career as a civil rights lawyer. He was a bright, moody, private person who turned up at all the civil rights demonstrations and

1. THE ORIGINS

student protests. But his marks were so mediocre ("I was more interested in chasing women and the real world than in math") that his Harvard scholarship was canceled and he was turned down after graduation by two law schools.

Abandoning a law career, he took a job writing children's textbooks for the Educational Development Center in Newton, Mass., and while working on an animal volume was struck by a photo of baboons disciplining their young. It looked so much like human parents dealing with their children, recalls Trivers, "that it was possible to imagine language as just so much froth on the ocean, and that there was something else underlying human discipline. It occurred to me that to understand human behavior, it would be very helpful to examine the behavior of other organisms."

At the time, Trivers knew little about evolution and nothing at all about biology, but he plunged into the literature and sought out mentors. "Once I learned what natural selection was," he says, "it was clear that for one hundred years since Darwin, almost no work had been done in applying Darwin's reasoning to social behavior. It was an incredible opportunity to be able to move into this enormous vacuum."

Excited by his new interest, Trivers borrowed money and went back to Harvard as a special student in biology, gaining his Ph.D. and a faculty appointment in 1972. Zoologist Ernest Williams, one of his teachers, describes him as a brash, brilliant student who turned in papers with slashing attacks on well-known biologists, some of whom have not forgotten—or forgiven. Brashness is still part of Trivers' character. He derided an anthropologist (who, incidentally, admires his work) as too old to understand the implications of sociobiology. The anthropologist was then 38.

The second of seven children, Trivers admits that the problems of growing up in a large family and the arguments he had with his father helped to point him toward his theory that parent-child conflict is biologically certain. Trivers believes that the child shows a selfish interest in itself and seeks to get more than its fair share of the energy and resources of parents. But the parent has only a partial genetic interest in each child and thus is preoccupied with sharing resources. The result, according to Trivers, is biologically certain conflict between the child, who tends toward selfishness, and the parent, who insists that the child share.

Another example of the conflict, in a variety of mammals, is weaning. When the benefit to the child begins to be outweighed by the cost to the mother (reduced ability to bear or care for other offspring), the mother will deny milk, though the offspring will continue to demand more. But parents have an edge.

(Says Trivers: "An offspring cannot fling its mother to the ground at will and nurse.") So evolution has provided a defensive weapon for the offspring: psychological warfare. Some fledgling birds will scream with hunger—even when they are reasonably well fed—to induce the parent to bring more food. Dogs withhold tail-wagging to get more food. Children withhold or provide smiles—as a means of reinforcing maternal behavior they need. Says Trivers: "Strong selection pressures tend to favor the infant's efforts to express its own self-interest. Once you explore the stratagems of parent and child, I think you can see that the child is not just an empty vessel to be filled by the parents but a sophisticated organism capable of acting in its own self-interests from early on."

So early, Trivers thinks, that the action may actually begin before birth. He believes there are "chemical tactics" that the fetus uses on the mother to increase its size and fitness while still in the womb. Even more surprising is Trivers' theory (for which he admits there is yet no evidence) of genetic conflict between egg and sperm before conception: under some conditions, the egg may try to repel sperm with female-producing X chromosomes in order to be fertilized into a boy rather than a girl.

Parents, as well as children, have genetic interests that emerge as manipulation. One of Trivers examples: a parent may be overprotective in order to keep a grown child at home helping with the other offspring—something that promotes the self-interest of the parents and the younger kids but diminishes the chances of reproductive success for the older child. Says Trivers: "Humans are caught in an intense co-evolutionary struggle with their closest relatives. Parents, siblings and offspring are our allies as well as our opponents."

In fact, sociobiologists believe, conflict—both in the family and with outsiders—is the essence of life. But they do not think that man is at the mercy of an irresistible aggressive instinct, as Lorenz (*On Aggression*) and Author Robert Ardrey (*The Territorial Imperative*) insisted in their popular books more than a decade ago. For sociobiologists the trick in becoming an evolutionary winner is to hit just the right level of aggression. Too little, and the organism may be muscled out by competitors. Too much, and it may die in battle without reproducing, or use up time and energy in fighting while competitors steal its food or mate. Aggression, in other words, pays off only when the cost-benefit ratio makes it a workable strategy.

Sociobiology seems to have an explanation—usually a deflating one—for nearly every human phenomenon. Maternal love is a genetic investment policy. Friendship and law are probably

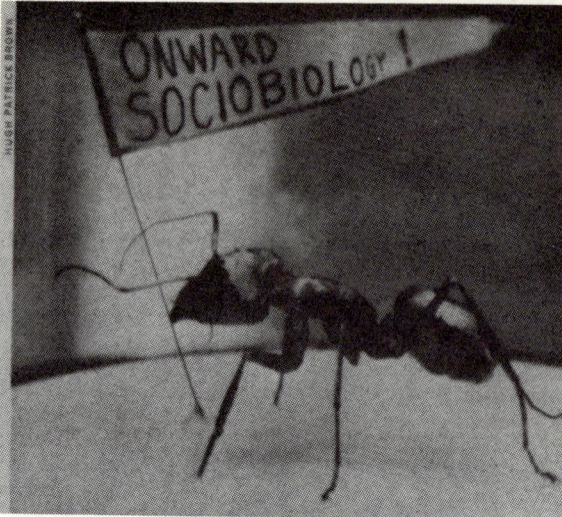

EDWARD WILSON'S INSECT MASCOT AT HARVARD
Giving his life for eight cousins.

rooted in reciprocal altruism and its calculus of self-interest. The socialization of children, at home and school, is as much forced indoctrination in reciprocal altruism as it is genuine teaching. Ethnic pride (as well as racism) can be viewed as an irrational generalization of the biological tendency to distrust strangers and prefer the company of individuals who look like ourselves. Says Wilson: "We are likely to see some of our most exalted feelings explained in terms of traits which evolved. We may find that there is an overestimation of the nature of our deepest yearnings."

Sociobiologists argue that those yearnings are so encrusted with self-deceit and rationalizations that only a rigorous evolutionary analysis will make them clear. Wilson, in fact, calls for "ethics to be removed temporarily from the hands of the philosophers and biologicized." Though Wilson is hazy about what a biologicized ethic might be, he suggests there could be different moral

strictures for males and females, old and young. An ethic of children, he says, might account for their genetically based resistance to parental control, as well as for the tendency of teen-agers to band together and set their own rules.

Wilson, 48, curator of entomology at Harvard's Museum of Comparative Zoology, is currently writing a book on the

NATURALIST CHARLES DARWIN
The revolution completed.

evolution of ethics in relation to sociobiology. A specialist in the social insects, he wrote *The Insect Societies* (1971), then put in three years of 90-hour weeks working on his sociobiology text. Says he: "I wanted to synthesize and draw the boundaries to shape sociobiology into a discipline."

In the spectrum of current theories about human behavior, that discipline falls between the thinking of Harvard Psychologist B.F. Skinner, who regards people as pliable beings whose behavior can be almost entirely shaped by their environment, and Lorenz, who believes that man is a prisoner of his aggressive instincts. Like Freudian psychology, sociobiology stresses the innate but allows for the influence of environment. Indeed, sociobiologists concede the possibilities of a Freudian connection. Trivers says that he can think of 16 ways the discipline could "revitalize" the teachings of Freud, who also had something to say about inevitable parent-child conflict and the role of self-deception.

Many social scientists are now contributing to the development of sociobiological theory. Anthropologist Napoleon Chagnon of Penn State University (TIME, May 10, 1976) reports that the Yãnomamö tribes of southern Venezuela and northern Brazil seem to be engaged in almost continuous war over the right to reproduce. The tribes "invest" more heavily in raising boys, practice female infanticide and constantly raid other settlements for women. Anthropologists Lionel Tiger and Robin Fox (*The Imperial Animal*) insist that evidence points to a "biogram," or biological program, guiding human behavior.

Harvard's Irven DeVore, already one of America's leading anthropologists when he converted to sociobiology, now says he will go back and redo all of his major primate studies. He has gone to Africa this summer to conduct the first real test of sociobiological theory on primates.

Donald Campbell, former president of the American Psychological Association, believes that psychology must adapt itself to evolutionary theory, if not sociobiology. He thinks religious teachings have evolutionary importance —an idea a few theologians have picked up from sociobiology. Says Unitarian Ralph Burhoe of Chicago's Meadville/Lombard Theological School: "The truths in religion have been selected because they are necessary and essential to man." Though no sociobiologist has yet worked out a full theory of religion, the general view is that the golden rule about love of neighbor evolved out of reciprocal altruism.

All told, sociobiology seems to have won the first round with its critics —largely because their accusations were overblown and based on emotional response rather than hard evidence. "Our rhetoric was at fault," admits Biologist Stephen Gould, an opponent of sociobiology. Lewontin adds glumly: "Other people may have listened more if we had presented our arguments differently."

Still, Trivers agrees that the critics have a point in being concerned about the social implications of what sociobiologists preach. "Social theory," he says, "ought to be looked at from the standpoint of what its implications are. It's not like particle physics." Wilson's book, for instance, raises some unsettling questions that most social theorists shy away from: Is it possible that social classes reflect genetic differences? Do the upper

classes gradually accumulate a separate and superior gene pool? After stating that the idea has "plausibility," Wilson goes on to say there is "little evidence" of its truth: culture moves too fast, and even the 2,000-year-old castes of India are not genetically different in any measurable way. Still, Wilson believes there is a "loose correlation of some of the genetically determined traits with success." Such beliefs worry many readers, so Wilson often devotes himself to reassuring audiences that sociobiology is not threatening. He says, for example, that only about 10% to 15% of human social behavior is genetically based. (After this less-than-scientific guess, Sahlins replied with some dry academic mockery that human behavior cannot be reduced to 10% biology, 5% physics, 3% chemistry, .7% geology, 81% symbolic logic and .3% the action of heavenly bodies.)

Wilson also stresses that genes need not always be obeyed. He notes that man has "a genetically inherited array of possibilities. Some of these possibilities set limits on man's aspirations, others do not, and the search should be for where biology pushes mankind and where man can resist the push." He also admits that "genetic constraints evolved during the millions of years of prehistory, under conditions that to a large extent no longer exist." It would be foolish, he says, to rear as many healthy children as possible in today's crowded world, no matter what the genetic push.

Despite the weaknesses in sociobiological doctrine that required these concessions, opponents have been slow to mount a scientifically based counterattack. A major reason for the delay: few critics feel competent to cut across all the disciplines involved, from ethology and mathematics to anthropology and game theory. But a more sophisticated opposition is beginning to take root in the academic community.

Anthropologist Sahlins in *The Use and Abuse of Biology*, the only anti-sociobiology book published to date, contends that kinship patterns among humans do not—as sociobiological theory predicts—always follow bloodlines. He also argues that Trivers' theory of reciprocal altruism simply does not work: an individual may help himself by behaving altruistically, but he also helps one of his competitors. Thus there is no net advantage to altruistic behavior, and it should be selected against by evolution.

Another common objection: human sociobiology is long on theory, short on proof. Some sociobiologists concede that large chunks of the theory may have to be modified as studies proceed.

But the strongest argument against sociobiology is that it underrates the emergence of the human brain, consciousness and culture. Said Columbia

1. THE ORIGINS

Anthropologist Marvin Harris to an M.I.T. audience last year: "Sociobiologists tend to drastically underestimate the result to which human cultures represent an emergent novelty." His point: even simple organisms show great variation in behavior, but only the genes can pass it on. Among humans, learning can be passed on by culture, thus overwhelming the genetic contribution to behavior.

The fear of many of sociobiology's opponents is that it will prove nothing but leave a heavy political impact anyway. Sahlins fears it may disappear as a science but go on and on in the popular culture.

Indeed, few academic theories have spread so fast and with so little hard proof. Apart from the Hamilton-Trivers work on altruism, there has been little to impress the skeptics, and no hard evidence has been presented to show that genes influence human cultural behavior. The power of sociobiology comes from its astonishing promise to link the physical sciences with the human sciences and to bring all behavior from Drosophila to Homo sapiens under one great discipline.

What is more, sociobiology may have appeared at the right cultural moment. The 1970s have brought with them growing impatience and disillusionment over failed educational and environmental experiments designed to alter social behavior. The concept of social theorists that man is infinitely malleable and perfectible has fallen into disfavor. At such a time the emergence of a doctrine preaching that man is caught in history, able to exercise free will only within the limits set by his genes, may do very well indeed.

Sociobiology and Sex

Q. Why do men go to war?
A. Because the women are watching.

This classic exchange may not be the last word on human aggression, but sociobiologists would admire the insight into male psychology. In their view, male displays and bravado—from antlers in deer and feather ruffling in birds to chest thumping in apes and humans—evolved as a reproductive strategy to impress females. Machismo is biologically based and says in effect: "I have good genes, let me mate."

But such male bluster works only if females allow it to work. Among many monogamous birds, a female will mate only with a male willing to build nests before copulating. Presumably, human females have much more power to breed machismo out of the population. At cocktail parties, women often ask Anthropologist Irven DeVore when men will give up machismo. His immodest —but sociobiologically correct—reply: when women like you stop selecting high-success, strutting men like me. "Males," says DeVore, "are a vast breeding experiment run by females."

■

In evolutionary terms, sex is the central game in life, and the aim of all players is to get as many genes as possible into the next generation, at the lowest cost. Some of the best low-cost players are female fish, which deposit their unfertilized eggs in front of a chosen male. Then, while he is inseminating the eggs, they flee, leaving the poor male to protect his genetic investment by nurturing the young himself.

But in most species, including humans, the female has no such advantage. Men have far more chances to play the reproduction game: each male can start thousands of pregnancies; each female can start a maximum of about 30. More important, the female must invest far more heavily in each pregnancy—nine months of time, energy and eating for two. The male must invest only sperm, and promiscuity may pay off for him as a workable reproductive strategy. If he spreads his genes widely and refuses to nurture at all, he can still reasonably assume that some of his offspring will be likely to survive. Sociobiologists say this is why promiscuity is more popular among men, and why the urge to nest is stronger among women.

Why, in the vast majority of species, does the male aggressively pursue the female, instead of the other way round? According to Sociobiologist Robert Trivers, the sex that invests more is a "limiting resource." In other words, because women do most of the work to bring children into the world, they are in the position of sellers in a scarce market, and men must line up to buy. This principle explains the natural evolution of what DeVore and his colleague Joseph Popp have called "prostitution behavior" in higher species. A female chimp in estrus will use a sexual come-on to get more than her share of food. Even a very dominant male cannot afford to alienate the most precious of all resources—a willing female. Sociobiology also explains why, in most human societies, men are older than their mates: older men are more likely to control resources of value to a reproducing female. Males go along with the system because it is to their reproductive advantage to pick young females with many childbearing years left.

In general, males are the high rollers in the sex game. They take greater risks than females (death in combat over a female, exclusion from breeding by a stronger male), but they also have more to gain (spreading their genes far and wide). Still males have one overpowering disadvantage—they can never be sure that the offspring are their own. A cuckolded male is a biological loser, tricked into investing his time and energy in another male's genes. Thus sexual jealousy evolved among monogamous males as an adaptation. So did courtship rituals. By monopolizing a female's time, but not copulating, a courting male waits long enough to make certain that the female is not already pregnant. Among ring doves, a male turns from wooing to aggression if the female responds to his courtship too soon; that is a good sign that she may be pregnant.

For females, coy behavior makes sense if it elicits some sign of good genes or commitment to nurturing. Sociobiologists believe estrus disappeared in humans as a female strategy to cement monogamy: a year-round sexual attractiveness helped keep mates from wandering off. Menopause may have evolved to turn aging females away from breeding and toward protecting their genetic investment by caring for grandchildren.

Sociobiologists think that evolution has produced different physiques, behavior and attitudes in males and females—a touchy subject for feminists. Trivers says the female is not equipped for the chase and shows no interest in it. And Edward Wilson reminds readers that in the million-year hunter-gatherer period of evolution, men hunted and women stayed home. Adds Wilson: "This strong bias persists in most agricultural societies, and on that ground alone appears to have a genetic origin."

■

Comments like these have irritated some campus feminists, who fear sociobiologists are telling them to stay home and mind the babies, but sociobiologists have some calming news: hunter-gatherer women were economic equals. Says DeVore: "The female is an absolutely integral part of the society, because only her gathering makes it possible for the male to indulge in the gamble of the hunt." Sociobiologists stress that the sexes are genetically equal and can evolve different strategies as conditions change.

It has been argued that the rise of feminism could be a genetic adaptation. Robert Trivers, however, has a sobering thought: if more feminists take jobs and have fewer children, more of the childbearing may be left to nonfeminists. In evolutionary terms, this would mean that feminism is being selected against and will either die out entirely or start from scratch in every generation.

Shapers at Work
by Kenneth Goodall

THE MOTHER OF A CHILD who attends a big-city school rarely gets a phone call from the principal. When she does, she can expect the worst: very likely, her child is being suspended or expelled for tardiness or truancy or rowdiness.

A call from Ronald E. Brown, principal of Bryant elementary school in Kansas City, Kansas, almost always is a pleasant surprise. "I'm glad to see that Larry made it to school on time again today," Brown might say. Or "Larry hasn't skipped a class all week and he's doing much better on his tests."

When I visited Bryant school on a recent cross-country tour of large-scale projects in Skinnerian human-behavior control, Brown's associates told me that he always had preferred to pat parents and children on the back—it just came more naturally to him than chewing them out or punishing them in other ways. Now, with guidance from R. Vance Hall, a pioneer developer of behavior-shaping technology for use in public schools, Brown was patting people systematically throughout Bryant school—teachers as well as students and parents.

Brown is a young and enthusiastic administrator whose smile and openness convey a playful feeling of joy in his work. He doesn't fit the fantasy of a faceless and threatening behavior controller conjured up by the antibehaviorists' persistent question, "But who will do the controlling?" Nor did Vance Hall when I talked with him in his storefront office in Kansas City's black ghetto and over a lunch of cornbread, ham, and black-eyed peas in a tiny lunchroom nearby. Nonetheless, both Brown and Hall are in the vanguard of a rapidly expanding movement that aims to make Skinnerians of us all.

Aversion. I started studying the movement a year ago after editing B.F. Skinner's book, *Beyond Freedom and Dignity*, for *Psychology Today*, which published the major part of the book in the August 1971 issue. In one way the editing job was a distasteful assignment because of my long-standing aversion toward behaviorism. But it also was rewarding because I quickly realized that I was working with a rare masterpiece in the literature of psychology. Above all, it was frustrating, for Skinner stayed on a philosophical plane with his argument for the development of a technology of human behavior; only occasionally did he allude to the ways this technology might work.

"A technology of operant behavior is already well advanced and it may prove to be commensurate with our problems," he wrote. It isn't ready yet to solve all of them, but it "continues to develop and is in fact much more advanced than its critics usually realize." Behavioral technologists still cannot design "a successful culture as a whole"—Skinner's *summum bonum*—"but we can design better practices, piecemeal."

Advance. These and other tantalizing allusions to the human applications of behavioral technology needed probing, I felt. If Skinnerism with its reinforcements and its contingencies really were advancing at such a rapid rate, I didn't want to be taken by surprise along with the general run of Skinner's critics.

I passed the next several months reading, observing, and listening to the behaviorists who are systematically applying Skinner's operant psychology in all kinds of places with all kinds of people to change all kinds of behaviors. The experience helped me to flesh out Skinner's allusions and put faces on his followers, a new breed that I think of as the post-Skinnerians. Both facts and faces argued against the fantasies of Skinner's critics.

Today's band of human-behavior controllers, I found, still marches to the sound of many pigeons pecking. It is a distant sound, however. Behavioral experimentation began a slow move out of the traditional campus psychology laboratory some 20 years ago, and few of the post-Skinnerians spend much time there anymore. In fact, they can be found almost anywhere *but* there—in classrooms, kitchens, mental hospitals, rehabilitation wards, prisons, nursing homes, day-care centers, factories, movie theaters, national parks, community mental-health centers, stores, recreation centers, and right next door. Nevertheless, the basic principles that guide them in their work with human beings are the ones B.F. Skinner and a few associates formulated by observing pigeons and rats in Skinner boxes.

Bit. The most basic of these principles is that behavior is affected by its consequences. If a tasty bit of food falls into a Skinner box after a pigeon pecks a button or a rat presses a bar, the pigeon or the rat is likely to peck or press again. In Skinner's psychology, the food is a natural or *primary reinforcer*, the act of eating it is an *unconditioned response*, the pecking or pressing is a learned or *conditioned response*, the environmental conditions that determine the response are *contingencies*, and the whole process is *operant conditioning*.

Beginning. In 1949, more than a decade after Skinner published his first book, *The Behavior of Organisms*,

1. THE ORIGINS

> "In civilized society, personal merit will not serve you so much as money will. Sir, you may make the experiment. Go into the street, and give one man a lecture on morality, and another a shilling, and see which will respect you most."
> —Samuel Johnson (In Boswell's *Life of Johnson*)

> "It is not the youngster who has failed, but it is the public-school system and the ecology that maintains that school system that has failed; it is not the youngster who is mentally bankrupt, but it is the public-school system that is bankrupt."
> —Harold L. Cohen (in a paper, "Educational Therapy")

a graduate student at Indiana University (where Skinner headed the psychology department before he moved on to Harvard) showed that the human organism is just as apt as the avian when it comes to operant learning. Paul R. Fuller taught an institutionalized "vegetative idiot" to earn food by raising his right arm to a vertical position. Fuller used a *shaping* technique, first reinforcing random upward movements of the arm and then reinforcing movements that brought the arm closer and closer to the vertical position. After only a few experimental sessions the youth, who according to his doctors hadn't learned anything in his 18 years of life, was raising his arm and swallowing his reinforcer (a warm sugar-milk solution) as fast as he could.

Fuller's report on this experiment ended prophetically: "While of normal human parentage, this organism was, behaviorally speaking, considerably lower in the scale than the majority of infrahuman organisms used in conditioning experiments . . . Perhaps by beginning at the bottom of the human scale the transfer from rat to man can be effected."

Bound. Two of Skinner's graduate students at Harvard, Ogden R. Lindsley and Nathan H. Azrin, helped effect the transfer. Lindsley, working closely with Skinner at Boston's Metropolitan State Hospital in the mid-'50s, set up experiments with psychotic patients that closely resembled earlier animal experiments. He found that he could control human operant responses (in this case, pulling a lever to obtain reinforcements of candy or cigarettes) by varying the reinforcement schedule. (*Continuous reinforcement* speeds up the learning of a task. But once the task is learned, human beings, like animals, will work harder and longer when the prize comes at an intermittent schedule than when it comes with every pull of the lever.)

Though Lindsley was working with a group of psychotics, his primary interest at the time was in gathering data on operant conditioning of human beings, not in modifying their sometimes bizarre behavior. It was Azrin who took a giant step into *behavior modification* in the early '60s after he became director of behavioral research at Anna State Hospital in southern Illinois. To help him he brought in a *Wunderkind*: Teodoro Ayllon, who had a brand-new Ph.D. from the University of Houston.

Bananas. Ayllon first did some ingenious experiments with individual psychotic patients. To treat a woman who had a nine-year history of towel hoarding, he had nurses deliver towels to her room by the dozens until, satiated by what she had once found reinforcing and exhausted by her customary folding-and-stacking routine, the woman carried 625 towels out of her room, never to hoard again. Ayllon then undertook the behavioral management of an entire ward of 40-odd severely disturbed patients.

Over the next few years, Ayllon and Azrin moved the experimental analysis of human behavior forward on two fronts. They demonstrated the efficacy of a *token-economy system* of reinforcement, and they devised an operant model that enabled clinical psychologists to work with large groups of persons who suffered from various behavioral disturbances as well as with single cases or small groups. [See "Mimosa Cottage: Experiment in Hope" by James R. Lent, PT, June 1968.]

The token economy, like most techniques used by the human-behavior controllers, had its origins in animal experiments. Chimpanzees started it all in the late '30s by showing that they could learn to 1) place a poker chip in a slot to obtain grapes, 2) press a bar to obtain a chip, and 3) save up a specified number of chips to exchange for grapes after a specified time interval. The chimpanzees also learned an unrelated task—weightlifting—to obtain only chips, which meant that the chips had become *secondary reinforcers*. In other words, a chimpanzee would work for a chip that wasn't worth a grape. It was a delightful development for the Skinnerians, since chips have distinct advantages over grapes: they are less perishable, less satiating (for the chimpanzees) and less limited in their appeal once the chimpanzees learn they can use them to buy bananas as well as grapes.

Cookies. More than 20 years later, when Ayllon set up the token system with patients at Anna State Hospital and Arthur W. Staats and Montrose M. Wolf experimented at Arizona State University with a similar system for children, they used these advantages to good effect. Just as chimpanzees tire of grapes, children tire of M&M candy. But, as Staats and Wolf found, even children with little love for reading will do a lot of it if their reward is a bunch of tokens that they can trade in later for cookies, pieces of cake, toys—or M&Ms. That such a system amounted to bribing a child for doing something he ought to get into the habit of doing was once a common charge. It usually came from authoritarian types who were blind to their own double standard. Behavior-therapist Israel Goldiamond once made this comeback: "If they stopped paying me for coming to work, this nice ingrained habit I have might quickly vanish." The charge is heard less often these days.

Chores. Ayllon and Azrin's application of the token system is commonly regarded as one of the most significant achievements to date in human-behavior control. Like Ayllon, other researchers had used experimental techniques to modify specific behaviors of individual psychotics like the woman who hoarded towels. "But,"

> "Our enthusiasm was not derived from reading persuasive reports or theories. It is rather based on the pleasurable experiences which follow from our efforts to help families. The fact that these experiences are so readily translated into data is an additional source of reinforcement."
> —Gerald Patterson (unpublished paper)

> "Indeed, behavioral education may create the very kind of people needed to cope with the extremes of technical advancement and social crisis characteristic of the 20th century."
> —Roger Ulrich, Stephen E. Louisell, Marshall Wolfe (in *Educational Technology*)

as Ayllon and Azrin recall, "none of us had yet attempted to design a total environment that would deal with all of the behavioral problems in a mental hospital."

This engineering feat showed that long-hospitalized and idle psychotics, when they were properly reinforced, could learn how to care for themselves, do housekeeping chores, and even hold down jobs around the hospital. The trick was to learn which reinforcers worked with which persons—one patient might spend tokens to sit in a favorite chair, another to attend religious services —and to find an efficient way to deliver the rewards. Hospital staff members had to look at each patient's individual behaviors and overcome the stereotyped images that went with "schizophrenic," "mental defective," and other labels the patients had acquired. Staff members also had to keep records of how each patient spent the day and had to hand out reinforcements systematically.

The token system proved to be so effective that Ayllon and Azrin predicted that it "will probably find great applicability in many different disciplines concerned with human behavior." They were right. Their example inspired many similar programs in the United States and abroad—with retarded children, slow learners and juvenile delinquents as well as with adult psychotics in mental hospitals.

Chaos. The most notable program was created by Harold L. Cohen, an artist and designer who, as head of the design department at Southern Illinois University, had been greatly impressed by the behavioral approaches of Israel Goldiamond, who was also at Southern Illinois University, and of Ayllon and Azrin at nearby Anna State Hospital. Cohen later succeeded Goldiamond as executive director of the Institute for Behavioral Research (IBR), a private company in Silver Spring, Maryland. IBR's CASE Project at the National Training School for Boys (then located in Washington, D.C.) successfully extended the token system to a new age group (adolescent boys), new behavior problems (juvenile delinquency and failure in school) and a new setting (prison). In general, the youths they worked with made academic gains three times greater than the standard gains that are expected of public-school children. *A New Learning Environment*, the book Cohen wrote with his colleague James C. Filipczak, tells how they did it.

Ayllon's name has become almost synonymous with the token system, especially since the publication in 1968 of Ayllon and Azrin's *The Token Economy*. His reputation led me to suspect, before I visited him last December, that his current work with children in the Atlanta schools (he moved to Georgia State University in 1968) probably involved the wholesale use of token systems. I was surprised to learn from one of Ayllon's graduate students, William Skuban, that in working with a highly disruptive seventh-grade class they had set up a token system only as a last resort after more traditional methods had failed to end the chaos. When I asked why, he replied, "Why use tokens if something else will work?"

That seemed heretical until I realized that Ayllon was less interested in promoting "his" method than in spreading the benefits of any successful behavioral technique. At one point in our conversation about his work and its shift in focus from psychotics in mental hospitals to ordinary children in ordinary classrooms, Ayllon referred to *Walden Two*, Skinner's fictionalized account of a community that was run on behavioral principles. "*Walden Two* is visionary," he told me. "It's going to come."

Ayllon's shift in focus is no accident. In the last five years behavior controllers increasingly have moved away from the laboratorylike settings of mental hospitals, correctional institutions and special classrooms and have set up programs—sometimes large-scale ones—in public schools, halfway houses, private homes and community-mental-health centers. In Kansas, they have helped vitalize a large urban ghetto housing project; in Maryland, they even talk confidently of a plan to convert the governmental, educational and law-enforcement systems of a huge suburban county to the use of behavior modification.

Dealing. "Behavior modification," however, is a catch-all term that is fast losing whatever meaning it once had. In popular usage, it generally refers to psychotherapeutic methods that sprang from experimentation and theory in the two main branches of scientific behaviorism: Pavlovian *classical conditioning* and Skinnerian *operant conditioning*. But Leonard Krasner, a leading behaviorist, uses "behavior modification" to cover what he calls evocative psychotherapies, including psychoanalysis, as well as the behavioral therapies. Albert Bandura, another major behaviorist, contends that "all forms of psychotherapy, regardless of their self-conferred honorific titles and noble aims, effect behavioral changes through either deliberate or unwitting manipulation of controlling variables." (To complicate matters further, Bandura himself has contributed a distinct therapeutic technique, *modeling*, to the behavior-modification armory.) To me, it seems simpler to discard "behavior modification" and to think instead in terms of two major movements that attempt to deal with human problems from a behaviorist orientation: *behavior therapy* and *applied behavior analysis*.

Design. Behavior therapy, a mid-century outgrowth of

1. THE ORIGINS

     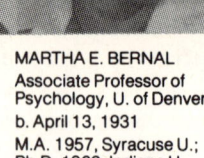

TEODORO AYLLON
Professor of Psychology and Special Education, Georgia State U.
b. April 25, 1929
M.A. 1955, U. of Kansas; Ph.D. 1959, U. of Houston

Joined Georgia State faculty in 1968 after six years as clinical research director at Anna State Hospital and professorships at Southern Illinois U. and U. of Pennsylvania. Pioneered use of behavioral techniques, including token economy, with severely disturbed mental-hospital patients. Author, with Michael, of article that sparked applied behavior movement ("The Psychiatric Nurse as a Behavioral Engineer," 1959) and coauthor, with Azrin, of *The Token Economy*. Current work is mainly with children in Atlanta public schools.

NATHAN H. AZRIN
Professor at Rehabilitation Institute, Southern Illinois U., and Director of Behavior Research Laboratory, Anna State Hospital, Anna, Illinois
b. November 26, 1930
M.A. 1953, Boston U.; Ph.D. 1955, Harvard

Moved to Southern Illinois in 1957 after conducting research at Harvard on childhood psychosis and, with Skinner, on automated teaching methods. Azrin and Ayllon set up first large-scale token-economy system. His other coresearchers have included Lindsley, Goldiamond, Ulrich and Sulzer-Azaroff. Developed technology for treating many behavioral problems, including cigarette smoking, posture, stuttering, self-medication and incontinence [see "Pain and Aggression," PT, May 1967]. Coauthor, with Ayllon, of *The Token Economy* (Appleton-Century-Crofts, 1968).

DONALD M. BAER
Professor of Human Development, U. of Kansas
b. October 25, 1931
Ph.D. 1957, U. of Chicago

Joined Kansas faculty in 1965 after teaching and conducting research for eight years at U. of Washington. Trained in developmental psychology, not in operant conditioning. With Bijou he pioneered use of applied behavior analysis with severely disturbed children. Principal author, with Wolf and Risley, of paper that defined the field—"Some Current Dimensions of Applied Behavior Analysis," reprinted in Ulrich, Stachnik and Mabry's *Control of Human Behavior*. [See "Let's Take Another Look at Punishment," PT, October 1971.]

ALBERT BANDURA
Professor of Psychology, Stanford
b. December 4, 1925
M.A. 1951, Ph.D. 1952, U. of Iowa

Joined Stanford faculty in 1953. Has spent entire career there, teaching and conducting research on social-learning theory and applications. Outstanding contribution has been in modeling (or imitative-learning) techniques. Behavior therapists use them to modify phobias, and applied behavior analysts use them as shortcuts in the shaping process. Bandura did important studies on TV and aggression, more recently on self-control mechanisms and individual and collective aggression. Author of *Principles of Behavior Modification* (Holt, 1969). President-elect of American Psychological Association.

WESLEY C. BECKER
Professor of Education, U. of Oregon
b. March 17, 1928
M.A. 1953, Ph.D. 1955, Stanford

Joined Oregon faculty in 1970 after 15 years at U. of Illinois, where he and Siegfried Engelmann developed Engelmann-Becker model curriculum for compensatory-education classes. Former consultant to U.S. Office of Education's Follow-Through program and now codirector of Follow-Through planned-variation project using E-B model. Did research with O'Leary and Madsen. Author of *The Empirical Basis for Change in Education* (Science Research Associates, 1971).

MARTHA E. BERNAL
Associate Professor of Psychology, U. of Denver
b. April 13, 1931
M.A. 1957, Syracuse U.; Ph.D. 1962, Indiana U.

Joined Denver faculty in 1971 after teaching and conducting research at Indiana, U. of Arizona and UCLA's Neuropsychiatric Institute. Major work has been in modification of "brat" behaviors and training parents to modify their children's behaviors. Studied autistic children and psychosomatic problems. Coauthor of "Behavior Modification and the Brat Syndrome," reprinted in Ulrich, Stachnik and Mabry's *Control of Human Behavior*.

SIDNEY W. BIJOU
Professor of Psychology and Director of Child Behavior Laboratory, U. of Illinois
b. November 12, 1908
M.A. 1937, Columbia; Ph.D. 1941, U. of Iowa

Joined Illinois faculty in 1965 after two years at Indiana U. and 17 years at U. of Washington, where he was instrumental in building the university's reputation as a top-flight center for application of behavioral techniques to problems of children. Conducted and directed numerous studies that led the field [see "The Mentally Retarded Child," PT, June 1968]. Former editor of *Journal of Experimental Child Psychology* and coeditor, with Baer, of three-volume *Child Development* (Appleton-Century-Crofts, 1961, 1964 and 1967).

ROBERT L. BURGESS
Associate Professor of Sociology, U. of Washington
b. June 24, 1938
M.A. 1964, Ph.D. 1969, Washington U., St. Louis

Joined Washington faculty in 1963. He and Bushell (also a St. Louis product) are a rare breed: operant sociologists. They coedited *Behavioral Sociology: The Experimental Analysis of Social Process* (Columbia U. Press, 1969). With Roger N. Clark and John C. Hendee, Burgess pioneered open-setting studies to control littering behavior. Book in progress: *Environmental Pollution: An Experimental Model for Its Analysis and Treatment*.

WILBERT E. FORDYCE
Professor of Clinical Psychology, U. of Washington School of Medicine
b. January 3, 1923
M.S. 1951, Ph.D. 1953, U. of Washington

Joined Washington faculty in 1959 after five years as clinical psychologist at VA Hospital, Seattle. Reported successful use of behavioral techniques in physical rehabilitation of patients. Most impressive work has been in reduction or elimination of long-standing chronic pain through operant-conditioning. Author of excellent overview in *Rehabilitation Psychology* (American Psychological Association, 1971).

PAUL R. FULLER
Professor of Psychology, Western Michigan U.
b. January 16, 1923
M.A. 1949, Ph.D. 1952, Indiana U.

Joined Western Michigan faculty in 1970 after several years as psychologist in industry, where he supervised work in America's manned space-flight programs. As graduate student at Indiana U., he conducted pioneer experiment in human operant conditioning. Taught at Indiana and Florida State U. A behavioral engineer for nearly 20 years, he focused on the integration of applied behavior analysis into total-systems analysis. Author of "Parameters of Man-in-Space—The Psychophysiology of Manned Space Flight," a Martin Company technical report.

ISRAEL GOLDIAMOND
Professor of Psychiatry and Psychology, U. of Chicago
b. November 1, 1919
Ph.D. 1955, U. of Chicago

Joined Chicago faculty in 1968 after teaching and conducting research at Southern Illinois U., Arizona State U. and Johns Hopkins U. Executive director, Institute for Behavioral Research, 1963-1968. Important early work on stuttering (with Azrin) and the control of other verbal behaviors. Pioneered use of self-control procedures to solve personal behavior problems [see "Moral Behavior: A Functional Analysis," PT, September 1968].

R. VANCE HALL
Associate Professor of Human Development, U. of Kansas
b. December 4, 1928
M.Ed. 1960, Ph.D. 1966, U. of Washington

Joined Kansas faculty in 1965 after several years as elementary-school teacher and principal. Now director of Juniper Gardens Children's Project in Kansas City ghetto. Studied use of behavioral techniques in classrooms. Through seminars and packaged responsive-teaching model, he and his graduate students have spread techniques across U.S. Author of *Managing Behavior* (H & H Enterprises, 1971).

4. Shapers at Work

DONALD G. BUSHELL Jr.
Associate Professor of Human Development, U. of Kansas
b. June 22, 1934
M.A. 1958, Kent State U.; Ph.D. 1964, Washington U., St. Louis

Joined Kansas faculty in 1967 after teaching sociology and conducting research at Washington U. and Webster College in St. Louis, U. of Washington in Seattle. Directed projects in design of instructional systems at Central Midwestern Regional Educational Laboratory and use of contingencies in college classrooms at U. of North Carolina. At Kansas he was codirector of Juniper Gardens preschool and now heads Follow-Through and Head-Start projects using his own behavior-analysis model. Author of *Classroom Behavior: A Little Book for Teachers* (Prentice-Hall, in press) and coeditor with Burgess, of *Behavioral Sociology*. (Columbia U. Press, 1969).

HAROLD L. COHEN
Executive Director of Institute for Behavioral Research, Silver Spring, Maryland
b. May 24, 1925
B.A. 1949, Illinois Institute of Technology

Joined staff of Institute for Behavioral Research in 1964 and succeeded Goldiamond as its executive director in 1968. Spent nine years as chairman of Southern Illinois U.'s department of design. With James A. Filipczak, he set up a token-economy environment for inmates at National Training School for Boys. Current projects include PICA to shape interpersonal and academic behaviors of students in trouble, two preventive delinquency programs called BPLAY and TARR, and a whole-system use of behavioral techniques in public schools. Coauthor, with Filipczak, of *A New Learning Environment* (Jossey-Bass, 1971).

CHARLES B. FERSTER
Professor of Psychology, American U.
b. November 1, 1922
M.A. 1948, Ph.D. 1950, Columbia

Joined American faculty in 1969 after teaching and conducting research at Harvard, the Yerkes primate laboratories, Indiana U., Arizona State U. and Southern Illinois U. Preceded Goldiamond and Cohen as executive director of Institute for Behavioral Research. Coauthor, with Skinner, of operant-conditioning classic, *Schedules of Reinforcement* (Appleton-Century-Crofts, 1957). Did influential early work with autistic children and behavioral control of overeating, more recently with language teaching, college instruction, self-control and Skinnerian analysis of the psychoanalytic process [see "The Autistic Child," PT, November 1968].

NORRIS G. HARING
Professor of Education and Director of Experimental Education Unit, U. of Washington
b. July 25, 1923
M.A. 1950, U. of Nebraska; Ed.D. 1956, Syracuse U.

Joined Washington faculty in 1965 after five years at U. of Kansas Medical Center. Specialist in education of exceptional children and associate editor of journal *Exceptional Children*. Worked on new curriculum designs and precision-teaching model for training teachers in contingency management. Author of preface to H. P. Kunzelman's *Precision Teaching: An Initial Training Sequence* (Special Child Publications, Seattle, 1970) and coauthor of *Analysis and Modification of Classroom Behavior* (Prentice-Hall, 1972).

ROBERT P. HAWKINS
Associate Professor of Psychology, Western Michigan U.
b. February 10, 1931
M.S. 1963, Ph.D. 1965, U. of Pittsburgh

Joined Western Michigan faculty in 1966 after a year's research at U. of Kansas under supervision of Baer. Spent a year working with Bijou at U. of Washington's Child Development Clinic and did pioneer study in training parents to modify their children's behavior. At Western Michigan he directed research program for emotionally disturbed children sponsored by Kalamazoo public schools. Advocates "universal parenthood training" in behavioral techniques to prevent mental-health problems [see "Stimulus/Reponse," page 28]. Founding editor of journal for teachers called *School Applications of Learning Theory* (SALT).

LLOYD E. HOMME
Self-employed
b. December 5, 1917
M.A. 1948, Southern Methodist U.; Ph.D. 1953, Indiana U.

Formerly head of behavioral-systems research for several organizations, including Teaching Machines, Inc., Westinghouse Learning Corporation, and most recently, Individual Learning Systems in San Rafael, California. Taught at Indiana U., U. of Pittsburgh and U. of New Mexico and conducted research in programmed instruction with Skinner at Harvard. Pioneered use of Premack Principle in schools; helped develop "reinforcing-event menu" and contingency contracting. Author of *How to Use Contingency Contracting* (Research Press, 1969). Now writing book on humanistic behaviorism.

---

classical-conditioning experimentation and the learning theories of psychologist Clark Hull, retains many of the trappings of older psychotherapies: a predominantly one-to-one, therapist-client relationship; scheduled sessions in the therapist's office or clinic; fees paid by clients. Its techniques—systematic desensitization, assertive training, covert sensitization and other, mainly aversive, conditioning methods—differ considerably from those used in psychoanalysis, but both therapies have the same limitations: their practice usually requires extensive training; they can reach only a small fraction of the people who are in need of them, and they are designed to alleviate problems, not to prevent problems.

Applied behavior analysis is a direct descendant of Skinnerian operant-conditioning experimentation. It has retained many of the scientific trappings (such as close observation and precise recording of behaviors) and most of the jargon of the rat-and-pigeon days. It also has added some trappings of its own, such as interval recording and new observation procedures and research designs. Though many of its practitioners are therapists, and many have done work in one-to-one and small-group situations, its milieu more closely resembles an educational setting than a doctor's office. Unlike psychoanalysts, who use a battery of techniques but seldom refer to them as a technology, applied behavior analysts spend a great deal of time developing, packaging, disseminating and talking about behavioral technology. They have not given up experimentation, but their laboratory is the real world; they still treat individual problems, but they attempt to do it on an increasingly massive scale; and their technology, usable to a large extent by just about anybody, permits them to emphasize prevention rather than cure. In short, they are becoming behavioral engineers.

Deviance. Freed from built-in restraints of most psychotherapies, applied behavior analysis is an aggressive and radical reform movement that already has stepped into a vacuum of failures left by traditional methods of teaching and healing. And, like the potential victor in an evolutionary struggle, it has several built-in advantages that make it a likely alternative in the present search for social programs that refuse to set limits on an individual's possibilities for growth.

Though Skinner's philosophy, with its unabashed insistence on the need for planned control of human behavior, is the bane of humanists, the implicit assumptions of the post-Skinnerians have a strangely humanist ring.

For many applied-behavior analysts, as for humanist heroes like Thomas Szasz and R.D. Laing, mental illness

1. THE ORIGINS

FRED S. KELLER
Adjunct Professor of Psychology, Western Michigan U.
b. January 2, 1899
M.A. 1928, Ph.D. 1931, Harvard U.

Joined Western Michigan faculty in 1968 after 26 years at Columbia, three years at Arizona State U. and a year at the Institute for Behavioral Research. In many ways, Keller has had even more influence on the development of behavioral engineering than has Skinner, his long-time friend. His experimental and applied research in human learning and communications training inspired classroom-instruction techniques that are used in many behavioral programs, and his operant psychology program at Columbia turned out many Skinnerians.

LEONARD KRASNER
Professor of Psychology, State U. of New York at Stony Brook
b. December 17, 1924
M.A. 1947, Ph.D. 1950, Columbia

Joined Stony Brook faculty in 1965 after eight years as a professor at Stanford and coordinator of training and special research projects at VA Hospital in Palo Alto. Taught at U. of Washington. Pioneered use of reinforcement in psychotherapy, and published many important articles in theory and practice of behavior therapy and human operant conditioning. Introduced token-economy systems at mental hospitals in California and New York. Coeditor, with Ullmann, of *Research in Behavior Modification* and *Case Studies in Behavior Modification* (both Holt, 1965).

OGDEN R. LINDSLEY
Professor of Education, U. of Kansas
b. August 11, 1922
Sc.M. 1950, Brown U.; Ph.D. 1957, Harvard

Joined Kansas faculty in 1965 after teaching and conducting research at Boston U. Medical School and Harvard Medical School. With Skinner, he did pioneer studies in human operant conditioning and coined term "behavior therapy." Devised simplified system for precise behavioral management ("pinpoint, record and consequate") and precision-teaching model. His Behavior Research Company in Kansas City has set up computerized Behavior Bank to store and retrieve data on how to change behaviors.

O. IVAR LOVAAS
Professor of Psychology, U. of California at Los Angeles
b. May 8, 1927
M.S. 1954, Ph.D. 1958, U. of Washington

Joined UCLA faculty in 1961 after teaching and doing clinical and research work at U. of Washington. Leading authority in treatment of autistic children with a combination of behavioral techniques, including operant, imitative (modeling) and aversive (electric shock). Did research on tension, aggression, verbal behavior and self-destructive behavior, principally with children. Planning new study on childhood gender problems. Coeditor of *Readings in Behavior Modification with Deviant Children* (Prentice-Hall, in press).

CHARLES H. MADSEN Jr.
Associate Professor of Psychology, Florida State U.
b. March 28, 1933
M.A. 1964, Ph.D. 1965, U. of Illinois

Joined Florida State faculty in 1967 after two years as research professor at Illinois and as staff psychologist of mental-health clinic in Champaign. Did extensive research with Becker, Ullmann and others, mainly in modification of child behavior. With Clifford K. Madsen, also at Florida State, he explored use of music and other innovations in behavioral technology. As consultant to schools and child-care centers in Illinois and Florida, he helped spread classroom use of behavioral techniques to more than 6,000 teachers.

RICHARD W. MALOTT
Associate Professor of Psychology, Western Michigan U.
b. October 3, 1936
Ph.D. 1963, Columbia

Joined Western Michigan faculty in 1966 after teaching and conducting research at Indiana U., Columbia and Denison U. Pioneered use of contingency management in introductory psychology course for college students. Coauthor, with D. L. Whaley, of programmed textbook, *Elementary Principles of Behavior* (Appleton-Century-Crofts, 1971). Now doing pilot research on behavior-oriented experimental college. His Behaviordelia firm produces pop-culture, multimedia works such as *Big-New-Mother Mind-Boggling Behavior Expander* (1972) and *The First Fly-by-Night Underground Experimental College of Kalamazoo* (1971).

is a myth. Labeling persons as schizophrenic or retarded is useless and often harmful. The illness, or medical model, which perpetuates the myth and the labels, is no longer valid. Neither are the tools—I.Q. tests, attitude scales, questionnaires—that facilitate the pigeonholing process.

If a person exhibits "deviant" behavior, the failure is in the social and physical environment that determines his behavior, not in the individual; changing the environment will change the behavior. If "treatment" is necessary, the best place to do it is in the home or school, not in some artificial or perhaps permanent place of confinement. And the best persons to provide the treatment are parents, teachers, friends—not medicine men. Therapy, even with large groups, must concentrate on the individual or it will not be effective; and its concern is with the here and now, not with some past trauma or some statistical prediction about future performance. But therapy itself should take a back seat to prevention, which is far better and less expensive. Above all, the process of changing human lives must be evaluated continually; and it must be accountable to its consumers, the persons who are affected by it and the persons who pay for it.

Essence. This is my own summary, distilled from talks with several applied behavior analysts and a great deal of reading between the lines of their scientific reports. The analysts themselves spend little time denouncing traditional clinical and teaching methods. But if my overview is accurate, the new breed of Skinnerians has a lot in common with many of the younger radical and humanist professionals who are challenging the traditionalists in psychiatry, psychology, education, counseling, social work, rehabilitation and correction. This conclusion, which practically forced itself upon me after I noted point after point of similarity, was the most personally surprising outcome of my trip beyond *Beyond Freedom and Dignity*. I suspect that if it weren't for their own curtains of mutually exclusive jargons and mutually reinforcing labels, the humanists and the behaviorists might be surprised at how near they are to being bedfellows.

Editors. The applied behavior analysts meanwhile keep themselves busy writing prescriptions for change and producing results that astonish almost all who behold. The program at Bryant school, for instance, is just one of the numerous ongoing projects that make Kansas probably the world center of applied behavior analysis. The state leaped into behaviorism in a big way in 1965,

4. Shapers at Work

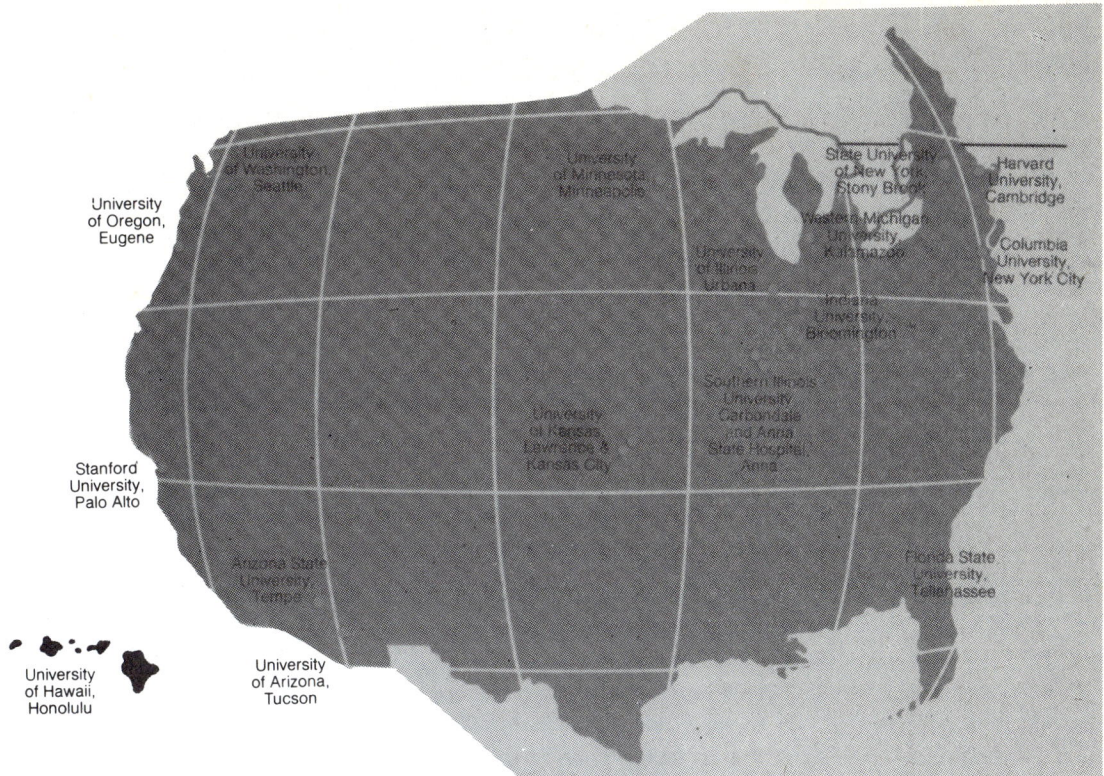

Washington lost Bijou, Baer and several other top-flight applied behavior analysts in the mid-'60s, but it remains an active center. Also highly active are the State University of New York at Stony Brook, the University of Oregon in Eugene, and the University of Hawaii in Honolulu.

Some centers have been chiefly doctorate-producers. Forty-one of the 42 leading behavior shapers hold doctorates, half of which (21) came from just five schools—Washington (six), Harvard (five), Indiana (four) and Columbia University and the University of Minnesota (three each). These figures reflect the influence of Skinner at Harvard, Indiana and Minnesota; of Bijou at Washington; and of Fred S. Keller at Columbia.

Other centers owe their present status to the work of one or two outstanding individuals—Bijou at the University of Illinois in Champaign; Nathan Azrin at Southern Illinois; Albert Bandura at Stanford; Ralph Wetzel at the University of Arizona; Charles Madsen at Florida State. A few once-busy centers have grown quiescent, including Arizona State University, which was known in the early '60s as "Fort Skinner in the desert."

The next few years will see the flowering of new centers. Best bets are Drake University in Des Moines, where Jon E. Krapfl, W. Scott Wood and others are developing behavior-modification and educational-engineering training programs; and the University of Utah in Salt Lake City, where Howard Sloane, Gabriel Della-Piana and others have a wide range of programs under way, including one that uses behavioral techniques to train poets and sculptors.

1. THE ORIGINS

HUGH S. MCKENZIE
Associate Professor of Education, U. of Vermont
b. May 10, 1935
Ph.D. 1966, U. of Arizona

Joined Vermont faculty in 1967 after a year as research fellow at U. of Kansas Bureau of Child Research. Developed consulting-teacher model for training school psychologists and special-education teachers in behavioral techniques. Current research in Vermont public and parochial schools involves behavior-shaping techniques and natural reinforcers in learning language, arithmetic, self-care and social behaviors. Author of "Special Education and Consulting Teachers," in *Implementing Behavioral Programs in Education and Clinical Settings* (Research Press, 1972).

MERLE L. MEACHAM
Associate Professor of Educational Psychology, U. of Washington
b. Feburary 22, 1920
M.A. 1956, U. of Washington; Ed.D. 1964, Washington State U.

Joined Washington faculty in 1966 after several years as psychologist and guidance counselor in Washington secondary schools and colleges. Specialist in use of reinforcement techniques by school psychologists and counselors. Coauthor of *Changing Classroom Behavior: A Manual for Precision Teaching* (International Textbook Co., 1969).

JACK L. MICHAEL
Professor of Psychology, Western Michigan U.
b. January 16, 1926
M.A. 1952, Ph.D. 1955, U. of California at Los Angeles

Joined Western Michigan faculty in 1967 after teaching at U. of Kansas, U. of Houston and, for seven years, at Arizona State U. With graduate student Ayllon he published seminal study, "The Psychiatric Nurse as a Behavioral Engineer," in 1959. Pioneered use of behavioral approach in rehabilitation, counseling and college instruction. Has been influential as teacher, consultant and lecturer at workshops and conferences across the country. Coeditor, with Charles Neuringer, of *Behavior Modification in Clinical Psychology* (Appleton-Century-Crofts, 1970).

K. DANIEL O'LEARY
Associate Professor of Psychology, State U. of New York at Stony Brook
b. October 3, 1940
M.A. 1965, Ph.D. 1967, U. of Illinois

Joined Stony Brook faculty in 1967 after a year of teaching and research at Illinois. With Becker, Susan G. O'Leary and others, he did extensive research in use of token reinforcement and other behavioral techniques in public schools. Coordinator of the Child Clinic and director of the University Laboratory School at Stony Brook. Coauthor, with Ronald Drabman, of "Token Reinforcement Programs in the Classroom: A Review" *(Psychological Bulletin,* June 1971) and coeditor, with Susan O'Leary, of *Classroom Management* (Pergamon Press, 1972).

GERALD R. PATTERSON
Research Professor of Education, U. of Oregon
b. July 24, 1926
M.A. 1951, U. of Oregon; Ph.D. 1956, U. of Minnesota

Joined Oregon faculty in 1957. He is also research associate at Oregon Research Institute and president of the Association for the Advancement of Behavior Therapy. Pioneer in teaching behavioral techniques to parents, teachers and student peers. Now developing engineering technology in work with juvenile delinquents. Developed intervention techniques for use in marital conflict. Author of *Families: Application of Social Learning to Family Life* (Research Press, 1971) and coauthor of *Living with Children: New Methods for Parents and Teachers* (Research Press, 1968).

DAVID PREMACK
Professor of Psychology, U. of California at Santa Barbara
b. October 26, 1925
M.A. 1951, Ph.D. 1955, U. of Minnesota

Joined Santa Barbara faculty after nine years at U. of Missouri. Taught and did research at the Yerkes primate laboratories in Orange Park, Florida, and at UCLA and Harvard. Primarily an animal experimentalist, he formulated the Premack Principle of operant reinforcement, which applied behavior analysts have found invaluable in contingency management ("Toward Empirical Behavioral Laws: I. Positive Reinforcement," reprinted in Ulrich, Stachnik and Mabry's *Control of Human Behavior*). It was Premack who taught Sarah, a chimpanzee, to "talk" [see "The Education of S*A*R*A*H," PT, September 1970].

How Behavior Shapers Move

	HARVARD UNIVERSITY	INDIANA UNIVERSITY	COLUMBIA UNIVERSITY	UNIVERSITY OF MINNESOTA	SOUTHERN ILLINOIS UNIVERSITY	STANFORD UNIVERSITY	UNIVERSITY OF WASHINGTON	ARIZONA STATE	UNIVERSITY OF ARIZONA	UNIVERSITY OF ILLINOIS	FLORIDA STATE UNIVERSITY	UNIVERSITY OF KANSAS	WESTERN MICHIGAN UNIVERSITY	UNIVERSITY OF HAWAII	SUNY STONY BROOK	UNIVERSITY OF OREGON
1955	*Azrin *Ferster Homme *Keller *Lindsley Skinner	Bijou Ferster *Fuller Homme Malott *Sarason Skinner	Bijou *Ferster Keller *Krasner	*Patterson *Premack Skinner	Azrin Cohen Goldiamond Ulrich	Bandura *Becker *Ullmann	Baer Bijou *Fordyce *Hall *Lovaas Meacham Sarason Wahler Wetzel	Staats		Becker Ulrich	Fuller Turner	Ayllon Michael				Patterson
1960	Lindsley Skinner	*Bernal Ferster Ulrich	Keller *Malott		Ayllon Azrin Cohen Ulrich	Bandura Krasner Ullmann	Baer Bijou Fordyce Hall Krasner Lovaas *Risley Sarason Wahler Wetzel Wolf	Goldiamond Keller Michael Staats *Wolf	Bernal *McKenzie Tharp Wetzel Wolf	Becker *Madsen *O'Leary Ullmann	Risley Turner	Haring				Patterson
1965	Skinner		*Sulzer		Ayllon and Sulzer	Bandura	Burgess Bushell Fordyce Haring Hawkins Meacham Sarason	Keller Michael	McKenzie Tharp Wetzel	Becker Bijou Madsen O'Leary Ullmann	Madsen	Baer Bushell Hall Hawkins Lindsley McKenzie Risley Wolf	Hawkins Keller Malott Michael Ulrich	Staats Tharp	Krasner O'Leary	Patterson
1970 TODAY	Skinner				Azrin	Bandura	Burgess Fordyce Haring Meacham Sarason		Wetzel	Bijou	Madsen	Baer Bushell Hall Lindsley Risley Wolf	Fuller Hawkins Keller Malott Michael Ulrich	Staats Tharp Ullmann	Krasner O'Leary	Becker Patterson

4. Shapers at Work

TODD R. RISLEY
Associate Professor of Human Development, U. of Kansas
b. September 8, 1937
M.S. 1963, Ph.D. 1966, U. of Washington

Joined Kansas faculty in 1965 after a year at Florida State U. Director of preschool research at Juniper Gardens Children's Project. Director of living-environments projects for infant, preschool and day-care centers, an urban recreation center and a nursing home; develops packages telling how to design, select and organize facilities, equipment, materials and personnel for complete environments that will maintain appropriate behaviors for various populations [see "Learning and Lollipops," PT, January 1968]. Risley is editor of the *Journal of Applied Behavior Analysis*.

IRWIN G. SARASON
Professor of Psychology, U. of Washington
b. September 15, 1929
M.A. 1953, State U. of Iowa; Ph.D. 1955, Indiana U.

Joined Washington faculty in 1956. Has done research on personality and problems in clinical psychology, including test anxiety and verbal conditioning. Outstanding work was the introduction of modeling techniques in behavior modification of test-anxious students, juvenile offenders and parolees. Author of *Personality: An Objective Approach* (Wiley, 1966) and coauthor of *Reinforcing Productive Classroom Behavior* (Behavioral Publications, 1971).

B.F. SKINNER
Professor of Psychology, Harvard
b. March 20, 1904
M.A. 1930, Ph.D. 1931, Harvard

Joined Harvard faculty in 1948 after teaching and conducting research at U. of Minnesota and Indiana U. Formulated operant-conditioning paradigm in first book, *The Behavior of Organisms* (Appleton-Century-Crofts, 1938). Generally considered the father (through Azrin and Lindsley) of applied behavior analysis, though some members of movement prefer to pay direct allegiance to Bijou and Baer. One of the few operant psychologists who has written books for general public—*Walden Two* (Macmillan, 1948), *Science and Human Behavior* (Macmillan, 1953), and *Beyond Freedom and Dignity* (Knopf, 1971) [see PT, August 1971].

ARTHUR W. STAATS
Professor of Psychology and Educational Psychology, U. of Hawaii
b. January 17, 1924
M.A. 1953, Ph.D. 1956, U. of California at Los Angeles

Joined Hawaii faculty in 1967 after 10 years at Arizona State U. and two years at U. of Wisconsin. Pioneered use of token-economy system in special education, behavioral techniques to correct reading disabilities. Did extensive research in human learning aimed at developing unified theory of social behaviorism. Author of *Learning, Language and Cognition* (Holt, Rinehart and Winston, 1968) and *Complex Human Behavior* (Holt, 1963).

BETH SULZER-AZAROFF
Training Consultant, Mansfield Training School, Mansfield Depot, Connecticut
b. September 6, 1929
M.A. 1953, City College of New York; Ph.D. 1966, U. of Minnesota

Joined Southern Illinois faculty in 1966 after several years as elementary-school teacher. Left in 1972 to take present position. Completed three-year study on use of token systems to raise academic-achievement level of public-school children. Directed in-service teacher-training workshops in behavior-modification procedures. Coauthor of *Behavior Modification Procedures for School Personnel* (Dryden Press, 1972).

ROLAND G. THARP
Professor of Psychology and Director of Clinical Studies, U. of Hawaii
b. June 6, 1930
Ph.D. 1961, U. of Michigan

Joined Hawaii faculty in 1968 after five years at U. of Arizona and two years as field selection officer for Peace Corps. Specialist in marriage problems, use of behavioral techniques by family therapists and probation officers. Author, with Wetzel, of *Behavior Modification in the Natural Environment* (Academic Press, 1969) and, with David Watson, of *Self-Directed Behavior* (Brooks/Cole, 1972). In earlier years he won several literary awards, including the *Atlantic Monthly*'s Grand Prize.

How Behavior Shaping Grows

		TARGET SUBJECTS	BEHAVIOR SHAPERS	TARGET BEHAVIORS	ENVIRONMENTS	BEHAVIORAL PRODUCTS
1935	Experimentation	animals	experimental psychologists	operant responses	campus psychology laboratories	Skinner box, operant paradigm, experimental designs, token incentives
1960	Treatment	individuals	clinical and school psychologists	severe disturbances, learning disabilities, physical handicaps	mental institutions, clinics, special-education classrooms	treatment and learning techniques for human subjects, token economy
1965		small and large groups, families	psychologists, teachers, special therapists, parents	social and educational disturbances	prisons, regular classrooms, halfway houses, homes	applied-behavior-analysis model, teaching techniques and models for professionals and paraprofessionals, new environmental designs, evaluation research, accountability techniques
1970	Prevention	whole schools, neighborhoods, whole counties, general public	administrators, teacher aides, employers, students, families, selves	mild disturbances, normal	mental-health centers, social and welfare agencies, businesses, open settings	packaged learning programs for university classes, schools, homes, institutions, child-care centers, nursing homes, halfway houses
2001		everyone	everyone	all kinds	everywhere	a happy, productive culture without war, poverty or pollution

1. THE ORIGINS

A. JACK TURNER
Research Director, Huntsville-Madison County Mental Health Center, Alabama
b. January 19, 1932
Ph.D. 1962, Florida State U.

Moved to Huntsville-Madison center in 1970 after six years as professor of psychology at Auburn U. Planned and coordinated conversion of center to whole-system use of empirical—chiefly operant—techniques and now directs three-year implementation and evaluation program.

LEONARD P. ULLMANN
Professor of Psychology, U. of Hawaii
b. May 28, 1930
M.A. 1953, Ph.D. 1955, Stanford

Joined Hawaii faculty in 1972 after nine years at U. of Illinois. Also taught at Stanford and San Jose State and was coordinator of Psychiatric Evaluation Project at Palo Alto VA Hospital. Major work has been on normal and schizophrenic responses to emotional stimuli, problems of psychodiagnosis and modification of verbal behavior. Author of *Institution and Outcome: A Comparative Study of Psychiatric Hospitals* (Pergamon, 1967) and coauthor, with Krasner, of *A Psychological Approach to Abnormal Behavior* (Prentice-Hall, 1969). Also coeditor, with Krasner, of two collections of major behavior-modification articles (see Krasner).

ROGER E. ULRICH
Research Professor of Psychology, Western Michigan U.
b. August 30, 1931
M.A. 1957, Bradley U.; Ph.D. 1961, Southern Illinois U.

Joined Western Michigan faculty in 1965 after teaching and conducting research at Anna State Hospital, Illinois Wesleyan U. and Illinois State U. Studied at U. of Illinois and Indiana U., worked with Azrin and Goldiamond. Set up and directs Learning Village, a private, behavior-oriented school for children in Kalamazoo. Does experimental analyses of aggression in animals and people. Coeditor, with T.J. Stachnik and J.H. Mabry, of two-volume collection of important papers in behavior shaping, *Control of Human Behavior* (Scott, Foresman, 1966 and 1970). Third volume is in press.

ROBERT G. WAHLER
Professor of Psychology, U. of Tennessee
b. October 1, 1936
M.S. 1960, Ph.D. 1962, U. of Washington

Did post-doctoral work at U. of Washington Child Development Clinic under supervision of Bijou and Baer. Moved to Tennessee in 1964. Specialist in use of behavioral techniques in evaluation and treatment of deviant child behavior. Best-known work is with "oppositional" children—or "brats," as Bernal calls them—and with parents as therapists. Current work, on generality of behavior changes, takes ecological approach. Coeditor, with O.H. Milton, of *Behavioral Disorders: Perspectives and Trends* (Lippincott, 1969).

RALPH J. WETZEL
Professor of Psychology, U. of Arizona
b. June 11, 1933
M.S. 1958, Ph.D. 1961, U. of Washington

Joined Arizona faculty in 1962. Chief work has been in training parents, teachers and paraprofessionals to use behavioral techniques with children. Former consultant to Head-Start and Follow-Through programs. Current research involves change processes in educational and mental-health systems. Coauthor, with Tharp, of *Behavior Modification in the Natural Environment* (Academic Press, 1969).

MONTROSE M. WOLF
Professor of Human Development, U. of Kansas
b. May 29, 1935
M.A. 1961, Ph.D. 1963, Arizona State U.

Joined Kansas faculty in 1965 after teaching and conducting research for two years at U. of Washington and a year at U. of Arizona. As graduate student, he was a research assistant to Goldiamond and Staats; his dissertation adviser was Michael. Developed behavioral techniques for modifying problems of normal, disadvantaged and retarded children and adolescents. Created Achievement Place, a community-based home for predelinquents, and the teaching-family model.

---

when Ogden Lindsley moved from Harvard to the University of Kansas to coordinate research at the Medical Center's Child Rehabilitation Unit in Kansas City. That same year, a top-notch group of young researchers who had done work in child development with Sidney W. Bijou and Florence Harris at the University of Washington—Vance Hall, Montrose Wolf, Donald M. Baer and Todd R. Risley—moved en masse to the main campus at Lawrence, Kansas, and tapped a generous supply of funds flowing from the Federal Government through the University's Bureau of Child Research. (Risley alone has received nearly a million dollars in grants.)

This group, which *Behavior Today* lightheartedly referred to as "the Kansas Mafia," has dominated the chief post-Skinnerian scholarly publication, the *Journal of Applied Behavior Analysis*, since its founding in 1968. (JABA is the prodigal son of JEAB, the *Journal of the Experimental Analysis of Behavior*. Its conception saved JEAB from overcontamination by the real world and hastened JEAB's return to the laboratory purity of its Skinnerian birth.) Wolf was editor-in-chief of JABA's first three volumes, and the current editor, Risley, took over the post from Baer. JABA's very first volume opened with an article by Hall and two associates that was the first published account of the application of behavior analysis in a regular classroom, and it featured an article by Baer, Wolf and Risley that established the model for applied behavioral research and, by implication, the criteria for getting published in JABA.

"An *applied* behavior analysis," they warned, "will make obvious the importance of the behavior changed, its quantitative characteristics, the experimental manipulations which analyze with clarity what was responsible for the change, the technologically exact description of all procedures contributing to that change, the effectiveness of those procedures in making sufficient change for value, and the generality of that change."

Efforts. In Kansas, the group immediately started testing their ideas at Juniper Gardens, a black housing project in the poorest section of Kansas City. Baer, a 1957 Chicago Ph.D. who had taught at Washington for eight years, was the mentor and theorist. Hall, who had been an elementary-school teacher and principal for 13 years before completing his Ph.D. at Washington, focused his efforts on the public-school setting. Wolf, whose research at the University of Houston, Arizona State (Ph.D., 1963) and Washington had ranged so widely that it practically paralleled the field's development, concentrated on home-style settings. Risley, the youngest, arrived in Kansas even before he received his Ph.D. (Washington, 1966); he took charge of the Juniper Gardens community center, running the recreation, preschool and day-care programs and organizing the tenants.

Force. The seven-year association has proved to be mutually fruitful. For the area's residents, it has resulted in better schooling for the children; new, well-run preschool classes; a new day-care center; a clean, well-managed recreation center that, unlike such centers in other areas,

4. Shapers at Work

Margaret, Age 10, and Martha, Age eight—

A Sample Case of Behavioral Engineering

"We are well aware that good teachers had been using these same techniques effectively long before B.F. Skinner formulated the principles of operant conditioning," R. Vance Hall points out in his handbook *Managing Behavior.* Some parents had used them, too. But most had not done it precisely and systematically—which is what applied behavior analysis is all about.

Many parents hand out allowances on a noncontingent basis; they do not make the amount dependent on completion of homework or routine chores. Then they wonder why the homework and the chores don't get done. Some children, of course, find sufficient reward in performing the tasks—or in the praise they collect for doing them. For other children, parents may need to use more elaborate measures.

The following brief research report illustrates several techniques used by applied behavior analysts like Vance Hall. The experiment, done with parents by Hall and student Lois Cox, is similar to experiments conducted in classrooms by the teachers I visited at Bryant school in Kansas City. It involves the same five-step procedure. The token-economy system, though it is less complex than the one I saw in operation at Montrose Wolf's Achievement Place, makes use of the same principles.

—Kenneth Goodall

THE EXPERIMENT

Margaret and Martha are sisters aged 10 and eight. Their mother had difficulty getting the girls to do daily work and personal chores in the home.

The mother made a chart for each girl listing nine tasks they were expected to do each day. The tasks listed on Margaret's chart were: make beds, brush teeth (a.m.), brush teeth (p.m.), turn off night light, hang up clothes, put dirty clothes in hamper, practice music (30 minutes), clean bathroom after bath, read. Martha's chart was identical except that it required only 20 minutes of music practice.

The mother checked daily on whether the girls completed the tasks. Her husband made an independent check. Their records always agreed 100 percent.

Baseline 1: During a two-week baseline phase in which no contingencies were in effect, except the usual parental requests and urgings to do the assigned tasks, the mean number of tasks completed for both Margaret and Martha was 1.3 per day.

Pay for Duties 1: In this phase the girls were asked to keep the chart record by placing an X in a blank after completing each task each day.

Each girl received five cents a day for each day she completed all the duties for that day. If she failed to complete all duties, she received nothing for that day. However, if she completed all duties for an entire calendar week she received a bonus of 15 cents. In other words she could earn 50 cents a week by doing all of her daily tasks. She received no other allowance.

In the first week under these conditions each completed all duties and received 50 cents. In the second week each failed to complete one task and received only 30 cents for that week. Neither failed to complete all tasks through the remainder of the phase. The mean levels of completing tasks for both girls was therefore almost nine per day.

Baseline 2: In the eighth week of the experiment the girls were told that they should continue charting task completions but that they were doing so well that they would receive their 50-cent allowance even if they forgot to complete all tasks. In these conditions Margaret completed an average of 2.4 tasks per day, Martha two per day.

Pay for Duties 2: The following week, allowances were again made contingent on completing assigned tasks. Doing tasks returned to high rates. Over the next three weeks the mean number completed by Margaret was 8.9 and by Martha 8.8 per day.

THE PROCEDURE

1 Select target behaviors that need changing. As Hall says, "The behaviors must be clearly defined."

2 Keep a baseline record—a notation of each behavior as it occurs—to find out how strong the behaviors are before any attempts are made to change them. To ensure accuracy, behavior-analysis experimenters use an independent observer.

3 Set up the experimental conditions and record and reinforce correct behaviors. The purpose is to attempt to modify the behaviors by rearranging the consequences that follow the behaviors.

In some cases, when the purpose is to decrease incorrect behaviors, an extinction technique is used—that is, the consequences are the withholding of reinforcements.

In this case, when the purpose was to strengthen correct behaviors, the consequences were reinforcements: tokens (marks on a chart) that were exchangeable later for money. Thus the girls were put on a token-economy system.

In this phase, as in the baseline phase, each correct behavior was recorded. According to Hall, this record "provides continuous feedback as to the effectiveness of the modification and indicates if further modification procedures are necessary." They weren't.

4 Return to baseline conditions by briefly discontinuing reinforcements. This technique—reversal—is one of two main research designs used by applied behavior analysts. If the behaviors return to their former level, as they did in this experiment, the behavior analysts are just a step away from what they consider to be scientific verification that reinforcement was instrumental in increasing correct behaviors.

5 Reinstitute the conditions that were successful. "If this again results in a change," Hall says, "a cause-and-effect relationship has been demonstrated."

1. THE ORIGINS

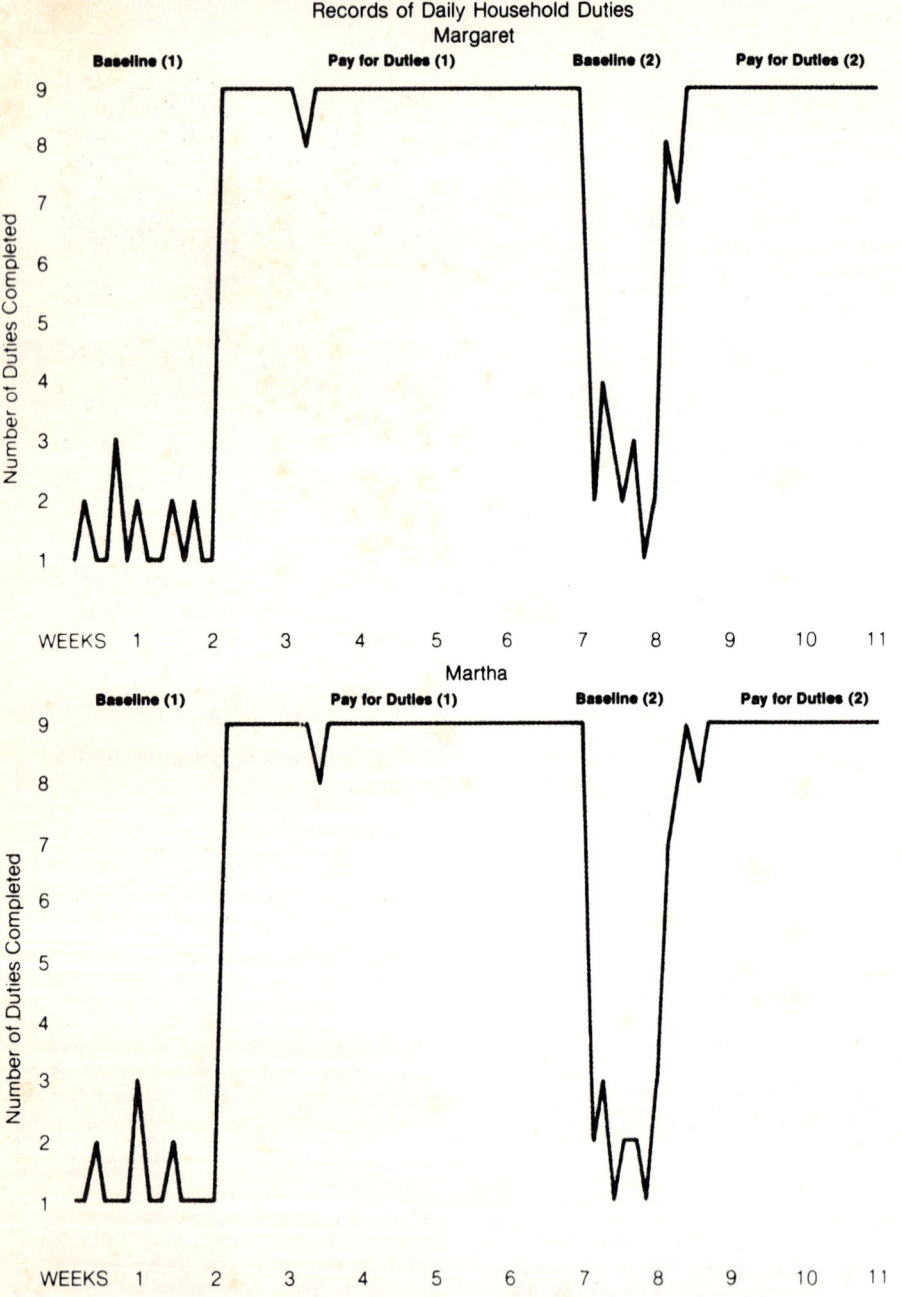

Discussion: This study demonstrated that a token system (marks on a chart) backed up by money was effective in getting two girls to complete home tasks. A brief reversal provided scientific verification that contingent allowances resulted in desired changes. The parents reported that they were pleased with the fact that the girls were doing their expected duties without being nagged and because they were "accomplishing far more on their musical instruments." The girls were also reported to be pleased by their accomplishments.

Charting gives graphic record of behavior changes. Dramatic increase in performance of target behaviors with institution of experimental conditions, followed by an equally dramatic drop when experimental conditions are removed, gives chart lines a shape that is typical of successful experiments in applied behavior analysis.

is much more used than abused; a reading-tutoring program; several paraprofessional jobs; and a new tenants' association that is using behavioral techniques to solve neighborhood problems, including one problem the police had ignored: speeding motorists. For the researchers, Juniper Gardens has provided a natural laboratory in which to gather data, develop new technologies, and bolster their group's credentials as a guiding force in human-behavior control.

Farm. One of the most impressive fruits from Juniper Gardens is Achievement Place, a large and rambling old farmhouse in Lawrence that is a home away from home for adolescent boys who have got into trouble with their parents, their schools, or the law. The idea was Wolf's, and he spent more than three years perfecting it. It employs an elaborate token-economy system and the learning techniques first tested at Juniper Gardens. Up to eight "uncontrollable" boys live in the home with two "teaching parents," Elery and Elaine Phillips, who trained for their jobs in graduate study with Wolf. The Phillipses and the boys themselves make videotapes of what happens at the home as they work to change various behaviors. One tape caught what might be called a Skinnerian doubletake—a new arrival's almost instantaneous behavior reversal, from adamant refusal to sit still and do his homework to rapt absorption in the task after Elaine Phillips explained the token system and put him on it. The Phillipses also have published extensive data showing increased cooperation, lessened hostility, greater tidiness and punctuality, and better school work among the boys, who seemed anything but uncontrollable last winter when they took me on a guided tour of the home and gave me a concise explanation of how their token system works.

Finance. Wolf has established a special graduate program at the University of Kansas to train teaching parents, and he has outlined his *teaching-family model* carefully in a handbook so that other communities can set up their own homes for delinquent children. A.S. Neill's *Summerhill* is "a great and inspiring book about working with kids," Wolf told me, "but it provides no technology. That is why attempts to replicate it have not been successful. We do have a usable technology."

Although Achievement Place is costly to operate, it is "much less expensive than traditional programs in large state institutions," according to a brochure Wolf put out this year. He estimated that last year's operating costs for the community-controlled home were $3,600 for each boy—considerably less than the $8,500 to $9,000 spent annually for each boy at the Kansas Boys Industrial School. Replications of Achievement Place in Kansas City and elsewhere reportedly are doing well, though one in Lawrence—for girls—has run into some unique problems, perhaps because girls usually have to be much more "uncontrollable" than boys to be labeled delinquent.

Graduates. Hall, too, has developed and packaged a teaching model, based on pilot studies at Juniper Gardens. Hall had noticed that some teachers who were involved in early classroom experiments "soon reverted to less effective practices once the experimenters withdrew." His *responsive-teaching model* makes it possible for teachers to learn the essentials of applied behavior analysis in a week-long workshop, usually for college credit, and to devise their own experiments without esoteric equipment or outside expertise.

Hall told me that there is a "terrific demand" for the workshops. He runs many of them himself through his H & H Enterprises, Inc., but his graduate students usually do the teaching. Some 200 participants paid $135 each, plus travel and lodging expenses, to attend his workshop last June in Kansas City, Missouri. A few of the participants returned home and set up workshops to spread the new techniques among other teachers in their districts. H & H Enterprises has sold more than 18,000 copies of Hall's three-part responsive-teaching package, *Managing Behavior*, at $1.55 a copy; and he recently added three more parts that cost up to $4.95 a copy.

Gist. The teachers at Bryant school showed me how they use Hall's model to conduct classroom experiments:

1. They select *target behaviors* that need changing, such as poor attendance, tardiness, or low academic performance;
2. They keep *baseline records* to find out how often the unwanted behaviors occur;
3. They set up *experimental conditions* during which they record each "correct" behavior and reinforce it with praise (a smile for the student, for example, or a phone call to the parent), with a token (a smiling-face sticker, perhaps, that will buy a lollipop or a crayon) or with the opportunity to do something enjoyable (go to a ball game or work in the school lunchroom, for instance);
4. They return to baseline conditions (withdrawing the rewards) to find out whether reinforcement was instrumental in increasing correct behavior; and
5. Finally, they reinstitute the conditions that were successful.

Richard Fox and Rodney Copeland, who worked with Hall as graduate students, were overseeing the Bryant program when I visited there. They took me on a tour of the school; and the principal, Ronald Brown, and his teaching staff spent a couple of hours outlining their recent projects. The teachers sometimes used a token-economy system with individual students, I learned, but rarely with entire classes. One teacher, who does use it, told me she dropped it at one point but reinstated it because "the kids wanted it back." Fox and Copeland said they don't believe in "expensive" token systems and prefer instead to use "available consequences"—that is, objects or activities that are both reinforcing and readily at hand—such as crayons, an extra five minutes of recess or, for the younger children, a "squeezy hug" from the teacher.

Genesis. The idea of using natural reinforcing events came from animal research, just as the token-economy idea did. In the laboratory, researchers generally used food as a reinforcer and kept their animals hungry to make sure they worked to get it. In 1959, animal behaviorist David Premack developed a hypothesis that anything with a good probability of eliciting a response would reinforce a response of lower probability. When this *Premack Principle* was applied to children, as it was by behavioral engineer Lloyd E. Homme and others in 1963, it gave teachers an almost unlimited supply of reinforcers that cost the schools little or no money. Teachers could keep boisterous children quiet during a 10-minute study period, for instance, by giving them as a reward a two-minute period in which they could run and scream all they wanted to.

Hooky. One Bryant teacher told me she had run into what seems to be a fairly common problem in choosing reinforcers—their short half-lives. A 10-year-old boy in her class for the educable mentally retarded had stopped playing hooky after she let him work in the lunchroom as a reward for attendance; now, grown weary of the work, he had started cutting classes again and she was looking around for a new reinforcer. Another teacher expressed discouragement over the meager results of her first attempt to reinforce a child's academic performance and got a quick reinforcement herself; after all, Brown told us, a correct-response rate of 2.6 (out of a possible 52) *was* better than 0, the baseline rate.

And the Bryant counselor told me she had tested Brown's old practice of phoning parents and had found that it was indeed effective. It improved the attendance of several target students who frequently were absent and it also improved the attendance of their sisters and brothers.

Help. Kansas has spawned other teaching packages besides Hall's and Wolf's. Lindsley devised a course in "precision teaching" at the University of Kansas School of Education; and his colleagues, including Merle Meacham and Norris Haring of the University of Washington, have packaged a *precision-teaching model* that is used in many parts of the country. A former member of the University's Bureau of Child Research group, Hugh S. McKenzie, has spread applied behavior analysis all over Vermont with his *consulting-teacher model*. In a two-year master's program at the University of Vermont's School of Education, he trains experts who in turn work in local school districts training elementary teachers and parents. The *behavior-analysis model* devised by Don Bushell Jr., a University of Kansas sociologist, was used last year by coordinators, teachers, teachers' aides and parents in 279 classrooms across the country with nearly 7,000 students enrolled in a Follow-Through program that Bushell runs from his offices on the Lawrence campus.

Half. Schools are a natural testing ground for learning techniques, of course, and this circumstance, combined with the willingness of funding agencies and school administrators to let them experiment, is why most applied behavior analysts have chosen to work there. A good half of the 200 or so accounts of token systems published in the last decade involved classroom use, and work with teachers and parents has intensified in the last three years. Daniel G. Brown, a former consultant for the National Institute of Mental Health, keeps track of such things; he said that more than two thirds of the total literature covering work with teachers and parents was published after 1968.

Most of the studies have reported successful behavior changes that range from significant to astounding. The best ones, in keeping with the applied model set forth by Baer, Wolf and Risley, are highly replicable. Nevertheless, it is difficult to compare the outcomes with those achieved by other techniques because most of the experiments compare a subject's behavior not with a control subject's but with his own, before and dur-

1. THE ORIGINS

ing the experimental conditions. While this practice may be convincing enough for a teacher who can see the changes with her own eyes, it often leaves skeptics unconvinced.

Improvement. Two major efforts, the Head Start and Follow-Through planned-variation studies, are under way to compare behavioral and other specially designed approaches to compensatory education. The results, highly tentative so far, indicate that the two behavioral approaches—Don Bushell's behavior-analysis plan and the E-B program designed and run by Siegfried Engelmann and Wesley C. Becker at the University of Oregon—outstrip all the others in improving the academic performance of preschool and first-grade children. This outcome is no surprise; the behavioral programs are designed specifically to achieve this goal, and their highly structured, no-nonsense format led Follow-Through evaluators at the Stanford Research Institute to nickname them "pricklies." Still, even with less tangible objectives such as positive shifts in attitudes toward school and learning, these two approaches seem to be about as effective as humanist programs—the "gooies"—that talk more about the growing awareness of the whole child than about test scores.

Increase. Bushell and Becker told me that their own statistics show significant academic gains by poor children in urban and rural areas as well as by middle-class children. For instance, poor children in Becker's program raised their reading level by 4.1 grades in three years. "Keep in mind," Becker said, "that the expected gains for economically disadvantaged children have typically been reported at about .6 grade levels per year."

In Waukegan, Illinois, children in Bushell's kindergarten classes raised their reading grade-levels in a year's time from .25 to 1.35 as measured by the Wide Range Achievement Test. In spelling they went from .10 to 1.35 and in mathematics from .40 to 1.80. Comparable gains by children in two Waukegan schools that were not in the Follow-Through program were from .05 to .75 in reading and spelling and from .25 to .90 in math. Bushell also reported that children in his first-grade program on the Northern Cheyenne Indian Reservation in Montana advanced from .80 to 2.07 in reading, .87 to 1.90 in spelling and .76 to 2.30 in math.

These gains do not come cheap. The Government spent $728 last year to put each child through Bushell's program. Development expenses accounted for more than half of the total, however. Once the program is past the development phase the cost will drop to $300, Bushell said. The Kansas operation will fade out, and control will pass to the local schools.

Input. "Control" is the right word. Television cameras film the action in each classroom, and Bushell and his colleagues view the tapes in Kansas. Each local program also phones in a periodic report on each child's progress to be fed into a computer in Lawrence. In return, the teachers get regular feedback on their own performance as well as that of their students. Theoretically, Bushell told me, if such a system were set up in a local school district, a superintendent could keep a daily check on every student. He also could give a reinforcing bonus to the teacher whose students made the biggest gains—a practice that Bushell favors. Even now, Bushell's program exemplifies on a large scale the built-in advantages that applied behavior analysis has for the continuous evaluation of ongoing programs, for making them accountable, and for changing them if necessary before it is too late.

If behavioral technology has any possibility of fulfilling Skinner's high ambition to redesign the whole culture, its use should extend practically from the cradle to the grave. And it does, as I learned when I took a look at Todd Risley's "living-environments" programs in Kansas. They included crawlers and toddlers at day-care centers, beginning learners in preschool classes, juveniles at the Juniper Gardens recreation center, adults in the tenants' association, and old persons in a private nursing home for the retarded in Lawrence. Risley already has contributed such techniques as Placheck and the "zone" concept to simplify the problems of behavior control, and he intends to package day-care and nursing-home models to add to the available technology.

Thousands of parents have learned to use applied behavior analysis, since all of the teaching models recognize the large part that parents can play in their children's learning process. Some parents get a fairly detailed course in the principles of operant conditioning. But it really is not necessary, according to several recent studies.

One of Wolf's colleagues, Edward R. Christopherson, found that parents need no formal training to use a point system to modify their children's behaviors, though they do need to be "cooperative and motivated," he told me. A graduate student of Ayllon's, Michael D. Roberts, used a simple "cookbook" method to teach mothers who had completed only three years of elementary school how to help their own and other children develop language skills.

Jump. Parents and thousands of their neighbors in Huntsville, Alabama, are learning behavioral techniques in the largest and most exciting of the current programs. The Huntsville-Madison County Mental Health Center, which serves nearly 200,000 persons, uses the techniques in all aspects of its operation—screening, diagnosis, treatment, consultation, prevention and staffing. It switched from a traditional approach in January 1971, and six months later the National Institute of Mental Health, after much debate over this wholesale jump into a nonmedical model, gave the center a three-year, $150,000 grant to study its effectiveness.

According to William H. Goodson Jr., a psychiatrist who directs the center, the new system "injects into the therapeutic relationship a healthy 'positive' approach, in which the patient's strengths are valued and considered much more than the weaknesses." Research psychologist A. Jack Turner, who devised the system and oversees it, told me that "our commitment is to empiricism, not to behavior modification, which I believe is a fad." The system uses tokens, modeling, desensitization or any other behavioral technique whose effectiveness can be shown empirically.

Jeopardy. Putting the emphasis on empiricism was a politically wise move in heavily science-oriented Huntsville, a space center. It was part of Turner's deliberate use of Skinnerian shaping techniques in the community to avoid the furor that sometimes accompanies the introduction of behavior-control programs. He had the community pretty well shaped, he told me, until the "ill-timed" publication of *Beyond Freedom and Dignity* put the programs in jeopardy. The book stirred up opposition and forced him to do some further shaping.

The center's services are wide-ranging. They include therapy with inpatients and outpatients, day treatment, community consultation and education, emergency calls, care of patients before and after confinement in state mental hospitals, a satellite operation in Huntsville's

4. Shapers at Work

Model Cities area, an alcoholism program, research and evaluation, and training. In its first year, it provided care for 1,019 patients and consultation and education for 32,419 other persons.

Keenness. Goodson and Turner have assembled a young, turned-on staff that is fully committed to behaviorism. Their keenness, spirit and enthusiasm were infectious last spring when I saw them in Atlanta at the Southeastern Psychological Association convention, which gave them their first chance to tell other professionals about their accomplishments. In just one year they had made clear-cut progress toward meeting several specified goals. In one area, admissions to state hospitals, they reported a 55-percent reduction.

Psychologist Daun Adams coordinates the high-priority consultation and education service. In 1969, George A. Miller, as president of the American Psychological Association, called on his colleagues to "give psychology away" to anyone who needs it. [See "On Turning Psychology over to the Unwashed," PT, December 1969.] This is exactly what Adams is doing. Professionals and paraprofessionals in local schools and social and welfare agencies are learning how to use behavior control, and so are parents, husbands and wives, and ministers. This outreach program aims to prevent "illness," and if it succeeds "we could work ourselves out of a job," Turner said with a smile.

Knowing. An ambitious plan to manage the behavior of a whole community is also under way in Prince George's County, Maryland. Prince George's, one of the largest suburban areas in the country, has a "mixture of all kinds of people" that makes it "a model of America," according to Harold Cohen, the one-time artist who no longer restricts his talents to designing good chairs.

Somehow Cohen has managed to combine the ideas of the two men who have influenced him most—B.F. Skinner and Buckminster Fuller, both of whom are associated with his Institute for Behavioral Research—into a pragmatic whole. "Fred and Bucky are quite alike," he told me in his Silver Spring office. "But they go to opposite ends of the pendulum." From Fuller he borrowed an ability to think audaciously about doing things as they have never been done before, and from Skinner the techniques to make new environments work. The pragmatism is his own. "I'm against any kind of aversive control," he said, "I'm not a moralist, it just doesn't work." He believes in structure because "discipline is the way to freedom." And what is freedom? "Knowing the limitations of the system."

Kaleidoscope. There is much more to Cohen's current three-year Prince George's project than IBR's official description of it reveals. It is a kaleidoscope that includes two programs—Teenagers' Rights and Responsibilities (TARR), a packaged course to teach "social problem-solving" skills, including the ins and outs of the legal process, to eighth-graders; and Behavioral Programs in Learning Activities for Youth (BPLAY), which includes after-school social-problem discussions and practical sessions in such activities as auto maintenance, sewing and film-making. The project also has set up a teen-age coffee-house, the Renaissance.

What Cohen really hopes to do is to convert the county's establishment—schools, police, courts—to behavior-control methods that are reinforcing rather than aversive. Like Turner, he uses a shaping treatment to gain acceptance for the idea, especially from county officials. "I first approached the school superintendent when it looked as if some ugly incidents might result in the police coming into the schools," he said. "And I told him, 'You'll be blamed, but the total environment is responsible.'"

He is using a similar approach with police and judges, and it seems to be working.

Locked in a safe at IBR are copies of the confidential records of teen-agers who are arrested in the county, which the police turned over to him. These records provide baseline and experimental data, with which he hopes to show over the next few years the favorable effects of TARR, BPLAY and other projects he has in mind. Someday, if things work out as he expects, policemen will go around handing out token rewards for correct behaviors instead of making arrests. He told me he hadn't yet let them in on his idea to change their title from law-enforcement officer to reinforcement officer.

Looks. The large-scale programs in Kansas, Maryland and Alabama are only a few of hundreds in operation or in planning stages across the country. Western Michigan University in Kalamazoo, the State University of New York at Stony Brook, and the Universities of Oregon, Washington and Hawaii are major centers of activity, and new ones spring up each year.

Although they are impressive, these programs are the products of a science and a technology that are still in their infancy. Skinner, in *Beyond Freedom and Dignity*, compared human-behavior analysis to physics, suggesting that it is just slightly beyond the time of Newton. Though the number of applied behavior analysts swells as they turn out more and more Ph.D.s, they remain a close-knit, almost incestuous band whose harmony seems to be a defense against the Skinner-scared Philistines. They have waded together into the complexities of human behavior, and they know that going deeper will require more sophisticated equipment. Montrose Wolf told me, "We have research techniques that look like the best around, but we only have pieces of technology." His statement seemed less a lament than a reminder of work to be done.

Latitude. The direction that work will take seems clear:

WHOLE SYSTEMS. For the post-Skinnerians, things still work best in a Skinner box. Skinner, who has done little of the field work himself, dreams of a box as big as the world. Others, who know the problems firsthand, will be content to "put walls around neighborhoods," as Todd Risley is doing, and to wrap up packages for use in special environments.

"The time is ripe for experimentation with new organizational schemes involving whole schools," a special work group on behavior analysis has reported to the United States Office of Education. A few such innovations already are under way: Hall's at Bryant school in Kansas City, Cohen's at schools in Maryland, and Roger E. Ulrich's at Learning Village, a private school in Kalamazoo, Michigan. With new support expected from the Office of Education, the list will grow.

NEW TERRITORIES. In education, the behavior analysts will move up the ladder to design more packages for high-school and college classes, as Charles B. Ferster at American University in Washington, D.C. and Richard W. Malott and Jack Michael at Western Michigan already have done.

The business world is practically virgin territory for behavior analysis. However, there are signs that the businessmen's long honeymoon with humanist T-groups is ending, and some will follow the post-Skinnerian lead taken by Emery Air Freight.

1. THE ORIGINS

ecological problem, that of nonreturnable bottles.

Behavior analysts also will find new ways for persons to practice self-control. Wilbert E. Fordyce, who uses operant techniques in physical rehabilitation at the University of Washington School of Medicine, has called self-control "one of the more important relatively undeveloped aspects" of applied learning methods. Nathan Azrin and Israel Goldiamond pioneered this field, and it will burgeon.

NEW RESEARCH. If the United States Office of Education follows the recommendations of its work group, behavior analysts will have funds for longitudinal and follow-up studies to look into the long-range effects of their programs.

They will also investigate side-effects. Behavior-control methods sometimes change nontarget behaviors as well as target behaviors, and Robert G. Wahler of the University of Tennessee is mounting a computerized effort to document the interrelationships. It may one day be possible for behavior controllers to change one behavior by working on a totally different behavior.

Psychotherapists of all persuasions have attempted to change "deviant" behaviors with almost no knowledge about what "normal" behavior is. Behavior analysts like Stephen M. Johnson of the University of Oregon at Eugene, are beginning to gather data on the behavior of "normal" families, and other investigators will extend this work into new areas.

* * *

Applied behavior analysis, which came into existence only a decade ago when the operant conditioners stepped out into the real world, is entering a new era. "We are now ready for phase two," according to Gerald R. Patterson of the University of Oregon, a leader of the movement. "While continuing to use operational language, observation data, and a functional analysis, phase two will also become more analogous to social engineering," he said.

As behavioral engineers, the post-Skinnerians will need to concern themselves much more than they have with the penultimate item in Baer, Wolf and Risley's definition of applied behavior analysis: "in making sufficient change for value." They will need to translate their methods into viable programs that the public will find worth the cost. If they do not provide this kind of reinforcement, no amount of shaping will keep the public from spending its tokens elsewhere.

SPECIAL EDUCATION

Designed to follow the introductory course in special education, it is also a book which can be used as the first course book for Exceptional Children, Foundations of Exceptional Children, and the overview course for students entering special education departments.

For more information about this book and other materials in special education, contact Joseph Logan, Editor, Special Learning Corporation.

Special Learning Corporation

42 Boston Post Rd. Guilford, Connecticut 06437   (203) 453-6525

Behavior Modification in the Classroom

Overall knowledge of basic stimulus control procedures is the key of behavior modification for the teacher in a classroom setting. Nursery school and elementary school children can be affectively modified behaviorally through the use of social reinforcers. Behaviors which need strengthening are given praise and attention, while those which need weakening are given withdrawn attention. The learned process of not responding to disruptive behaviors is the most important tool for effective teaching.

A teacher's verbal behavior directly creates "bad" or "good" classroom behavior among students. The crucial key to the teacher is the use of his praise for a particular behavior, regardless of the frequency of use of positive social reinforcers as a consequence relating to improved behavior on the part of the student.

Possible withdrawal of reinforcers, use of threats as involving aversive stimuli and other forms of punishment are not usually feasible in the classroom setting, as the resulting generation of fear and possible anger will set up aggression models for the student to act upon. If you "condition" the threat, or the reprimand in an effective manner, it may then be backed up with an effective punishment as required.

How might this be accomplished and where: In various settings . . . the emotionally-disturbed classroom, the autistic classroom, or the "normal" classroom . . . the procedure remains the same, with the tools proving most effective as punishers: time-out and response cost procedures. Both require use of the loss of reinforcers, followed by positive reinforcement which eventually leads to the student's acquisition of desired behavior. With the occasional use of such techniques, the teacher can then effectively use these positive reinforcers and make them work for him, thus making punishment unnecessary in the process.

Other considerations to be taken into account in dealing with classroom behavior modification involve stimulus control technology for classroom uses, basic methods of teaching, good classroom management and solid design procedures of curriculum. Each of these combine to form stimulus control principles for effective means of behavior changes in students in an educational setting. All being very basic in principle, and known to us now. The future can only yield further innovations in behavioral psychology for relevant learning principles in all levels of teaching and education.

How can this child be helped?

Four types of troubled learners and how to help them

Hugh Carberry

HUGH CARBERRY, director-psychologist, Sterling Area Child Study Center (Somerdale, Magnolia, Sterling High Schools), Magnolia, New Jersey.

Each child is a unique and complex arrangement of personality, behavior, and learning patterns. We acknowledge that individual differences should be recognized and met, but to put individual diagnosis and prescription into a realistic perspective, some generally descriptive ground rules are necessary.

The following models describe four distinctly different types of behavior which apply to children in normal as well as exceptional learning environments. Each description is followed with suggestions on how to help each child make an adjustment to a more effective behavior pattern. However, no child is a "pure" example of any one pattern, rather a composite with one style of behavior being predominate.

The *passive-dependent* child perceives the teacher as doing the work and presents himself as the helpless receiver, never taking the initiative for learning. He is usually highly conforming and not a behavior problem in the acting-out sense. Learning potential is not actualized and he often appears as a dramatic underachiever. If the displayed helplessness is fed, this reinforces the passive-dependent stance and encourages the development of a life-style marked by a lack of healthy assertiveness. Such reinforcement eventually produces anger in the child which may be expressed through resistance, stubbornness, dawdling, and procrastination.

This child rarely asks a question when he does *not* understand, but he may ask many when he *does* understand. While fairly good at rote memory tasks such as spelling or memorizing the multiplication tables, he has great difficulty with tasks requiring more assertiveness such as problem solving, or logical reasoning.

One ramification of this behavior pattern is a defensive-extension referred to as the "Help Rejecting Complainer." He asks for help, then rejects it. "I've already tried that and it doesn't work."

This child needs to increase his risk-taking behavior and to increase his assertiveness in interpersonal situations. The teacher must first identify his behavior pattern, ignoring the undesirable behaviors whenever possible. Then, the more appropriate risk-taking behaviors must be reinforced as the child exhibits them.

Make an individual profile of the child, listing behaviors rather than attitudes. Then you can systematically know what to reinforce and what to ignore. For example, the undesirable behavior might be, "John rarely asks questions when he doesn't understand the material." The desirable behavior would then be, "John asks questions when he doesn't understand the material."

The third step is to meaningfully reward any behavior that approximates the assertive, risk-taking behavior desired. Remember, however, that a child cannot move from one type of behavior to another in one jump. View his behavior on a continuum and reward at different points that approximate the final goal.

Involve the child in the process from the start. Accurate communications, accompanied with warmth and understanding, will go a long way in establishing the relationship necessary to bring about change and make the child a more efficient learner. For many children this is the core of the reward system.

The following types of activities can be used with the passive-dependent child.

• Reinforcement of risk-taking behavior in other children serves as a vicarious reinforcement for the child.

• "Assertive Training" through the use of role-playing activities helps. Have the child role play getting the attention of a store clerk when he is waiting and has been overlooked; have him bring to someone else's attention that they have mispronounced his name. Start with simple tasks and gradually increase the difficulty.

• Assign him the role of "question formulator" for a small group activity.

In general, using a step-by-step approach, direct him toward development of the desired behavior using constant positive reinforcement.

The *negativistic* child typically pouts and refuses to begin work or gets antagonistic when things go against him or he experiences failure, and quits. He may then become violent if pressure is exerted. His negativism is indirectly expressed by such things as getting around to the task at hand, making excuses, losing his pencil.

Some negativistic children initially appear very pleasant and charming. They try to get along through their appealing ways rather than through work. Personal charm is used to get help, but little progress is evident. Sometimes, the more you help, the slower the child becomes. Typically, there is no correlation between the child's school behavior and nonacademic tasks where he comes across as bright and alert.

The negativistic child generally needs the following structure.

"Exceptional Children: Can This Child Be Helped?" by Hugh Carberry reprinted from *Instructor*, copyright © January 1976 by The Instructor Publications, Inc., used by permission.

5. Can This Child Be Helped?

- Initial focus on situations in which he is usually cooperative with reinforcement of this behavior.
- A step-by-step approach, steps small in the beginning, starting with a task you know he will do.
- Avoidance of confrontations which result in a will struggle. Such confrontations only reinforce his negativism.
- Initial reduction of the criterion for correctness.
- Guaranteed success in learning.
- Settle for a "thimbleful" of accomplishment. Don't look for a "bucketful."
- Creation of a predictable learning environment where he is rewarded for his accomplishments and not rewarded if he fails to meet reasonable expectations.

Once progress is evident, gradually introduce situations in which his behavior is usually negativistic. Tell him you appreciate the fact he is changing his behavior. Discuss goals and rewards with him. Be prepared to back up, modify tasks, and reset expectations if he fails or reverts to negativism. He needs direction in the change process, and change is hardly ever a straight-line process.

In addition, this child is typically supersensitive to any perceived unfairness and, while he may not overtly express anger, he may sulk and brood when he should be working. Group discussion on themes such as teacher unfairness, favoritism in the classroom, and feeling like you're always picked on can be very helpful in reducing his angry, hostile feelings. Listening to other children discuss their feelings can help alleviate some of the guilt feelings the angry child may have. It also helps him understand that it is not the end of the world if he is treated unfairly. Participation in these discussions should help build empathy for the needs of others and reduce his supersensitivity.

The *impulsive* child typically cannot focus either his auditory or visual attention long enough to learn. He guesses at work, misreads addition and subtraction signs, starts work before he really understands directions, and is often a disruptive behavior problem. He has not learned to wait, to look, to listen, or to control his own behavior. His mistakes and errors are initially due to the above behavior, but as he falls behind in his work he often gives up in academic areas and finds satisfaction through fooling and clowning.

The impulsive and distractable child generally needs the following structure.
- Increased individual attention through task structure, with definite limits set for acceptable behavior.
- Decreased permissiveness and less opportunity for choicemaking.
- Concentrated training in desirable habit formation—checking work, organizing work, following step-by-step directions.
- An atomistic, step-by-step approach rather than a holistic, Gestalt approach to learning.
- Minimum pressure for immediate academic achievement at grade-level standards, but definite expectations at his level.
- Reduced environmental stimulation.
- Learner tasks which are concrete rather than abstract.

Since the impulsive child usually has a problem with order he can be helped through tasks which have a defined starting point and a series of steps leading to a conclusion which is scorable as complete or incomplete. Decrease the amount of teacher talk and involve him in tasks of the "doing" variety. Require student involvement and aim for tasks which provide a novel and satisfying activity and appeal to his interest level.

For example, have him name or list the items missing in various situations, ordered in a sequence, which happen during the ordinary course of a day. Use a scene showing a family at breakfast with something missing from the picture. His task would be to identify the missing part and then create a time sequence that is logical in order and/or has a logical conclusion.

At recesses and noon periods try to direct him to the less strenuous, less competitive games. Free play in unsupervised, large group activities can be disastrous for him since he is easily overstimulated.

Avoid nagging him. For years he has been nagged, reprimanded, punished, and disciplined. This approach hasn't worked, only led to further confusion, frustration, anxiety, and unhappiness. Also, it negatively reinforces the undesired behavior.

Save work samples so that he can chart his individual progress. Give much positive reinforcement for the gains he does make. Seat him where he is accessible for your attention and help when he needs it. Set up a den, office, or cubicle for him to work in. This cuts out excess stimuli and extraneous distractions. Develop an individualized, highly structured curriculum with precise goals, definite instructions, fairly rigid routines, and few choices. This can be done while maintaining a good relationship with the child.

The *apprehensive* child can best be described as one who sets about most learning tasks by being frightened. He decides in advance that learning is too difficult for him and is petrified when asked to answer a question. He is particularly frightened when faced by anything new, strange, or complex. He equates learning with anxiety and anxiety tends to confuse and disorganize his thought processes. He does learn that if he can't perform, the adult will do it for him. By second or third grade his unresponsiveness presents itself to the casual onlooker as retardation. In a sense he gets off the hook by taking refuge in apparent dullness. As a result he receives the bonus that he is no longer pestered by people who want answers and he no longer needs to be anxious.

The apprehensive child generally needs the following structure.
- Reduction of the criterion for correctness of his response.
- Guaranteed success in learning.
- A specific starting point with a series of steps leading to a conclusion which is scorable as complete or incomplete.
- Removal from competition with other children for a period of time. Include individual tutoring if necessary.
- Initial reduction of pressure to participate through assurance that he is only competing with his own past performance rather than the whole class. This can free him to respond with more security.
- Elimination of letter grades and reduction of any demands for perfection. Discuss this with his parents so that they understand what is being done.

Offer him a variety of short tasks, rather than single, longer ones. Give him assignments which draw on information he has readily available and which capitalize on his major interests. This will encourage increased response.

Emphasize the "you can do it" approach, rather than reinforcing the dependency relationship. Stories told by the teacher which emphasize that it is not a catastrophe nor the end of the world to make an error, followed by class discussion can serve as an indirect and helpful way to reduce his anxiety. Getting other children to discuss their apprehensions can give the anxious child a sense of not being alone nor strange with his feelings and fears.

For some apprehensive children, physical contact or physical expressions of affection can be extremely threatening and produce further anxiety. If the child tenses physically, this is a good cue that another avenue of communication will be less threatening. If he does exhibit this kind of tension there are a number of rhythmic exercises which can be used to help reduce body tension. For example, have him scribble or draw in time with music; use selected deep-breathing exercises; increase the amount of general physical activity. Know the child and be selective in the technique chosen.

To generally help children exhibiting one or more of these ineffective patterns of behavior the teacher must first identify the major behavior pattern of the child. Then develop an individual profile listing undesirable and desirable behaviors so that it is possible to tell when the child is approximating the desired behavior. Involve the child in establishing goals and rewards. Work in small steps and give constant reinforcement as his behavior is directed toward more effective learning patterns.

YOUR PRAISE CAN SMOTHER LEARNING

DAVID L. MARTIN

In classrooms throughout the country, teachers are popping jellybeans into students' mouths for any conceivable reason: to reward correct answers, to encourage more answers, in response to incorrect answers, to reward the motivated students, to motivate the unmotivated; and perhaps most often, jellybeans are given on a random basis, out of habit, for no special reason at all. Tons of jellybeans are being dispensed and consumed. Having discovered this widespread use of candy in the classroom, a few researchers are asking pointed questions: Does the candy aid or disrupt learning? What effects does it have on children and what they learn, how they learn, and their attitudes about learning? Should it be used at all?

Farfetched, yes. But if you substitute *praise* for candy, this scenario is an accurate one, including the part about researchers who currently are studying praise as it's used by teachers. And what the researchers say they are finding is startling: Praise is used in massive amounts; praise is ineffective in helping children learn and can actually sabotage learning; praise can hook kids on external rewards and can weaken their self-motivation; praise is used to control low-achieving students; praise perpetuates unequal treatment based on race and ethnic background.

Praise? Are the researchers talking about common, everyday, run-of-the-classroom praise? "That's a good answer." "You did really well." "Good, good." "Oh, that's excellent." That type of praise?

Yes.

How One Researcher Found Praise
In the 1960s, University of Florida professor Mary Budd Rowe tried to find out what variable could make children in elementary grade science programs develop the type of scientific inquiry into ideas and relationships that the courses were designed to provoke. A lot of things *didn't* seem to make a difference: science background of the teacher, type of science curriculum being used, size of class, age of child. What Rowe finally discovered to be the most effective variable in eliciting inquiry from students is something she calls "wait-time," which is the amount of time a teacher waits for an answer after posing a question (wait-time I) and the amount of time a teacher waits after a student answers a question (wait-time II). Rowe found that when teachers stretched out their wait-times to an average of three seconds (instead of the overwhelmingly typical wait-times of one second or less), several things happened: students gave longer responses and more unsolicited but appropriate responses; students' confidence in their responses increased; students' failure to respond decreased; students interacted and exchanged more information with each other; and students asked more questions. In other words, student performance improved, or at least there was an increase in the types of student actions that we often associate with improved performance.

But there was a wasp in the wait-time ointment: praise. While examining the different patterns of wait-times given to students in a class, Rowe found that teachers praise certain students more than others. She then went back to her data to see how and how much teachers praise. Rowe discovered that praise is "habituated" in the speech of many teachers and that, for some teachers, one out of every four words uttered in a classroom is a word of praise. Rowe also found that teachers' heavy praise of students sabotaged the beneficial effects of longer wait-times. "Thus," Rowe explained in a 1974 issue of the *Journal of Research in Science Teaching*, "we were forced to pay attention to rewards whether we wished to or not, since they frequently confounded the interpretation of the early wait-time investigations."

Rowe's experiments are backed up with nearly 1,000 tape recordings of classroom exchanges. Her interpretations of experiments, observations and those recordings are contained in reports she's written for the *Journal of Research in Science Teaching* and in her McGraw-Hill book, *Teaching Science As Continuous Inquiry*. What

6. Your Praise

Students are conditioned to go for a quick payoff of praise.

Rowe has uncovered is a stunning indictment of praise: it cuts into students' task persistence; it undermines students' confidence in their answers; it lowers the number of alternative explanations offered by students; and it cuts down on cooperation and exchanges among students.

How Praise Gets in Learning's Way
One of Rowe's primary contentions is that heavy praise from teachers makes children more dependent on a system of extrinsic, rather than intrinsic, rewards. Constant praise "teaches" a child that reward will come from one external source (the teacher), and this interferes with a child's development of self-satisfaction from learning itself—from understanding new ideas or completing new tasks.

Rowe's speculation seems to be borne out in her experimental findings and in the work of other researchers, such as Martin L. Maehr and William M. Stallings of the University of Illinois, Urbana-Champaign. In a 1972 report published in *Child Development*, Maehr and Stallings said that their studies of eighth graders indicated that conditions in which students relied on internal evaluations (doing a task because it is fun or interesting to the student, for example) "seemed to spawn greater motivation to [continue] performance at difficult tasks." Students preferred to do easy tasks when they knew that their work was going to be evaluated by an external source (the teacher).

Heavily praised students have less confidence in their answers, Rowe maintains. She found that students from high-praise classrooms (when compared with students in low-praise classrooms) did more of the following three actions, which Rowe infers are signs of students' lowered confidence: eye-checking with teachers, which Rowe says is done by students who are unsure of themselves and who are trying to confirm that what they are doing or saying is OK with the teacher; making responses in an inflected, self-doubting tone; and exhibiting low task persistence, which indicates to Rowe that students are unwilling to keep plugging at something in which they have little confidence.

In one of her experiments, second graders from inner-city schools were tested on how confident they would be in continuing to give explanations when Rowe's experimenters disagreed with those explanations. The experimenters wanted to see how many students could survive three disagreements. Although the small number of students involved in the experiment precludes one from making generalizations, Rowe did find that most of the students from classrooms with a heavy praise schedule failed to survive two disagreements; five out of the ten students tested quit after the first disagreement. Most of the students from classrooms with a low schedule of praise survived all three disagreements.

Rowe suggests that students accustomed to high amounts of praise will not get involved in innovative or complex reasoning because they've been conditioned to go for a "quick payoff" of praise. When the primary reward system in a classroom is teacher praise (instead of the rewards of discovery, internal satisfaction, or even praise from peers), students also are less likely to share information with or to listen to other students. In one set of high-praise classrooms, Rowe found that "students tended to guard results until the teacher asked for them. This behavior was especially pronounced in middle-class populations."

In a study of 30 classrooms, Rowe compared the students of the five teachers who praised the most with the students of the five teachers who praised the least. Here's what she discovered:

The low reward schedule produced more student-student encounters. Task persistence is higher under the low schedule. Under the high schedule, the students tend to stop at stages and call for the teacher. Thus there is also a lot of waiting around for the teacher to reach them. The amount of spontaneous sharing of ideas between students is greater in the low reward condition. The number of alternative explanations and suggestions for new experiments favored the low reward group. Inflected responding was almost three times as frequent in the high reward group as in the low. . . .

In some high-praise classrooms, Rowe found, students would "tease or mock" kids who had been praised: "This behavior was common in both suburban and ghetto groups but was especially pronounced in some ghetto classes." This negative peer pressure also was evident in a study done by Georgia M. Gabor, curriculum adviser for the San Marino School System in Pasadena, California. Gabor conducted two experiments with junior high school math classes; one experiment was with students from an "underprivileged, minority community, inner-city" school, and the other study was with students from a middle-class suburban school. Using the students' performance on a math test as her basis, Gabor sought to examine the effect of several variables, including two teaching methods, praise, reproof and no feedback. Before taking the math test, some students were praised for their performance on a previous test, some students were criticized for their past performance, and some received no feedback. Gabor hypothesized that children who were praised would perform better than children

2. IN THE CLASSROOM

Teachers substitute praise for challenging academic standards.

who received no feedback from the teacher or who were criticized. She struck out on teaching methods and "no feedback"—those variables didn't seem to have a significant effect on performance. But, she wrote in a 1975 issue of the *California Journal of Educational Research*, "the effect of reproof and praise were highly significant in the studies." Gabor said that "reproof had a significantly facilitating effect" on the suburban students and that praise affected "performance of both sets of students very negatively."

Some of the suburban students in Gabor's experiment said that the praise made them overconfident and that they didn't concentrate on the test. And, as in Rowe's observations, some inner-city students "felt annoyed to irate about having had been praised in front of their peers."

Whom Praise Hurts Most
In her testing samples, Rowe discovered that teachers praised students whom they rated as their "top five" differently than they praised students whom they rated as their "bottom five." The bottom five students, according to Rowe, were praised more and received more nonpertinent praise; teachers praised their top students for correct answers but they praised their bottom students for both correct and incorrect answers. For the students classified (by teachers) as being in the bottom of the class, "as much as 50 percent of the praise did not seem to be attached to correct responding. The bottom five generally receive[d] an ambiguous signal system."

This nonpertinent praise, according to another study, is the most disruptive type of praise. In a 1970 issue of the *Journal of Research in Science Teaching*, Francis X. Lawlor of Columbia University's Teachers College in New York described how he tested 191 second grade students (from a middle-class, suburban school) on their ability to perform a simple sorting and grouping task. The children were split into groups that performed the task under different reward conditions: pertinent reward (praise for acceptable solutions), no reward (the experimenters quietly observed the children), and nonpertinent reward (children were praised on "a fixed time schedule"). Lawlor said that the nonpertinent reward condition "is most analogous to observed classroom practice." He looked at the second graders' performance in several areas (number of solutions, number of acceptable solutions, perseverance time, for example) and here is what he found:

The conclusion seems justified, on the basis of the data reported in this study, that the use of verbal rewards which are not congruent with behavior will result in less efficient problem-solving than either a neutral, no-reward situation, or the use of rewards which are congruent with the problem-solving behavior. The giving of rewards which are congruent improves the problem-solving efficiency of girls but not of boys.

It would seem that Lawlor's finding that pertinent reward can be helpful is in conflict with Rowe's conclusions, but she told *Learning* that it is not. Rowe has been studying more complex learning activities (inquiry into and exploration of ideas, for example), and the effect praise has on this type of learning is vastly different from the effect praise has on the type of simple task that Lawlor's subjects were performing (he said the tasks "were of low conceptual complexity").

Some studies, Lawlor's included, seem to indicate that praise has a different effect on girls than it does on boys. Girls *may* be more tuned into or susceptible to praise, but this has not been proven, and Rowe says she is cautious about concluding that praise has a sexist effect.

Researchers from Stanford University's School of Education are not, however, at all cautious about concluding that praise has a special—and negative—effect on minority-member students. Celestino Fernández, Rubén W. Espinosa and Sanford M. Dornbusch questioned 770 San Francisco high school students about the students' attitudes toward school and opinions of their achievement in school. The researchers wanted to know what was perpetuating "the low academic status" of Chicano students. One of the leading culprits apparently is praise.

Chicano and black students responding to the questionnaire said they did think school was important, they did think they were working hard in school, and they did think they were doing OK in school. But these minority-member students were neither working hard nor doing well in school when compared with other students. Fernández, Espinosa and Dornbusch said that the minority students' "misperceptions were a product of a faulty evaluation system, which substituted teacher warmth and praise for challenging academic standards."

Excerpts from the Stanford report:
- *Chicano and black students were the two groups with the lowest achievement levels, yet they were receiving the most academic praise.*
- *Teachers' failure to set challenging standards led Chicano students to a false view of their own level of effort and skill. Their faulty self-assessment helped perpetuate a pattern of institutional discrimination. The warm and positive acts of teachers led to the preservation of the existing structure of inequality.*
- *Chicanos and blacks, the ethnic groups who were doing less well in*

6. Your Praise

If you praise too much, slow your pace and be silent more often.

school, saw teachers as more friendly and warm than did the other ethnic groups. Most teachers are "Anglos," yet other white students (and Asian students) perceived teachers as less friendly and warm.

• Upon reflection, it is not surprising that receiving praise for work that is not very creditable leads to distorted images of the level of effort and achievement each student believes he or she is putting forth.

In their conclusion, the Stanford researchers say they are not blaming teachers (who are trying to be responsive to students) but that they are revealing "institutional discrimination in which the agents of discrimination, the teachers, are warm and positive in their relations with their students, and the students are deceived about their current position and their destiny."

How Not To Praise

All these findings about praise are, to say the least, unsettling. And they're confusing, too. In our minds we may link praising students with helping and being supportive of them. There also seems to be a conflict between what behavior modification studies conclude about the effectiveness of positive reinforcement (praise) and what the research cited in this article says about praise. But no conflict, in fact, exists. Rowe's work concentrates on praise's effect on inquiry, exploration of new ideas, investigation into relationships. She points out that praise for simpler tasks or for drills (multiplication tables, for example) or for acceptable social behavior is or can be effective. (The Lawlor study indicates that even for simple tasks, praise must be pertinent.) The decision to praise or not to praise, therefore, probably should be based on the type of learning students are engaged in: if it's simple or rote learning, praise (or jellybeans, for that matter) probably will work. For more in-depth learning, neither praise nor candy is likely to be effective.

Here are some ways to determine if you praise heavily, and if you do, how to stop:

1. Make tape recordings of your exchanges with students. While listening to these tapes, count the number of verbal rewards you hand out. Do words like "good" and "excellent" and "fine" constantly pop up in your speech? Do you seem to be giving more praise to low-achieving students? Is the praise you give low-achieving students less pertinent or accurate than the praise you give high-achieving students? Watch your students for other actions which may indicate that you (rather than the students or learning itself) have become the sole and central source of reward in your classroom: students do not share information with each other, they answer you in a questioning tone, give short and incomplete answers, watch you constantly, and seem extremely eager (jumping up and down, frantically waving their arms) to get *your* attention and to give answers to *you*.

2. If praise does seem to be a main ingredient in your classroom, try to slow down your pace. Be silent more often. Give kids a chance to answer questions and a chance to follow up on their answers. (Rowe has found that most teachers give wait-times of one second or less.) Heavy praise simply may be an unconscious part of your speech. You might, for example, say "good, good" after a student's answer in much the same way each of us says "uh, uh" when we pause during our conversations. One way to break this praise-speech habit (and to lengthen wait-times as well) is simply to be silent after you ask a question and after a student answers your question. Effective wait-times begin at three seconds.

3. Do not always be the one who sets goals and tasks for students; encourage them to set their own goals and to determine their own tasks. Encourage them to set goals for themselves that are not easily reached. Some studies have shown that students who work toward their own specific, difficult goals accomplish more and build more self-motivation than do students who work toward goals that have been set by an external source and that are rather easy to meet. The Stanford research study notes that praise or teacher friendliness alone is not effective in helping children maximize their efforts; challenging standards must be set.

Maryann Gatheral, supervisor of teacher education at the University of California at Davis, sees heavy praise as a symptom of poor teaching techniques. Gatheral says that an effective teacher can convey a positive attitude without using words of praise (which she calls "flattery"). Gatheral also speculates that teachers who criticize heavily need praise as a counterbalance, and if the criticism stops, so will the praise. Rowe would argue that both types of external evaluations (praise and criticism) get in learning's way.

Here is some of Gatheral's advice for teaching without flattery:

• In response to a student's answer or comments, be specific and put the focus on the material being covered or on other students—or just look at the student and wait for him to elaborate or for other students to chime in. Ask another question. Ask about the topic being discussed. Ask, "How does that relate to what we're talking about?" Ask another student, "What do you think of this answer?" These questions won't come across as put-

2. IN THE CLASSROOM

Praise is least harmful when it's specific and directed toward tasks, not persons.

downs, Gatheral says, if the teacher's tone and attitude is supportive.
- If a student gives a correct answer and you feel compelled to praise (maybe the answer was especially insightful or perhaps this specific student usually doesn't answer correctly, or at all), make these kinds of comments: "That's getting us someplace." Or: "That gives some depth to our conversation." Gatheral says, however, that in a classroom with a positive tone and in which students know it is safe to respond, the teacher probably won't "feel compelled" to praise.
- If a student makes a response that is completely off the track, a teacher can say, "I don't understand what you're getting at." Or: "What facts do you have to back that up?" (Again, the teacher's supportive attitude is the key to making these types of questions nonthreatening to students.) The teacher can pick up on specific parts of the student's remark:

Teacher: "You say witches are bad. Why?"
Student: "Because they're ugly."
Teacher: "Is ugliness bad? Can you be ugly and good? Does anyone know of a person who is ugly and good?"

Gatheral says that this type of response to a "wrong" answer teaches a child that he must have reasons to support his opinions. When children can't support their contentions, the incorrectness becomes obvious to them—the judgment does not have to come from the teacher.
- Praise should not be used to encourage reluctant students to participate in classroom discussions, says Gatheral. Instead, she suggests, a teacher, in circulating around the classroom, should talk casually and privately with the reluctant student. Get him accustomed to talking, to making comments, to sharing his opinions. Choose topics (in your private conversations with the reluctant student and in classroom conversations) that interest him. Keep getting to him in this private, casual, nonthreatening way, Gatheral says, and don't attempt to praise him into responding.

No one is suggesting that you never, ever again utter a word of praise during classroom exchanges with your students. But you and your students will be better off if you do not praise heavily, inaccurately or habitually. And it does seem that some types of praising are more disruptive than others. Gatheral argues that praise may not be so harmful if it is based on specific, clear and well-understood standards. If you praise a student for not being noisy, say: "You're doing a good job of being quiet and that'll help us finish our discussion." Do not say: "You're being a good student."

Mary Budd Rowe makes a similar point: Praise of tasks, when it is specific and detailed, is not as disruptive as generalized praise of persons. If you tell a student, "That's good that you've set up this experiment in a new way," then other students know what is being praised and can even attempt to duplicate the praised task. Non-praised students have less of an idea what is praiseworthy and can become resentful when teachers praise persons ("You're a good experimenter") or when teachers use praise in other unclear and nonspecific ways: "Good. Good." Or: "That's an excellent job!" (Does everyone know what is being praised and why it's excellent?)

If you manage to stop praising students and then find that the urge to praise is building up inside you and that you absolutely must relieve the pressure by praising someone, lay it on your colleagues. Overt, heavy, person-oriented praise has not yet been found to have deleterious effects on teachers.

"I'm Just Plain Dumb!"

—how to change negative self-concepts in low-ability children

JAMES R. WATSON,
fourth grade teacher, Eastgate Elementary School, Bellevue, Washington.

□ **Few teachers would be insensitive enough to tell** a child that he has below average intelligence. In our culture, we rarely tell children directly that they are not intelligent, but as educators we tell them in innumerable ways—red marks on their papers, poor reports to parents, extra individual teacher help, visits to reading specialists, and nonverbal signs of teacher annoyance or disapproval.

Other children naturally make their contributions, in varying degrees of subtlety, to convincing low-ability pupils of their inadequacy. By the time parents and other adults have done their part, most children with below-average intelligence are thoroughly convinced they are not capable of anything.

How can we change these feelings of inadequacy? Try these suggestions:

• Low-ability students are often successful as tutors for younger children. They sometimes have more patience and understanding with young children than do their more academically capable peers; they can especially identify with children who are slow to catch on.

Intellectually slow fourth grade children could listen to first graders read or work with second and third graders on their addition and subtraction facts. This arrangement would give the tutors feelings of worth and importance and also assist younger children in reading and math.

Where would these less able students find the extra time for tutoring? It isn't necessary for them to do all the assignments required of their more capable peers. With proper planning, they can participate in tutoring without neglecting their own schoolwork.

Low-ability students should also work together with their own classmates—tutoring each other. It is important that they feel capable of helping and being helped by children their own age.

• Emphasize the positive qualities of all youngsters, but especially the less able, during parent-teacher conferences or contacts. For example, student tutoring activities could be more fully explained and praised at this time. Parents are usually aware of the poor academic quality of their children's work. You needn't dwell on this unpleasant fact. You should mention the moments of academic success (a well-written report or presentation) as well as successful experiences in nonacademic areas.

Try to restrain yourself from informing parents that "Johnny will never make college because he doesn't have the necessary intelligence." This omniscient evaluation is not only damaging to many parents and children but may well be untrue.

• Don't feel obligated to cover the papers of low-ability students with red check marks. You may believe that marking out all the mistakes will somehow help teach the child the error of his ways. Unfortunately, it teaches him that he must really be incapable.

It might be more desirable for you to work individually with a student on the particular assignment in question. Possibly marking only the correct problems —emphasizing the positive—would be a good approach. You might use several different colors of ink. From their past experiences, many less able students look on red ink as an indication of mistakes and failure. Also, it isn't necessary to correct every single assignment. Many assignments need no evaluative mark, especially those dealing with opinions, attitudes, feelings. Teacher comments or reactions indicating interest in the children's papers would be more appropriate.

• Avoid classroom situations in which low-ability children are compared with high-ability students in academic areas. Continually being last, lowest, or behind the other students does little for developing a positive self-concept. You can help avoid situations of this nature by primarily displaying work with no right or wrong answers, working privately (whenever possible) with children who have academic difficulties rather than always revealing their ignorance to the entire class, and employing heterogeneous grouping whenever possible.

• Give academically low students both public and private reinforcement for good academic work. Since this type of academic performance may be rare, it is important to shower praise and attention on these stu-

2. IN THE CLASSROOM

dents during their moments of success.

Receiving approval from parents, teachers, and other students for academic performance is an unusual and cherished occasion for less able children. Even though students shouldn't work hard in school just for approval, this approval may be the only positive reinforcement these children get. Also, it may be required initially in order to keep them from completely giving up in school.

Take a hypothetical situation: John, a low-ability student, takes a real interest in elephants. He gets books from the public and school library. He reads extensively and develops a good report, complete with pictures and a discussion of elephants. He proudly turns in his work to the teacher.

To take full advantage of this situation, the teacher could read the report carefully and make comments revealing interest (no marks for misspelling, etc.), ask him to share it with the class, praise him in front of the group, see if another classroom might be interested in having John share his report, and mention it to his parents.

- Attempt to discover the specific skills or talents of your low-ability students. Often children can compensate for poor academic performance by excelling in some nonacademic area. It might be worthwhile to encourage students to display their particular skill for the other children. Peer and teacher approval do much to develop and maintain a positive self-concept. One teacher kept a couple of tumbling mats in the room for the benefit of a girl who was gifted in acrobatics. Her peers were impressed by her performance, and her self-confidence soared.

- Display a genuine interest in student activities and interests. Most children are quick to spot apathy in teachers, and some may react to your lack of interest in a very personal way: "I am an inadequate, boring person of no real interest to the teacher."

Do teachers really like all their students equally well? This seems unlikely. It is only natural to respond more positively to some students than to others. Children are individuals, and some are more interesting to converse with than others.

Although it is not necessary or even possible to like all youngsters to the same degree or in the same way, you can have a real interest in each one and make an effort to interact with even the least interesting, who may need your attention most. Low-ability students are frequently found in this group because they may not be the most adept conversationalists and often do not relate well to teachers.

Especially in the upper elementary grades, the teacher is sometimes the symbol of the failure encountered in school and is not always a sought-after friend. You should be aware of this possibility and try even harder for successful social interactions with less able students.

Our society places great emphasis on intelligence and academic excellence. Many students with high ability and some with average ability have been receiving constant reinforcement that they are worthwhile, important, and capable ever since they started school. On the other hand, students with low ability are subtly and directly getting the message that they could and should be doing better—that they are not doing as well as their teachers and parents would like.

That these students often see themselves negatively, especially in school related areas, is understandable.

It is possible, however, by employing some of the previously mentioned approaches, to counteract and contradict the perpetual message throbbing in the brains of many low-ability students, "I am not capable. . . . I am not capable. . . . I am not capable. . . ."

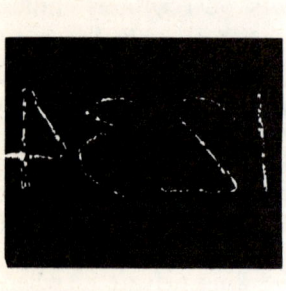

LEARNING DISABILITIES

Specifically designed to follow an introductory course in learning disabilities, this book provides a comprehensive overview.

For further information about this book and other special education materials, contact:

Joseph Logan
Editor
Special Learning Corporation

Special Learning Corporation
42 Boston Post Rd. Guilford, Connecticut 06437 (203) 453-6525

AN APPROACH TO EDUCATION OF YOUNG CHILDREN WITH LEARNING AND BEHAVIOR DIFFICULTIES

WILLIAM I. GARDNER, Ph.D.

Consulting Professional Director, Child Development Center, Easter Seal Society for Crippled Children and Adults of Milwaukee County, and Professor, Department of Studies in Behavioral Disabilities, University of Wisconsin

The behavior modification approach seeks to provide the child with rewarding experiences that will be satisfying to him and make him eager to learn more.

1. The Problem

A number of different labels have been used to describe children who present learning and behavior problems. The more frequently used ones are those of emotional disturbance, learning disability, and mental retardation. Let us meet three children who have been so labeled.

Tracy has a *learning disability*. She is a petite six-year-old girl of above-average intellectual ability who has difficulty in consistently maintaining her involvement in activities of the developmental education program that she attends. Although on occasion she is quite animated and involved, she more characteristically is easily distracted. She is quickly frustrated and not too infrequently will burst into explosive temper tantrums when things become too difficult for her. Activities do not hold her interest for very long. Perceptual-motor difficulties are evident in many of her activities. She gives the impression of being overly stubborn about becoming involved in new tasks and relationships that require her to maintain her attention and to exert some consistent effort. She seems unwilling, almost

2. IN THE CLASSROOM

fearful, of committing herself lest she fail. The teacher alternates between feelings of compassion and aggravation toward Tracy—compassion because the child appears so fragile, and aggravation because Tracy seems to have the resources for more successful learning, but appears actively to refuse to use these resources. The child gives the impression at times of wanting to learn, but on most occasions seems bent on doing those things that not only insure failure for herself, but also disrupt the learning activities of her peers.

Todd's parents have been told by a group of professional people that their son is *emotionally disturbed*. He is one of those beautifully handsome children who is an instant puzzle. His physical appearance creates the impression of a confident, active, and strong boy who should enthusiastically dive into school activities. This impression is quickly dissipated by observing Todd as he comes into the classroom. He is painfully shy. He seems suspicious, almost fearful, of peers and teacher alike. He speaks only after considerable encouragement and then only in such low tones that he is difficult to understand. He is curious about little, becomes involved only when given specific and consistent support, and quickly withdraws into inactivity when the structure is withdrawn. He is without energy or interest. His greatest satisfaction seems to be in leaving the program at the end of the day.

Beth is quite different from both Tracy and Todd. A psychological evaluation at the university clinic resulted in a diagnosis of *mental retardation*. In the developmental education program she tries to please. She attempts to learn. She does persist, but the tasks all appear too difficult for her. She may seem to grasp something one day, but when the teacher moves on to other things, Beth soon forgets what she had learned before.

These and numerous similar labels focus on the deficiencies or difficulties that are assumed to lie within children—Tracy's learning *disability*, Todd's emotional *disturbance*, Beth's mental *retardation*. None of these offers specific assistance to teachers or parents as they attempt to create more successful learning experiences for children like Tracy and Todd and Beth.

The booklet describes an approach, *behavior modification*, which focuses on the child's assets as he learns and behaves in his present social environments. The approach is the same regardless of the label placed on different children. Although recognizing that many children do have difficulties in learning and in behaving, the approach focuses neither on these difficulties nor on the deficits, disabilities, disturbances, or retardation assumed to underlie these. Rather, it identifies the child's present learning and behavioral assets, whatever these may be, and designs educational experiences that build on these.

2. What is behavior modification?

Behavior modification refers to a set of educational procedures for influencing the development and occurrence of a wide range of language, social, emotional, cognitive, motor, and perceptual behavioral patterns of children.

3. What is the major objective of behavior modification?

The basic objective of behavior modification is "to insure that the child learns and uses positive behavioral skills." As the child with learning and behavior difficulties becomes successful in a variety of experience areas, his attitudes and feelings toward learning, school, and teacher will become more positive. He will begin to enjoy learning new ways of behaving if the educational environment is so structured that he is in fact successful in acquiring a range of desirable behavior patterns.

The major focus, thus, is on the arrangement of a learning environment in which both new behaviors will be acquired and desirable behaviors presently in the child's repertoire will be strengthened and maintained.

4. Is behavior modification useful in managing any problems that a child may present?

Yes. Behavior modification may be used successfully with problems that represent behavioral deficits, patterns of excessive behavior, or a combination of these. In each of these situations, a discrepancy exists between what the child does and what a situation requires.

Problems of deficit behavior refer to those in which a child is expected to behave in a certain manner, but cannot because the expected behavior is not in his repertoire. As examples, a child may be unable to read, to discriminate red from green, to dress or undress himself, or to focus his attention for long periods of time. He either lacks the necessary skills or, if these are present, performs them in an inconsistent and unacceptable manner. The goals of a behavior modification program in these instances are: 1) to provide appropriate learning experiences that will result in the child's acquiring those desired behavior patterns that he does not have, and 2) to insure that these patterns become sufficiently strong to be maintained and to occur with consistency under appropriate conditions.

Other behavior patterns create problems due to their *excessive* nature. Children who are too demanding, who cry too easily or too frequently, who talk too much or are too loud, who are too fearful, or who are too aggressive toward other children demonstrate excessive behavior patterns. The goals of a behavior modification program for excessive behavior patterns are those of:

1) Teaching the child new discriminations so that desired behaviors will occur under appropriate conditions.
2) Reducing the frequency or intensity of excessive behaviors to an acceptable level by teaching the child a range of behavioral alternatives.
3) Eliminating highly inappropriate behaviors so that these will seldom or never occur.

5. What is the basis for behavior modification procedures?

The educational procedures that collectively are known as behavior modification have been derived from a number of learning theories and principles denoting the manner in which a) desired behavior is acquired and maintained, and b) undesired behavior is eliminated.

6. What are these learning theories and principles?

There are numerous concepts that represent aspects of various learning theories. The central concept may be called the *rule of positive reinforcement*. This rule states that any behavior (e.g., reading behavior, social interaction behavior, curiosity behavior, dressing behavior, spontaneous behavior, polite behavior) will be strengthened when followed by positive consequences, that is, will be more likely to occur in the future under the same and similar circumstances.

2. IN THE CLASSROOM

Another aspect of this rule suggests that behavior which is rather unlikely to occur will be strengthened if it is followed by activities the child enjoys. This has been called *Grandma's Rule*: "You do what I ask you to do and then you can do what you wish to do." As examples, "After you finish dressing, you may listen to your favorite record." "As soon as you put your toys away, you may join the play group." Such arrangements facilitate the development of the new skills.

Other rules to follow in influencing the child's behavior will be described after further discussion of the concept of positive reinforcement.

7. What are positive consequences?

Positive consequences are those events that the individual child finds pleasing. One child may enjoy praise, a smile, a warm caress, approval, or even just physical closeness. Other children at various stages in their social-emotional development may require more tangible objects such as toys, trinkets, candy, food, etc. Some of these things that may be used to strengthen and maintain behavior are naturally rewarding to a child and are called *primary or unlearned reinforcers*. Food and beverages such as candy, cookies, cereal, bread, soft drinks, and milk, along with other primary types of events such as physical stimulation, may serve without the influence of prior learning to reinforce behavior.

Other events may have little or no reinforcing effect when initially presented to a child (e.g., a smile, approval, acceptance, a gold star, money, educational toys, music, the opportunity to be teacher's helper). These may, however, become reinforcing events through a process of learning. When these previously neutral events do become reinforcing ones they are called *secondary or learned reinforcers*.

8. How do neutral events become reinforcing ones?

Events may become effective *secondary reinforcers* if they are associated frequently with consequences that are reinforcing to the child. A smile or praise may become pleasing to a child if paired frequently with the presentation, consumption, or manipulation of such tangibles as food, drink, toys, or play activities that already are reinforcing to a child. The steps to follow to insure this learning are:

1. Identify items or events that are reinforcing for the child (food, an activity, a toy).
2. Present simultaneously with the item an event that is neutral in terms of its reinforcing effects (a smile, "very good!"). For example, after a child's desired behavior, smile and say "very good!" while presenting the child with a toy.

After a number of such associations, the smile and "very good!" will acquire reinforcing characteristics and then, independently of the toy, can be used as a reinforcer to strengthen behaviors. The critical factor in this procedure is the close and frequent association of the neutral and the reinforcing events.

9. How can I determine what will be reinforcing to a child?

Reinforcing events may be identified by observing what the child prefers to do or selects when provided a choice. He may be presented with a wide variety of potentially reinforcing objects or activities and requested to identify those that most appeal to him. The final test of the reinforcing qualities of any event is whether or not that par-

8. An Approach

Time with an activity he enjoys reinforces the child as he learns new behavior patterns. Social reinforcement in the form of affection, a hug, and praise is used frequently by the teacher in efforts to teach positive behavioral skills.

ticular consequence does strengthen or maintain the behavior that produces it.

10. **When should reinforcement be provided? Can it wait until the end of an activity or the end of the day?**

For optimal learning to occur, reinforcement should be provided immediately following the occurrence of the behavior you wish to strengthen. If a child who typically does not pay attention to your verbal requests, for example, does look at you when you call his name, reinforce him immediately. This immediate reinforcement will likely result in the child's being more attentive when you call his name in the future.

11. **How frequently should reinforcement be provided?**

In addition to the requirement of immediate reinforcement, the most rapid learning will occur in the initial phases of teaching a new behavior if this behavior is reinforced *every* time it occurs. Thus, in the initial stages of teaching a child a new behavior be prepared to reinforce the behavior immediately each time it occurs. Fulfilling these two requirements is essential for the child with learning difficulties. As such children typically acquire new behaviors at a slow rate, success can best be achieved by a consistent use of these two procedures of providing *immediate* reinforcement *every time* the desired behavior, or an acceptable approximation of it, occurs. It is true that children do learn many behavior patterns even though reinforcement is delayed or is presented haphazardly. However, such learning will be inefficient and will require considerably more time than would be necessary under more appropriate conditions of immediate and frequent reinforcement.

12. **But must I continue to provide reinforcement every time a child behaves in a desired manner?**

No. As the child begins to demonstrate some consistency in a behavior pattern that is being taught, the *schedule or pattern of providing reinforcement* should be changed. Begin to reinforce the behavior less and less frequently. Eventually only infrequent reinforcement will be sufficient to maintain the behavior. In fact, after behavior is learned it is best maintained (remembered and thus repeated at appropriate times in the future) if it is reinforced in an irregular manner.

2. IN THE CLASSROOM

13. How much reinforcement should be provided?

The amount of reinforcement required for effective learning to occur will vary considerably from child to child. Some children will require a great deal; others will require much less. It also will depend upon how difficult the behavior to be learned is for the child. To insure attention and persistence more reinforcement would be required for a difficult task than that needed for behavior that is easy for the child. Try out varying combinations to determine both the type and the quantity of reinforcing events required for each child to learn and/or to perform.

14. In working with children who demonstrate learning and behavior difficulties, should I be aware of any special reinforcement characteristics of such children?

Yes. Children with severe and/or chronic learning and behavior difficulties in comparison with typical children of similar age are:

a) Likely to respond to a smaller range of secondary reinforcing events. Events that have become secondary reinforcers generally are relatively weak.

b) More likely to find tangible events most reinforcing. Material reinforcers, in comparison with social and intrinsic ones, are disproportionately strong for many children with severe and chronic learning and behavior problems.

c) Less likely to find social attention in its various forms of praise, affection, approval, and acceptance to be highly reinforcing.

d) More likely to be highly selective in the social consequences that are reinforcing. Certain specific persons (mother, father, older brother or sister) may be reinforcing, but not most other people.

e) More likely to require more immediate, greater frequency, and greater amounts of reinforcement for learning and performance to occur.

f) Less likely to find a broad range of activities to be reinforcing. Novel experiences, being successful, competing in a game, becoming involved in cooperative endeavors, etc. are less likely to hold reinforcing qualities.

These differences in reinforcement characteristics of children with severe learning and behavior difficulties emphasize the critical need to identify reinforcing events that do influence each child and to initiate a systematic program of creating new sources of positive reinforcement. (See Question 8 for the procedure for establishing new positive reinforcers.)

15. Can a child ever be expected to learn or to do something just because he wants to or enjoys it, or must the teacher or parent continue to provide reinforcement?

The goal of behavior modification is to render the child as independent as possible of external reinforcing events. As implied in Question 7, the types of events, activities, and personal relationships that are reinforcing to a child change as the child moves from one stage to another in his social-emotional development. Initially, a child may need primary rewards. Next, the child may learn under immediate and frequent parent-teacher attention or approval. Later, attention and approval may be necessary only on occasion. At a higher level, peer approval and group acceptance become quite reinforcing. Finally, a child will find that mastery and accomplishment will become rewarding.

This independence, however, will take place gradually—and then only after the child has been successful in many activities and relationships, that is, after his behavior has produced frequent externally provided positive consequences of a tangible and social nature. Gradually, the child will come to enjoy—will find reinforcing—such activities as task involvement, cooperation, task completion, creating things, interacting with others, etc. These and similar activities that have resulted in success will acquire intrinsic reinforcing qualities. These behavior patterns will then occur without the necessity of frequent extrinsic reinforcing events.

The child learns to "pat himself on the back" and to engage in other self-directional activities for initiating, maintaining, and strengthening, and thus controlling, his own behavior.

16. How can I teach a child something new?

The child with learning and behavior difficulties frequently fails to learn because the educational program requires the child to learn too much at a given time. The child is unable to make the transition from what he presently is able to do to what the program is requiring him to do. The child may well be quite capable of learning new patterns of behavior or more complex combinations of his present behavior when the learning tasks are presented in a sequential order in smaller steps.

If the child is unable to do what you wish (e.g., complete a puzzle, copy geometric forms, pay attention, write his name, or any other behavior pattern that represents a reasonable expectation for him), a procedure of behavior *shaping* should be used. This means reinforcing successive approximations of the desired behavior. The initial approximations that are reinforced may be quite different from the final behavioral objective. At each stage in the shaping procedure, the behaviors for which reinforcement will be provided are increasingly similar to the goal behavior.

The teaching procedure used with a child with severe learning difficulties is described by two educators as follows:

> ... we usually teach him bit by bit. For example, if we want to teach him to work a puzzle, we wouldn't try to teach him to do the whole puzzle at once. Instead, we would start with one piece and make sure that he knew where it went before going on to the second. We would continue this way until he knew all of the pieces. The same thing is true in teaching a retarded child to dress himself. We would not give him his pants and tell him to put them on. Instead we would start by putting them on his legs and pulling them almost all the way up, teaching him to just pull them up the last inch or so to start with. Gradually we would teach him to pull them up further and further until he could pull them up from the floor. Then we would start teaching him to put on one leg of the pants, after we had already put the other one on for him. Finally, we would teach him to put on both legs and pull them up by himself. It is very important to notice here that *we always teach good behavior in small steps*.[1]

17. How can I best teach more complex behaviors?

By following the same general procedure. More complex behavior patterns usually are comprised of a number of similar behavior segments. First teach these smaller segments and then integrate these

---

1. Larsen, L. A. and Bricker, W. A. A manual for parents and teachers of severely and moderately retarded children. IMRID Papers and Reports, Vol. V, No. 22. p. 24. Nashville, Tenn.: George Peabody College, 1968.

2. IN THE CLASSROOM

into the more complex pattern of behavior. A teacher may be concerned with teaching such behavior patterns as following classroom routine, successfully engaging in language lessons that require a variety of separate skills, developing independence in lunchtime activities (sitting, eating, clearing table, remaining at table until the group is dismissed) and following directions involving use of various separate skills.

In shaping of a desired behavior, successive approximations of a complex behavior are reinforced until a final goal is attained. In cutting, below, the child:

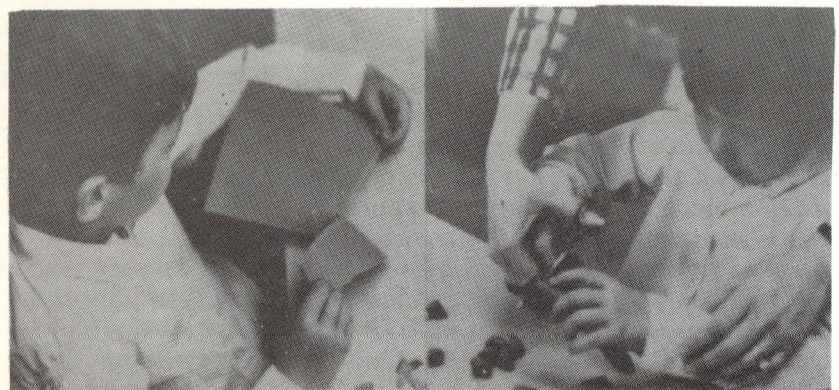

1. Begins by tearing paper . . .   *2. Next uses scissors to cut soft clay . . .*

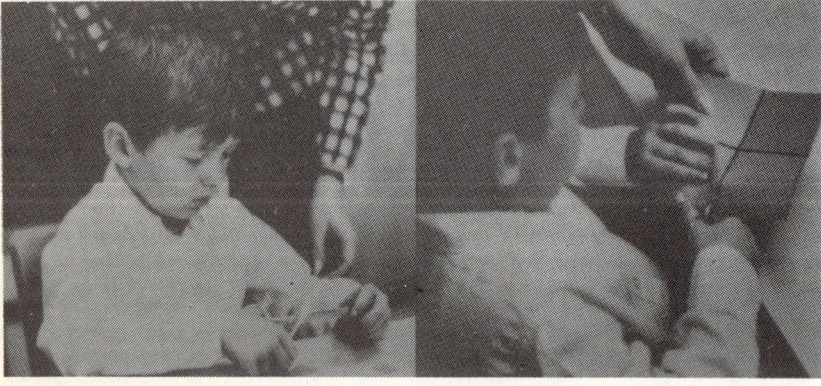

3. Learns to cut bits of paper . . .   *4. Receives help . . .*

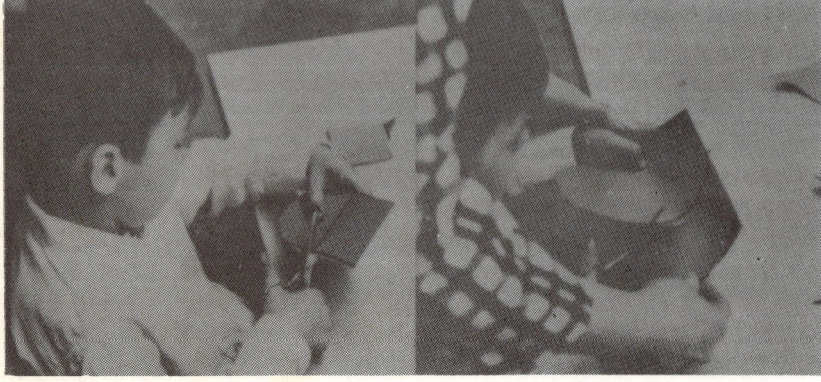

5. Cuts straight lines without help . . .   *6. Is guided to more complex cutting.*

A child may be able to engage in the separate behaviors that make up a more complex pattern, but still be unable to put these together on his own. For example, a child may know how to sit in a chair, to work on a puzzle, to sit and begin work when requested to do so, to put his completed tasks away, and to remain at his desk until requested to dress for outdoor play. Or, the child may know how to get out of bed when mother calls in the morning, to dress for school, to place bed clothing in the closet, to eat breakfast, and to get ready for the bus. However, considerable monitoring may be required to get each of these behaviors to occur and to insure smooth progression from beginning to end of the pattern. The child has each of these components in his repertoire, but is unable to integrate them into a pattern.

Learning frequently is facilitated by beginning with the last segment of a behavior pattern and reinforcing it immediately as it occurs. As this final behavior segment begins to occur consistently, the segment that precedes this final behavior is required prior to reinforcement. In teaching a child to complete a six-part picture puzzle, the puzzle is presented to the child with the final piece removed. As the child is able to place this piece successfully and receive reinforcement on a few occasions, two pieces are removed. Following successful completion of these two pieces, the child is presented with three, then four, then five, and finally six pieces. The pleasant consequences presented following correct placement of the final segment of the puzzle serve to strengthen the entire sequence from beginning to end. Each step serves as a signal for the next steps, which eventually result in reinforcement. By gradually increasing the number of segments, the final reinforcing event comes to influence and maintain more and more preceding behavior.

18. If the child does not learn when this procedure is used, can I assume that his learning difficulty is caused by his mental retardation, emotional disturbance, or learning disability?

No! Remember that learning difficulties frequently are a result of an inadequately designed educational program. If the child fails to make progress, ask yourself:

1. *Have I set the standard for reinforcement too high?* If so, the child is unable to demonstrate the behavior required for reinforcement. He will make little progress and become highly frustrated over his lack of success. He will quickly lose interest in the program.

2. *Am I moving from one step to another too rapidly?* If so, the preceding behavior has not been reinforced sufficiently to become strong. The child will soon forget the behavior he once demonstrated.

3. *Are my steps too simple?* If so, the program is inefficient, and the child may become bored and refuse to participate.

19. Are other procedures useful in getting desired behavior to occur?

Yes. A desired behavior, or an approximation of it, may be in the child's repertoire, but may occur only infrequently at the right time or place. In other instances the child may be able to behave as desired if he is told or shown what to do. There is no need in such instances for shaping of the desired behavior by the procedure of reinforcing successive approximations of it. The more appropriate procedure in these cases is to arrange for visual and auditory prompting to insure that the desired behavior will occur at the appropriate time and place and then to strengthen it through positive reinforcement.

2. IN THE CLASSROOM

Children will learn a behavior pattern more quickly if they can be guided in a manner that insures few errors. Practice does not make for effective learning if excessive errors are being made. Considerable assistance, which may be called for initially to insure the occurrence of the desired behavior, should be gradually removed as the child is able to behave appropriately in the presence of more natural cues. For example, while teaching a child to write letters or to draw geometric forms, numerous visual and mechanical prompts may be introduced, then gradually removed as the skills develop. In teaching a child to color within the lines of a drawing, heavy thread may be used as an outline of the picture. The size of the thread can be progressively reduced as the child learns to color within the lines.

For any particular child, select those prompting procedures that hold greatest promise of producing the desired behavior under the appropriate situation. Some children are quite skillful at following verbal directions and can engage in the desired behavior patterns after these are described to them. In other instances various forms of physical guidance may prove invaluable. For example, take the child's hand and move him through a cutting, coloring, drawing, or writing task, then gradually decrease the guidance as the child begins to behave on his own. In teaching a child to copy the letter A, numerous visual cues may be provided initially and gradually faded or removed as follows:

It frequently is valuable for someone to demonstrate or *model* the desired behavior as the child observes. Show the child how to complete certain tasks, how to pronounce a word, how to draw a circle, how to tie a bow. Speech, for example, could not be learned without models for the child to imitate. Immediately following observation, the child should be encouraged to imitate what he has heard or seen. As the desired behavior occurs, reinforcement should follow.

20. Does a child imitate everything he observes?

Children are more likely to imitate the behavior of those whom they like—those who provide, or are associated closely with, positive consequences. Other children, especially those of the same sex, frequently become the most influential models for imitation. Boys and girls who are leaders or who otherwise enjoy some status in the observer's eyes, close friends, someone with characteristics similar to those of the observer or whose behavior frequently results in positive consequences are more likely to be attended to and imitated.

21. Does a child learn to behave inappropriately just as he learns desired ways of acting?

Yes. The same general rules involved in the development and continuation of desired ways of behaving also are involved in a child's learning of inappropriate behavior patterns. For example, if placed in an environment with others who exhibit an excessive number of inappropriate behavior patterns, it is highly likely that the child will imitate some of these behaviors. This is especially true if the inappropriate behavior results in positive consequences. He will be more likely to imitate behavior that he sees resulting in pleasing consequences than he would be to imitate behavior that does not result in positive consequences to the model.

Attention of others in a classroom is highly reinforcing to many children. A child may imitate another child who engages in excessive activity, loud disruptive talk, or clowning behaviors as these actions are attention-getting. The teacher may attempt to ignore the behavior, but it may continue to occur as a result of the reinforcing attention it draws. This observation emphasizes the desirability of placing a child with learning and behavior difficulties in an environment with those who provide good behavior models. At the same time the teacher should always display her best behavior as it is likely to be imitated by the child. The teacher who moves about too quickly or who is too loud or too jumpy presents a poor behavior model.

In other instances, a child may find that attention from adults may best be obtained when he misbehaves. Thus, such behaviors as negativism, temper tantrums, and aggressiveness may be learned if these are followed consistently by adult attention.

22. What is the rule of negative reinforcement? How is it involved in the development of inappropriate modes of behavior?

The *rule of negative reinforcement* states that behavior which results in the removal or termination of events that are unpleasant to the child will be strengthened. Behavior, thus, will be strengthened if it results either in pleasurable consequences (positive reinforcement) or in the removal of unpleasant conditions (negative reinforcement). A child whose temper tantrum stops the teacher or the parent from requesting that he put his toys away (when he still wishes to play with them) will be more likely to throw a temper tantrum the next time he is requested to. A child's inattention and hyperactivity will be strengthened if it results in the removal of a difficult task that he had been asked to complete. Again, behavior that results in the termination of unpleasant conditions will be strengthened, that is, more likely to reoccur under similar conditions in the future.

23. How can inappropriate behavior be reduced or eliminated?

There are a number of procedures that can be used in efforts to reduce or to completely eliminate undesirable behaviors. The initial step is to evaluate the conditions under which inappropriate behavior occurs. Frequently, inappropriate behavior can be reduced significantly with only minor changes in a classroom routine. Excessive frustration, excessive noise or movement on the part of teacher or others, fatigue, and failure are among conditions that may greatly increase the likelihood of inappropriate behavior.

One teacher described the positive behavioral effects that resulted from changes in her classroom environment:

> As a result of training in behavior modification principles, I attempted to change my classroom environment completely. I previously scurried about, chattered constantly, and often found myself yelling at the children. It came to me . . . that I was teaching the children, through modeling, the exact frenzied behavior I could not control. I began to walk about the room more slowly; I talked more softly, distinctly, and slowly. I carefully explained what I wanted and waited for questions . . . I began deleting all useless words and unnecessary parts of lessons . . . The results were astounding. My class now works quietly for long periods of time and is able to clean up much more quickly than before. The children are more relaxed and speak more quietly . . . In general a calm atmosphere prevails. This has reduced my fatigue and tension. This is extremely important because as my tension rises, so does the noise level in the room.[1]

Another major approach to use in reducing inappropriate behavior may be described as one of *reinforcing alternative behaviors*. This involves the strengthening of those desired behaviors that will com-

2. IN THE CLASSROOM

pete with and eventually replace undesirable patterns of behavior. For example, rude behavior could be ignored and polite behavior reinforced in a systematic manner. A child who is out of his chair excessively could be reinforced for remaining seated and for engaging in an assigned task.

It is easy to punish inappropriate behavior as it occurs; it is more difficult to identify and to provide positive reinforcement for appropriate ways of behaving. Ask yourself, "What should the child be doing at the times he is behaving inappropriately?" Then plan to strengthen such alternative behaviors through positive reinforcement.

In selecting alternative behaviors to be reinforced, choose behaviors that will be most beneficial for the individual child. A child who is aggressive toward younger children could be taught to stay away from these children. However, this alternative behavior pattern does not reflect constructive social skills. Instead, the alternative behavior pattern to replace the aggressive one should consist of skills such as playing and working cooperatively with those who are younger.

24. What are other procedures of dealing with undesired behavior?

Another procedure is that related to the *rule of extinction*. This rule states that behavior can be eliminated or decreased in its likelihood of occurrence by removing the reinforcing events that have previously followed the behavior. This rule is based on the observation that behaviors, desirable or undesirable, will continue to occur if they are reinforced on occasion. If reinforcing events are removed and thus no longer follow the behavior, the behavior will soon disappear.

John, a five-year-old nonverbal child with severe developmental difficulties, had learned to forcefully take toys and books away from his younger brother. This aggressive pattern had been learned and continued to occur because of the reinforcing consequences it provided: John got the toys and the books. Mother, although inconsistent in her reaction to John's behavior, generally thought that this was acceptable because "John can't talk and has no other means of making his wishes known." When John entered a developmental education program he behaved in a similar aggressive manner toward his classmates. However, such behavior did not work as these children would not give in to John's aggressiveness. The behavior gradually disappeared in the new setting, even though John was quite upset initially. The behavior disappeared in the school setting because it was not reinforced as it had been in the home. The teacher then taught John other more appropriate ways of making his wishes known.

As another example, four-year-old Terry engaged in frequent disruptive whining and shouting in the home whenever he did not have his way. This behavior produced considerable attention from his parents. They speculated that the inappropriate behavior was being reinforced by both their attention and the fact that they would "give in" to Terry on occasion and let him have his way. After determining that these episodes occurred on an average of ten times daily, the parents began a new approach of immediately turning away from their son and occupying themselves with other activities when Terry whined or shouted, but attending to him when he behaved appropriately.

Following consistent use of this extinction procedure in combination with their giving of frequent social attention, approval, and praise following a variety of other desirable social behaviors, the disruptive whining and shouting became infrequent. More appropriate means of social interaction and of expressing disagreement were

---

1. Becker, W. C., Engelmann, S., and Thomas, D. R. *Teaching: A Course in Applied Psychology.* p. 169. Chicago: Science Research Associates, 1971.

learned. This example emphasizes the procedure of using an extinction approach in combination wtih one of reinforcement of appropriate behavior. An extinction procedure used in isolation does not strengthen those desired behaviors that should replace the ones extinguished.

25. What about the use of unpleasant consequences to discourage undesired behavior?

The use of negative consequences represents another approach to reducing the strength of undesired behavior patterns. Directions for using negative consequences represent aspects of a law of nature indicating that behavior resulting in unpleasant consequences will be less likely to be repeated under similar circumstances in the future. These "unpleasant consequences" rules refer to both 1) the occurrence of unpleasant events following behavior and 2) the removal or withdrawal following undesired behavior of positive consequences the child either has or finds available to him.

These negative consequences may be 1) naturally occurring unpleasant results of various behaviors, or 2) unpleasant events that are provided by peers, parents, teachers, and others. Just as certain rules of nature suggest that some behaviors should be avoided (eating excessive candy produces a stomach ache, playing in snow without gloves produces hurting fingers, touching a hot coffee pot produces a burned hand), certain rules of social living discourage various behaviors. The child hits another child and gets hit in return. He is rude to other children and they no longer play with him. As a result of these unpleasant consequences, the child learns to abide by certain rules in his interaction with his social environment. It is sometimes necessary for parents and teachers to arrange for unpleasant consequences to occur whenever the child ignores these rules. These rules should not be imposed arbitrarily nor should they be presented in a harsh, punitive, or derogatory fashion. The rules of social living and the resulting consequences should be logical and understandable to the child. *In every case, the child should have a choice.* Adherence to the rules of social living results in positive consequences; if the child does not choose the appropriate behavior of which he is quite capable, specific unpleasant consequences may be arranged to follow.

Procedures involving negative consequences should be minor and infrequently used aspects of a behavior management program. The excessive use of negative consequences can only result in aggressive outbursts or in excessively inhibited and overly emotional children— hardly behavioral characteristics to encourage. The parent or teacher who uses aversive consequences in a punitive, harsh, hostile, or aggressive manner when angry or aggravated merely provides an aggressive model for children to imitate. Children exposed to such behavior become apt to use these same modes of behavior when they become angry or have control over others. When used in skillful combination with procedures based on positive reinforcement, however, the selective use of unpleasant consequences may contribute to the positive behavior development of young children.

A child development program should teach a child to choose between those behaviors that produce positive consequences and those unacceptable to significant others. Unpleasant consequences following unacceptable behavior may assist the child in making a discrimination between acceptable and unacceptable behavior. Although a child may be shown and told what to do, inappropriate behaviors may still be quite strong occasionally. Permitting the child to experience unpleasant consequences immediately following undesired behavior,

2. IN THE CLASSROOM

and at the same time insuring him of experiencing frequent pleasant consequences for alternative appropriate behavior, may serve to facilitate positive behavior development.

To emphasize, it must be recognized that *no new appropriate behavior* is being taught when negative consequences are used to discourage undesired behavior. The behavior management program must always use other procedures for teaching the desired means of behaving. This is best done by frequent and systematic use of positive reinforcement.

26. Children with learning and behavior difficulties frequently exhibit emotional problems. Are these learned?

Children with learning and behavior difficulties frequently experience considerable problems in emotional expression and control. Some respond emotionally too frequently and intensely to too many aspects of the home and school environments. Other children are emotionally bland and show an insufficient amount and variety of emotional responsiveness. In most instances, these emotional behaviors are learned reactions resulting from excessive failure and related unpleasant experiences.

But children also can learn more appropriate and enhancing patterns of emotional responsiveness. They can learn this in the classroom through exposure to an emotionally expressive adult who provides carefully designed program experiences that produce plentiful sources of positive reinforcement following desired behavior. Whenever a child is provided positive reinforcement for desired behavior, he learns positive emotional reactions.

Social experiences in a structured environment that insures successful interpersonal contacts and systematically reduces the negative emotional impact of previous frightening and unpleasant experiences will reduce the general adjustment difficulties of young children with histories of learning and behavior difficulties. A child who is able to approach and interact with his school environment in a relaxed and trusting manner is a child who is free to learn and to be enthusiastic about learning. These general response patterns result from numerous experiences that provide consistent and predictable positive consequences.

More specifically, a child can become emotionally comfortable and less likely to engage in disruptive emotional responsiveness in a program that is structured and predictable. A program with routine and well-defined limits provides the consistency that results in security (freedom from excessive fear or apprehension) and enjoyment. The child in this environment is able to be successful. He can develop generalized positive emotional patterns. He can learn to tolerate increasing amounts of frustration and interpersonal conflict without resorting to intense and disruptive emotional outburst. As the child acquires a wider range of positive emotional reactions through the success a highly structured program brings, he can then be exposed gradually to less and less structure. He can be taught to make decisions and to accept the consequences of these decisions. This can be done through demonstrations, by guided practice of the observed behaviors, and by joint participation with others in successful solution of numerous social and nonsocial problems.

In providing a program for influencing the emotional behaviors of children, it is essential that the adults involved consistently demonstrate those emotional behaviors they wish the child to acquire. If the child is to learn to be relaxed, enthusiastic, or cheerful, the teacher and parents must demonstrate consistently these behavior patterns in a spontaneous and natural manner. The child must also be provided with many opportunities to engage in various emotional behaviors and to label or describe them. This can be done with role-playing experiences or be injected into other social situations to which the child reacts throughout the school day.

To employ role-playing, introduce a game requiring the child alone, or in a group, to show how he would feel in various situations. A puppet may be used to enhance attention and participation. Describe the puppet as being in situations causing him to be sad, happy, apprehensive, pleasantly surprised, pleased, contented, angry, etc. Guide the child into acting out the various feelings depicted and encourage him to describe his own feelings.

27. What steps are followed in developing a behavior modification program?

1) Describe what the child *does do* to create some concern—that is, what does the child actually do in situations that require a level or type of behavior he does not demonstrate? The problem may represent either excessive or deficit behaviors.

Although it is easy to focus on what a child *does not do*, a program can be based only on what a child *does do* in situations that require behaviors other than those exhibited by the child. A description such as "He does not sit still" does not indicate what he does do. Does he move about excessively while remaining in his chair? Does he move out of his chair? What does he do when away from the chair?

Stating that a child is unable to label pictures of common objects, cannot identify basic colors or shapes, or cannot copy simple forms is equally inadequate as descriptions of the child's behavioral skills. What does he do when presented with pictures of objects or when shown colors? Is he able to match pictures with objects or colors with objects of similar colors? Does he have the verbal labels for the objects and colors and does he use these, although inappropriately, when requested to label objects and colors? These current behaviors are the ones with which the behavior modification program must begin in order to teach more desirable or complex forms of the behaviors.

2) Describe the behavior of concern in specific objective terms. Reporting that Susan is "spoiled" is much too vague. Such a description does not indicate what Susan actually does. This general description must be translated into specific behaviors such as: "She cries when she cannot be first in a classroom activity." "She whines when required to clean up her mess." "She does not share her toys with others." Also, the behavior must be described as it occurs in specific situations. These requirements are illustrated in the table below.

3) Describe how you expect the child to behave. These *should do* behaviors become the program goals or objectives. These behavioral objectives are intimately related to how the child presently responds to specific situations. If the general program goal is to insure that the child becomes independent in dressing himself, description must be made of what the child does when presented with a request to dress himself. These behaviors form the beginning steps in a program designed to teach more complex dressing skills.

4) Develop a specific behavior modification approach to teach the "missing" behaviors, that is, those that will fill the gap between what the child *does* and what he *should do*. This emphasizes that a specific behavior modification approach for a child cannot be delineated until the *does do* and the *should do* behaviors have been specified. The program begins with what the child presently does and continues until the child reaches the desired should do behavior objectives.

The program will consist of two closely related aspects, the *ex-*

2. IN THE CLASSROOM

The following illustrates these first three steps in developing a program for a child:

Physical and Social Situation	What Does the Child Do?	What Do You Wish the Child to Do?
1. In a classroom with five children sitting at a table, he is presented with colors and asked "What color is this?"	1. He looks at the colors, reaches for them, and shakes his head "no" when prompted to name them.	1. Correctly name the colors red, blue, green, yellow, black, and white.
2. During lunchtime when seated with five children and teacher, he is asked to use his knife, fork, and spoon in eating his food.	2. He uses his spoon and fork appropriately, but spills food on the table when he attempts to cut meat with his knife.	2. Use all eating utensils appropriately during mealtime.
3. At the end of school day he is provided coat, overshoes, and gloves and requested to get ready for the bus.	3. He puts his coat on and attempts unsuccessfully to get his overshoes on. He gets his gloves on the wrong hands.	3. Dress himself completely and satisfactorily in preparation for going home at end of school day.
4. At home following play, he is requested to put his toys away and get ready for bath and bed.	4. He begins to whine and engage in other negativistic behaviors.	4. While being free on occasion to express disagreement, typically comply with parental requests.

posure and the *consequence* components:

a) The *exposure* component refers to those things that will be involved to insure that the desired behavior, or a reasonable approximation of it, will occur. This includes the arrangement of the physical setting, what the teacher will do, and the materials or other stimulus events that will be provided.

b) The *consequence* component refers to the specific consequences that will be provided after the behavior occurs, the manner in which these will be presented, and the schedule by which these will be provided. Desired behavior is best acquired when the consequences are of specific interest to the individual learner.

28. A behavior modification program requires considerable planning. Is this feasible in working with more than one child?

The approach does require the teacher to know each child, to set specific program objectives for each child, and to tailor the educational experiences to coincide with the specific needs of each child. These are time-consuming activities. But with experience, the teacher can tailor the educational experiences to the individual needs of each child in her class. She is reinforced for her hard work, for in such an environment young children with learning and behavior difficulties do learn—and do come to enjoy it because they are being successful. Numerous experiences of parents and teachers support the use of a behavior modification approach in implementing educational programs for groups of children. (*See reading list for examples.*)

29. But if I must be so analytical and objective, will this not interfere with my spontaneity and inhibit my being natural?

No. Once understood and practiced, the use of behavior modification procedures should not interfere with your being natural. A teacher or parent can be just as warm, spontaneous, and enthusiastic in a program of behavior modification as in any other program of child development. A person can be systematic and spontaneous at the same time. Only a skilled observer will be able to identify a teacher who is systematically using behavior modification procedures. Within a few minutes in interacting with a group of children, a teacher may be reinforcing four or five different behaviors by using various types and arrangements of positive consequences, may be extinguishing other undesired behaviors, initiating the development of needed discriminations, and discouraging other behaviors by skillful shaping of more appropriate competing ones. The teacher can be calm but confident, relaxed but organized, warm but consistent, and flexible but specific in determining individual expectations for each child.

The behavior modification approach is a most humanizing one. But just as with any approach, an essential ingredient is an adult who cares for children and who is willing to invest energies in the experiences provided for them.

30. How can I learn more about the approach?

Numerous books describing the approach and its application to children are available. The following references will provide the interested reader with a more detailed discussion of the topic of behavior modification.

SUGGESTED READINGS

Parents and Lay Readers

Becker, Wesley C. *Parents are Teachers: A Child Management Program.* Champaign, Ill.: Research Press, 1971.

Deibert, Alvin N. and Harmon, Alice J. *New Tools for Changing Behavior.* Champaign, Ill.: Research Press, 1970.

Gardner, William I. *Children with Learning and Behavior Problems: A Behavior Management Approach.* Boston: Allyn & Bacon, Inc., 1974.

Kozloff, Martin A. *Reaching the Autistic Child: A Parent Training Program.* Champaign, Ill.: Research Press, 1973.

Patterson, Gerald R. *Families: Application of Social Living to Family Life.* Champaign, Ill.: Research Press, 1971.

Watson, Luke S. *How to Use Behavior Modification with Mentally Retarded and Autistic Children.* Columbus, Ohio: Behavior Modification Technology, 1972.

Introductory Materials for Professional Persons

Becker, Wesley C., Engelmann, Siegfried, and Thomas, Don R. *Teaching: A Course in Applied Psychology.* Chicago: Science Research Associates, 1971.

Clarizio, Harvey F. *Toward Positive Classroom Discipline.* New York: John Wiley & Sons, Inc., 1971.

Gardner, William I. *Children with Learning and Behavior Problems: A Behavior Management Approach.* Boston: Allyn & Bacon, Inc., 1974.

Haring, Norris G. and Phillips, E. Lakin. *Analysis and Modification of Classroom Behavior.* Englewood Cliffs, N. J.: Prentice-Hall International, Inc., 1972.

Kozloff, Martin A. *Reaching the Autistic Child: A Parent Training Program.* Champaign, Ill.: Research Press, 1973.

Krumboltz, John D. and Krumboltz, Helen. *Changing Children's Behavior.* Englewood Cliffs, N. J.: Prentice-Hall International, Inc., 1972.

Kunzelmann, Harold P., et al. (Eds.) *Precision Teaching.* Seattle: Special Child Publications, Inc., 1970.

Macmillan, Donald L. *Behavior Modification in Education.* New York: Macmillan Company, 1973.

Neisworth, John T. and Smith, Robert M. *Modifying Retarded Behavior.* Boston: Houghton Mifflin Co., 1973.

O'Leary, K. Daniel and O'Leary, Susan G. *Classroom Management: The Successful Use of Behavior Modification.* New York: Pergamon Press, Inc., 1972.

Steucher, Uwe. *Tommy: A Treatment Study of an Autistic Child.* Arlington, Va.: Council for Exceptional Children, 1972.

Sulzer, Beth and Mayer, G. Roy. *Behavior Modification Procedures for School Personnel.* Hinsdale, Ill.: Dryden Press, Inc., 1972.

Watson, Luke S. *How to Use Behavior Modification with Mentally Retarded and Autistic Children.* Columbus, Ohio: Behavior Modification Technology, 1972.

It was 1:30 p.m. on Thursday and time to add up the reward points earned during the day. The conversation went something like this:

"Well, Jack, it looks as though you really had a good day. You earned 36 points. How did you do it?"

Jack shrugged his shoulders and replied with a grin, "I don't know. Just worked hard, I guess."

"You've earned enough points to go outside, Jack. Is that where you want to go?"

"Yes," said Jack as he zipped up his jacket.

"Let's see now, Laura. How many points do you have here?"

"Yesterday, I earned 33 points and I went to quiet games but today I earned 34 points. I want to go to blocks with Roberta because she earned 34 points, too."

"Very good. Let's see where it is that you didn't earn your two points."

"Oh, I missed my behavior point in ego group and my 'coming in quietly' point in phonics."

"I bet you'll earn them tomorrow, won't you?"

Laura answered with a grin.

"Now, who's next? Oh, yes, here's Michael. How did it go, Michael?"

"Well, I got 32 and I'd like to go out, but I guess I'll go to coloring."

"O.K., Mike, maybe you'll earn enough tomorrow. What kept you from earning your points?"

Michael responded with a shrug.

"Well, we can't be perfect every day. You're doing so much better than when you first came here, aren't you? After all, 32 is good enough for a reward, so we must think that's pretty good."

Just then Ronald came into the room. "Well, here I am," he declared. "I got only 31 points, so I have to go to counseling." Ronald proceeded to the counseling area and sat down to wait for the counselor and any other students who had not earned enough points to go to one of the reward centers.

■ Scenes like the one described above can be seen and heard every school day at 1:30 p.m. at the McVey Diagnostic Impact Center in Newark, Delaware. The center was started in 1971 to diagnose and treat kindergarten through 5th level children with social, emotional, intellectual, and/or learning difficulties, using a nongraded, noncategorical approach.

After the center was established, it did not take long for the four teachers and three aides to determine the need for a behavior modification technique to teach children new academic, social,

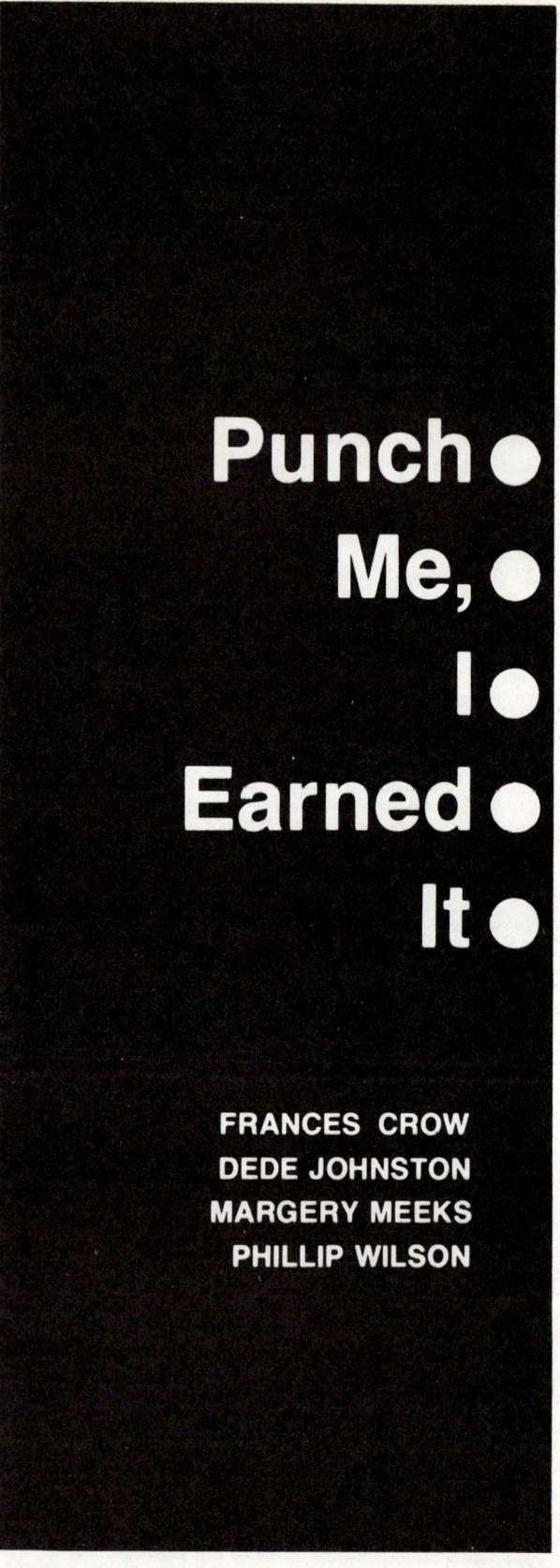

Punch Me, I Earned It

**FRANCES CROW
DEDE JOHNSTON
MARGERY MEEKS
PHILLIP WILSON**

Frances Crow, Dede Johnston, Margery Meeks, and Phillip Wilson are a teaching team at the McVey Diagnostic Impact Center in Newark, Delaware.

9. Punch Me

36 35 34	33 32 31	30 29 28	27 26	25	24 23	22	21 20 19
Homeroom	Spelling	Language	Recess	Hall	Lunch	Hall	Math

NAME _____ DATE _____

Homeroom	Class	Class	Class	Phonics	Reading
1 2 3	4 5 6	7 8 9	10 11 12	13 14 15	16 17

FIGURE 1

and emotional behavior. Various methods were applied but not consistently or successfully.

Finally, the center's principal, Willis A. Proctor, suggested the use of a punch card to reward good behavior. Since that time, and with several modifications, the present punch card system based on earned points for rewards and interval reinforcements has evolved. It has proved quite successful and easy to use when the staff has good cooperative rapport and consistency.

USING THE PUNCH CARD

The staff and children at the McVey Center understand that each child may earn three points in each 20 minute work period. The first point in each class is punched for coming into the area quietly; the second point is punched if the assigned task is completed; and the third point is punched for acceptable behavior (see Figure 1).

Every morning the teacher sits on a large rug as the children arrive. She has a punch card for each child, which has been prepared in advance by writing in the child's name and the date. She also has a paper puncher which she uses to punch the earned points. A paper puncher with a metal strip attached to catch the paper is available commercially. This type of puncher avoids pieces of punched paper being scattered around the school. The teacher empties the puncher into a wastebasket at her convenience during the day.

Each child is expected to walk off the bus into his class, hang up his coat, and take a place quietly in the circle on the rug. If the child successfully completes these steps the teacher punches the first point on the child's punch card while complimenting the child on the completion of his task. If a child chooses not to follow through on the expected steps, the teacher will simply mention when he does join the circle that he did not earn his first point, but that he can still earn the others. Sometimes more explanation is given as to why the point was not earned or, in order to place more responsibility on the child, he might be asked if he earned the point.

Because of the class routine, the children do not have to ask the teacher to "punch me." They know their first point will be punched at the beginning of each class period. The teacher then holds the punch cards until the end of the period when the children again sit in a group to receive their punch cards. They know their work and behavior points will be punched at that time if they have been earned. If the child has worked to his capacity during the work period, the second point will be punched. If his behavior has been satisfactory (e.g., sitting still, minding his own business), the third point is punched. The same verbalization is used as with the first point. The teacher and aides are careful to be consistent about the requirements for each point.

At the end of the day, the teacher and the child

2. IN THE CLASSROOM

count earned points. The child may choose a reward center based on the number of points earned during the day (see Table 1). The staff decided that 32 points or more out of a possible 36 would constitute a reward. If 36 or 35 points are earned the child may choose any of the four rewards. If 34 points are earned he may choose any of the rewards for 34 points or below. If 33 points have been earned the child has two choices, and with 32 points he has only one choice.

The punch card is the child's ticket into the reward area. It must be presented to show the correct number of points were earned. If a child earns 31 points or less, he goes to counseling, which is an opportunity for the teacher and the child to talk about what happened during the day and how the child can earn more points the next day. The punch card is particularly useful here because it is a tangible indication of behavior patterns. It may also indicate a need to reexamine the task requirement.

Many of the children take their punch cards home at the end of the day. Because the parents have had the point system and the use of the card explained to them previously by the teachers, they may praise the child for his good day.

ADAPTING THE PUNCH CARD

The flexibility of the punch card meets the needs of the individual students, the group contingency needs, and the communication needs demanded by a team teaching situation.

Individual student needs, as embodied in behavioral or academic problems, are concisely and tangibly handled with the McVey punch card. For example, a child who consistently has difficulty controlling his temper may earn an additional point each 20 minute period that he controls his scheduled to meet with a speech therapist at 11:10. His card may be circled at the appropriate punch number and marked *Speech,* thus reminding both the teacher and the child of the appointment.

Individualized contingencies are communicated to the team members by using the available space at the bottom of the punch card. An example of this might be a child whose behavior point is specifically defined (e.g., the child must come directly to the work area and remain seated for the entire period). A notation to this effect on the card facilitates consistent action among the team members.

temper (e.g., does not cry, scream, or lash out at others verbally or physically). A graph recording the number of points he earns daily for controlling his temper may be created by the teacher and the child, with a reward for a designated number of perfect scores.

A child who is nearing the completion of his stay at the center may be placed on a long term point contingency to determine the exact date of his or her departure. For example, the child may be permitted to color in one block of a maze each day that 36 points are earned. When the maze is completed, the child may be considered ready to depart.

Communication needs among the team members are met through the tangible nature of the paper punch card. A child may verbalize in the morning what he intends to work on that day to earn his points; for example, "I am working on saying full sentences" or "I am working on raising my hand and not calling out." The teacher may then write this on the available space at the bottom of the punch card for the child and other teachers to see.

Events to be remembered can easily be recorded on the card. For instance, a child may be

Effects of Touch and Verbal Reinforcement on the Classroom Behavior of Emotionally Disturbed Boys

J. EUGENE CLEMENTS
D. B. TRACY

J. EUGENE CLEMENTS is Associate Professor of Special Education, Division of Clinical Studies, West Virginia University, Morgantown; and D. B. TRACY is Associate Professor of Educational Psychology and Research, University of Kansas, Lawrence.

The potential of tactile stimulation as a reinforcer has been suggested by Bailey and Meyerson (1962) and Siqueland and Lipsitt (1966). Although various forms of touching, such as patting and hugging, are often a part of everyday teacher-pupil interaction, they are seldom applied systematically with definite goals in mind. The present study attempted to investigate the relative effects of tactile and verbal reinforcement and a combination of both on attention to task and accuracy of performance in solving arithmetic problems.

Subjects and Method

The subjects were 10 boys of normal intelligence, ranging in age from 9 to 11 years, who had previously been diagnosed as emotionally disturbed and placed in a special education classroom operated under the structured approach (Haring & Phillips, 1962; Whelan & Haring, 1966). The female teacher initiated each treatment by giving the subject an arithmetic work sheet, instructing the student to work the problems, and giving the appropriate cue to the subject. The tactile cue consisted of firm hand pressure applied to both shoulders of the subject, and the verbal cue consisted of telling the subject that he would do a "good job." Cues were repeated by the teacher at approximate 4 minute intervals during each 20 minute work session while the subject was attending to task. Each subject received each of the following treatments on four different occasions in a random order: tactile, verbal, both verbal and tactile, and control (no cue).

Results

Attention to task as measured by observer counts of 15 second intervals of attention or inattention (Martin & Powers, 1967) and arithmetic performance (percentage correct on the arithmetic work sheet) were analyzed by the extension of Friedman's test (Conover, 1971, p. 273). Pairwise comparisons among treatments were made by the method of adjusted significance levels (Ryan, 1960).

For attention to task both the combination of tactile and verbal cues (Mdn = 88.5%) and tactile cue alone (Mdn = 88.0%) were significantly ($P < .05$) higher than either verbal cue alone (Mdn = 73.0%) or control (Mdn = 68.5%). The verbal cue alone was also significantly higher than the control in attention to task. For arithmetic performance, the combination verbal and tactile treatment (Mdn = 91.5%) was significantly higher ($P < .05$) than the tactile only (Mdn = 85.5%), verbal only (Mdn = 76.0%), and control (Mdn = 65.0%) treatments. Both tactile only and verbal only were also superior to the control treatment on arithmetic performance.

Discussion

The present study demonstrated that tactile stimulation is potentially valuable as a reinforcer, especially when combined with verbal praise. Since no special apparatus or token system is needed, systems application of tactile and verbal reinforcement should be especially easy to apply in classroom settings.

Because the present study was limited to a single classroom of 10 subjects and a single teacher and there are possible cumulative effects from repeated treatments applied to the same subjects, the present results must be interpreted with caution. Further research in other settings with other types of subjects, teachers, and materials would be needed for wide generalization.

References

Bailey, J., & Meyerson, L. Vibrations as a reinforcer with a profoundly retarded child. *Journal of Applied Behavioral Analysis*, 1962, 2, 135-137.

Conover, W. *Practical Nonparametric Statistics.* New York: John Wiley & Sons, 1971.

Haring, N., & Phillips, E. *Educating Emotionally Disturbed Children.* New York: McGraw-Hill, 1962.

Martin, G. L., & Powers, R. B. Attention span: An operant conditioning analysis. *Exceptional Children*, 1967, 33, 565-570.

Ryan, T. Significance tests for multiple comparison of proportions, variances, and other statistics. *Psychological Bulletin*, 1960, 57, 318-328.

Siqueland, E., & Lipsitt, L. Conditioned head-turning in human newborns. *Journal of Experimental Child Psychology*, 1966, 3, 356-376.

Whelan, R. J., & Haring, N. G. Modification and maintenance of behavior through systematic application of consequences. *Exceptional Children*, 1966, 32, 281-289.

Pseudo-Retardation as a Form of Learning Disability: The Case of Jean

Denis H. Stott Ph D

In a preschool for the retarded, a four-year-old girl was suspected of playing the role of a low-grade retardate, controlling her social environment by means of extreme dependance and helplessness. Rehabilitation was sucessful through a behavior modification program in which this role was not reinforced and through use of the Flying Start Learning-To-Learn Program, which positively reinforces good learning behavior. The child showed herself to have good learning ability and her IQ was raised to within the normal range. It was noted that her choice of the dependent was not arbitrary, but was an understandable aftermath of early handicaps.

The subject of this report is a four-year-old girl who had assumed the role of retardate as a way of life, and had been diagnosed as such and placed in a nursery for the retarded. Through a rehabilitation program she was persuaded to abandon this role and function at a normal level of mental ability. Experience with children in retarded settings suggests that such cases are not uncommon, even though the reasons for their choice of the retardat's role may differ. The condition of pseudo-retardation may thus often remain undiagnosed, so that the child continues to be treated as a retardate, the evidence to the contrary being too dissonant with our conceptions and with the role that we have provided for the child as retardate. The definition of mental deficiency given by the Manual of the American Association on Mental Deficiency (Heber 1959) has been critized (Garfield and Wittson 1960, Halpern 1970) for laying the chief stress upon current functioning. It sees social adjustment, broadly conceived, as one of the criteria for mental deficiency. Whereas it is recognized that failure thereof may result from intellectual deficit, no attempt is made to differentiate between the individual's intrinsic inability to meet the requirements of an in-dependent life due to cognitive impairment and malfunctioning which is due to motivational aberration. It is on this distintion that the concept of pseudo-retardation rests. In terms of current functioning, the pseudo-retardate is in deed mentally retarded, but may not be "truly" retarded in the cognitive sense in that, once the motivational aberration is removed, he may be able to function at a normal intellectual level.

What makes us suspect in some cases that the child is not truly retarded is the apparent ability to function at a normal level at certain times or in some areas. This is the basic concept underlying Benton's (1962) discussion of pseudo-feeble-mindedess or psychogenic mental dificiency. He points out that among normal people a "subject matter disability, as in mathematics or literature" is acepted without question. In other words, a normal person is permitted to be learning disabled in some areas. If, however, the areas of disabilities reach a certain size or impring upon functions that traditionally are associated with low intelligence, the person is classified as retarded.

The detection of pseudo-retardation requires, in consequence, the systematic study and recording of an individual recording of an individual's functioning in a variety of situatons over a period of time. The observed behaviors then can be classified as, on the one hand, demonstrating ability to function at a level of complexity which enables the individual to operate effectively and to achieve his goals or, on the other hand, inability to cope with situations at such a level. If there is a underlying consistency in this inconsistency of function, we may begin to suspect pseudo-retardation.

The criterion of complexity enables us to differentiate between cognitive (true?) retardation and socially maladaptive behavior. In the case to be described, the child operated at a high level of complexity in order to maintain a socially maladaptive, and indeed a "retarded" role. Normally such a role would be judged highly detrimental to the child's best interests in the long run, she was achieving an effective manipulation of her environment.

MOTIVATION FACTORS

Benton likewise suggests that pseudo-feeble-mindedness - that is, an assumed learning disabili - may arise from motivational factors, notably avesive conditioning by early unpleasant or traumatic experiences. "Motivation" is here defined as comprising the factors which determine the individual's choice of goals - more precisely, the types of relationships which the person seeks to establish between himself and his world (Nissen 1958). What looks at first sight to be extremly ineffective functioning may, in the light of his chosen goals, be highly effective and "intelligent." The person may decide to avoid coping with certain situations either because they are deemed unrewarding or because other goals demand noncoping. In the case of this girl, maintenance of her rewarding dependency role required consistent noncoping in everyday - situations - above all, those in which an adult demanded some achievement.

11. Pseudo-Retardation

Reduced to ultimate objectivity, the motivational variable is a matter of whether behaviors of a certain class occur or not. This applies also to cognitive processes. De facto mental retardation may arise either because such processes are grossly impaired, or because they do not occur (or a combination of both). It is suspected that much pseudo-retardation and other forms of learning disability result from non-use of cognitive functions, that is to say, is of motivational origin. Since the efficiency of the cognitive processes only comes in question if they occur, the motivational factor can be the overriding one. An intelligence test score does not distinguish between motivational and cognitive impairment. Failure on an item — and hence the IQ as a whole — may be due either to the subject's inability to operate at the requisite level of complexity or to a failure to initiate the cognitive processes. In the present case study the apparent retardation was entirely of the latter sort. Once the cognitive processes were brought into play, they were seen to be of normal quality.

It is tempting to accept the possibility of motivational handicap as an exceptional phenomenon while retaining the convenient traditional diagnosis in terms of "mental level" or minimal brain dysfunction. However, experience with many cases in a remedial clinic to which children were referred from primary departments of schools as slow learners or learning disabled led us to the view that practically all such cases are of motivational origin, without significant impairment of the cognitive processes as such.

If, as argued above, occurrence or non-occurrence of a process is more fundamental than its quality when it does occur, the first step in the diagnosis of any kind of impaired performance should be the assessment of the motivational variable (Stott 1971b). Such an approach requires the means of identifying and classifying temperamental factors in learning disability.

CASE REPORT — JEAN

Just before her fourth birthday, Jean, the subject of the present case study, was admitted to a nursery for the mentally retarded on the recommendation of a psychologist and a public health nurse. No intelligence test was given because she was patently untestable. As director of the Centre for Educational Disabilities in Guelph, I had been invited by the director of the preschool for the retarded to work with some of my graduate students to identify any children in the preschool for the retarded who might benefit from our early education program. Jean was one of those whom I identified and continued to work with. To all appearances she was severely retarded, and her extreme helplessness was the cause of considerable concern to the nursery director. Any attempt to bring her into an activity was met by turning away, lying on the floor, and a pose of pity-exciting misery. This style of behavior was reinforced by the good-hearted but untrained helpers, who would pick her up and nurse her patiently whenever she adopted it, with the result that the greater part of her time in the nursery was spent in someone's arms. She never mixed with other children or played with the available toys.

Jean became the subject of clinical study at the age of four and a half. Interviewed at this time, the mother reported somewhat similar lethargy and miserableness in behavior at home, but added that she indulged in temper tantrums followed by sulking when she could not get her own way. However, she played well on the whole with her brother, one year younger than herself, and, most surprisingly, usually took the lead.

The family consisted of five children ranging in age from 3 to 13 years, all of whom were stable and functioning well except Jean, the fourth. The parents were sensible and stable, and led a well-organized, middle-class life. The mother did not work, but was taking extension courses at the university. She had the warm, protective, maternal style found in many traditional cultures. She accepted the view that Jean was retarded and reinforced her dependence strategy in much the same way as did nursery helpers.

Observed from behind a one-way mirror in the nursery, Jean's general manner certainly gave the appearance of severe retardation. There was, however, one telltale contradiction. Even when lying inert on the floor she would be following one adult or another with her eyes, presumably to gauge the effect of her behavior.

THERAPY BEGINS: BEHAVIOR MODIFICATION

The first therapeutic objective was to halt the reinforcement of Jean's dependence strategy. A meeting was held with the nursery helpers at which it was pointed out how she was able to command constant attention and, in fact, very effectively controlled their behavior. They were led to see that as long as she was allowed to enjoy this form of fulfillment she would not progress, and there would be no means of finding out whether she was retarded or not. Very specific guidance was given to them never to pick her up when she collapsed whimpering on the floor, and if she did not care to participate in the musical and other social activities, she simply was to be ignored. With one or two lapses, the helpers faithfully carried out this program.

A similar explanation and similar counseling were given to the mother. It was not anticipated that she would be able to carry out such a radical change of attitude without further guidance, but throughout the treatment she showed the most commendable determination to cooperate.

The behavior modification treatment in the nursery began to show good results within a matter of days. Bored with lying unattended on the floor, Jean made her way over to the toy corner and occupied herself with the toys. Within a short while she began to interact with other children, utilizing the same pattern of interaction as with her younger brother.

THERAPY CONTINUES: FLYING START

At this stage she was included in a group of children about her own age who were beginning the Flying Start Learning-to-Learn Program (Stott 1971a). This consists of a programmed series of puzzles and other play activities for kindergarten and prekindergarten children, so designed that success can be achieved only if the requisite perceptual and cognitive processes are brought into play. It thus represents an adaptation of the principles of behavior modification in the direction not of reducing undesirable but of producing desirable behavior. The types of activity correspond to the kinds of behavior which a child naturally seeks to achieve in order to be effective (White 1959, Stott 1961) and thus spontaneously are motivating. Since occurrence of cognitive processes is consistently reinforced, the program serves to correct those problem-solving strategies which for one reason or another (avoidance, impulsivity, etc.) result in nonoccurrence.

The first item requires merely that the child join the two halves of a boldly drawn picture. In order to preclude mere trial-and-error fitting and to reinforce attention and cognitive rehearsal, the picture is divided by a straight rather than by a curved cut such as usually found in play materials for the retarded. When presented with this task, Jean showed no sign of comprehending what was expected of her. Her lack of response could easily have resulted in failure on an intelligence test. However, despite her moping she followed closely with her eyes the successful efforts of the other three children. She resisted all cajoling to participate. Then the therapist, in the course of handing out fresh pieces of pictures to the others, laid in front of her the two halves of a picture only a short distance apart. He made no comment and paid no further attention to her. The other children joined their halves into pictures and were duly praised. Jean, forgetting momentarily her role of nonparticipant, could not resist pushing the two halves of her picture together. Attention was drawn to her accomplishment and she was fulsomely praised. In the next round another picture was placed in front of her with the halves similarly almost joined, and again without any injunction to participate. She put them together quickly this time. It was obvious that they presented her with no perceptual or other mechanical difficulty. Finally each half was presented to her separately, and she completed the picture straightaway.

The next week she completed the same picture cut into quarters. She began playing happily with other children and began experimenting in the use of an active, initiative-taking

2. IN THE CLASSROOM

lifestyle. With little hesitation she embarked upon the next of the Flying Start tasks, which consists of "mailing" small cards, each bearing a letter of the alphabet, into mailboxes bearing similar letters (see Fig. 1). She concentrated on this activity with what the research assistant described as "super-focus." At the same time, as would be expected of a normal child, she became bored with the picture completion task.

A week later she was beginning to become more assertive and to exploit her new life style to the point of being described as disruptive. She was reported as frequently smiling, and even laughing heartily, and showing an "exaggerated independence." In group activities she became competitive, trying to build a "biggie, biggie, biggie tower." The research assistant noted that "she does not lack competence in meddlesome activity."

The next week she had a partial relapse. The volunteer who had ministered to her all too affectionately returned after several weeks off duty and there was not time to brief her adequately in the new therapeutic strategy. Her presence evidently reactivated Jean's desire for control through dependence. She refused to answer her name in the circle. Half her time during the play activities she spent watching the movements of her favorite volunteer. Yet, to quote from the nursery director's daily notes, "participation and enjoyment amounted to a much greater part of the morning than nonparticipation and unhappiness." Notably, she did extremely well at the mailboxes.

Four days later she definitely opted for the outgoing, participating style as evidently bringing greater rewards. She sang a verse of a song by herself in the circle, became very affable and, after correctly identifying the numbers one through ten, became quite "hyper" at her accomplishment. The only contretemps was when she cried at having to lie on a mat alone instead of having a volunteer beside her, but she stopped after two minutes of being ignored. During this period she began to wet her pants but desisted when she was made to visit the bathroom every hour.

THIRD MONTH: PROGRESS

At this time, some two months after the beginning of the treatment, her behavior was rated on the Effectiveness-Motivation Scale (Stott & Sharp 1968). Descriptions of typical levels of effectiveness are scored from zero to four in 11 areas of functioning, such as Building, Creative Play, Make-Believe Play, Appeal to Novelty, Helping Others, Reactions to Strangers. She scored 30, which is half a standard deviation above the mean of 24 for a normal nursery school sample. This result showed that, contrary to first appearances, she could not be rated as in any way an undermotivated child. Her occasional reluctance to tackle new tasks stemmed, in so far as this was not normal, from her harking back to a dependence/incompetence strategy.

A week later the nursery director was writing of Jean, "Behavior practically normal, very happy playing in a group with small cars. The quartered cards and the mailboxes seem too easy for her when she is in a cooperative mood." The next day she had her "best day ever" in the swimming pool, not only undressing and dressing herself but attempting to help dress the volunteer. She jumped into the pool willingly and bobbed her head under the water, which is anything but characteristic of a temperamentally apprehensive child.

During the following weeks she maintained her happy, outgoing, participating style with only slight lapses. She did not mind which volunteer worked with her, and she helped to organize the children for various games and songs. On arrival she ran off from her mother eagerly in order to show how well she was doing at her activities. She made no attempt to interrupt her mother's socializing at the end of the sessions but busied herself by putting on her coat, hat, and boots. This transformation in her behavior and level of mental functioning had taken not quite three months. During the next few weeks it was apparent that Jean was out of place and had reached the limit of her progress in the retarded nursery. Also, since she was just turned five, it was important to prepare her for entry to a normal kindergarten. It was therefore decided to introduce her to the kindergarten group at the Centre for Educational Disabilities, composed of children referred as slow learners, but, like Jean, showing for the most part faulty styles of learning behavior rather than poor ability.

SPECIAL KINDERGARTEN

On her first visit to the Centre she was brought by a nursery volunteer who had been firm with her, and she settled down well to the learning activities. By now she could do the six-piece puzzles and worked with a good, thoughtful strategy. However, she decided to test her earlier strategy of moodiness and fretting on the Centre volunteer, and whined for her mother, whom she knew would be fetching her. On subsequent visits she made sporadic, albeit successful efforts with the learning materials, but continued to behave in a petulant way. The crisis came when we asked the mother to leave her at the Centre and return for her at the end of the session. This she was prepared to do, but Jean clung to her, crying, and the mother was in a helpless state of conflict between her old and new methods of handling the child. She was told, in defiance of orthodox therapeutic practice, to give Jean a smack on the bottom, send her into the playroom, and then leave herself. She administered the smack in a half-hearted way and one of the Centre staff pulled Jean screaming into the playroom. This tactic was used in the confidence that Jean suffered from no genuine apprehensions but was making a last desperate effort to maintain an unprogressive strategy of control. Once in the room she stood against one of the playhouses whimpering, but characteristically watching the activities of the other children. After a minute or two she gave up the whimpering and just stood, sporadically making indecisive movements to join them. After just over five minutes a kindergarten girl came up to her and said, "Do you want to come and play or stand there crying?" When the other child took her by the hand, Jean followed, and after a few minutes she participated in the cutting of paper shapes. During the subsequent learning activity sessions she made further attempts to manipulate the teacher by pouting, but when she saw this had no effect became friendly and talkative. She mentioned her wish to have yellow shoes to match her yellow dress (she could distinguish all the basic colors). By now she had reached the eight-piece animal puzzles, could do them surprisingly quickly, and was delighted with her success.

On subsequent visits the same alternation of strategies persisted, but with the dependent, moody one becoming progressively less frequent. She could quickly see when the "game was up." One might say that she was now behaving like any rather spoiled five-year-old.

Intellectually she made great strides. She needed very little encouragement to do the final set of animal puzzles of ten pieces, and they presented no difficulty to her. She overcame her resistance to the Matchers game and eventually completed the first ten series. This item of the Flying Start Program demands not only good problem-solving strategies but the use of fairly complex cognitive processes. For example, a picture of a pirate has to be matched from among a row of six which contain systematic variations (see Fig. 2). In three of the pictures, the pirate wears a hat, in three he is bareheaded. The distinction has to be held in mind (cognitively "stored") while the child examines the feet. In two pictures the pirate's feet are intact, in two there is a wooden peg in lieu of the right leg, and in two a wooden peg in lieu of the left. Thus the child has to withhold his choice until he has made two successive discriminations, and for four out of six, the additional one of sidedness.

It is part of the compensatory program for slow-learning kindergarten children in this Centre to help them attain the elementary concepts of quantity and numeration, and also the phonic principle that letters represent sounds. Jean had already mastered the idea of counting, and played the Number Games with success and enthusiasm. She provided us with our biggest surprise by her rapid mastery of phonic encoding. The method used is based on the little-recognized fact that the learner must associate the letter symbol not with a separately pronounced "sound" but with the phoneme as actually pronounced in the word context. This method of teaching the phonic basis of reading, although more realistic and efficient, means that the child has to learn to listen to words and to associate their various beginning sounds with letters. In the course of a game of some 15 minutes it is usual to teach a group of children only four such associations. In her first session, Jean learned all nine of the first set, showing no lack of confidence or

FIGURE 2. Flying Start Matchers game.

hesitation, and demanded to be allowed to go on to the next set of ten. She got all these correct except the "k" (having previously had the same sound for "c").

If, at the end of her two months in the Centre's kindergarten group, she still had any temperamental handicap, it was that she never became a compliant child. She wanted to control her own world and to follow her own motivations. She would agree to do the things that pleased her, or, when pushed, what was necessary to assure being allowed later to do what she wished. If she rejected one learning activity it was usually because she preferred another. She had a wide range of strategies, such as feigning fatigue, or wanting to go to the washroom, and continually appraised her chances of having her own way. One might attribute this defect, if that it be, to her high effectiveness-motivation combined with a lack of social conditioning within the permissive atmosphere of her home. Her behavior resembled that of an intelligent younger child.

Two weeks before the end of her time at the Centre, Jean was given the Slosson Intelligence Test. She earned an IQ of 91-93. Curiously, her main area of failure was that of numbers, in which she used elaborate avoidance techniques. Nor would she collaborate in the repetition of sentences. It was typical of her that although she could not, or would not, tell the tester how many apples there were when there were only three, when the testing was over she drew ten apples (see Fig. 3) and counted them correctly. She then drew the members of her family, with the correct number of children. Seeing the long ears she had given them she imaginatively called them pet rabbits. The drawings had good detail for a child just over five years of age, and there is no sign of any impairment in muscular control.

KINDERGARTEN
In September Jean entered kindergarten without fuss, and all went well for a few weeks. Thereafter she made another attempt at "control" by temper tantrums, and the teacher found her unmanageable. She was admitted to a children's psychiatric hospital some distance from her home, where she stayed for two months and attended school. After two months back at home she again proved unmanageable. She was readmitted to the hospital and this time the mother was taken in with her for three weeks and given training in how to manage her. This training followed the behavior modification procedures that had been previously successful. During this period, the mother learned the behavior modification principle of rewarding the child only when she behaved well. The next September, Jean entered first grade. There had never been any doubts about her mental ability. In the fall of 1975 Jean was in a regular Grade 4/5 class and was maintaining average attainment.

DISCUSSION
Up to this point Jean's temperamental abnormality and consequent impaired performance have been discussed in terms of her volitions, that is to say, her chosen way of controlling her world. For the planning of a therapeutic program the chief desiderata are the patient's life style and, when it is a question of combatting dysfunction, the learning style. In thus emphasizing the understanding and modification of behavior, there is nevertheless a danger of falling into a purely behavioristic position where everything is viewed in terms of conditioning from a tabula rasa. In fact, individual differences of temperament and hence of motivation cannot be wholly explained along such lines, and serious errors in treatment may arise if such assumptions are made. Notably, the extent of any constitutional impairment has also to be assessed, although this may become apparent only in the course of treatment. The style of behavior which the child is using at any time is not necessarily the only one at his disposal. It may have been chosen in very early childhood owing to impairment or uneven development of the central nervous system; but over the ensuing years the damage or dysfunction may have been made good by the development of alternative structures, maturation, or biochemical stabilization. In such cases the potentiality for a more effective behavioral style may be present but lies dormant because the earlier style has established itself as the dominant one. This is particularly noticeable among impulsive hyperactive children of kindergarten age whose problem-solving strategies are those of guessing or — in the event of difficulty — avoidance by distractibility. By means of a program which "punishes" such tactics and reinforces cognition, it is often possible to bring the hitherto dormant good strategies into operation. In sum, the clinician has always to be assessing the potential repertoire of the child at a given stage of development.

Almost certainly, any grossly abnormal style of behavior in a child reared within a stable home environment can be traced to some initial impairment which has limited normal development. The diagnostic problem is that the subtle derangements of those parts of the nervous system which govern behavior are not anatomically observable. All we can do is note other indications of similarly subtle derangement in cognate structures, such as the motoric, speech, and endocrine, and the reflexes controlling physical homeostasis.

Comprehensive diagnosis therefore requires as full an account as can be obtained of the child's developmental history. In Jean's case we had to inquire why she alone of the five siblings chose such an incapacitating life style. It is true that the mother reinforced her dependency and acted on the conviction that she was retarded. But the other four children resisted the temptation to exploit her overprotection, at least to the point of complete dependence.

Review of Jean's Developmental History. In effect, Jean's history was characteristic of many handicapped children. Her mother had had an unhappy pregnancy. During the second month her father had to have surgery for a ruptured appendix. In the seventh month the family moved, to accommodate the husband's change of job, into a house that was cold and run down. They moved again when her mother was eight and a half months pregnant. With her anxiety-prone temperament, these events made the mother feel low and discouraged. During the year before Jean was born she had a duodenal ulcer and during the whole of the pregnancy suffered from indigestion.

Jean had a breech birth although she had been turned a week previously. Two weeks before the birth, an amniocentesis was done to determine whether blood transfusion would be required, the mother being Rh-negative. For 48 hours after birth, Jean was incubated owing to mucous congestion, and a slight jaundice was

2. IN THE CLASSROOM

FIGURE 3. Jean's drawing following intelligence testing.

noted for the first five days. She lay passive without spontaneous flexion and extension of the limbs.

Her childhood was free of serious illnesses, but she had chronic, nasal colds and an allergy to cow's milk that caused eczema. At two and a half years, she suffered a single short grand mal seizure (her mother had a series of such at exactly the same age).

Her development milestones were retarded. She did not crawl until 12 months, nor walk across the room unaided before 27 months. She began to put two or three words together at 24 months. At four years she was sometimes difficult to understand because, as the mother put it, "the words seem to come all together," but she could speak clearly if she took the time. She had been more inclined than her siblings to hurt herself by falling or bumping into things, although by four years of age this was becoming less frequent. Just before this age, a psychiatrist diagnosed her as a mild case of cerebral palsy, but as we knew her she was normally coordinated. This clumsiness and the jumbled speech suggested a sequencing derangement rather than impairment of motor function as such.

Perhaps the most telltale impairment for the understanding of her later dependency needs was that she did not smile or show evidence of affection until she was 18 months old. From then on she became very clinging and could not bear to have her mother or other members of her family out of her sight. At about two years of age, she lost her unnatural placidity and lethargy and developed her pattern of temper tantrums followed by sulking. This excessive need for dependency and social interaction is not uncommon in children who fail to display normal early attachment behavior. It is tempting to conclude that the child is belatedly making her way through the infantile phase of extreme dependency. All one can say for certain is that there was some derangement of the social-attachment behavior appropriate to each age.

A review of Jean's history suggests that she had suffered multiple congenital impairments of a minor character, affecting the central nervous system and especially the structures governing social behavior. However, these impairments seemed to be of the nature of faults in maturation. Given these, it is understandable that with her excessive need for attachment, she became conditioned by her mother's overprotectiveness to exploit dependency and a guise of retardation as a means of social control. Such a strategy pervertedly satisfied her more-than-average need for effectiveness. In this sense she could be said to have "chosen" retardation as a life style, but in another sense it could be argued that it was determined for her by a combination of congenital impairment and facilitating environment.

CONCLUSIONS

In this article the term *learning disability* is used in the literal sense, without implications as to either specific dysfunctions or the classical discrepancy between achievement and IQ. Thus learning disability, or poor academic performance, may, following Kirk (1962), arise originally from many kinds of delayed development, handicap, or disorder, including impairment of motivation or of temperament (Chess 1967, 1968). Included also might be social disadvantage, of which the results in terms of classical learning disability symptoms may be indistinguishable from those of actual brain damage (Deutsch 1963, Grotberg 1970).

Nearly always the original handicap generates secondary motivational impediments to learning. These may take the form of avoidance, by seeking distractions or by retreating into an attitude of nonresponse which may be mistaken for mental incapacity. Thus, as Forness (1974) points out, the use of categorical labels, implying mutually exclusive categories, is now being abandoned. In my experience such exclusivity does not represent the true state of affairs, and is indeed conceptually not feasible. The typical development of learning disability, as illustrated by the case of Jean, is one, first, of some initial handicap or disadvantage (which may be far removed from the mechanics of perception or cognition). Whatever it may be, it results in adverse conditioning and a consequent emotional avoidance of learning situations, or the establishment (as in Jean's case) of alternative coping goals.

The final stage is the development of an inappropriate style of learning (Stott 1971b). Besides being more realistic, this approach offers a methodology of diagnosis which leads naturally to a prescription for remediation, that is to say, the correction of the faulty learning style. In the course of such remedial work with the child, any persisting handicap will be uncovered. Work along these lines has shown, however (Stott 1974, O'Neill 1975), that in many cases the child has outgrown the initial handicap, or that this was merely a matter of environmental adaptation. The conditioned faulty learning style then responds rapidly to remediation, even though the outward appearance is one of extreme handicap. — *30 Colborn St., Guelph, Ontario, N1G 2M5, Canada*

Behavioral Disorders: Teachers' Perceptions

THOMAS J. KELLY
LYNDAL M. BULLOCK
M. KAY DYKES

A variety of procedures have been used in attempting to determine more accurately the incidence of behavioral disorders in school age children and youth. Reported incidence figures range from 2% to 69.3% of the populations under consideration (Glidewell & Swallow, 1968). Probably the most frequently cited estimate of the incidence of behavioral disorders is that of Eli Bower (1960). According to Bower, approximately 10% of the school age population need professional assistance of some type during their school years. However, less than 1% of school age children have severe emotional problems which require intensive intervention programs.

Researchers have sought the assistance of classroom teachers, parents, and mental health professionals—including psychologists, counselors, social workers, and psychiatrists—to make determinations about the mental health of children and youth. A variety of behavior rating scales, standardized test instruments, physical examinations, and direct observation systems have been employed. The results of studies have been reported in terms of mild, moderate, and severe behavioral disorders as well as in terms of traditional psychiatric labels such as schizophrenia, autism, and depression. In general, the use of numerous methods and associated variables has contributed to the confusion about the nature and scope of the incidence of behavioral disorders in school age children and youth.

The purpose of the present investigation was to sample an extensive number of regular classroom teachers and determine their individual perceptions of the behavioral status of their students. The regular classroom teachers perceptions of behavior were particularly important to the investigators since these same teachers spend a considerable amount of time with their children and in many cases are the major available change agents for the child. An additional impetus for undertaking the present investigation was the study by Ullmann (1952) in which he concluded that teachers are frequently in agreement with other mental health professionals regarding the mental health of children and youth.

Method

A specially designed research checklist was submitted to a total of 2,664 regular classroom teachers in kindergarten through grade 12 in 13 Florida school districts. Each teacher was asked to categorize the behavior of their students in terms of no perceived behavioral disorder or mild, moderate, or severe behavioral disorder. Specific behavioral dimensions and psychiatric terminology were not provided to the teachers as they responded to the checklist. The teachers were also instructed to avoid reporting children who had been previously diagnosed as having certain other primary handicapping conditions such as mental retardation and hearing impairment.

Definitions

Rather than attempting to relate the terms mild, moderate, and severe behavioral disorders to specific behavioral dimensions, a continuum of services or special programs were matched with the terms as a guide to the participating teachers. Each of the major special programs or services was selected and defined on the basis of general acceptance by special educators as educational alternatives for children and youth with mild, moderate, or severe behavioral disorders.

1. *Mild behavioral disorders:* Children or youth with behavioral disorders who can be helped adequately by the regular classroom teacher and/or other school resource personnel through periodic counseling and/or short term individual attention and instruction were defined as having a mild behavioral disorder.
2. *Moderate behavioral disorders:* Children or youth with behavioral disorders who can remain at their assigned school but require intensive help from one or more educational specialists (e.g., counselors and special educators) and/or specialists from community agencies (e.g., mental health clinics and diagnostic centers) were defined as having a moderate behavioral disorder.
3. *Severe behavioral disorders:* Children or youth with behavioral disorders who require assignment to a special class or special school were defined as having a severe behavioral disorder.

Results and Discussion

Considerable data relative to regular classroom teachers' perceptions of behavioral disorders in children and youth were compiled. The researchers focused attention on several teacher characteristics including their race, sex, experience level, and formal educational preparation. The race, sex, achievement level and the grade level of the children and youth were also considered. The following selected research findings are presented for consideration:

1. The total mean percentage of children and youth perceived by their teachers as exhibiting behavioral disorders was 20.4, with 12.6% placed in the mild category, 5.6% considered as having moderate disorders, and 2.2% indicated as having severe behavioral disorders.
2. A gradual increase in the perceptions of behavioral disorders was noted between kindergarten (19.4%) and grade 5 (25.1%). A downward trend was evident between grade 6 (22.0%) and grade 12 (8.8%), with the exception of grade 9 (26.0%).
3. Approximately two male students for every female student were perceived as exhibiting behavioral disorders. The female teachers generally perceived higher percentages of both male (26.6%) and female (15.0%) students as exhibiting behavioral disorders than did male teachers (21.1% males and 11.8% females).
4. Approximately two Black students for every White student were perceived as

Behavioral Disorders Teachers Perceptions, *Exceptional Children*, February 1977. ©1977 The Council for Exceptional Children.

2. IN THE CLASSROOM

exhibiting behavioral disorders in kindergarten through grade 7. Differences between Blacks and Whites were minimal between grades 8 and 12. In general, White teachers perceived more Black students as exhibiting behavioral disorders when contrasted with the perceptions of Black teachers.

5. When the teachers' educational backgrounds and years of teaching experience were considered as factors in teacher perception, virtually no association was noted.

Conclusion

When classroom teachers were given the opportunity to freely report their perceptions of the behavior of their students, a number of serious problem areas were highlighted. The mean percentage of 20.4 that was perceived by the participating teachers as exhibiting behavioral disorders is obviously cause for concern. Although 12.2% of the children were assigned to the mild category, another 7.8% were perceived as exhibiting moderate or severe behavioral disorders. In view of the service related definitions used in the present investigation, the need for specialized services as determined by the participating teachers is substantial.

An awareness of how teachers perceive the behavior of their students is essential in determining the needs of both students and their teachers. Data of this nature are particularly relevant since teachers' ability to make accurate judgments regarding the behavior of their students has received some support in the research literature (Ullmann, 1952; Nelson, 1971). However, the task of judging the appropriateness of human behavior is complicated by many factors. In the present investigation, the sex and race factors exerted an influence on how the teachers perceived their students.

The need for more specially trained personnel in the area of behavioral disorders is evident. However, an equally important priority is the upgrading of the training of both inservice and preservice regular classroom teachers. Through additional training and experiences in behavioral disorders, regular classroom teachers should be better prepared and more confident in their ability to assist that large number of children and youth who are perceived as having mild behavioral disorders. Additional training may also make it possible for teachers to more accurately judge the behavior of their students and make more appropriate referrals of children in need of specialized services.

References

Bower, E. M. *Early identification of emotionally handicapped children in school.* Springfield IL: Charles C Thomas, Publisher, 1960.

Glidewell, J., & Swallow, C. *The prevalence of maladjustment in elementary schools.* Chicago: University of Chicago Press, 1968.

Nelson, C. M. Techniques for screening conduct disturbed children. *Exceptional Children,* 1971, 37, 501-507.

Ullmann, C. A. *Identification of maladjusted school children* (Monograph No. 7). Washington DC: US Public Health Service, 1952.

THOMAS J. KELLY *is Director of Northwest Indiana Special Education Cooperative, Crown Point;* LYNDAL M. BULLOCK *is Professor in Exceptional Learner Education, University of Oklahoma, Norman;* and M. KAY DYKES *is Assistant Professor of Special Education, University of Florida, Gainesville. This investigation was supported by the Florida Educational Research and Development Council, University of Florida, Gainesville.*

WE WELCOME YOUR COMMENTS

Only through this communication can we produce high quality materials in the Special Education field.

Special Learning Corporation
42 Boston Post Rd. Guilford, Connecticut 06437

Behavior Modification: Teacher Training and Attitudes

William A. Stewart
Gay Goodman
Brad Hammond

WILLIAM A. STEWART is Chief Psychologist, Samuel A. Anderson Child Development Clinic, Richmond, Virginia; GAY GOODMAN is Assistant Professor, Department of Special Education, Virginia Commonwealth University; and BRAD HAMMOND is a teacher of the learning disabled for the Virginia Commonwealth University, Richmond.

Behavior modification has been demonstrated to be effective in modifying or treating numerous behavior problems and seems to be a valuable tool for those dealing with special problems in education, the social sciences, and the helping professions. It is advocated that to the extent behavior modification is not being used with children who could benefit by it, those children are not receiving the maximum possible assistance. It should be made a part of the special education teacher's repertoire of skills, through teacher training at the college level and inservice training for those already in teaching positions.

It may be reasonable to suspect that various degrees of unfavorable attitudes and lack of understanding regarding behavior modification often inhibit its proliferation as an effective tool. This premise is supported by Grieger (1972), who considers teacher attitudes an important variable in implementing a behavior modification program in the public school classroom. The purpose of the present study was to determine, within a moderately large metropolitan school system, the number of special education teachers using behavior modification (as well as the number of behaviors with which they were willing to use it), the number of teachers who had received some training or a learning experience in it, the attitudes of teachers toward behavior modification, and any relationship these variables might have to each other.

Procedure and Results

A questionnaire designed to obtain the above information was submitted to the 192 special education teachers in the Richmond Public School System and 124 teachers responded by completing and returning the questionnaire. The questionnaire used a semantic differential scale to assess teacher attitudes toward behavior modification.

It was expected that the attitudes of the teachers would be related to their use or nonuse of behavior modification and that among those using behavior modification the degree of use would also be related to their attitude. Both expectations were confirmed. A significant positive correlation of .36 (point biserial correlation; $p < .001$) was obtained between use/nonuse of behavior modification and attitude. Further, among teachers using behavior modification, a significant positive correlation of .20 (Pearson r; $p < .05$) was obtained between the number of different behaviors for which it was used and their attitude toward behavior modification.

The expectation that the attitudes of those who had a formal training experience in behavior modification would be significantly different from the attitudes of those not having such an experience was not confirmed (t test). Also not confirmed was the expectation that the frequency of using behavior modification among those who had had a formal learning experience in behavior modification would be significantly different from the frequency of use among those not having such an experience (t test).

It was encouraging to find that approximately 90% of the teachers who responded had had some learning experience in behavior modification and had used it to some extent in their classroom; however, it was also found that 75% of the teachers surveyed had never used behavior modification techniques to improve math skills, and 62% of the teachers surveyed had never used these techniques to improve reading skills.

Conclusion

It appears that when the special education teachers responding to the questionnaire in this study use behavior modification techniques, it is associated with a relatively positive attitude toward behavior modification. Conversely, when they do not use this technique, it tends to be associated with a less posi-

2. IN THE CLASSROOM

tive attitude toward behavior modification. Moreover, having chosen to use behavior modification, the number of behaviors with which the teacher is willing to use it appears to be somewhat associated with how positive his attitude is toward behavior modification.

Teachers of exceptional children must be sufficiently trained in behavior modification techniques that they view this method as one of the viable alternatives for improving classroom behavior and increasing the achievement levels of the pupils they teach. It would appear that a significant portion of such teacher training could profitably focus on the development of positive attitudes toward behavior modification in special education teachers. Further research to determine the generality of the results of this study is suggested.

Reference

Grieger, R. M. Teacher attitudes as a variable in behavior modification consultation. *Journal of School Psychology*, 1972, 10, 279-287.

MAINSTREAMING LIBRARY

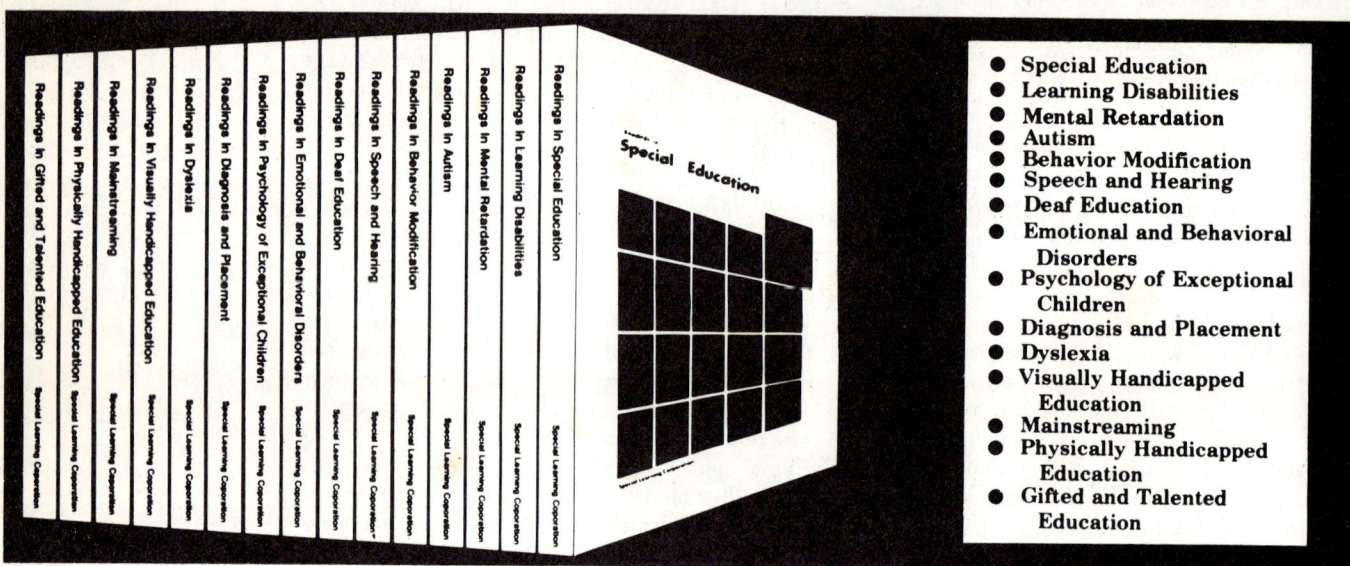

- Special Education
- Learning Disabilities
- Mental Retardation
- Autism
- Behavior Modification
- Speech and Hearing
- Deaf Education
- Emotional and Behavioral Disorders
- Psychology of Exceptional Children
- Diagnosis and Placement
- Dyslexia
- Visually Handicapped Education
- Mainstreaming
- Physically Handicapped Education
- Gifted and Talented Education

NOW $120.00

*individual books $8.75

For Teachers

For Administrators

For School Librarians

This set of highly useable professional books is published by Special Learning Corporation--a publisher of high quality special education materials.

The mainstreaming library provides the concerned professional a comprehensive resource for exceptional children. Each book deals extensively with a specific disability; providing a concise perspective and insight into the area.

Innovative methodology techniques are provided as an aid for the teacher concerned with providing quality education for the special child.

To order these books or for more information on these and other college and professional books, contact Joseph Logan, Special Learning Corporation.

SPECIAL LEARNING CORPORATION
42 Boston Post Rd. Guilford, Connecticut 06437   (203) 453-6525

Monkeying Around, or How to Make Mistakes Pay Off

Bill Hardin and
Bonnie Bernstein

A way to get away from the 'test, grade and hurry on' trap

It has been said that if you set an infinite number of monkeys at an infinite number of typewriters, one of them must eventually produce *Hamlet*. It's doubtful that those many monkeys would learn much from their many mistakes, but if we or our students are not afraid to monkey around with language and make mistakes, infinite learning can take place.

Did you ever stop to think that the most important tools of education may be mistakes and the way we deal with them? Certain kinds of learning require instant 100 percent success, no mistakes allowed. A mother calling to her toddler to come quickly out of a busy street is an obvious example. But school subjects, even the most basic, involve exploration, experimentation, refinement and reflection. Thus, schools and classrooms have to be established as long-term "mistake-making" environments—places where youngsters can feel comfortable and free to take the risks that sometimes lead to errors that they can learn from.

What If...

Few teachers would contend that learning means doing something right the first time or that its value depends on how fast the idea is grasped or even that skills or facts be absorbed with total accuracy. Learning begins with trying something and then carefully examining our own performance for flaws and "what ifs." "What if I tried it this way...." This process leads to alternate solutions and recognizing ways of improving the performance.

From this perspective, learning bears a remarkable kinship to Dewey's description of truth as "a series of successive approximations." It's no coincidence that the basis for most effective learning in any subject follows the scientific method of inquiry, which has so greatly changed the world in so short a time. The student becomes committed to the study of a specific problem, acquires information, uses it to predict a tentative solution, which he or she then tries, and carefully examines the results. When the child repeats later phases of the cycle, he or she achieves power, precision and success. It

2. IN THE CLASSROOM

all boils down to a basic routine: Do something, look for and at your own mistakes and monkey around with the results.

The Pressure Procedure

As logical as this process may seem, the classroom and curriculum setup and their accompanying pressures often encourage us to present, test, grade and then hurry on to the next thing. The kids who make the highest grades have "learned." The others haven't. How often do we hand back the completed assignment or test and ask the kids to locate and monkey around with their own mistakes? After all, this is what they'll be doing again and again in different ways and under different circumstances all through their lives.

Many of us are convinced that the formal "test" paper is peripheral to actual learning. We have seen that, given the chance, kids can test most of their learning hypotheses more quickly and more effectively by using logic and visual clues or asking someone who already knows how to do the "trick." Fortunately, most kids like to look for different solutions. They like to try different answers to a riddle. They like to uncover successive clues that they can see are bringing them close to an answer.

Try, Try Again

A key aspect of the teaching art is making sure that the problems assigned are ones that the kids stand a good chance of attacking with success. Then our basic question for evaluating learning might shift from "How many answers did you get right?" to "How many mistakes did it take before you got them all right?" In fact, it's worth considering whether the better "grade" should go to the kid who got it right the first time or to the one who made it after 75 tries.

However we mark, it's important to always keep in mind the value of "what if . . ." and to remember that an experimenting, questioning, exploring and rebuilding approach cannot exist when any disgrace whatever is attached to making mistakes. Mistakes are the raw material of learning. Tinkering with them, monkeying with them and improving on them is what learning is all about. If we are serious about teaching and learning, this kind of monkey business becomes very serious business indeed.

Strategies that encourage kids to monkey around with language and capitalize on mistakes

1
Make a list of "mistakes" in the English language (words that are not spelled as they are pronounced), such as *business, do, hour, knight, head, one, done, through*.

2
Write how words should be spelled according to their pronunciation, such as aks (*axe*), kat (*cat*), wuz (*was*).

3
Have the kids proofread to find mistakes without risk to self-concept. Give them a list of 10 words, five of which you have spelled incorrectly; an unpunctuated paragraph; an uncapitalized paragraph; a paragraph with 10 punctuation errors; a paragraph with 10 spelling errors; wrong directions for getting from school to a specific building. Then have them correct the errors, see who can find the most proofreading mistakes in three minutes or who can write an article and sneak the most mistakes past a proofreading committee. You might want to divide into groups or teams for contests or activities that would otherwise intimidate some youngsters.

4
Let the kids catch you in deliberate mistakes. Extra bonus: You won't be so embarrassed when you make a real one.

5
Have the kids write sentences substituting the wrong homophones, such as *hear* instead of *here*. See who can do the most in 10 minutes.

6
Have the kids substitute antonyms in the same way.

7
Slip in mistakes as you read aloud. See who can jot down (not call out) the most in three minutes. (Assign a penalty for each correct word a student says is wrong.)

8
Have some students scramble TV show titles or slogans, such as *Starsky & Cher, Don't Squeeze the Tenille, Gilligan's Heroes* and *Hogan's Island*. (Have a contest for the best.) Then ask the others to unscramble them.

9
Scramble and unscramble proverbs or quotations, like "A bird in the hand makes Jack a dull boy."

10
Scramble and unscramble sentences.

11
List some words that have more than one meaning and have the kids make up sentences using each of the meanings. For example, "I have to *run* home"; "I got a home *run*"; "I have a *run* in my panty hose."

12
Ask the youngsters to alphabetize scrambled letters.

13
Together read dialect, such as Hyman Kaplan's stories and Irish and Italian poems by T.A. Daly and show that these uses of language are ungrammatical, yet correct.

14
Make up, or have the students make up, cartoons with incongruous captions.

15
Make scrambled comic strips.

16
Scramble holiday names with incongruous symbols for them; for example, Fourth of July with a New Year's hat.

17
Crosswords, codes and ciphers, two-minute mysteries, short plays and mazes are all good fun ways to experiment with language.

IN PRAISE OF PRAISE

REGINA HACKETT

"YOU'VE GOT TO AC-SEN-CHUATE THE POSITIVE"
MIGHT BE THE THEME SONG OF AN OREGON
PROGRAM DEVISED FOR HYPERACTIVE CHILDREN

Six-year-old John was the kind of child who could give a teacher prematurely grey hair and a compelling urge to try for a living in some other profession. The youngster could sit still for no more than a few minutes at a time, during which he continually talked out of turn, a disturbance to be preferred over the wild temper tantrums he threw or the fist fights he provoked when he wasn't sitting. What's more, he was impervious to criticism.

Speaking of John, his teacher confesses, "He was my dead-end kid, my cross to bear. I simply didn't know what to do with him. If our school district had started special classes for behavior problem children, John's name would have been first on my recommended-for-transfer list."

Children like John have been described as hyperactive, hyperaggressive, acting-out, or even emotionally disturbed. Abrasively wearing on their teachers, disruptive to their peers, and a cause for worry and dismay to their parents, such children are heading pell-mell toward the brink of failure. "At six or seven years old, acting-out children already tend to be outsiders," says Hill Walker, director of the Center at Oregon for Research in the Behavioral Education of the Handicapped, which developed Contingencies for Learning Academic and Social Skills (CLASS), a program designed to change disruptive children's negative behaviors. "These children are very difficult to manage," Dr. Walker continues. "They are accustomed to peer rejection and teacher dislike. Usually, it doesn't faze them. What's more, principally because of their acting-out behaviors, they're often below grade level in academic skills."

With regard to the latter point, Sharon Beickel, a program consultant for CLASS, describes the disheartening cycle that faces the acting-out child who falls behind in school: "The disruptive behavior and decreased academic performance lessen the amount of praise or rewards received. This, in turn, leads to a further reduction in the quality and quantity of work, which leads to still fewer rewards."

Then Ms. Beickel explains: "Children need help before they enter this downward spiral. The cycle must be interrupted early in the educational process. This involves both social and academic adjustments for these students. They must learn that fighting and destroying property are not tolerated. They must also recognize that certain behaviors such as paying attention and following instructions are necessary for acquiring academic skills. I think the CLASS program helps children to learn these survival skills."

The Center at Oregon staff's confidence has roots in the success the CLASS program has recorded to date. After a year of experimental testing, the techniques developed in CLASS were incorporated into a standardized treatment package that was applied for a 30- to 45-day period to 32 acting-out children enrolled in 24 regular primary classroom settings in the Eugene-Springfield area during the 1971-72 school year. Even in this short period, significant changes were noticed in teachers' attitudes toward children in the study, the acting-out child being seen not so much as a defiant troublemaker but rather as one needing special help in adjusting to others. Equally important, observational data indicated the program was successful in changing the appropriate behavior rates of children to whom it was applied. Subsequent field testing of the program showed similar results.

In all cases the children's gains were achieved in their own classrooms, without special class placement. While the program produces rapid and dramatic changes in disruptive children's behavior, this is not the only goal of CLASS. The program is intended "to help classroom teachers maintain the initial gains children make and to extend the procedures to additional settings such as the playground, lunchroom, and other classrooms," explains Dr. Walker. "The changes produced are intended to be substantial and lasting."

The CLASS program was developed using a basic tenet of social learning theory as a first principle: Behaviors are learned and maintained as a result of the presence of reward or reinforcement and weakened in its absence. "CLASS takes that idea and runs with it," says one resource teacher. "We teach children what acceptable behaviors are and reinforce these behaviors every time they are displayed. We don't reinforce unacceptable behaviors. If that sounds simple, it's because it *is* simple. And it works."

The procedures themselves are a bit more precise. First, a teacher nominates for admission to the program a child considered unacceptably disruptive in regular class work. The CLASS consultant in the school or school district—usually a school counselor, psychologist, or resource teacher who has

2. IN THE CLASSROOM

been trained by CLASS personnel—discusses the referral with the teacher, asking him or her to be as specific as possible about the character, number, and frequency of behaviors considered undesirable. The ensuing list almost always includes items like "doesn't follow instructions," "uses physical and verbal coercion on peers," "destroys property," "talks out of turn," "throws spit balls," and "has temper tantrums." The child is always rated in relation to his or her classmates and not to an abstract ideal of a "normal" student.

Next, the consultant arranges to observe the target child for 20 minutes in a group activity and 20 minutes during individual seat work, selecting periods of the day in which the child is especially troublesome. During each visit to the classroom, the consultant evaluates precisely the amount and frequency of the disruptive child's undesirable behaviors. For every ten-second interval, the consultant tallies a plus when the child is working as instructed or a minus whenever his or her behavior varies from the rules that the teacher has established as acceptable for the classroom. The consultant then totals the "plus" tallies and computes their percentage of the total number of tallies. Children who are "on task," that is, behaving properly, less than 60 percent of the time and who display high rates of unacceptable behaviors, hitting and destroying property, for instance, are considered appropriate candidates for the program.

The consultant then explains to the principal, classroom teacher, parents, child, and anyone else potentially involved in CLASS exactly how it works and what responsibilities each will be expected to assume. Unless each individual involved, including the child, agrees to full participation and cooperation, the program is not initiated.

During the first five days of the program, the consultant assumes the major responsibility, the first step being to let the other children in the class know what's about to take place. Especially careful to avoid describing the procedure as an attempt to bring the class cut-up into line, the consultant tries in a positive and straightforward manner to get the entire class into the program. The consultant tells the class that the program is a means to help children learn faster and better, and that John or Mary (the target child) has volunteered to help. The consultant then explains to the children what they are expected to do, which essentially, according to Ms. Beickel, is to help the student by working on their own assignments and not

THE CLASS PROGRAM'S BASIC PRINCIPLE: BEHAVIORS ARE LEARNED AND MAINTAINED AS A RESULT OF REWARD OR REINFORCEMENT, AND WEAKENED IN ITS ABSENCE

bothering the student when he or she is working.

When the consultant is satisfied that the children understand what is expected of them and are willing to cooperate, the program begins. Take the case of John. For two 20-minute periods the consultant sits with him, cueing by means of a red/green point card when he is behaving in a way that earns points (green side up) and when he is not (red side up). John is observed at predetermined random ten-second intervals and awarded a point if he is behaving appropriately. The points are paired with praises to enhance the effectiveness of praise when points are removed. For every four points earned, John is praised at least once. In all, he can earn 40 points and be praised ten times, nine of the latter given by the consultant and one by his teacher.

"We do not expect a child to earn every possible point or to behave perfectly," says Ms. Beickel. "Research has shown that the 'normal' student attends to the teacher and to work about 80 percent of the time, so this is the goal of the CLASS program. Thus, if a child earns 80 percent of the possible points available, which is the established criterion for a reward in each period, he or she is immediately rewarded with some brief activity in which the entire class shares, such as a game or extra recess time." Thus, the child can earn two such rewards for the class each day.

When John earns 80 percent of the possible points for both his group activity and individual seat work, he is given the point card to take home, which indicates to his parents that he has earned a home reward as well. His parents have been instructed to praise *and* reward him when this happens. If he does not reach the 80-percent criterion, however, his parents are asked to praise him for bringing the card home, and simply not provide a reward that day.

An additional feature of the program is designed to handle emergency situations. If at any time during the school day John breaks a school rule—destroys property, for example, injures another child, or repeatedly refuses to follow directions—he is removed from the classroom and given enough school work to keep him busy the rest of the day. If one of his parents is at home, he is sent home to work. If not, a study room in the school can usually be found, preferably one close to the counselor's office so that his progress can be regularly and frequently checked. This procedure is called systematic exclusion.

A few of the children "test" the program to see if what they were told would happen really *will* happen. This occurs usually once or twice only, for when target children are in the classroom and working, they are central figures, earning extra privileges for the whole class and getting more approval than they have probably ever had before. Thus, it becomes unpleasant for them to be removed from this situation, and, therefore, they learn to suppress behaviors that result in exclusion.

But getting back to John, the time during which he is required to be "on task" in order to earn a point is gradually increased. His teacher does more praising and the consultant less, until by the sixth day of the program, the teacher is in charge, awarding all the points and praises. By the tenth day the program is extended to include the entire school day; that is, John must be behaving appropriately 80 percent of the day to earn his points.

If at any point in the program John fails to meet the 80-percent criterion after two tries, he is recycled to an earlier stage where he has experienced success. The recycling procedure is built into the program to account for individual differences in progression through the program, and to insure that a student is not allowed to experience failure for a prolonged period of time. As he progresses, points and tangible rewards are gradually phased out, and by the end of the program, he is able to maintain his behavior at a "normal" level and for praise and rewards that occur naturally within a classroom setting.

It does not necessarily follow that because this program seems to be successful with the great majority of the children who take part in it, it is an easy one to administer. Initially, some teachers,

15. In Praise of Praise

parents, and even school principals have reservations about both the basic premises of CLASS and the methods used to implement it.

"Getting the people who will be involved in CLASS to understand it and cooperate can be one of the most difficult parts of the program," says Dr. Walker. "Observational data have shown that problem children receive a much greater amount of teacher attention than do their peers; further, the largest part of that attention is negative. In our society, praising doesn't come naturally, especially when we think of changing the behavior of children. How many of us instinctively reinforce a child's positive behaviors with praise rather than address his negative behaviors with censure?

"School personnel who have been controlling children by largely aversive means, such as criticism and physical punishment, are often hard to convince that they should now begin a totally alien behavior pattern of praising and approving."

Unfortunately, no matter how useful a tool Dr. Walker thinks praise is in changing behavior, some teachers just don't feel comfortable with it. One confided that even though she had seen the CLASS program effectively change the problem behavior of a child in her school, she still felt that praising and rewarding a child for doing what he or she should be doing anyway is bribery. "It's like paying a terrorist protection money for *not* blowing up city hall," she says. "Look at it this way. Today you didn't knock down any old ladies or set fires in a national forest. Do you want me to praise you for that?"

"It isn't often that these objections come up," explains Ms. Beickel. "When they surface it is important to listen to the teacher and understand that in addition to having to cope with the acting-out child—in itself a handful—the teacher has an entire classroom of children to teach. When the topic of 'bribery' is broached, it is sometimes helpful to point out that bribery is defined as an inducement to act dishonestly or illegally, and then contrast that with praise, an expression of approval for desirable behavior."

Some teachers neglect to share their misgivings about the program with the consultant working with them, but let their doubts come out in other ways. One teacher managed by her voice and facial expressions to turn praises into condemnations. Another teacher made the unaccountable mistake of making the target child stand in front of his class and explain what he'd done wrong that day instead of praising him for his points earned. "Some teachers really dislike the child in question, and sometimes with understandable reason," says Hyman Hops, Director of CLASS. "Many of these kids have made the teachers miserable. But, our research shows that teachers change their perception of the child after their involvement in the program. Their praise feels more 'natural' and the child's new behavior 'praiseworthy.' Furthermore, our data indicate that the teacher's increased praise also generalizes to the other children in the class, so that there is a definite change in the overall classroom atmosphere."

Not all teacher problems arise from difficulties in praising students or liking them. One teacher states a different objection to CLASS: "The program deals with symptoms, not causes of behavior," this teacher says. "That's typical of behavior modification programs. What if John isn't sitting in his seat because he was whipped severely on his bottom the night before? No one would ask why he wouldn't sit down; observers would just take note that John wasn't in his seat. And he'd lose points for being off task. Also, what if he yells and swears because that's the way his parents taught him to communicate?"

Dr. Walker listens carefully to such objections and has a logical reply for most of them. "If John were physically unable or too uncomfortable to sit down," he says, "he wouldn't be expected to do so, even if remaining seated were one of his target behaviors. Our program is at least that flexible. And it would be highly unlikely for a condition that was so severe as to prevent a child from sitting or performing any other simple physical activity to go unnoticed, particularly by people accustomed to working with children.

"As for John picking up a pattern of using foul language from his home situation, it doesn't follow that he can continue using it at school. He's got to learn that different behaviors are expected in different situations. That's an important socialization rule.

"On the point of CLASS dealing with symptoms and not the causes of behavior, I suppose that's true on one level if you consider overt behavior to consist only of symptoms," Dr. Walker admits. "But trying to locate the past causes that may be accounting for a child's present behavior is difficult. Who can say for sure if an early sickness or difficulty with toilet training or some almost forgotten traumatic event is in fact accounting for John's throwing blocks now? These reconstructions require a lot of faith and can be pretty arbitrary. But let's assume for the sake of argument that the past trauma that is now causing an acting-out child's present difficulties can be reconstructed. Even with that first cause firmly in hand, there will still be an acting-out child. Finding the deep-seated, historical reasons for behavior doesn't change the behavior. What is important is to identify the conditions or events (causes if you will) that are currently maintaining the child's behavior."

Some parents have the same difficulties accepting CLASS that some teachers have. Many don't have a lot of faith in praise as a means of altering behavior. Others resent school personnel telling them how to deal with their children. Still others are sorely tempted to punish their children when they come home with a card that indicates they didn't make the criterion that day.

In the CLASS program, the child learns that certain behaviors are expected and that he or she is rewarded for achieving according to the rules established by his or her classmates and the teacher. In addition, the teacher is given an opportunity to work with a consultant in the classroom on a problem specific to that setting. Parents are also helped to see effective ways of providing assistance in their child's school-related problems.

But as well as CLASS seems to work, it can't possibly defuse all complaints. One parent had a criticism that couldn't be explained or praised away: He saw the program as an attempt on the part of the school establishment to make his child conform to white, middle-class standards. Dr. Walker argues that "behavior modifiers have been accused of imposing their value systems on others who may come from a different orientation. Because it is a powerful tool, the potential for abuse of behavior modification procedures have been used deliberately to change someone's value structure."

Critics who become involved with CLASS are usually won over as they see the program succeed. As one student teacher who collects observational data for CLASS says, "At first I was ambivalent about working here with these behaviorists. I was afraid of 'Brave New World' and brain control. But as I began to see the children before and after participation in the program, I decided that if CLASS does in fact represent behavioral technology, then lead me to the future."

Altering Schedules of Reinforcement for Improved Classroom Behavior

RONNIE N. ALEXANDER
CATHY H. APFEL

Token reinforcement programs have been used with good results on a variety of target behaviors and with a wide range of populations. Clark, Lachowicz, and Wolf (1968) pointed out that a major benefit is that the token can be used for immediate reinforcement of response and that it gains its effectiveness by being paired with backup reinforcers either outside the classroom setting, (e.g. candy and trinkets) or within the educational setting itself (e.g. stars, grades, and teacher approval) (O'Leary, Becker, Evans, & Saudergras, 1969; Broden, Hall, Dunlap, & Clarke, 1970).

Subjects and Setting

At the time of this investigation, a behavior disorders class of 5 boys, ranging in age from 7 to 13, had been on a token economy system for academic remediation for 4 months. Each period was divided into 15 minute sessions, at the end of which tokens were distributed contingent on the child's behavior. Tokens were in the form of play money and could be exchanged at the end of the day for small toys, candy, or free time. Observation and discussions with the teacher indicated that this system had some degree of effectiveness for all the children for the majority of the day, excluding a 15 minute period before work began and an hour period at the end of the day called "communicative skills," where the children watched science experiments, played games, or did art projects. During this last period, tokens could be received at the end of the hour rather than every 15 minutes.

The purpose of this investigation was to attempt to improve attending and study behaviors of the children during the communicative skills period by the use of a variable interval schedule of reinforcement.

Procedure

All children were observed during the communicative skills period from 1:00 to 2:00 in

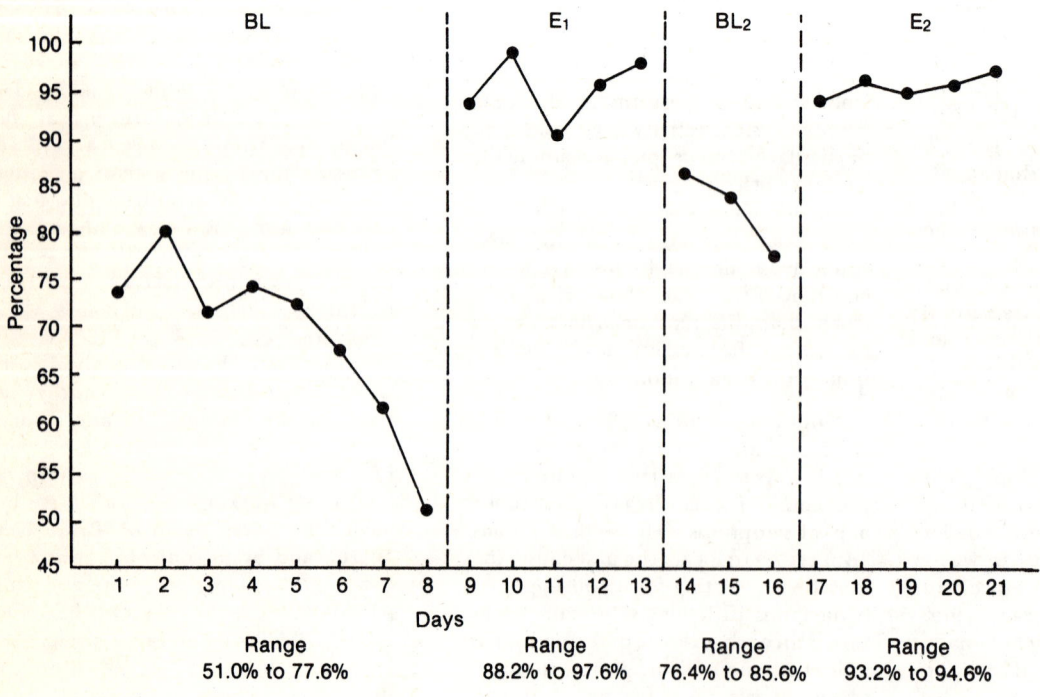

FIGURE 1. Daily mean percentage of attending for five subjects for each experimental phase.

TABLE 1

Average Frequencies of Disruptive Behaviors per 45 Minutes

Subjects	Nonattending behaviors	BL	E_1	BL_1	E_2
1	Daydreaming	3.3	.2	2.7	.2
2	Motor	4.6	1.2	3.3	.6
	Verbal	4.1	1.8	3.3	.4
3	Motor	8.4	2.0	4.0	.8
	Verbal	5.8	1.4	2.3	.4
	Daydreaming	2.4	.4	1.6	1.0
4	Motor	2.4	.2	.3	.0
	Verbal	2.0	.4	.3	.4
5	Motor	8.9	2.4	4.0	.8
	Verbal	2.8	2.2	2.7	.8

the afternoon. Time sampling was used as a means of noting attending behavior. At the end of every 3 minutes the observer looked around the table (in the same order each time) and noted who was attending to task and who was not.

Nonattending behaviors were of three types: (a) motor behavior (being out of seat without permission, hitting, pinching, rocking), (b) verbal behavior (talking to others in a loud manner, yelling, name calling), and (c) daydreaming (looking away from the task). During the 45 minute period, every time a child exhibited one of these behaviors it was noted. Thus both a percentage of intervals for attending and a frequency of nonattending behaviors were obtained, as shown in Figure 1 and Table 1, respectively.

For the baseline phase (BL) data was recorded for 8 days during the communicative skills period. During the first experimental condition (E_1), conditions were relatively simple. Rather than receiving the tokens at the end of the hour, for the first 2 days every 3 minutes a bell would sound and the teacher would look around the room and specify who had earned his token during the 3 minute time (Wolf, Hanley, King, Lachowicz, & Giles, 1970). After 2 days token delivery was changed to a variable interval schedule of approximately every 3 minutes. There was no alteration of the backup reinforcers. Only the timing of the distribution varied.

For the second baseline phase (BL_2), or reversal phase, the children were told that they were doing so well they were going to return to the old system of receiving tokens at the end of the period. During the second experimental condition (E_2), reinforcement was instituted on a 3 minute schedule. The mean percentage of attending for individual subjects for each experimental phase is shown in Table 2.

TABLE 2

Mean Percentage of Attending for Individual Subjects for Each Experimental Phase

Subjects	BL	E_1	BL_1	E_2
1	78.8	98.6	83.3	98.6
2	66.6	88.0	83.0	89.0
3	56.6	92.0	69.3	93.4
4	82.9	96.0	96.7	98.6
5	58.0	89.6	75.0	90.6

Results

By providing immediate reinforcement on a 3 minute schedule, problems with the unstructured communicative skills period were ameliorated. Immediate token reinforcement (contingent on behavior) was effective in increasing attending behavior and decreasing disruptive behavior for all of the subjects. The reversal design indicates that the variable interval schedule accounted for the improvements in behavior.

Discussion

As noted earlier, these children had been under a token system since the beginning of the year (4 months). Receiving tokens at the end of each academic period was effective for those periods *only*. There seemed to be no generalization to the afternoon period of communicative skills. Classroom activities that are less structured and not amenable to programed materials often produce more disruptive behavior than is generally desirable when fixed intervals of reinforcement are used. By the use of variable interval schedules of reinforcement, these behaviors may be brought under control by the teacher. Further studies might measure the effects of increasing and decreasing variable intervals of reinforcement.

Some general guidelines for use of this procedure are:

1. Use extremely short intervals initially in order to immediately "shape up" the behaviors.
2. Work toward using longer intervals at the end of the period and over time (week, months).
3. Involve the children actively and consciously in efforts to control their own behavior to a greater degree.
4. Verbally "prompt" longer periods of effort and study behavior while delaying reinforcement and gratification.
5. Use "rich" schedules and ratios of social reinforcers paired with stronger reinforcers to enhance their value and bridge the delay or gap of longer intervals.

References

Broden, M., Hall, R. V., Dunlap, A., & Clark, R. Effects of teacher attention and reinforcement in a junior high school special education class. *Exceptional Children*, 1970, *36*, 341-349.

Clark, M., Lachowicz, J., & Wolf, M. A pilot basic education program for school dropouts incorporating a token reinforcement system. *Behavior Research and Therapy*, 1968, *6*, 183-188.

O'Leary, K. D., Becker, W. C., Evans, M. B., & Saudergras, R. A. A token reinforcement program in a public school: A replication and systematic analysis. *Journal of Applied Behavior Analysis*, 1969, *2*(1), 3-13.

Wolf, M. M., Hanley, E. L., King, L. A., Lachowicz, J., & Giles, D. K. The timer-game: A variable interval contingency for the management of out-of-seat behavior. *Exceptional Children*, 1970, 37, #2, 113-117.

PSYCHOLOGY OF EXCEPTIONAL CHILDREN

Designed for the introductory courses of study in special education, this book provides an overview of the exceptional child. The social, emotional, linguistic and cognitive development of handicapped children are looked at, along with a special section dealing with support systems for the exceptional child, specifically family relationships.

For more information about this book and other materials in special education, contact Joseph Logan,

Special Learning Corporation
42 Boston Post Rd. Guilford, Connecticut 06437 (203) 453-6525

Classrooms for the Autistic Child

WAYNE SAGE

Once it seemed hopeless to send autistic children to school. Now a pioneering group in California is finding that these children can learn in a public classroom. And, in turn, they can teach us a lot about themselves.

Wayne Sage is a contributing editor to HUMAN BEHAVIOR.

There is one type of child that does not belong in school, his parents have always been told. His presence would be useless, even dangerous, said educators, administrators, social workers and most psychologists. But a small vanguard of autistic children seem to have proved the experts wrong.

The mere suggestion of enrolling an autistic child in a public elementary school would be enough to terrorize most principals. No kid gets kicked out of school these days for being slow to learn. Special classes for the retarded and the emotionally disturbed absorb those who cannot keep up with their peers. But once the word *autism* is written on a child's folder, he is viewed as little more than a dangerous vegetable, and until recently not even special education programs, public or private, would touch him.

The autistic child was thought dangerous because he is often self-destructive and sometimes does not confine his assaults to his own body. He may bite, kick, scratch, throw things at or urinate on any therapist who comes near. He was considered impossible to teach because of his self-stimulatory behavior, compulsive but mindless babbling, rocking, running, flailing of the arms or perhaps just obsessional study of his own fingers. In California, classes for the "educationally handicapped" are required to have at least 12 students

recognizing letters

to a classroom. Even one autistic child in such a setting would bring all instruction to a screeching halt.

Schools for the retarded and the emotionally disurbed are probably not the place for the autistic, anyway. They are often not retarded and the evidence is mounting that they are not emotionally disturbed (see "Autism's Child," HB, Feb. 1974). Revolutionary laboratory and clinical studies are discovering that they can be both tamed and taught, and the parents of the last children to be fenced out of the schoolyard are demanding that they be let in at last.

2. IN THE CLASSROOM

"We're going to win. No doubt about it," Dr. Harvey Lapin said last year, referring to a class-action suit filed by parents of autistic children against the state of California. Dr. Lapin, a dentist and the father of an autistic child, was then president of the Los Angeles chapter of the National Society for Autistic Children. Along with the California Association for the Retarded, the organization argued that every child has a constitutional right to an education regardless of his or her handicap.

"Probably the state will capitulate," said Dr. Lapin. "By the time they [the state] know they're going to court, the kids will have all we're suing for." According to Tom Gilhool, a law professor at the University of Southern California who acted as advisor to the suit, such battles are building legal standards throughout the country. Several mass lawsuits grew out of the California movement. Parental activism reached an all-time high when the mothers and fathers of autistic children demanded to be heard in news articles, on television and radio programs and through aggressive legislative lobbying efforts. All of a sudden, autistic children were in the classroom.

In California, education for autistic children is now mandated. Pioneering efforts there seem to have established that such kids do indeed belong in school.

"I knew that if I could put together an expert in language and an expert in behavior modification, I'd have something fantastic," says Florence Needels. Looking like the personification of compassionate determination, Needels is the project director of a program that is educating autistic children at three elementary schools in Southern California: Mark Twain Elementary School in Lawndale; Foster Elementary School in Bellflower; and Lassen Elementary School in Sepulveda.

Her Ph.D. language expert is Rookie Hirsch; the behavioral consultant is Alexander Tymchuk, an assistant professor of psychology at UCLA. The program that the three of them have put together is fantastic, to say the least. Four months after the program's inception, two of their autistic girls were working their way through standard reading and arithmetic manuals used in special education courses and even in regular elementary school classrooms. And one three-year-old autistic boy was reading.

When Mark Twain set aside three of its classrooms for the autistic in September 1974, the 20 prospective students were rated according to what services they might presently qualify for. Top priority went to "those who didn't have anything," Tymchuk remarks, "so we ended up with the worst." Community reaction was uncertain; backlash from the parents of normal children had already driven the program from one site while it was still in the planning stages. At Mark Twain, the atmosphere proved more accepting.

Even the worst autistic children have proven responsive to the controversial but undeniably effective punishment techniques developed in research laboratories. But transfer-

Students learn to make eye contact and kiss their playmates.

A tot does without lunch and is ignored after refusing the balanced meal.

17. Classrooms for the Autistic

ring such methods to a public school system was a trick the Mark Twain team knew would not be easy.

To most laymen, mere mention of the words *behavior modification* still conjures up images of sadistic assistants chasing screaming children with electric cattle prods. "There is just no way I could bring an electric cattle prod in here," says Needels. Even punishment and reward systems are not trusted by the general public. "It's like living in the Dark Ages," says one of the school's specialists. "They think teachers don't care. They do. They care desperately. But you can spend all day saying 'quit' [to an autistic child] with no effect. It's only when they [traditional teachers] see you save that time with 10 minutes of a highly structured program that their minds change."

"The proper use of punishment is a very important part of our program," Needels emphasizes. But instructors at Mark Twain have been able to establish control of tantrums and self-stimulation without electric shocks or corporal punishment. Yet those in charge have realized that the elimination, not just the reduction, of self-stimulating behavior is usually essential if learning is to begin. The only way to accomplish this is through operant conditioning. The responses of each child are carefully studied. Treatment is then prescribed for each, to be put into effect immediately when such behavior begins. In no case does the teacher decide what the punishment should be.

In some instances, a child's prescription called for a "startle response"—loud shouts of "no!" coupled with slaps on the table. The program is so finely tuned to each child's needs that there are three levels of "no!" that can be prescribed. The first is a simple spoken "no." The second is a loud, angry "no!" The third is the startle *"no!"* The prescriptions are written by consensus agreement at weekly staff meetings where each child's program is reviewed and possible alternatives for handling him are argued from every angle. "Anyone who says he knows how to handle autistic children, I feel funny around," says Needels. "We're finding out that some things work with many of the children and we usually try those first, but you never really know. There has to be a way of shifting."

So far, one of the three levels of "no" has proved successful with every child in the program. However,

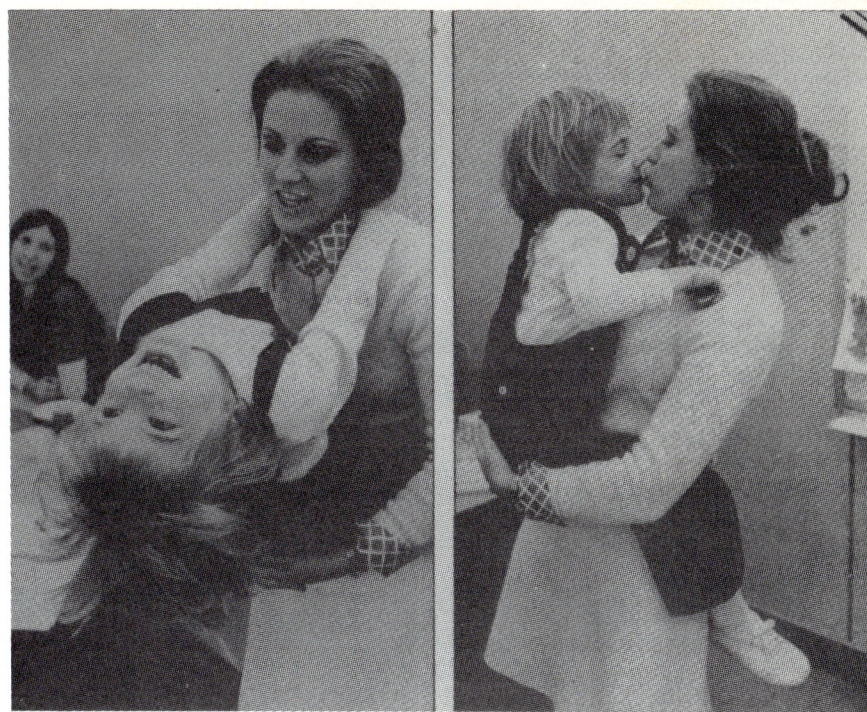

A therapist encourages a student to give affection and enjoy healthy play (above). Behavior therapy elicits direct eye contact and silence (at right).

"there is something about self-stimulation that is so perpetuating that when you insist on eliminating it they often slip over into a tantrum," Needels explains. "All my teachers have had their tetanus shots."

When the self-destructive behavior begins, the major weapon is isolation. The children are "trained to the wall." The teacher restrains the child, but she must not hold or console him. Either would only reinforce self-destruction. The teacher turns the child to the wall and spreads his arms out against it so that he cannot self-stimulate. Through conditioning, the wall thus becomes aversive and can be used to ward off the child's bouts with his own body. At first, screens were erected on each side of the child to block outside stimuli. Such screens are common in public school special education programs, according to Needels. "But our kids would knock over the screen onto another kid and go after the teacher to bite her."

For the extremely self-destructive child, hefty "time-out boxes" were constructed from wooden two-by-fours with open tops. The compartments were thickly padded and lined with black oilcloth so that the child could not bang his head against the walls or otherwise hurt himself once the door was tightly closed. Seven children's prescriptions called for these boxes. Although the huge structures still loom in two of the classrooms, the teachers have become so skilled at controlling such behavior, the boxes have not been used in over eight months. The program is limited to children two to nine years old. After that age, it is impossible for a single teacher to physically restrain a self-destructive autistic child.

When the simple "no" becomes enough to halt self-stimulation, the child is taught the prerequisites to instruction. Beginning with simple commands such as "sit down," "hands down" and "look at me," from here, his attention span is built and extended as his teacher rewards him with bites of his favorite food when he establishes eye contact with her.

A sampling of scenes at Mark Twain illustrates the success of inching from Point A to Point B.

"This is our biter, screamer, kicker, holy terror," says Needels, pointing out a beautiful little blonde girl. The girl looks around and smiles sheepishly. Needels goes over and puts her arm around the child. The girl nuzzles her face into her supervisor's neck. "Looks like I'm going to get a good loving this time and not a big bite," Needels remarks, still hoping she's right, and then turns the child back to face her teacher. "More work time now and then we'll love," Needels tells her.

In another part of the room, a boy

2. IN THE CLASSROOM

of four sits shivering as he fights to keep the tears in his eyes from falling down his face. His toddler-size chair has been pushed away from the table where his teacher sits ignoring him. Once the simple "no" has become enough to halt self-stimulation, if a child slides back into self-stimulation too often for instruction to proceed, he is removed from his desk and seated alone. He must bring himself under control before the teacher will attend to him. "He must learn self-control, not just manipulation," Needels explains, if the program is to have meaning.

In another room, a research assistant sits day after day in front of a boy of about five. "No, quiet," the therapist says and puts his hand to the child's lips. As soon as he takes his hand away, the child starts to babble in the monotone that blocks out the child's efforts at concentration. "No, quiet," the therapist says again and puts his hand over the child's mouth. "No, quiet . . . no, quiet . . . no, quiet. . . ." He continues the procedure again and again. Another research assistant seated beside him hits a stopwatch every time the therapist's hand is removed and records the time interval, continually only two or three seconds, before the child begins to babble. If the boy does remain quiet for even a few seconds, he is patted affectionately and told, "Good boy," but then as the babbling starts again, the therapist covers the child's mouth with his hand and insists on quiet. The procedure goes on and on. If over several days the data show that the babbling is beginning to extinguish, the procedure continues. If not, a new prescription will be written until one is found that works.

What will work, from token economics to sign language, is the overriding criterion for the methods that are used with each child. Those treatments that have no objectively discernible effect, such as psychoanalysis, are not considered appropriate for a public school program. "We don't worry about what caused it, whether it was organic or some psychological trauma. We just take in the kid as he comes and try to do something with him," says Needels.

Once self-stimulation and self-destruction are under control, the major goal is the development of useful language. But that stage often can be reached only through a tremendous number of minute steps. Not only can some children not associate or even

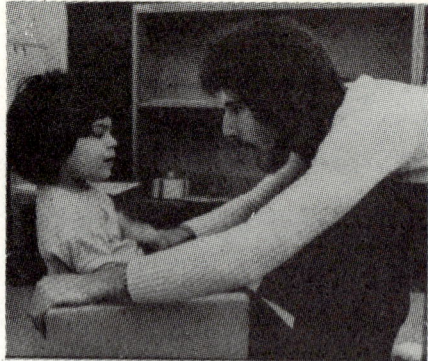

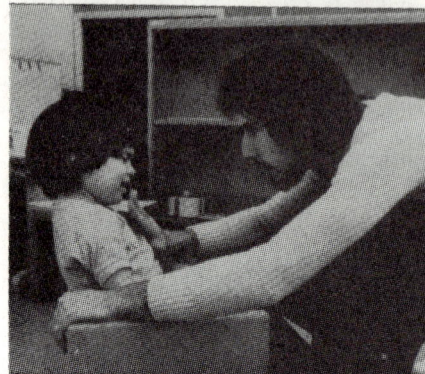

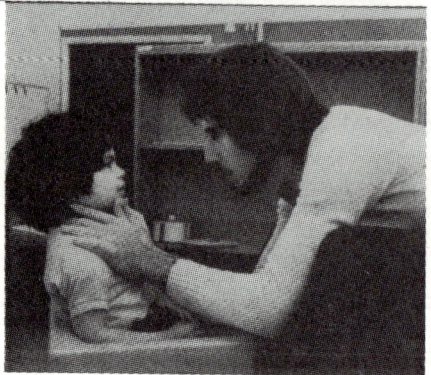

pronounce words, they sometimes do not have the cognitive skills that will allow them to benefit from language instruction.

Most theorists believe a child first organizes his world without language. He then learns to impose words upon it. Only after this receptive stage does he begin to use words symbolically to communicate with others. In order to draw an autistic child first into the receptive stage, his teacher seats him at a table before three objects, such as a toy chair, a doll and an apple. He is rewarded with bites of food when he picks up one of the objects and then when he hands it to the therapist. Once the command "Give me" is understood, the therapist will say, "Give me chair" or "Give me apple." If the child makes the correct response, he is rewarded with another bite of food and patted affectionately.

He thus learns to impose words on the objects, and the foundation of his receptive vocabulary is laid. Later, he will need to repeat the words himself. For some children, language must be built from the basics up, beginning with only vowel sounds, then going on to consonants and consonant blends and then to whole words. For others, symbolic gestures must be taught to communicate with the child until verbal language can be built.

The cognitive processes that allow even this instruction may be absent. If so, they must also be built. Simple concepts such as same versus different are developed by asking the child to match colored blocks to squares of the same color drawn on paper. And if the child is ever to read, he must be able to associate two dimensional representations with the three dimensional objects he is learning to name.

One characteristic of the autistic child is that he keeps experiencing every learning situation as though it were happening for the first time. Full color photographs are taken, for example, of the actual apple and toy chair to be used. The pictures are placed on the bottom of each compartment of an open box. The child is asked to put each object into the space where its picture lies. Photos of the same apple to be presented to the child must be taken because the child does not yet understand the concept of "appleness." That is, although he may learn to match the apple with its own photo, he may not be able to understand that the photo of a different apple is also an apple. As such generalization is taught, the cognitive processes are being built that will hopefully enable him eventually to use words meaningfully.

Although language is the key to higher learning, for the autistic, education also must include the basics of how to live. Some of the children were not even toilet trained at the beginning of the year. Instruction in buttoning and unbuttoning clothes, pushing and pulling doors and washing hands are all part of the curriculum at Mark Twain. At lunch time, eating a meal according to ordinary human custom is taught. The autistic are known for their bizarre eating habits—insisting on one brand of salami, for example, or living on Kentucky Fried Chicken only. In order to normalize their diets, children first are given food they ordinarily would not accept. The foods they like are used as rewards for eating. Here again the

17. Classrooms for the Autistic

obstacles to learning can be surmounted only by the teacher with supreme patience and skill. One boy sat nearly in tears as he sucked uselessly at a section of an orange, stuffing it sideways in his mouth and then spitting it out in his hand to try again. His teacher turned the section so as to bring only the edge of the morsel between his teeth and then nudged his jaw upward saying "bite." As his teeth finally went into the orange, he got the idea and continued to chew happily.

When their delicate attention spans begin to wane, the children are taken outside to learn to play. Each child's instructor accompanies him onto the grounds and structures his activities into the standard children's games such as riding a tricycle or throwing and catching a ball. As soon as the child has learned to play alone, he is taught to play alongside another child and, eventually, to play with him. Although, generally, the autistic children are kept completely separate from the regular school children, occasionally a normal child is brought in to play with the more advanced autistic children, to serve as a model. The regular kids consider it a treat to go over to play wtih the autistic children and compete with one another for the privilege of doing so. Recently, an integration program has gotten underway. A youngster from the regular classes at Mark Twain comes over and gets his friend from the classrooms for the autistic and takes him to lunch in the school cafeteria or to other school activities.

For the more advanced kids, a physical therapist is brought in for coordination exercises, which sometimes take the form of a game of Simon Says. "Simon says touch your left elbow," intones the therapist. Two of the verbal girls can now exchange places with the teacher in this game. "Simon says touch your head to your foot," says one autistic girl, and the therapist strains to obey.

Those social and emotional aspects of life that most of us experience without conscious effort must be taught to the autistic. They are nudged into camaraderie with one another, and the emotional coldness that supposedly marks them all begins to disappear. One teacher lifted an autistic boy from his desk to find herself caught in a joyful bear hug with his arms around her neck and his legs

Sensory exercises spur maturity in the autistic child (at left). In the rear is an isolation box for the very self-destructive—unused for many months. When attention wanes, it's time for a game of ball outside (above).

around her waist. "This is the autistic child who does not show love and affection," she said weakly.

One night a week, parents of the Mark Twain autistic children can attend workshops in behavior modification that will help them to extend their children's education into the home. With programs such as the one at Mark Twain, home life for the family of the autistic child is at last beginning to normalize. The state of California has closed down large numbers of its mental hospitals and therefore has tacitly taken the position that psychotic kids should be kept at home. Most experts agree that the home is the only place where autistic children, as well, can possibly progress. Yet by providing no community services or public school programs, the state forces parents into a Catch 22 situation—they have been forced to institutionalize their children, although it is cheaper to keep them at home where most parents and the state would prefer them.

But then the benevolence of neither the state nor society as a whole is to be thanked for the Mark Twain program, according to Dr. Lapin. "Society couldn't give a good flying fuck what happens to autistic kids," he says. "The handicapped are the most discriminated-against group in America. Hell, they don't even have civil rights." Certainly, the Mark Twain program has disproved any argument that autistic children cannot benefit from education. Probably other programs like the one in California can no longer be denied.

A few months after the program started, all of the autistic children at Mark Twain, their families and the project staff gathered for a potluck dinner to celebrate the program's successes thus far. The autistic kids took their seats at the table alongside their families and showed off their new social skills. "They were beautiful," says Needels proudly.

Afterward, Tymchuk gathered with the students' healthy siblings for a discussion of what it's like to be the brother or sister of an autistic child. Home life for the families is at last beginning to normalize. "We're very lucky to have a very good, very emotionally strong group of parents," Needels declares. "Some of the husbands and wives haven't been out for an evening alone together since the birth of their autistic child. Of course," she adds, "there was no getting a baby-sitter." Now that the kids are more manageable, that should change. A program for the summers and holidays has made state and county recreational facilities available to the autistic for the first time.

Parents of autistic children from across the country write in, some of them willing to move to California and live there for a year to establish residence in the hope of getting their children into a public school. Others have taken to activism in their own areas. "Hell, every child is deserving of an education," says one parent. "They can't lose."

Helping Teachers Work With "Unteachable" Children

W. Gregory Allard,
John M. Dodd and
Rowena B. Foos

W. Gregory Allard, a graduate student in special education at Eastern Montana College, Billings, participated in the 1974 summer workshop for teachers of handicapped children at the college. John M. Dodd, Ed.D., director of the Institute for Habilitative Services at Eastern Montana College, helped to coordinate public school and college efforts in the workshop while Rowena B. Foos, Ed.D., Associate Professor of Special Education, was director of the workshop.

The results of recent court litigation make it clear that most children have a right to be educated in the public schools. But while special education classes have long been offered, it is only recently that teachers have been asked to teach children with handicaps and/or mental retardation in their regular classrooms. This obviously places more demands on teachers as they try to work with children who were formerly excluded, because they could not walk or make their needs known, for example. Similarly, teachers of handicapped children in special classes will be asked to work with children with more severe problems.

If teachers are to be expected to teach such children successfully, more programs to prepare them to meet these new responsibilities must be initiated. In addition, to make certain that educational and other services are made available to handicapped children in the community, the public must be made aware that most children can learn when given appropriate opportunity and that they have a right to this opportunity.

During the summer of 1974, a special workshop, supported partially with funds from the Bureau of Education for the Handicapped, U.S. Office of Education, was conducted at Eastern Montana College's Institute of Habilitative Services in Billings to prepare teachers to work with severely handicapped children in their classrooms. The workshop was also designed to demonstrate—and publicize—the fact that most children, no matter how severely handicapped, can learn.

The workshop was divided into two 4½-week sessions, each attended by 10 full-time interns, 4 part-time students and 12 participating children. The students—who included special education and regular elementary school teachers, students at the college, a nurse's aide and a home economics teacher—worked with the children in the mornings and spent afternoons in discussion seminars. The workshop was conducted in a large classroom in the special education building near other college classrooms, a placement which guaranteed visibility to teachers from many communities who were attending summer school. On one side of the room were four cubicles equipped with one-way mirrors and sound equipment. These enabled students and other persons to monitor individual training sessions from an attached observation booth.

Public schools in the area identified children who could participate in the program and also provided transportation to bring them to the college.

The children ranged in age from four to 17. One child in the class was Jerry, a 10-year-old boy with D (13–15) Trisomy (a syndrome associated with a chromosomal abnormality) who had no receptive language skills, could not sit or stand and had a number of malformations including cataracts, hare-lip and cleft palate and congenital heart disease. His classmates included a 15-year-old boy diagnosed as autistic; two children with Down's Syndrome, one of whom also had some hearing loss; a 4-year-old who weighed only 12 pounds and had to be carried; and two other non-ambulatory children. Several had no expressive language and three children had never attended school before. Although this heterogeneity contributed to the teacher education program, it did complicate programming for the children.

Because the program was an educational one, only a minimum of necessary medical information was assembled. Each child's physician's name and telephone number, however, were kept readily available. Since it would have been impossible to test several of the children, and testing would not have been educationally useful for others, a crude screening device to test the general level of functioning of each child was developed by students attending the workshop sessions. An assortment of tasks, which included gross motor and eye-hand coordination skills, language usage, color and number recognition and ability to imitate, was assembled and each child was asked to perform tasks to determine his or her training priorities. The students then chose suitable tasks—tying shoes, naming objects, saying words and responding to simple requests, for example—which they would then teach the children assigned to them.

Using a behavioral task analysis model developed for the Madison, Wisconsin public schools,[1] along with other published training programs,[2] the students analyzed the particular task to be taught, separating the task into a series or chain of simpler tasks and integrating these into a teaching sequence. They then began training programs based on each child's needs.

The student working with Jerry, for example, wanted to teach him to sit up and to hold his head erect. Since Jerry

had spent most of his life in bed, mainly sleeping, it was difficult to keep him awake and his waking periods had to be increased sufficiently to make learning possible. Jerry was strapped into a chair and presented with a variety of stimuli and, after a short time, he was able to stay awake long enough for the student to begin working with him.

Since Jerry's hearing and visual ability could not be determined, tactile stimuli were used. The student said, "Jerry, sit up," into his ear so that he could feel the breath, even if he could not hear the words. This was paired with a physical cue—a light touch on the back of his neck. At first the student had to hold Jerry's head but each time his head was erect, even though it was primed, he was rewarded with a "spritz" of kool-aid or soda and hugged or patted.

As Jerry was rewarded for appropriate behavior, he began to respond and, within the first week, held his head erect without help. Soon the straps which held him to the chair were removed and, when he slumped forward, the student moved him to an upright position and rewarded him. After a few days he could sit unaided for a minute and, by the end of the 4½-week-session, Jerry was sitting alone for 40 minutes at a time. Gradually, Jerry learned to pick up objects and, ultimately, to drink from a cup.

Another student concentrated on teaching a young retarded girl, who had no expressive language and only limited receptive language, how to follow verbal directions and to develop imitation skills. These rudimentary skills were felt to be prerequisites for any future tasks.

Videotapes were made of the teaching sessions and reviewed during the seminars, and data-taking and charting were also discussed and demonstrated. To assure varied experiences, each student worked with three different children.

Half-hour individual training periods were alternated with juice and cookies, a group activity and "recess." Once each week the children were taken to the swimming pool.

Toward the end of the session, parents were invited to visit the classroom. After teaching procedures were outlined, they were taken to the observation room so that they could see and hear the procedures being employed. They were then invited into the classroom to more closely observe their own children being taught and to learn how they could carry out similar activities at home.

Jerry's parents were particularly surprised and encouraged by their son's progress, since when Jerry was born their doctor had predicted that he would never learn or develop and expected that he would live only a short time. Until a new physician recommended that he be placed in some kind of educational program, they had not been encouraged to seek help for Jerry.

Participants' Reactions

Many of the teachers who attended the workshop said that the new methods and techniques they had learned would be immediately applicable in their classroom situations. However, all of the participants agreed that the experience was particularly valuable in helping them to understand that many "unteachable" children really could learn and in giving them confidence in their own abilities to work with such children.

One special education teacher, who taught children with learning disabilities and who had had little contact with severely handicapped children, said: "I would suggest that all future teachers and those who are now teaching take a similar course. In this way some of the fear and apprehension about working with these children would be eliminated."

A student at the college said that when she enrolled in the course she had looked forward to "loving children who could respond only to love." After completing the session, however, she explained: "These children do need a lot of love and attention, but their abilities far exceed what just 'babying' them accomplishes. I spent many hard-working hours realizing that the more you expect from these children and the more dedicated and persistent you are, the more they will produce."

Publicizing the Program

Because one of our aims was to make the college and community aware of our efforts and progress, an open-door policy was maintained in the observation booth. College administrators and faculty members were specifically invited to observe the training sessions.

Since the children were taken to the student union for refreshments and to the pool, they were highly visible. Their daily arrival at the classroom was often a noisy processional—in fact, the children's presence was difficult to ignore.

The students in the workshop were also used to help publicize the program. Photographs were taken of each student working with a child and the photos, along with a brief story emphasizing the theme that severely handicapped children can learn, were sent to students' hometown newspapers. Most were printed.

The teacher education program at Eastern Montana College is continuing to strengthen its partnership with the public schools and, in Billings, the public schools are now practicing virtually "zero reject" in special education programming. Jerry is attending a public school special education class, the 4-year-old was enrolled in a preschool class for handicapped children, and others returned to classes for severely impaired children.

Until the recent development of behavioristic task analytic procedures, little technological information was available to help parents and teachers teach specific skills to severely handicapped children. However, now that this information is available, greater efforts must be made to make these procedures and the results of using them more widely known to teachers, parents and other community members. A similar workshop was held this summer and the program has expanded to include preparation in theory and techniques and a parent training component.

---

[1] Brown, Lou; Bellamy, Tom and Sontag, Ed (eds.), *The Development and Implementation of A Public School Prevocational Training Program for Trainable Retarded and Severely Emotionally Disturbed Children*, Madison Public Schools, Madison, Wis., 1971.

[2] Brown, Lou and Sontag, Ed (eds.), *Toward the Development and Implementation of An Empirically Based Public School Program for Trainable Mentally Retarded and Severely Emotionally Disturbed Children*, Madison Public Schools, Madison, Wis., 1972; and Longworthy, Ronald A.; Anderson, Chrys L.; Byrne, Kathy M.; Douglas, Margaret A.; Hathaway, Patty J.; Holem, Barbara L. and Swenson, Richard P., *Program Procedures Manual*, 3rd edition, Boulder River School and Hospital, Boulder, Mont., 1974.

Role Playing and Behavior Modification: A Demonstration with Mentally Retarded Children

L. GERALD BUCHAN, SALLY TEED, and CRAIG PETERSON

Within the last few years a "new wave" of therapeutic techniques for teaching the mentally retarded has emerged in this country. Two techniques which have been useful to the teaching professional are role playing and behavior modification. Not only do these methods modify learning behavior of the retarded, but also research has suggested they serve to improve adaptive behavior (Edwards and Lilly, 1966; Bryer, 1963).

Role playing procedures for the retarded have given them an actional dimension which is important in the total learning spectrum. Also, the "here and now" quality of role playing activities doesn't require a time perspective, yet specific situations can help the retarded plan for future events.

Behavior modification has been labeled variously as operant conditioning, reinforcement therapy, and behavior therapy. A primary principle involved is that of using reinforcement or reward to increase the probability of a response occurring again (Skinner, 1953). Operant conditioning also involves the principles of shaping or successful approximation where a response approximating the final desired response is rewarded. Another important principle is chaining responses. Gagne (1965) states that chaining is a matter of connecting together in a sequence two or more previously learned responses before reinforcement is presented. Eensburg (1965) has shown that chaining is an important technique for the severely retarded. Through chaining it is possible to have an individual learn complex and sometimes very difficult maneuvers in succession.

The mentally retarded individual should be prepared to the best of his or her ability to compete in society as an economically independent person. In the primary grades this involves learning experiences in the academic area. In junior and senior high levels, learning centers around practical application, prevocational, vocational, and avocational skills, and the utilization of academic subjects to assist in these skills. The teacher's job is to effectively prepare the students for the roles they will take in society.

In any classroom total individualized instruction between teacher and pupil is impossible. Therefore, when utilizing the principles of behavior modification, it is necessary to find a way to reinforce all children and yet allow this reinforcement to be as individualized as possible. Some goals of behavior modification in the classroom are to develop procedures whereby motivation, good study habits, cooperation, perseverance, and concentration can be developed (Birnbrauer, Tague,

---

Dr. Buchan is School Psychologist, Multnomah County Intermediate Education District, Portland, Oregon.

Mrs. Teed, high school teacher of EMR individuals, Highland High School, Pocatello, Idaho.

Dr. Peterson, School Psychologist, Vancouver Public Schools, Vancouver, Washington.

et al., 1965). If these goals can be established early in the child's academic career, then the possibility exists that these same principles will carry over into his or her adult life.

Combining Role Playing and Behavior Modification

Role playing situations and techniques can be adapted for use with the mentally retarded. Since many retardates exhibit a short attention span, as well as a limited verbal ability, situations with an actional base for the participants are preferable to those that are conversational in nature.

Two procedures will be examined which can be used with the mentally retarded: skill training and problem solving. These two procedures are the outgrowth of combining role playing and behavior modification.

Skill Training: When the director's purpose is skill training, guidance helps retarded individuals focus on acquiring skill in various tasks. If the situation is learning telephoning procedure, the teacher may provide the children with a model of appropriateness in using the phone. Later, the children may practice with other children or be given opportunity for "live" phoning.

Problem Solving: When the major purpose is problem solving, the director may focus on problems, feelings about handling these problems, and alternatives. More time may be spent delineating the problem or probing alternative proposals in an effort to get brief enactments and alternatives, and then helping the group choose one or two alternatives to explore in further detail. Time will also be spent in summarizing proposals for behavior and discussing the enacted sequences (Shaftel and Shaftel, 1967).

Both of these procedures are effective with the mentally retarded. They offer alternatives to problem areas in the classroom, as well as prepare the older retarded individual for experiences in the social world they will eventually encounter. An example of this would be to conduct a job interview and thereby give the student a chance to practice without fear of failure.

With a retarded individual, it is necessary to keep role playing situations relatively simple, especially at first. The individual needs to experience success and if the situations are too complex this is not possible.

Classroom Applications

This section will show how concepts of role playing and behavior modification can be utilized with the mentally retarded individual. The examples noted are for demonstration purposes only. It should be noted that the unfolding of role playing is generally spontaneous and consequently does not lend itself to orderly procedures, sequences, and so forth.

Two groups of mentally retarded individuals were selected for the demonstration. [The authors wish to thank the administration of the Pocatello public schools for providing time and space to conduct this demonstration.] Group one consisted of prevocational mentally retarded students; chronological age twelve to sixteen, mental age six to nine. Group two was composed of ten primary age trainable mentally retarded students; chronological age nine to twelve, mental age four to six. One day observation was given to each group to help identify the individual to be used in the demonstration, and also to decide which students in the group could be used as reinforcers. Peer reinforcements were used for both groups.

GROUP I: Robin is an educable mentally retarded individual, fourteen years of age. She has adequate verbal skills for a girl of her intellectual capacity. However, she is shy and withdrawn. She is easily intimidated by other class members and prefers to let them speak for her. This pattern of behavior was evident during the warm-up for role playing. It was noted that she would rather follow others than make any type of decision for herself. On the first day of the role playing situations several introductions were made, and as a role playing situation, students were given an opportunity to make applications for a job. Robin had an opportunity to view other students in this "pretend" situation and to get a feel for the mechanics of entering an interview situation.

She was then chosen to serve as an interviewee. Two students were chosen to reinforce Robin for appropriate interview behaviors; she was praised when she shook hands, asked questions in a clear voice, and when she left the office in an appropriate manner at the close of the interview. She was also reinforced verbally for not fidgeting with her hands while in the interview situation. During these particular enactments, several individuals were given an opportunity to serve as both interviewer and interviewee. Role reversal as a technique helped increase the reality of the situation. This also provided an opportunity for the individual to get a feel for the other persons point of view and also served to reduce anxieties in future job interview situations.

It was necessary for the director to serve as an auxillary and assist the individuals when they temporarily experienced difficulty in phrasing questions or responding to questions. It should be

2. IN THE CLASSROOM

noted that Robin was the only individual reinforced during this role playing situation.

On the second day of the role playing situation, additional interview-type situations were conducted in the classroom during a reading period. It was noted that Robin spoke loudly and clearly to the audience and to the teacher during this occasion in spite of a fellow student who spoke out of turn and exhibited rude behavior. As on the first day, Robin was the only individual reinforced in terms of techniques used during the two sessions. They included warm-up, role reversal, and mirroring.

Results with the group one students indicate that they had some difficulty in reinforcing Robin. They wanted to reinforce the model who initially gave appropriate ways to conduct the interview, and in the process the students became so involved in the role playing situation that they forgot their tasks. It was necessary for the director to signal them when she wanted Robin to be reinforced. As peer reinforcement was a vital part of this demonstration, the director stood behind Robin and nodded to the reinforcers when praise was to be given. Since immediacy of reinforcement is critical it was necessary to anticipate what Robin would say or do so adaptive behavior could be shaped. With reinforcement Robin did speak more loudly and clearly as she seemed to gain confidence each time she was placed in a role.

Using peer reinforcement techniques is necessary because behavior may be extinguished with little carry over value unless reinforcement and practice are frequent. In the author's opinion there was not an adequate amount of time to allow intermittent and secondary reinforcers to produce the desired behavior. With this particular age group, the lack of cohesiveness which prevailed and the factor of peer reinforcement did not appear to be entirely satisfactory. The group's lack of acquaintance with role playing techniques and the novelty of the situation may have caused some disorganization.

GROUP II: With the younger mentally retarded children, the director concentrated on one individual who had difficulty participating in group activities. Jane is a mongoloid child who appears to function much like an isolate in the class. Two of Jane's classmates were chosen to serve as reinforcers. The director talked to each of them independently and explained that when she nodded to them they were to praise Jane. They were to say, "That's good Jane," "Fine Jane," or "You're doing O.K. Jane".

Role playing for this class was more active than for group one. For warm-up, a story was told with each child taking part. The role playing situation centered around animals in the jungle (the children played the animals) and one individual was chosen to be king. In this particular story the children decided on their own to band together and manage a lion. The lion's behavior was dependent on the child who was portraying him. Jane was reluctant initially to enter into the story. However, when she did make moves or gestures indicating an interest, she was given pats on the back by peer reinforcers. With the use of successive approximation, she gradually became more interested in the story. During the first day of the demonstration, she did join in the group. However, this was all in a nonverbal manner.

On the second day of the demonstration, warm-up consisted of mirroring, and the students were given a chance to tell about vacation plans. Jane participated actively in mirroring (acting out facial grimaces pretending to be a tree, eating a banana, and so forth) but would not discuss vacation plans. A role playing situation was then developed with the activities centering on a "physical education classroom," with one individual being a leader and the rest of the class becoming participants. Jane was verbally reinforced for joining the group and participating actively. During this particular session, she did take part and even became leader for approximately thirty seconds.

Results of the demonstration with group two indicates that Jane's behavior changed dramatically. Jane had never before taken part in games at recess or worked with other individuals in the class, nor had she demonstrated a willingness to join a group. Verbal praise was reinforcing for Jane and reinforcement by her peers seemed to create more interest in group activities.

Results of these two demonstration groups suggest that mentally retarded individuals can utilize the accomodations of role playing and behavior modification to develop more appropriate social skills. Role playing gives the individuals freedom because it is like pretending while positive reinforcement gives incentive to go on and improve.

As the demonstration classes were only two sessions each, it is apparent that intermittent and secondary reinforcements had not become prominent. It is difficult to assess the long range value of role playing and behavior modification because of the brevity of the demonstration. However, it seems apparent that utilizing the peer group as reinforcers provided positive behavior changes in the mentally retarded individuals.

As the result of this demonstration, the teachers involved with these retarded individuals gained additional tools to utilize in reaching the growing, developing individual. Both role playing and behavior modification are important in the teacher's curriculum, and as professionals we have achieved only a modicum of the potential possible in helping students teach each other.

REFERENCES

BOOKS

Bandura, Albert, and Walters, Richard A. *Social Learning and Personality Development.* New York: Holt, Rinehart & Winston, 1963.

Buchan, L. Gerald. *Role Playing and the Educable Mentally Retarded,* Belmont, California: Fearon Publishers, 1972.

Chesler, Mark, and Fox, Robert. *Roleplaying Methods in the Classroom.* Chicago: Science Research Associates, Inc., 1966.

Shaftel, F.R., and Shaftel, George. *Roleplaying for Social Values: Decision-Making in the Social Studies.* Englewood Cliffs, New Jersey: Practice-Hall Inc., 1967.

ARTICLES—BEHAVIOR MODIFICATION

Edwards, M., and Lilly, R.T. "Operant Conditions, An Application to Behavioral Problems in Groups." *Mental Retardation.* 4, No. 4 (1966): 18-20.

Skinner, B.F. "The Science of Learning and the Art of Teaching." *Cumulative Record.* New York: Appleton-Century-Crofts, Inc.

ARTICLES—ROLE PLAYING

Bryer, S.J., and Wagner, R. "The Didactic Value of Role Playing for Institutionalized Retardates." *Group Psychotherapy.* 16 (1963): 177-181.

Long, Wilma J. "An Exploratory Study of the Use of Roleplaying with Severely Retarded Children." *American Journal of Mental Deficiency.* 3 (1959): 784-791.

Pankratz, Loren D., and Buchan, Gerald. "Techniques of 'Warm-Up' in Psychodrama with the Retarded." *Mental Retardation.* (May 1966): 12-15.

WE WELCOME YOUR COMMENTS

Only through this communication can we produce high quality materials in the Special Education field.

Special Learning Corporation
42 Boston Post Rd. Guilford, Connecticut 06437

Here, there and everywhere

Robert J. Trotter

When B. F. Skinner published his bible on behavior analysis, outcries reverberated through all segments of society (SN: 8/7/71, p. 96). Psychologists, psychoanalysts, poets, preachers and politicians charged that in Beyond Freedom and Dignity *Skinner had equated people with pigeons and rejected those qualities that set humans apart from animals. But the humanists weren't the only ones out to crucify Skinner. Some doubting Thomases among the behaviorists denied their master's philosophy while continuing to practice his techniques. One reason they and a host of pragmatic practitioners continue to operate in the Skinnerian mold is the immediate positive reinforcement it provides. In other words, the scientific model of behavior modification works. It produces the desired effects rapidly and efficiently. So, regardless of philosophical implications, behavior technology is being used increasingly on a variety of levels in a variety of areas.*

In a three-part article SCIENCE NEWS *looks at the widespread applicability of behavior technology and at some of the many ongoing examples of behavior modification at work.*

Achievement Place: A behaviorally oriented treatment program for juvenile delinquents

In the 1950's juvenile delinquents had greasy ducktails, black leather jackets, bicycle chains and zip guns. In the 1970's this particular stereotype is seen more often on the stage than on the street, but juvenile delinquency still exists and is a problem. It is a status characterized by antisocial behavior (truancy, waywardness or incorrigibility) that is considered to be beyond parental control and therefore subject to legal action. For many such youthful offenders (usually between the ages of 11 and 18) legal action means confinement in a state institution. This keeps them off the streets but does little to correct delinquent behavior or teach socially acceptable behavior. Researchers in Lawrence, Kan., are attempting to change this situation by reeducating delinquents in a controlled environment designed specifically to overcome behavioral difficulties.

The model environment they are using is called Achievement Place. It consists of a residential home, two teaching-parents and seven or eight boys or girls (11 to 16 years of age) who have been sent there by the Juvenile Court or the Department of Social Welfare in the community. The home is run according to the principles of behavior modification and its goals are to educate youths in academic, social and self-care or vocational skills.

Most youths sent to Achievement Place are having trouble in school. Truancy, tardiness and disruptive behavior have usually led to suspension or dropping out. A great many factors are involved in producing such behavior but lack of motivation is often the major problem. These students don't care about getting an education and see no connection between doing well in school and success in later life. One way to change the situation is to make the rewards of doing well in school more immediate and more tangible. Students at Achievement Place go back to or remain in their community school, but immediate feedback and positive reinforcement are provided by a token or point system. Each student has a daily report card. Teachers in each class sign the card and note whether or not the student has behaved in class, completed homework or other assignments and performed adequately on tests or exams. Back at Achievement Place the student is given points for all desired behaviors. Points, in turn, can be used to purchase a variety of privileges (free time, trips, spending money).

Elery L. Phillips, Dean L. Fixsen and Montrose M. Wolf of the University of Kansas in Lawrence helped design and put Achievement Place into operation. They report that before using the daily report card, students spent about 25 percent of their time in appropriate study behavior. Using the card and token system increased the figure to almost 90 percent. An average of one letter grade increase was common for most students after a nine-week period. Gradually, as appropriate behavior is learned, the supportive system is removed and students are returned to the normal feedback system.

School, however, is only part of the problem for many delinquents. In the Achievement Place home, teaching-parents (trained in human development at the University of Kansas) instruct their wards in such things as proper social interaction, personal cleanliness and community involvement. Specific behav-

20. Here, There, and Everywhere

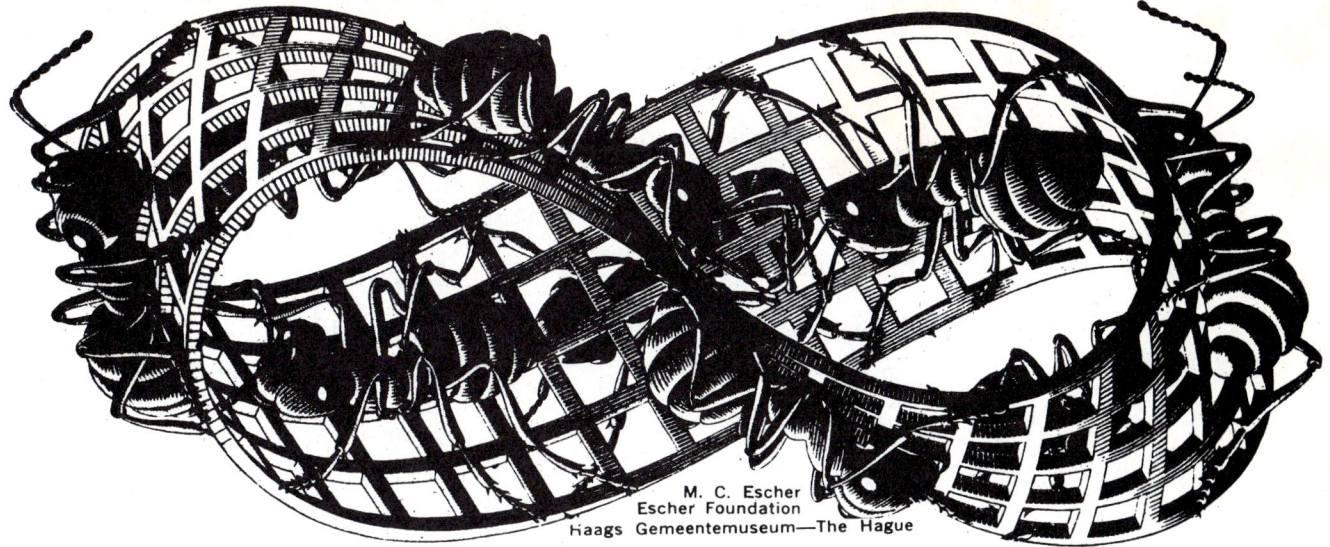

M. C. Escher
Escher Foundation
Haags Gemeentemuseum—The Hague

ior goals for each youth are based on behavior that members of the family, school, community and teaching-parents believe should be changed. Desired behavior earns points while speaking aggressively, arguing, disobeying, being late, stealing, lying and cheating lose points.

The immediate feedback provided by the point system helps the youths learn to respond to more natural rewards. When self-control, responsibility and the ability to work productively at home and school are demonstrated, the individual is ready to return to the community. Youths spend up to one year at Achievement Place.

Follow-up data indicate that the effects are long-lasting. The results can be seen in comparisons between Achievement Place delinquents, similar youths sent to a state institution and youths put on probation by the Juvenile Courts:

	AP	Inst.	Prob.
Offenses per year			
prior	3.8	3.6	2.6
during	0.4	0.5	1.3
1 year	0.7	2.4	2.5
2 year	0.0	1.4	0.8
Recidivism (%)			
1 year	6	13	31
2 year	19	53	54
School attendance (%)			
prior	75	75	77
during	100	100	84
1 semester after	84	58	69
2 semester after	90	9	37

In addition to being effective, Achievement Place is relatively inexpensive to operate. The average cost per bed to open such a home is $5,800. A state school or institution costs about $22,000 per bed. The yearly operating cost of Achievement Place is about $4,100 per youth; that of an institution is $9,800 per youth.

Because Achievement Place has had such good results, it has become a model for at least 15 similar homes in Kansas, Maryland, Arizona and California. North Carolina has made funds available to develop 11 such homes.

The Keller method: A personalized system of instruction

The token system used at Achievement Place is nothing new to educators. For years teachers have been giving gold stars for good grades or good behavior. But Skinner and behavior technology have taught more than positive reinforcement to teachers. Programmed instruction and teaching machines are the result of more sophisticated uses of behavior modification. One system in particular—based on Skinnerian conditioning and learning theory—is gaining increasing acceptance in universities and colleges. It is known as the personalized system of instruction (PSI), and was designed by Fred S. Keller (now at Western Michigan University in Kalamazoo).

In the early 1960's Keller was asked by the government of Brazil to set up a department within a university and study their system of education. The European lecture model was in use there. Keller saw major drawbacks in the system and proposed methods to overcome them.

The lecture system, for instance, assumes that all students have the same capability and can learn at the same rate of speed. Grading often depends on whether the student understood the material at the rate it was given. The lecture system has other drawbacks. In some ways it is too unstructured. Some lecturers follow a text or outline, but many discuss whatever comes to mind at a particular time of day. In other ways the lecture system is too structured. Students are required to be in a certain place at a specific time to hear the lecture. Final exams for all courses are usually scheduled within a short period of time and few exceptions are made for any outside problems or commitments (financial, social, personal) a student may have.

The lecture system can be trying in other ways. Some lecturers are admittedly brilliant entertainers and catalyzers of students' thoughts. Most, however, just don't have the ability to hold the attention of a class for an hour, much less three hours, a week. Even if students are interested, note taking detracts from concentration and concentration detracts from note taking. And finally, almost anything a lecturer can say is already written down someplace.

With these problems in mind, Keller devised a system of teaching that allows students to proceed at their own rate of speed. He decided that information should be presented in small sequential steps. Objectives should be clearly defined and behaviorally stated prior to each step and students should demonstrate complete mastery of material before moving on to the next step.

Following the Keller method, an instructor selects course material (from a textbook, variety of texts or any other appropriate source). On the semester system, the material is divided into 20 subunits—each a little less than one week's work. The instructor tells the

2. IN THE CLASSROOM

student to learn the material and gives objectives, study questions and important points to be aware of. Upon completing each section, the student asks to be tested. If the material has been learned, he goes on to the next section. If not, more study is indicated and an alternate form of the test is given when the student again requests it. In this manner a student takes the course in whatever amount of time is required.

Test questions in this type of course are usually the short essay type, and students are allowed to defend any errors or mistakes. One year is often allowed to complete a semester's work. Those who do not complete it are not further penalized with an F, but are allowed to withdraw from the course. Those who complete the material get an A. Anyone who finishes ahead of time can devote more time to other courses or can move on to the next course.

In this system no lectures are given. The instructor merely designs the course (and continually redesigns it as necessary) and is available to answer questions. Graduate students or advanced students act as proctors and are available at all times to give and grade the tests and act as tutors. The first sections of the course are highly structured in order to shape student behavior. As the student learns how to study, extract information and answer pertinent questions, the crutches are removed. PSI provides immediate feedback (tests are graded on the spot) and positive reinforcement (complete mastery always earns an A). Progress is charted in a public place and students are encouraged to complete and interact with each other as they would in a traditional course.

Upon his return from Brazil, Keller and J. G. Sherman of Georgetown University put PSI to use at universities in the United States. James R. Nazzaro of the American Psychological Association used the method for seven years at the University of Virginia. He sees it as a powerful teaching tool and says students learn more and enjoy courses more when taken under the Keller method. He, João Todorov and Jean N. Nazzaro reported in the December JOURNAL OF COLLEGE SCIENCE TEACHING that PSI not only works but works impartially for all students. They report that students have better recall five weeks after a PSI administered course than those who took the same course in the traditional method. They further report that the individualized approach gives the weaker student the necessary structure to improve study skills and continual success serves as a motivator.

Nazzaro admits that the Keller method may not be the best way to teach someone to interpret a poem of Shelley, but he says it is extremely promising in courses where a large body of information is to be conveyed. It is especially useful in the hard sciences but is also used in sociology, economics, psychology and introductory courses in all fields. At present more than 1,000 courses are being taught in the United States by the Keller method. Colorado Woman's College in Denver, for instance, uses PSI in 50 percent of its courses. The Massachusetts Institute of Technology uses it in 9 courses. Rice University, Denison University, the University of Texas, Michigan State and Lafayette are only a few of the schools using PSI. But Nazzaro says the whole field of behavior modification is burgeoning and the Keller method is sweeping the country.

Behavior modification in community mental health

In the mid-1960's the National Institute of Mental Health started a program aimed at replacing state mental hospitals with community mental health centers. Last year Ralph Nader's Center for the Study of Responsive Law charged that the 300 community centers in operation offered little more than a collection of traditional clinical services instead of the bold new approach originally intended (SN: 7/29/72, p. 70). The Nader group said there was too little accountability: Federal money is being funneled into a system that cannot prove it is doing its job.

William H. Goodson Jr. and A. Jack Turner of the Huntsville-Madison County Mental Health Center in Huntsville, Ala., disagree. They have an extensive system of accountability, and they say they can prove that they have an efficient, effective community mental health center. Their center operates almost entirely on the principles of behavior modification.

Since the advent of community mental health centers, the most popular therapeutic philosophies have been based on the psychoanalytical model. Goodson and Turner feel the psychoanalytical model has failed to generate data supporting its efficacy. In contrast, they say the behavioral model has mounds of data (behaviorists tend to count everything) showing how well it works in treating and preventing mental illness. "At the present state of mental health technology," says Goodson, "behavioral/learning methods offer the most accountable, empirical and practical approach to human problems."

In 1971 the Huntsville center received NIMH funding for a research project entitled "Behavior Modification as Applied to a Mental Health Center." Since then everything at the center has been done in accordance with the principles of operant conditioning. Inpatients, outpatients and even staff members are conditioned, rewarded, counted and evaluated. Goal setting, intervention (changing behavior), data collection and evaluation are the major components of the system.

F. S. Keller

Keller: "I can see the day when the length of a course depends on its natural content, when letter grades are gone, when everybody is a dropout at one time or another, when no one is moved up unless he deserves it and when teacher pay and tenure is dependent on teaching and not on scheduled presence in the classroom."

20. Here, There, and Everywhere

In the inpatient service, for instance, goals are set for each year: return of patient's behavior quickly to acceptable discharge state, reduction of admissions to jail on insanity warrants and reduction of admissions to state mental hospitals. These goals are reached by setting individual goals for patients. A major goal might be the return of a patient to work. Sub-goals could be an increase in conversation, increase in job skills and increase in out-of-bed time. Base-rate data are collected on these activities, and contingencies and reinforcements (such as tokens, social praise and passes to leave the grounds) are devised to increase them. As desired behavior is learned and established, patients are transferred to the outpatient service.

Two years of operation show that the system is working. The number of residents from Madison County in the state hospital has decreased from 153 in 1970 to 93 at the end of 1972. The number of admissions has decreased from 112 to 28. The frequency of jailings on insanity warrants has decreased from 74 to 13, and the number of days in jail has been reduced from 514 to 67. The number of patients admitted to the inpatient unit has remained almost the same, but the average stay has decreased from 18.4 to 12.5 days. This reduction alone has meant a savings of $40,219.

Similar achievements have been made in the outpatient service with clients whose behavioral problems are not severe enough to warrant intensive care. Behavioral therapies are successfully used with outpatients in the modification of such behaviors as phobias, marital problems, family conflicts, sexual anomalies, drug use, psychosomatic complaints and depression. Members of the patients' families are encouraged to learn behavior therapies and use them to maintain adaptive behaviors in the home. Using these and other behaviorally oriented therapies the Huntsville center is able, with a staff of 35, to effectively provide a variety of comprehensive mental health services to a population of 186,000 residents.

At a time when the Federal Government is cutting back on social programs and consumer protection agencies are calling for accountability, mental health centers will be fully funded and supported only if they are shown to be effective. Goodson and Turner feel they have met these qualifications and have taken the concepts of mental health out of the ephemeral realms and given them concrete meaning.

So, while behavior manipulation may have its drawbacks and detractors, the fact remains that the Huntsville center (like Achievement Place and the Keller method) has shown itself to be a workable and efficient operation.

MENTAL RETARDATION

Designed specifically for the course of study known as Exceptional Children or Mental Retardation. It is excellent for students and teachers who plan to work with the educable, moderate and severely retarded.

For more information about this book and other materials in special education, contact Joseph Logan, Editor, Special Learning Corporation.

Special Learning Corporation
42 Boston Post Rd. Guilford, Connecticut 06437   (203) 453-6525

A Comparison of Nonassertive,

It is often difficult to judge the effectiveness of our behavior when faced with a conflict of rights between ourselves and another person. Just getting what you want may not be the best criterion, especially if your approach has permanently antagonized your adversary or engendered feelings of guilt within yourself. A better indication is the way you and the other person feel about yourselves after the conflict has been resolved. Simply, assertive behavior, as opposed to submissive or aggressive behavior, generally makes you feel good and gains the goodwill of your opponent; it may even make that person your friend. The chart at right may be used to evaluate the

Item	Nonassertive Behavior
Characteristics of the behavior	Emotionally dishonest, indirect, self-denying, inhibited
Your feelings when you engage in this behavior	Hurt, anxious at the time, and possibly angry later
The other person's feelings about herself when you engage in this behavior	Guilty or superior
The other person's feelings toward you when you engage in this behavior	Irritation, pity, disgust

Assertive, and Aggressive Behavior

overall effectiveness of your actions and reactions to delicate or intimidating situations, with the middle column, Assertive Behavior, suggesting the most effective approaches and their emotional benefits. If you find that your actions consistently place you at the far right or left of the behavior scale, you may be a good candidate for Assertive Training. Either way, you should learn something interesting about yourself and the way you affect others.

Chart reprinted from *An Introduction to Assertiveness Training Procedures for Women*, copyright 1973, by the American Personnel and Guidance Association, reprinted with permission.

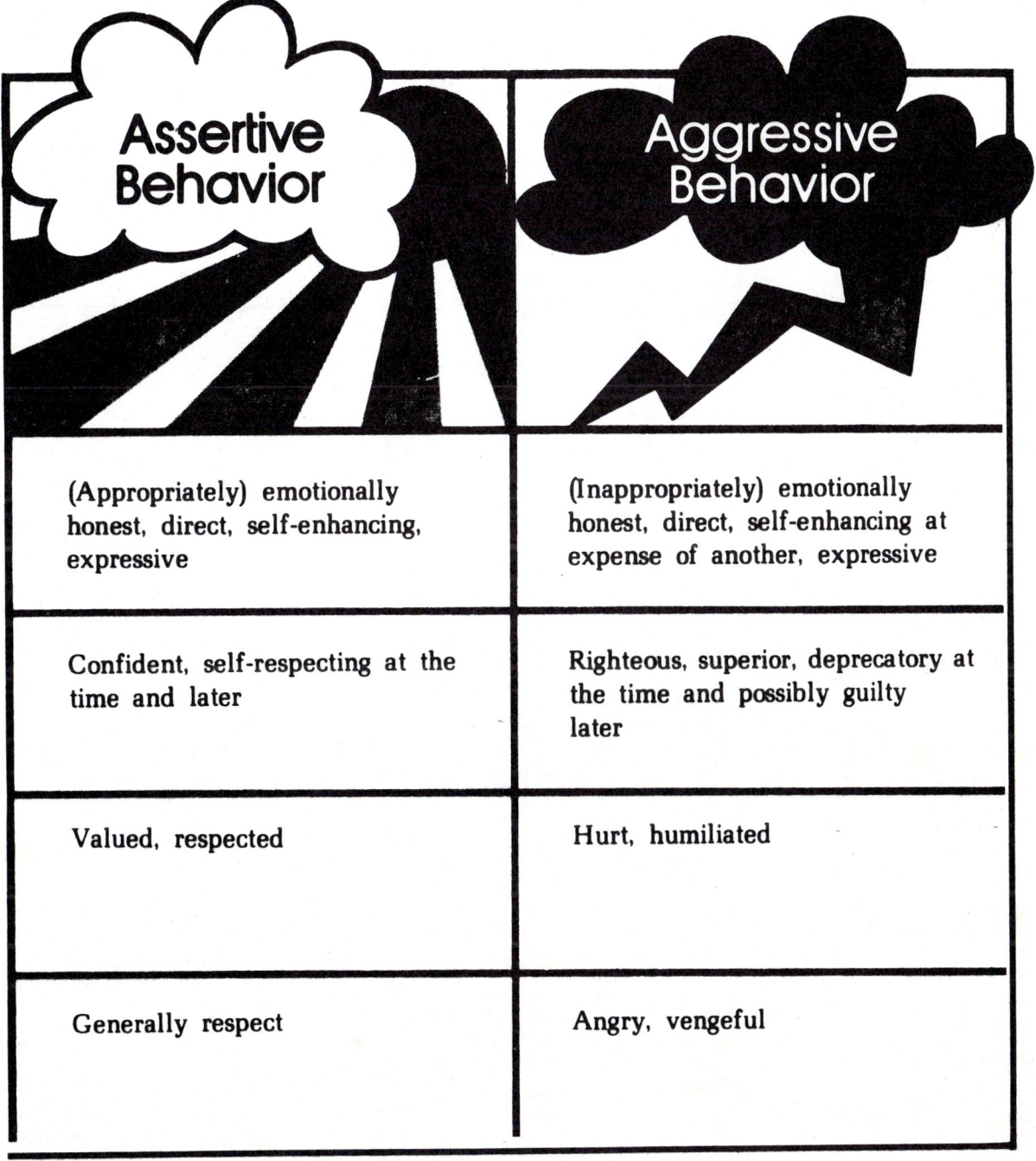

Assertive Behavior	Aggressive Behavior
(Appropriately) emotionally honest, direct, self-enhancing, expressive	(Inappropriately) emotionally honest, direct, self-enhancing at expense of another, expressive
Confident, self-respecting at the time and later	Righteous, superior, deprecatory at the time and possibly guilty later
Valued, respected	Hurt, humiliated
Generally respect	Angry, vengeful

Methods of Behavior Modification

In terms of reality, the world is a flowing tide of activities which are dependent on each other. Behaviorists pick only those things which can be seen and heard within that tide and determine the frequency of their occurrence within reflex and voluntary behavior. The end result is a system of measurement . . . or as Skinner stated: "Behaviorism abandons the idea of personality." From this measurement we progress to actual "terms" or "methods" of dealing with behavior. For instance, behavior is controlled by those consequences which immediately follow. If you control the consequences, you control the behavior. Thus the behavior becomes a reinforcer. In order to have that reinforcer become an effective tool, it must be immediately inforced in order to have it perform the desired consequences.

This principle can be readily applied to many fields of life . . . teaching and education, special education, crime prevention, prison rehabilitation, and personal growth and betterment. In order to accomplish this, behaviors must be catagorized and analyzed.

For the criminal, the act of criminality becomes distantly related in terms of time to the confinement of his prison sentence and it's consequences, that the consequences thus become ineffective.

In an educational setting such as an autistic classroom, behavior can be increased or decreased by manipulation of rewards. For correct action, thus continuous reinforcement changes behavior in the short term, with intermittent reinforcement becoming the ultimate goal.

In a personalized program of behavior modification for phobias, compulsions, lying, forgetfulness, hypochondria, or idiosyncracies in general, we set up concepts of learning where actions that would normally be rewarded are now punished in order that the behavior may be modified.

All these principles are ideas of applied technology. Where we apply them to the individual, with his circumstances and behaviors being unique in their own right, we can use these tools of education to reinforce satisfactory results. Proof of these results include Primal-Scream Therapy, Freudian Therapy, Games-People-Play Therapy, Group Encounter Therapy . . . all simple in form and based on testing through facts.

Growth and change with continuing revision are crucial reinforcers for the survival and refinement of the development of this comprehensive theory of behavior modification for social application in any given situation . . . be it in the prison, the hospital, crime detection, the business world, the home, and perhaps most importantly, in "problem schools" of education.

TEACHING INDEPENDENCE by Joanne Mitchell

At first our Greg was a model child. Healthy, happy, unfailingly sweet-tempered, he was a total joy as a baby. When he was one year old, he thought that everything mother and father wanted him to do was wonderful. His second birthday passed, and he remained cooperative and adorable. Aha, I thought, the "terrible twos" that everyone complains about must result from inadequate attention and discipline.

Then Greg turned 2¾ years old. Suddenly we had an obnoxious monster in the house. His favorite word was "No!" and he used it constantly. At the simplest request he would stamp his feet and cry. It took a battle to get him to put on clothing he had previously worn happily. Favorite foods were thrown on the floor. It became almost impossible to take him shopping because he would lie down in the store and refuse to move. There was constant tension in the house, and my husband and I became irritable, too. We felt as if we were living on the slopes of a volcano, and we found ourselves giving in to Greg too much in order to avoid the threatened eruptions.

Finally, we accepted the fact that Greg's attitude was really a healthy sign. He had stopped being a baby and was ready for more independence. However, I had continued to treat him like a baby. I decided what clothes he would wear, I decided the day's schedule, I planned menus, I arranged playtime with other children. In short, I organized his life for him, and he had very little say in it. He was protesting in the only way he knew, by having tantrums and crying.

After all, we wanted him to grow up to be self-confident and decisive. He was starting to show these character traits now, even though he wasn't old enough to handle all the decisions he wanted to make. We should have been encouraging his independence rather than fighting it.

We realized that the only way he could learn to make the big decisions in life was to practice making the small ones. There turned out to be many ways he could show his opinions with no inconvenience to us.

For a start, I told him that he was now in charge of deciding what he would wear every day. I would tell him if he needed short sleeves or long, but then he would choose the shirt, pants and socks he wanted. He and I moved his everyday clothing from the upper dresser drawers that had been convenient for me, into the lower drawers more convenient for him. He was thrilled with his new responsibility and took it very seriously. He was even inspired to try to dress himself and learned to wriggle into his pants without help. Of course, he came up with some unusual outfits, but if we told him how nice he looked when he did put together a pleasing color combination, he learned to repeat the combination.

We were amazed at how quickly Greg's personality changed when he was given more responsibility. His tantrums stopped almost completely. The cloud of tension that had been hanging over the household simply faded away. He was extremely proud of himself and all his new duties. "Me not baby now," he would say. "Me big boy." His favorite sentence of all was, "Me can do it all by myself!"

Greg was still too young to make all his decisions, of course. We learned that he could make limited decisions fairly easily but not open-ended ones. For example, if I said, "What do you want to do today?" he was likely to pick something impractical, like visiting Grandma, who lived 90 miles away. When I had to say no, a tantrum would result. Yet if I offered him a choice of two or three possibilities, he could handle the decision well. "Do you want to go to the zoo or for a walk by the duck pond?" "Do you want to paint, read picture books or listen to records?" These were decisions he could manage.

He also enjoyed making many decisions about our household. It became our custom to sit down together after breakfast to plan the day's menus. "Let's see," I would say. "If we have pork chops tonight, how about potatoes and a salad to go with them?" Greg would solemnly help me decide among mashed, baked or pan-fried potatoes and between a gelatin salad or tossed green salad. At dinner he would proudly point out his contribution to the menu. As an unexpected bonus, he also became more adventuresome about tasting new foods.

Baking was fun for Greg, too. We had a basic sweet bread recipe he particularly enjoyed making. While we were mixing and kneading the dough, he would decide whether we should make a large, braided loaf or any of a half dozen types of sweet rolls.

In the supermarket Greg was assigned the job of deciding flavors and brands. He would choose between shredded wheat and corn flakes, for example, or between Swiss and muenster cheese.

He learned other lessons while grocery shopping, too. At first he selected only the items he liked himself. With a little gentle hinting, he learned to pick strawberry yogurt for himself and vanilla yogurt for me, or strawberry jelly for himself and grape preserves for his father.

Once Greg could make decisions, he was eager to go on shopping expeditions. There was no time for him to lie on the floor and scream; he was too busy helping.

21. Teaching Independence

He especially enjoyed shopping for clothing after I explained the idea of "matching." He thought it was an exciting game and found it an incentive to learn the names of the colors. Whether he was helping to choose a necktie for his father or a blouse for Grandma, he would study the pattern and color and try to think of what it would match. He enjoyed this much more than he ever enjoyed any of the toys designed to teach colors and shapes.

I remember the day he selected a loud green and orange shirt for himself. When I wondered aloud if it would match the rest of his clothes (predominantly blue), he thought for a long time and then put it back. "This one be better," he said as he picked up a blue-and-white striped shirt.

On the few occasions when he still had tantrums, we ignored him. The tantrum would soon pass. One time when I was setting the table for dinner, Greg decided he wanted to paint a picture. When I said, "Later," he stamped his feet, screamed, and started punching my leg. I carried him to his room and told him that he could come out when he was ready to be quiet. He continued the tantrum in his room for a few minutes, but discovered there is no point to a tantrum if there is no audience. He came slinking out, very embarrassed, refusing to meet my eye. A quick hug and a few kisses made us friends again, and he was soon back to his usual sweet self.

Greg is six years old now. He has graduated to more involved decisions. This week he is trying to decide how to spend the dollar his grandmother gave him. Should he squander it on a glorious week of extra ice cream with his school lunches, or should he save it to get a special toy he has been wanting? It is his money and his decision. Someday he will have to choose between saving part of his salary for a special purchase or spending it on an immediate pleasure. We hope these small decisions now will help him then.

We have another two-year-old boy in the family now. Jeff is a very different person from Greg—more exuberant, less intellectually inclined. But the same general approach has worked to ease Jeff through the "terrible twos." Now he is the one to choose his own clothes, help plan menus, and decide on flavors and colors. He, too, is very proud to be treated as a real person who has opinions that matter, and he, too, is proud to say, "Me do it all by myself."

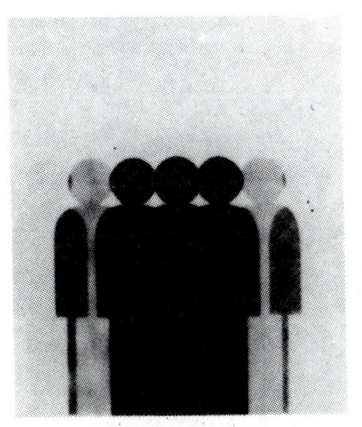

EMOTIONAL AND BEHAVIORAL DISORDERS

Designed to serve a specific course for the in-depth study of the psychology of exceptional children.
For more information about this book and other materials in special education, contact Joseph Logan, Editor, Special Learning Corporation.

Special Learning Corporation
42 Boston Post Rd. Guilford, Connecticut 06437 (203) 453-6525

Days of anguish, moments of hope for a child called Noah

Josh Greenfeld

The author and his family won't give up in their frustrating search to find the right kind of help for their autistic child—or in their efforts to adjust to Noah's illness.

August, 1971
... I still don't know exactly what's wrong with Noah. I only know something is profoundly wrong with him. I still don't know what to do—I only know I must do whatever I possibly can. Although Noah is too young for an institution now, I know I must still accept the very real possibility of his eventual institutionalization. I also know I must try not to feel more sorry for myself than for Noah, but some days I forget. . . .

It is a year, a long year, since I wrote these words about my autistic son, Noah. At that time he was four years old. He was neither toilet-trained nor could he feed himself; he seldom spoke expressively; his attention span was almost nil; he rarely played with toys at all; he never came when he was called by name; he was almost always lost in a world whose activities consisted solely of thread-pulling, lint-picking, blanket-sucking, spontaneous giggling, inexplicable crying, eye-squinting, finger-talking, wall-hugging, circle-walking, bed-bouncing, head-nodding and body-rocking.

Now Noah is five. During the past year he has received megavitamin treatment—heavy dosages of certain vitamins daily—and been exposed intensively to operant conditioning, a behavioristic carrot-and-stick system of rewards and punishments. And things have changed: he has become easier to manage. He is out of diapers, and if he does not always tell us when he has to go to the bathroom, he will try to go when we tell him to. He plays with toys when prodded, winding up his music box or bouncing his Slinky or pushing a car along the track on his Busy Box. He eats by himself and assists in his dressing, pulling on his socks and tugging up the zipper of his sleeper and poking his head through his T-shirts. He knows how to turn on the TV set and how to turn off the hot water in the bathtub.

Such feats may not seem the stuff of great otherwordly miracles, but judged in the context of the Noah we have known, we count each a blessing, marvelous as any grace. At the same time, though, we are too often reminded that Noah is still very much enclosed in a world of his own whose latch he makes not even the slightest attempt to jiggle—let alone lift. Again perhaps the best way for me to describe the experience of the past year, to communicate the changes in him—and us—the encouraging and hopeful baby steps forward he has made in certain directions and the sometimes agonizing and distressing lack of progress in other ways, is to go back and thumb through the pages of my journal.

July 1, 1970
Although the subject is little aware of it, a card from the chiropractor arrived informing us that today is Noah's fourth birthday. Noah had about a half-dozen chiropractic adjustments last fall—but with little effect. And when we saw that the chiropractor, for all of his good intentions, was gradually losing confidence in his treatments, was literally all but going through the motions, we stopped making appointments.

I set much greater store on Noah's daily regime of megavitamins. Diagnosed as a childhood schizophrenic—whatever that may mean—he now receives under the psychiatrist's supervision hefty doses of vitamins B-3, C and E among other things, along with an enzyme-producing catalyst called Deanor. These vitamins come in pills which Foumi or I pulverize with a mortar and pestle and then spike into his orange juice.

We're also proceeding along the lines of the best workaday-live-through-the-week advice we've yet received in regard to Noah. It came from one of Dr. Ivar Lovaas' students at UCLA, Bob, an operant-conditioning therapist whom we met on our visit to UCLA. He told us to make Noah pay attention, establish eye contact by saying, "Look at me." And to reward such "appropriate" behavior with a cookie or a potato chip. So whenever Noah starts jumping on the couch as he prepares to take off into his

3. METHODS

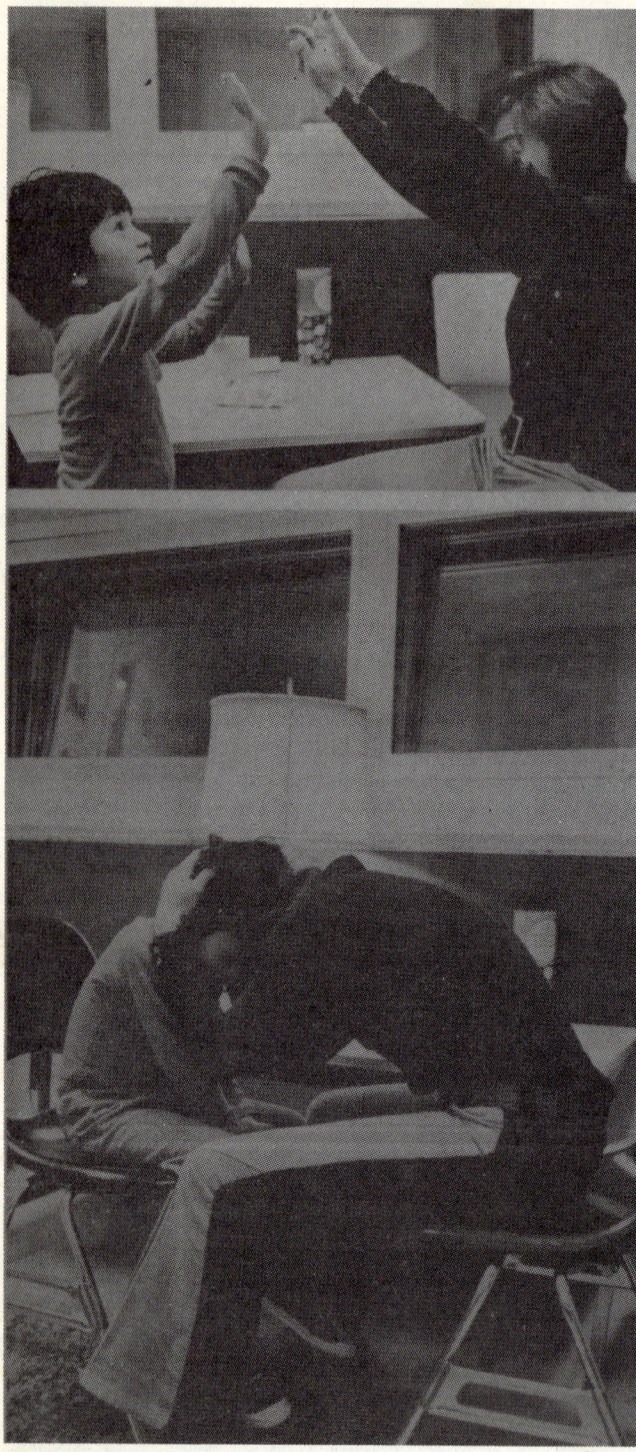

Working with Noah, a UCLA therapist employs operant-conditioning—a behavioristic carrot-and-stick system of rewards and punishments. First step for the therapist is to establish contact ("Noah, look at me!"); once this is done, the child is taught to imitate—the first step in the learning process (top). If he responds correctly to the command ("Noah, do this!"), Noah is rewarded with hugs and Fritos (bottom). Failure is greeted with sharp words or an occasional slap.

own world or starts to prance-dance about a room, I shout: "Look at me." If he persists in his self-stimulation, in his inappropriate behavior, I admonish him with a sharp "No," a "Stop it," and even an occasional smack as Bob suggested.

But it takes an awful lot of persistent energy to keep after Noah. So we're beginning to think of moving (from Croton-on-Hudson, New York) to a place such as Los Angeles, which has a setup with the proper operant-conditioning facilities and faculties. At the same time, we rebel at the idea of moving just because of Noah. We don't want to start dedicating our lives to him completely. We have three other lives in our family.

August 3, 1970

I sat down with pencil and paper this morning and figured out our financial position. We can afford to give the UCLA approach a shot. And if we can't manage Noah any better afterward, if nothing seems to work there, then we'll have to think hard about institutionalizing him. Otherwise our lives will be one long servitude. And that's something we cannot afford.

August 29, 1970

Foumi, out of guilt to both the young and the old, went into the city with her mother and Karl. I was left with Noah. Unremittingly. He had a b.m. and urinated twice, and, except for a two hour period in which I forced him to stay in his crib, he had me running, changing diapers, trying to curb his jumping, attempting to interest him in some kind of positive activity. I realized just how hard a day Foumi has every day.

A note came from UCLA. They won't exactly commit themselves to accepting Noah for therapy. They said if we'd come, they would see about it. But they all but intimated that they would accept Noah, though they would not accept the responsibility of telling us to come to California for just that purpose. I'm an old gambler; I'll take an "if-come" bet. We'll go to California.

September 9, 1970

We went to see the vitamin doctor again. Not much was accomplished by the visit. But we do have a clearer view of Noah as a schizophrenic; and now we have to begin to have a clearer view of schizophrenia. The chances are indeed slim that Noah will ever be cured, as things stand now. But there always remains the chance that some day a biochemical cure will be found. In the doctor's waiting room we spoke to a schizophrenic of about 20. She was blond and good-looking, and we noted how consciously she tried to talk. She said she lacked the ability to pay attention, to focus completely on any activity for very long, that it took her, for example, an hour to read a page in *Time* magazine. When she had schizophrenia attacks, she said, people were to her as things, assuming vague but threatening shapes. Since she has been receiving high dosages of vitamin C and Niacinimide, she told us, her attacks have become more infrequent. "Before, I used to have to have shock every couple of months, but now I can get by on just the vitamins."

The doctor also told us he would be getting a new product which he would like us to try on Noah. It has

22. Days of Anguish

been used with great success in the Soviet Union to help activate speech and is supposed to help more oxygen reach the brain cells.

October 18, 1970

We went to see the school in Connecticut. It's the best setup we've seen yet. An old Tudor stucco building at the edge of a park, with its own enclosed playground. The director is the mother of an autistic child herself. She understands the problems of a Noah implicitly. She has one teacher per pupil, has the school doors open 52 weeks a year, from 9:30 a.m. to 4:30 p.m., six days a week. Most special schools don't realize that since they are for special children they require special hours. Because these kids just can't go home and run around and play after school and cavort all summer long. They don't know how to.

We would have to move to Connecticut if we were to send Noah there. But right now Noah is too young for both the school and the director's educational theories. She believes—and she is a former teacher herself—that it is much easier to work with older kids. The youngest student in her school is seven.

But the physical layout of the place—the gym, the private instructional booths, the abundance of teachers—was reassuring to us. It was good to know that such a school exists. The director was also reassuring in her advice.

"These are the worst years," she told us. "Things will get easier as Noah gets older. Growth is optimum even in the abnormal. Even though sometimes for your own good you have to remember that Noah isn't a normal child. And just forget about him, ignore him; he won't have the normal reactions. So don't worry about it."

I still have California on my mind for the winter. And it is comforting to know that we might have a possible future in Connecticut. Just driving there, the golden-auburn trees made one feel there might be autumnal solutions for Noah. But we still have to look for some spring ones. I want to do *now* what can be done *now*.

November 1, 1970

Last night was a bad night. The cares of the day had piled in on Foumi: Karl sliding in sand piles, dirtying his clothes constantly. Noah his usual un-toilet-trained self. People dropping in unexpectedly in the early evening. And then the avalanche excitement of Halloween tumbling in with the noisy parade of kids at the door trick-or-treating. By bedtime she was done in, sobbing tiredly, uncontrollably, not even quite knowing why. Finally the sniveling stopped and she slept.

And then I got up at midnight and decided to check Noah. He was dry. I took him to the bathroom. He began to yell and howl. So the night wore on, with Foumi up and sobbing again.

November 13, 1970

Last Thursday I flew to California and met Dr. Lovaas at UCLA. He said they would accept Noah for therapy three times a week, for one-hour sessions in the afternoon. He also would be sending a student out to our house once we got there. And he told me of two nursery schools Noah might attend while there. I left his office in high spirits. But on Saturday morning I breakfasted with the father of a 12-year-old autistic child who had been through the UCLA treatment and had gotten "a little but not much out of it." The father, however, still seemed to think UCLA was worth a try. His son, though, is not as yet toilet-trained. Which struck me as a grim prospect. I asked him what he was trying to do for the kid now. "I'm an accountant," he said, "so I'm trying to lay in money for his future. That's the best thing I can do."

Lovaas himself told me: "I promise no miracles, I hold out little hope. A lot will depend upon the ability of you and your wife to learn the therapies. Because if the treatments are not kept up, no matter what advances your boy makes, he will eventually backslide."

As usual, the best part of my trip was the return: Karl running to the door somehow seeming inches taller than I remembered him; Noah, though yelping and bouncing, still a beautiful sight to behold; and Foumi, the last to come in view, wiping her hands on her apron, looking truly lovely as I took her in my arms.

November 18, 1970

We went to Connecticut. Again I was impressed with the facilities of the school. They even have a gym where motor problems can be dealt with. We watched the gym teacher roll a ball back and forth to a kid who couldn't concentrate because he has peripheral vision. So like a horse that tends to run wide, they had him in blinders, trying to focus his vision straight ahead.

A psychiatrist and a speech therapist observed Noah. They seemed to think he was not too badly off "in a comparative sense." Compared to what? I asked. Compared to what he could be, I was told.

November 21, 1970

We had another conference with Noah's teacher. She began by saying that she was applying a form of operant conditioning, using pretzels as rewards. She and her aide give the reward whenever he obeys a command such as "Stand up." And whenever he disobeys, they punish him. For example, if he crumples and picks at his sandwich at lunch, they throw it out. As a result, he has become much better at eating his sandwich by taking normal bites. He has also improved at taking off his coat and hanging it up and at pulling up his pants after going to the toilet.

The regime of the school is devoted to trying to give the children a practical and busy day. In the morning they are asked to take off their coats and push their chairs to the table. Then they go to the toilet. From 9:20 to 10:00 the teacher usually works with Noah on a one-to-one basis. Lately she has been working with a cup and spoon, asking Noah to give her the one or the other. When he gives her the cup, she rewards with a half-swallow of juice; when he gives her the spoon on command, he gets a piece of pretzel. And the idea, of course, is that he eventually does the command and is unmindful of the reward. If he pees on the floor, the teacher says, she makes no big deal of it. Mostly she believes in rewards rather than punishments. Ten o'clock is snacktime, a cheese or graham cracker and some juice. Toilet again. Ten-twenty to 10:35 is circle time. They sing songs which try to teach them their names, the parts of their bodies, concepts such as up and down. The teacher believes the children learn better from each other than from a teacher.

There are five children in Noah's group. Three other

3. METHODS

brain-damaged and/or autistic young boys and a mongoloid girl. She's by far the most advanced in the class. Group activity begins at 10:35. The youngsters fingerpaint, which Noah loves, or use plastic glue, which he also digs. Or bake a pudding or pie that they will eat in the afternoon. The teacher tries to keep the play constructive. For example, if Noah in the first period goes to the sandbox, he cannot merely run sand through his fingers. He must fill or empty a pail. And the approbation he enjoys most is not a hug or a kiss but an applauding: "Yea Noah!" Noah will get on a bike and pedal a few turns toward a pretzel. (Indeed, it was funny to watch Noah frisk the apron pockets of both his teacher and her aide before we left.) At 11:00 they put on their coats and go out to play on the swings. Lunch is at 11:30, and afterward is toothbrushing. It's as hard for them as it is for us to get Noah to brush his teeth, but at least he opens his mouth on the command in school now. Next, wash-up. And then each child brings his cot to his place—without getting a reward at this point. Noah usually sleeps from 12:25 to 1:15, and he tantrums there as he does at home when he is awakened; 1:15 is toilet time again, and the remaining time is a free activity.

The main thing, the teacher says, is to be consistent. Now they are trying to teach the children the nursery-school way of putting on their coats. Noah manages one sleeve before losing interest. But his interest span, she notes, has lengthened. He can sit for 15 minutes during the one-to-one session, whereas in the past he would start wandering off after 15 seconds.

Last night I reported all this to Foumi. She was pleased. We both wonder whether it is the "primitive" operant conditioning or the vitamins that are responsible for the changes; meanwhile, we'll continue with both.

November 23, 1970

Solutions pose problems. We planned to leave for California next week to get Noah into the operant conditioning program at UCLA. But yesterday the new acting director of Noah's school told me that there might not be a place for Noah upon our return, that another child on the waiting list would assume his place. She did assure me, though, that Noah would have an excellent chance of getting into the school in the fall again, that as a former student he would be given priority. But that still leaves us facing a hurdle when we return. We may have less than we started out with. I feel as I did in the army. One never knows when one is transferring into a worse outfit, into a lousier theater.

As for California we will apartment-hotel it for December. And then perhaps rent a house for three months. I do think at this point we'll be staying there until the end of March. It will be bad for Karl to be so dislocated; it will be good for Noah since he'll get more of the conditioning there and he'll miss less schooling when he gets back here, just two or three months. I feel I must make a different choice about what is best for either child. It is a choice I do not want to make. Because either way Noah or Karl comes out a loser.

November 30, 1970

I had lunch with a divorced concert pianist today who told me how much he missed the sound of children, and I was telling Foumi about it at dinner. "Let him have Noah for one night and see how much he misses the sound of children," she said. Karl, sitting at the table, put down his fork and looked up with wide imploring eyes: "Please don't give Noah away," he said. Foumi and I tried to keep talking, but we couldn't. And looked away....

December 1, 1970

Packing day. Foumi manages somehow. And even I do my small share. We wondered about our cat, Brodsky. Our next-door neighbor volunteered to take care of him. But then we decided that leaving him next door might be too dangerous, too confusing. We could see him freezing on our steps all winter long. So we're taking him with us.

But the big event for me today came this afternoon, when I picked up Noah at his school. He mumbled a greeting to me: "Daddy."

December 9, 1970

We took Noah over to UCLA to be videotaped. He was placed in an empty room except for a table full of toys. From another room behind a two-way glass mirror he was recorded by a camera and monitored for sounds. For the first 10 minutes he was left in the room to do as he wished by himself: Noah did nothing except for his usual babble song and jumping dance. For the next 10 minutes a student entered the room with a chair and sat there quietly, making no effort at all to involve Noah. Except for a moment or two, Noah barely noticed him. For the last 10 minutes, at one-minute intervals, the student actively tried to interest him in various toys. Noah could scarcely have cared less.

Afterward I spoke to Lovaas in his office. He told me the purpose of the videotaping and monitoring was to establish a "baseline" on Noah's usual pattern of behavioral responses—or lack of responses—to outside stimuli. Also, hopefully, the videotape could serve as a dramatic "before" to be contrasted with the "after" picture. But again he warned me that an autistic or schizophrenic child who undergoes behavior therapy will usually not end up anywhere near normal, that his progress at best can be compared to climbing the first step of a ten-step ladder. The goals would be to suppress Noah's self-stimulation—his senselessly repetitive motor acts which block out perceptions of the outside world and therefore impede learning; to teach him some elementary forms of language that he can use to express demands; to generally make him easier to live with at home by making his conduct more acceptable on a minimal social level.

Dr. Lovaas also reminded me that the treatment might sometimes call for the use of adverse stimuli such as spanking, slapping, weak electrical charges and food deprivation as well as the use of rewards—or reinforcers—such as candy and potato chips. And I signed a release granting my permission.

We discussed the difference between psychogenic therapy and behavior therapy. "Simple," said Lovaas. "Behavior therapy proceeds independent of etiology. A treatment based on etiology has to rest on very shaky grounds since we do not know exactly why these children become as they are. So in the absence of such information it seems pointless to me to implicate parents and make them feel guilty, which is at the basis of the psychogenic approach."

22. Days of Anguish

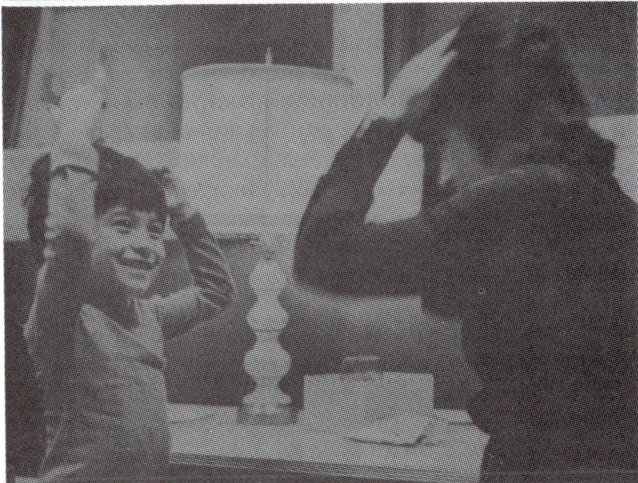

The author describes the goals of behavior therapy: "To suppress Noah's self-stimulation—senselessly repetitive motor acts which block out perceptions of the outside world and impede learning; to teach him some elementary forms of language that he can use to express demands; and to generally make him easier to live with at home by making his conduct more acceptable on a minimal social level." Dr. Lovaas of UCLA told the author that if the treatments are not kept up, Noah will eventually backslide.

I cracked a weak joke: "Every time somebody strikes Noah, I'm going to feel guilty."

Lovaas put his hand on my shoulder and looked me straight in the eye: "Look, the little that we can do is the only form of treatment which has scientifically demonstrated effectiveness. Besides," he laughed, "nobody is going to bat your kid around. Don't worry about it." He then bent over, picked up Noah, who had been prancing about his office, began to jiggle him playfully on his knee and, laughing affectionately, buried his blond Norwegian head in Noah's giggling face.

December 10, 1970

Noah started nursery school this morning. And I'm not sure we made the right choice. They didn't seem exactly 100 percent prepared for him, lacking proper potty facilities on the premises. He also had his first operant-conditioning session.

Foumi and I sit in a control booth like radio network vice-presidents. The treatment room is a mini-studio: two chairs, a table ledge with a cluster of keys, a model car, a bag of Fritos on top of it and a two-way mirror. From behind the mirror we observe. Laura, one of the two therapists who will work with Noah, walks in with him. She sits Noah down facing her. She cracks the Fritos into little pieces and arranges them beside her. Then she begins: "Noah, look at me." Each time he does so, or almost does so, she rewards him with a sliver of a chip, tufts his hair and says: "Good boy." Now she moves on, using the "Look at me" as a point of return and reward, asking him to clap his hands just as she is clapping hers: "Noah, do this." Once he does so and is lavishly praised and rewarded. But the other attempts fail. Laura returns to: "Look at me, Noah." When his attention wanders, when he begins to gleefully self-stim, getting lost in observing his fingers dance erratically, she rebukes him with a sharp, "Noah!" Now she lifts her hand: "Noah, do this." And once or twice he does, tentatively, but then ignores the rest of the commands. Again: "Look at me, Noah," the hair rub, the "good boy, Noah." Laura turns to the cluster of keys: "Give them to me, Noah." He does so: the "good boy," the hair rub, the Frito. Sometimes on the command Noah's hand absently wanders over to the object, the car or the keys she is asking for. Other times the task is dispatched with great alacrity. Now Noah suddenly acts as if he's very sleepy. He starts to tantrum. Laura looks away, does not comfort him, refuses to get involved with him. The tantrum passes, the sleepiness disappears, the tasks continue. Laura addresses us through the mirror: "You must never let him determine when you can stop working with him. The last thing he does must always be the obeying of a command—even if it's just a simple: 'Look at me.' Because otherwise, he'll think he can get out of doing anything by having a tantrum or acting sleepy or just self-stimming in general."

Afterward we see Lovaas. He tells us that Laura and Meredith, the other girl who will work with Noah, are two of his very best therapists. Meanwhile, I notice the battery-charged shocker, like a cattle prodder, on Lovaas' desk. I have heard of it, but still, seeing it is disconcerting. I wonder if it will be used on Noah. Just then a tired Noah wanders into the office. Lovaas bends down, placing his own knees on the floor, to tie Noah's trailing shoelaces.

3. METHODS

The gesture endears him to me enormously, counteracting the sting at the sight of the shocker.

December 26, 1970

Foumi has noted that Noah has all but stopped talking in California. But Dr. Lovaas said his speech was probably gradually fading out anyway. And I recall the Connecticut lady pointing out that as children like Noah move forward in one area, they generally fall back in another. I don't know what area he is quite progressing in at the moment, but I do feel he is more contented out here. And just as important, Foumi is more hopeful.

In the long run I've come to be less sanguine. Because what we're looking toward ideally is 10 percent of a normal human being, a child we can cope with about the house, whom we can keep at home as long as possible. If at this stage of the game Brodsky, our cat, functions more intelligently than Noah, it is a fact I have grown to accept. If most of operant conditioning is nothing less than old-fashioned dog training, it is something I do not scoff at. I must admit that on the rare occasions Noah is struck during a treatment, I flinch and clench my fists. Even though he is no ordinary child, he is my child, and I entertain the ordinary feelings of parental outrage. But then I remind myself that what love and affection can't always accomplish, perhaps a little fear and duress can.

Jan. 4, 1971

We moved on New Year's Day. Karl is pleased with the house we rented because it's in the same school district as the hotel, so he doesn't have to change schools. Noah is delighted with the panoramic view provided by our floor-to-ceiling windows. We're keeping him out of school for the moment.

This morning I tried to do a little operant conditioning on him for the first time. It was a frustrating experience; I was often tempted to haul off and sock him. At this point Noah will immediately put his hands over his head in an attempt to please and get an immediate reward. But he won't clap his hands for anything, or differentiate between commands. At every command he simply puts his hand over his head. This was comic but heartbreaking, the stuff of Beckettian comedy—and, of course, our own small human tragedy.

The purpose of these command exercises is to teach Noah how to imitate, the first steps in any learning process, the steps he has so far refused to take. But as I put him through these paces I thought again of placing him in an institution. Perhaps it is better to live at a remove from one's most personal problems.

January 11, 1971

For the past several days Noah has "self-stimmed" to an unusual degree before going to sleep. The theory behind "self-stimulation," or the repetition of stereotyped behavior, the constant repeating of the same simple action, such as jumping or head-shaking or finger-talking, is that for an organism to stay alive it must be stimulated. And if it doesn't receive stimulation from the outside world, it stimulates itself. And yet by the same destructive token, while it is stimulating itself it cannot receive stimulation from the outside world. It's all a vicious circle that a child like Noah can't possibly break out of.

If one has a child like Noah, one needs money. In order to get enough money, one must have the time and the energy to work. But a child like Noah drains away one's energy, takes away one's time. There is simply no way out.

I must confess something: Sometimes I hope Noah gets sick and dies painlessly.

January 31, 1971

Mrs. Harris, the teacher at Noah's school, tells me my son has been adapting very well. Yet as I watch Noah make his advances, his huge steps—such as simply responding to his name or "coming here" on signal—are infinitesimal. I realize that a dog in two nights at obedience school is still light years ahead of my boy. And no matter how inured I've become as I watch the kids at his school, various Noahs jabbing the air grotesquely, picking lint meticulously, rocking wildly on the swings, I still have to turn away after a few seconds. I really can't quite yet accept myself as the father of a Noah.

February 5, 1971

Lovaas worked with Noah. He got him to repeat simple respiratory sounds such as "ah" and "pip." He was certainly like the musician pushing his instrument by feel into new areas of expression. Usually he was gentle with Noah, but once when Noah reached out to take his reinforcer—the Frito—Lovaas slapped him down hard.

Another student is going to work with Noah in addition to the three sessions a week Noah has with Meredith and Laura. He's a kid named Tom who'll be concentrating on speech.

February 27, 1971

They "staffed" Noah at UCLA. At noon all of Lovaas' students gathered like an informal strike committee, paper-bag sandwich lunches before them, around a large conference table in a classroom to discuss Noah. Foumi and I testified like witnesses as to Noah's progress (great in visual imitations, minimal in speech therapies). Meredith and Laura and Tom issued their reports. A discussion followed as to what might be the next best step to help accelerate Noah's learning. Finally Lovaas suggested that Noah be put on a food-deprivation program of 36 hours to see how he would react, to show him dramatically that communications can bring him desired rewards.

Foumi and I agreed at the meeting. But then we've had second thoughts. Noah is young, he is not that withdrawn, 36 hours is a long time. And Lovaas himself pointed out that such a plan has only about a five percent chance of being effective. So I called him this evening and said we'd like to cut down the length of the food-deprivation period to the omission of a breakfast or a lunch for openers.

Lovaas explained the need for a long-term trial. At the end of 10 hours the child is dazed and dizzy; at the end of 20 hours he is searching for food; at the end of 36 hours he is desperate and will do anything to get food.

We finally worked out a compromise. Noah will be deprived of food—but not water or juice—from dinner one night to 3:30 the following afternoon.

March 3, 1971

The big fast day. Noah skipped breakfast, crying a little, as if he were sensing a lack, a missed beat, when I hustled him out of the house and on to school, but otherwise going without his usual food in a most submissive way. Picked him up at school before

22. Days of Anguish

Understanding the Autistic Child

Autism is not a common disorder, but it is a devastating one. It affects only three or four people in every 10,000, and the victims are always young children. Although the cause is undetermined, autism is often connected with schizophrenia in later life.

Autism is difficult to diagnose in a very young child, because the symptoms—sudden refusal to eat, tantrums, playing with only one toy for extended periods of time, staring into space, rocking back and forth, chattering incessantly or refusing to talk—are also behavioral patterns common to many normal young children.

The child's abnormal behavior patterns usually become noticeable when he is two or three years old. While other children his age begin to socialize and talk, he ignores everything, refusing to respond to visual or auditory stimuli. He lives in his own world, whether silent and withdrawn or hyperactive and inexhaustible. At times he may be violent, inflicting punishment on himself, beating his head against the wall, seemingly bent on self-destruction. He has little or no control over excretory functions and toilet training is almost impossible. He follows a rigid routine in the simplest matters and even slight deviations (such as rearranging the furniture in a room) can provoke a violent reaction. It is nearly impossible to communicate with an autistic child. He is locked inside himself and little is known on how to reach him. Eventually he will most likely be categorized as mentally retarded and put in an institution.

Some children come out of it themselves. At about eight or nine they begin relating to the world and assuming normal lives; however, they usually remain marked as different in one way or another. An autistic child may even excel in a specific field of interest such as music, display amazing aptitude for memorizing facts and details or acquire the habits of running and climbing better than a normal child. Why? No one knows the answer.

In 1944, Dr. Leo Kanner, a noted child psychiatrist, identified the disorder as "early infantile autism." He proposed that parental attitudes and personalities contributed to the development of autism in a young child. Today there are varied hypotheses about both the cause and the treatment needed. Child psychologist Bruno Bettelheim believes that autism is a withdrawal from a hostile environment. However, Dr. Bernard Rimland, who heads the Institute for Child Behavior Research in San Diego, attributes autism to a malfunction of body chemistry. Dr. James Simmons, psychiatric head of UCLA's Children's Inpatient Services, traces it to a genetic deficiency.

Today the autistic child has little chance of leading a normal life; public schools, even those with special classes for the mentally retarded, are closed to the autistic child. Private schools are few and expensive and accept children only up to the age of 13. Three court cases have been filed (two in California and one in Massachusetts) suing the state to provide educational facilities for autistic children. The cases are pending.

In 1965, Dr. Rimland founded the National Society for Autistic Children. Today some 3,000 parents belong to the organization, which is "dedicated to the education, welfare and cure of all children with severe disorders of behavior and communication." The society provides information to educators and parents, counsels parents on seeking professional help and establishing their own schools if none are available and lobbies for federal research funds. Although research is carried on at different institutions, there is still no center for research into the disease.

The autistic child is a study in frustration. He brings grief to his parents as well as love. He brings hope and the constant shattering of dreams. But he does all this unwittingly; he has been cast in a role that only he can play and only the world can help save him from.

12:00—didn't want him to see the other children having their lunches—and brought him home, where he seemed happy enough. At 3:30, over to UCLA. There they were all gathered in the observation room of the booth, Lovaas and his crew. (Lovaas: "This is an enormously rich country. Where else would eight adults gather to watch one four-year-old?") Meredith began to work with him, holding out spoonfuls of ice cream, pieces of bagel, as reinforcers. But Noah's reactions—or lack of them—were about the same as usual.

Then Lovaas asked if we would allow Noah to skip dinner and bring him back the next morning. "He's not hungry enough," he explained. And we agreed. So now it is nightfall and Noah hasn't had a bite to eat all day. Nor has he drunk any of the liquids we've offered him. But amazingly, he isn't at all ill-humored, still jumping and giggling.

The purpose of the food-deprivation program, of course, is to find out exactly how much Noah will put out if he wants something badly enough. To place, as Lovaas intimated to me, "a firecracker up his ass." But at this point, knowing Noah, I suspect the firecracker will only sizzle.

March 4, 1971

The starvation diet—or whatever its euphemism—is a bust. We awoke this morning to hear Noah hacking, and when I looked in his crib I noted his sheets stained with yellow vomit-like mucus. It reminded me immediately of the stuff my father emitted before he died.

We called Lovaas, and he called Meredith. She came to our house, looked at Noah quickly, and decided he couldn't be "worked with." We got some food into Noah—but he refused to drink anything—and took him over to the pediatrician, where he received a clean bill of health. He explained that Noah had up-chucked bile because there was no food in his stomach for the enzymes and juices to work on.

Somebody should have warned us about that. Foumi knows starvation, terminal starvation, too keenly from the war; and the death of Brodsky is still too omnipresent for us not to be unduly sensitive.

So the past two days have been given again to learning there is no quick path. There is only patience. And even a behavioristic concept has to take into consideration the individual child and the instincts—or fears—of his particular parents. Foumi and I know that Noah has no deep reservoir

3. METHODS

of will, no great desire to live, and that there is always the danger that he could pass on in his own otherworldly way, not even with a whimper, but with a quiet unfocused smile.

March 16, 1971

We watched Noah at school over a closed-circuit TV. Mrs. Harris conducts the class as if it were an ordinary class, so the whole process was like watching the patient construction and perpetual reconstruction of a sand castle that keeps slipping and falling apart. And the hours stretched out in slow motion.

Mrs. Harris thinks Noah should be treated like a two-year-old, a very slow two-year-old with a very low energy threshold, and she constantly talks to him as such. We'll try to do the same.

Noah also will begin a new regime at home. The accent will be on daily life, and the UCLA therapists will come to our house. Foumi and I will be instructed in how to get him through operant conditioning to do a little more for himself—eating, dressing, brushing teeth, toilet. Foumi will also learn how to teach him to play with toys; I will work with him on speech.

April 1, 1971

The first sound is the hardest sound. Noah has begun to grunt back an "ah" from me on cue. His sound is primitive, it comes from the throat, like one straining to defecate or vomit. But I esteem it as important a breakthrough as the "wah" of Helen Keller, the *"eau"* of *The Wild Child*. Yesterday I tried converting it into an "eat," the day before to an "oh." But it does not matter, whether he is speaking our precise language or not, he now knows that certain sounds will get him things he wants: food and approval.

And at school he now gets on the swing by himself, climbs up the slide. So perhaps here in California, before we prepare to return home, we have at last come in out of the cold.

May 26, 1971

A day with Noah: on the typical school day, Foumi, Karl, and I get up at about 7:50. We then breakfast together separately from Noah. Karl is entitled to begin a day as the center of attention, as the star attraction. Second, once Noah sees bread or toast on the table, it is impossible to get him to eat or drink anything else. So we try to get Karl, who has an 8:38 bus to catch, on his way before dealing with Noah. Meanwhile Noah, awakened by the alarm, is bouncing about on his bed. Once breakfast is over, I take him to the bathroom and try to get him to take care of his toilet needs, wash him if he's wetted during the night and change him. Noah then comes downstairs and is greeted by juice, eggs, fruit and toast, in that order. These days he eats well. While he is at breakfast, Foumi is preparing his lunch—a piece of fruit, peeled and placed in a plastic container; some meat; salad greens; and a thermos of either juice or chocolate milk, laced with his vitamins. At 9:10 I manage to get him out of the house, and we're at his school by about 9:15.

At school he removes his jacket or coat and hangs it in his cubbyhole and pushes his little chair toward his place at the table he shares with his classmates, a puzzle or a toy usually awaiting him there. From then on his class has the usual kindergarten routine: circle, songs, sandbox, block corner, outdoor play, lunch, rest—but not in quite that order. A teacher and a teacher's aide keep the children busy— except during the rest period— until 1:30. Then they prepare for the end of the school day.

Noah is usually home by 2:00, his old crony, the septuagenarian cab driver, delivering him in his stationwagon taxi. He then plays in our yard, making forays to the swing, the sandbox, but most often running the pebbles of our rock garden through his fingers repeatedly, as if he were looking for some rare gem among them. Foumi next prevails upon him to enter the house, where he is taken to the bathroom, offered some refreshment, and set to work on his therapies. Foumi tries to teach him how to play with toys, how to crawl á-la-patterning, how to distinguish the letter *A* from the letter *O*—all with the rewards and the prods of operant conditioning. She does so until Karl comes home at 3:30 and she has to supervise his reading and homework.

At 4:30 I usually arrive on the scene. And although I don't have a very good teaching personality, I sit down with Noah for a little speech work. It is still slow and frustrating, but I stay with it as long as we both seem productive.

By this time Karl is outside playing, Foumi is busy preparing dinner, and I, unfortunately, sometimes have a few phone calls to return. Left alone for even a moment, Noah is quick to resume one of his self-stim nonactivities—lying down on the couch, pouncing about the room, bouncing in his crib upstairs. And one of us duly admonishes and chastises him for it with a, "No. Stop it."

Since we are a rice-eating family, at dinner we do with rice as we did with bread at breakfast, withhold it until Noah has eaten his fill of the protein course. Then we all sit down and join him. Afterward, I generally play with Karl, always, though, looking over at Noah from time to time, playing with his Slinky or draped over a chair, until he seems to indicate that he might be in the market for a bowel movement. There are no sure signs, only vague indications—a move toward the stairs, a withdrawal into a corner, a downward tug at his pants. I then take him to the bathroom. We're successful about half of the time. The rest is clean-up time.

Next comes his bath, a change into p.j.'s, a decent wait, a final urination. And then bed. He climbs into his crib in a ritualistic sort of a way, first walking around it, pushing the chair that is his step away from it, ducking through the chair frame from the inside, and finally climbing up and in. We still keep him in a crib because it means smaller sheets to clean and has a waterproof mattress. The chances that he will wet during the night keep diminishing but are still present.

Lately, he sleeps the night through— without bedwetting—about 75 percent of the time. We're greatly appreciative of the change.

Gradually, I would say, we tend to ignore Noah more and more as the afternoon wears on. He drains a great deal of energy without recharging us as battery sources by means of the simple gestures of reciprocity—what the psychologists call "feedback." Noah appreciates affection, is all cuddly, but he never seems to initiate a hug or impulsively lavish a kiss. Foumi claims he sometimes comes over to her and presses his lips against hers. And at times he does the same thing to me. But I'm convinced he's considering more a bite than a kiss on those occasions—and sometimes I have the tooth nibble marks to prove it.

May 29, 1971

Foumi and I, after much discussion,

22. Days of Anguish

have laid down two basic ground rules about Noah. 1. We will go only to places we want to go to anyway in order to find better treatment for him. 2. We will not alter our lives, or life style, because of him alone; it is too great a load to place on his slender person.

June 2, 1971

Tonight for the first time Noah, receiving lavish praise every step of the way, got into the bathtub by himself—and stayed there. Until now one of us has had to get into the tub with him. And we often wondered what would happen when he became too big for that. Hopefully, that worry may now be over.

June 21, 1971

The picnic season continues. We went to one yesterday, and many friends whom we hadn't seen in a long time were amazed at the changes in Noah—and us. We could leave him alone, did not have to worry about his wetting himself; we could be loose. Indeed, someone remarked how wonderful it was that we could be so relaxed with a child like Noah. "That's because," said Foumi, "since California we know what to do."

June 23, 1971

We saw the vitamin doctor, and he noticed a marked improvement in Noah. And whether the improvement is attributable to the vitamins, or to operant conditioning, or to the natural course of maturation, or to a combination of these factors, the doctor did not care. "What matters is that Noah is more responsive."

July 1, 1971

It wasn't until after I dropped him off at his school's summer camp this morning that I realized today was Noah's birthday. Five years old. And I thought back to the hot day of his birth and wondered where the five years had gone, how quickly they all seemed to have passed—just like with any other kid.

And Noah is so funny now about going to his room and getting into bed at sleep time. When we tell him to do so, he does so, but his evasive acts, delaying tactics—such as going to the bathroom, pulling a paper cup out of the dispenser, and holding it against the cold-water tap—are just like those of any other kid.

But now finally he and Karl are off to sleep. The house is quiet. Foumi's put a pie into the oven, and now she's at her desk writing—lately she's begun a new sideline career, having published two articles in two of Japan's leading magazines. And I've just gone to the bookcase to check on that first sentence of Tolstoy's, and come away shaking my head. "Happy families," I know, "are *not* all alike."

Editor's note:
Eleven months later. Noah has progressed, slowly. He can match shapes, build blocks, hold a pencil correctly; but, says his father, "You always have to push him. He won't initiate any action." Karl realizes that Noah holds him back a little. He sometimes asks "Why don't we put Noah in an institution?" then backs down when his parents call his bluff. But the Greenfelds will probably institutionalize Noah eventually. They are currently looking for a school that will accept him on a permanent basis. "One can dream," says Greenfeld, "but one has to prepare realistically for the future."

AUTISM

The history of Autism is looked at along with a prospectus on the course and current methodology, research and diagnosis.

For more information about this book and other materials in special education, contact Joseph Logan, Editor, Special Learning Corporation.

Special Learning Corporation
42 Boston Post Rd. Guilford, Connecticut 06437   (203) 453-6525

Does Your Quirk Irk You...
and others, too?

NEAL ASHBY
Neal Ashby, who writes often on medical and psychological problems, didn't think he had any idiosyncracies—until he started researching this article.

During the 50's, a New York City drama critic managed to circulate about town without ever punching an elevator button with his bare finger. When not wearing gloves, he accomplished the job with a stiff piece of rolled up newspaper. Another idiosyncracy was his daily mail retrieval system: He'd stop at the office and stand before his secretary's desk with an open magazine into which she was required to drop the day's correspondence. According to some acquaintances, the critic also had the unpleasant habit of reprimanding all those who coughed or sneezed in his presence. Despite these quirks, he was considered quite normal. He had many friends (who judiciously avoided him when they had colds), and his work was respected.

Although it is very difficult for us to define "normal" behavior, we often have a quick sense of what is "abnormal" about the people around us. Sometimes, too quick. In fact, our unprofessional judgments are frequently unfair. Everyone, after all, has peculiarities that one person defines as extremely abnormal, which another sees as endearingly eccentric. Was the drama critic emotionally disturbed or just strange? How can we tell the difference? Can we help ourselves and those close to us understand the motivations behind "unusual" behavior? And when should we consider seeking or suggesting professional help?

This month FAMILY HEALTH has sought the assistance of two psychiatrists, Dr. Arthur Zitrin, professor of psychiatry at New York University, and Dr. Dominick Calobrisi, chief of psychiatry at St. Francis Hospital in Roslyn, New York, and of two clinical psychologists, Lewis Bernstein, PhD, professor at Wisconsin Medical College in Milwaukee, and Bonnie Jacobson, PhD, associate director of the Park East Psychological Associates in Manhattan, in order to present a compendium of some of the most common behavioral quirks. With each example, our panel of experts has offered guidelines for understanding and judging when a minor disturbance in behavior might be signaling a deeper psychological problem that requires professional attention.

Phobias

"Bacteriophobia" is the word psychiatrists use to describe our drama critic's dread of germs. As defined by Dr. Zitrin, phobias are "exaggerated fears for which there is usually little realistic basis." Common phobias include fear of heights (acrophobia), fear of closed spaces (claustrophobia), and fear of open spaces (agrophobia). But obsessive fear can become attached to almost any object or condition—pain, blood, cancer, death, snakes, insects, foreigners, fire and flying—and achieve phobic proportions.

Where do such fears originate? Our panel tells us that phobias are generally related to other psychological problems, often an anxiety that is too difficult to face. The drama critic's fear of disease, which reached such dimensions that his peculiar behavior left a trail of jokes behind it, was really a disguised anxiety about failing at his work. It was easier for him to worry about some outside threat than to face his insecurities about his qualifications.

Other phobias, those triggered by an accumulation of temporary anxieties, are less deeply ingrained and tend to pass once the pressures responsible for them have lifted. Dr. Bernstein recalls a patient, Susan Slater, who developed a driving phobia following two minor accidents. Although most of us would return to the wheel and, after a period of caution, become ourselves again, Susan shunned driving, despite her acute dependence on a car for transportation. Dr. Bernstein attributed this phobia to displaced feelings from two other anxieties plaguing her at the time: Her parents were unemployed and unable to pay her college tuition, and her boyfriend had recently transferred to a different school. Instead of facing and dealing with these unpleasant realities, she subconsciously chose to fret over the possibility of being hurt in another accident. That fear was a more controllable focus for her sense of impending doom.

According to Dr. Jacobson, phobias that develop after a traumatic incident —such as a fear of dogs after a vicious attack and claustrophobia after being trapped in an elevator for eight hours— frequently clear up on their own. Why? Because, unlike the obsessive fears of the drama critic and Susan Slater, they are not surface cover-ups for deeper psychological upsets.

When trying to determine whether professional help is needed in order to cope with a particular phobia, ask yourself just how badly the fear impairs an individual's functioning. How much distress does it cause the sufferer and those around him? Clearly, if a person has a phobia about public speaking, but is never called upon to do it, he'll do quite well without any therapeutic attention.

Compulsions

A young accountant, tortured by jokes about his uptightness, asks, "Just because I return things after borrowing them, keep my checkbook balanced and review my appointments calendar each evening, does that mean I'm uptight?" Since he also looks as neat as a pin and always likes everything in his life arranged just so, most people, to his dismay, think he is.

Behavior that not so many years ago might have been called "meticulous," "fastidious" or "conscientious" is nowadays apt to be labeled "compulsive." Is everyone who keeps a clean desk and follows the rules a true compulsive? Obviously not. Some of these habits clearly help us organize our lives. But if you constantly pack, unpack and repack your suitcases in pursuit of some "forgotten" item, you've ventured beyond mere organization.

Compulsive behavior of both the benign and malignant varieties is a way of exercising control. According to Dr. Bernstein, who calls it "a form of mental bookkeeping," compulsive actions usually coincide with obsessive thoughts. The classic example is Lady Macbeth's constant hand-washing, a reflection of the clawing guilt she felt about her part in the plot to kill King Duncan. Of course, your own obsession may be less dramatic in nature: You may fret about your image, your comfort or your fear of failure.

Adjusting to a spouse's or co-worker's compulsive behavior is a generous act—up to a point. That point is passed when idiosyncracies become so intense that they permeate every aspect of the person's existence as well as that of everyone with whom he comes in contact. Because compulsions are usually accompanied by inhibitions and an inability to relax, they may well sap the pleasure from life. When this happens, help is needed.

Overtalkativeness

"Once I had two patients—a husband and a wife—who both talked incessantly," says Dr. Jacobson. "When friends tried to interrupt, they would respond with a perfunctory, 'Oh really?'—and then rush on with their own opinions and stories. Both of them were plagued with self-doubts, one professionally, the other as a parent. Their young daughter was hyperactive —an emotional condition that I believe was aggravated by the atmosphere the parents created at home. In turn, the youngster's hyperactivity presented her parents with another problem to worry about, and this only increased their chatter. It was a nasty cycle."

Talking too much, a compulsion that rates a category of its own, is one of the common ways we have of compensating for feelings of low self-esteem. Who hasn't experienced that inner sagging as he realizes, say, in an important meeting with the boss, that the rapid motion of his jawbone is digging him deeper and deeper into the ditch? Unfortunately, for some people, constant chattering is a way of life. They think that if they speak in a domineering, commanding way, they will appear more knowledgeable and interesting—precisely the qualities they fear they lack. But such behavior usually has the opposite effect and forces people to keep their distance.

Not all overtalkativeness is compulsive. Sometimes, Dr. Bernstein points out, it is a symptom of manic behavior —behavior that is characterized by wide mood swings. Talking takes over when the manic individual's inhibitions have flown, and the spontaneous, aggressive portions of his psyche are suddenly let loose. A milder version of this phenomenon may take place with any of us when we are feeling "up" or energetic or determined to get things off our chests.

As for the compulsive talker, nothing would be more beneficial than to take him aside and let him know how his behavior affects you—that is, if you can get a word in edgewise.

Lying

The braggart who's always caught a bigger fish, the wife who continually fabricates tales of her husband's great devotion, the co-worker who, by his own account, always tells everyone off and never gets the short end of a verbal exchange are all compensating for intolerable feelings of inferiority or inadequacy. They are addicted to lying, another compulsion that reflects deep emotional insecurity.

If you care enough about the person who's plagued with this habit to try to help him face and break it, be tactful, considerate and careful in the way you bring the matter to his attention. Even the most aggressive quirks cover soft vulnerabilities.

Where To Get Help

Dr. Bonnie Jacobson, associate director of the Park East Psychological Associates in New York City, suggests four ways to find a mental health professional:
1) Ask your family doctor for advice. He's accustomed to referring patients to other specialists.
2) When seeking help for a child, consult the school psychologist, guidance counselor or principal for the name of a psychotherapist whose work and reputation is known to them. 3) Check your local mental health clinic, where social workers, psychologists and psychiatrists provide therapy at sliding-scale rates based on a family's income. These clinics are often associated with a hospital or fraternal organization. 4) Ask a friend who's been in therapy and whose judgment you trust. This is the way people usually choose a therapist, although it's not necessarily the best procedure.

"Psychotherapist" is the general term used to describe people who treat patients with emotional problems. Keep in mind, though, that some people who call themselves psychotherapists have no training whatsoever. In most states, the term "psychologist" is protected by law against such abuse and refers to an individual with a certain amount of advanced training. Requirements for licensing therapists vary from state to state and unfortunately some states have none at all. Try calling your local social service agency to find out exactly what qualifications your state law demands and whether or not the therapist you're considering is indeed licensed. In general, psychiatrists (who have medical degrees and are able to prescribe medicine), psychologists with PhD's and social workers with masters' degrees are better trained to handle patients than therapists with masters' degrees in fields such as counseling or psychology—but individual quality still varies greatly. Dr. Jacobson stresses that the most important criterion is how comfortable you feel with whomever you choose. "Have faith in your own judgment," she says, "and don't worry too much about labels. Because therapy is an intimate activity, you have to be able to trust your therapist—and you're the only judge of that."

3. METHODS

Seductiveness

"I have a male friend," says Dr. Jacobson, "who always manages to be coming out of the shower just when company—especially female company—is arriving. Of course, his route to the bedroom takes him through the living room where he stops to chat—a towel wrapped around his dripping body, his smile terribly engaging."

Seductiveness is usually manifested by emphasizing secondary sexual characteristics like breasts, voice and posture, and according to Dr. Calobrisi, it's symptomatic of "very low self-esteem and forever trying to be likeable." Yet, no matter how it's achieved, or what it's caused by, habitual seductiveness is one of the most infuriating, sometimes even dangerous, types of idiosyncratic behavior.

Some people are seductive with their dress—letting a skirt ride up enticingly on the thigh or wearing tight slacks and sweaters. So is talking in a come-hither voice or gazing piercingly into the eyes of someone of the opposite sex. Although Dr. Jacobson reports that seductive people sometimes do practice what they seem to preach, frequently such behavior actually masks a person's fear of sex. Unknowingly, the habitual flirt may be sending out a false signal—one that can lead to unpleasant encounters with spouses, friends of the same sex or over-excited "victims" who may be so frustrated by such teasing that they react violently.

Sometimes just pointing out a behavior pattern like this is enough to set the perpetrator on a reforming course. But if the habit is deeply ingrained, seduction addicts may require the self-awareness that comes with therapy before they can even recognize they're doing anything peculiar.

Forgetfulness

Dr. Bernstein recalls a patient who was incapable of remembering the names of people to whom she was introduced, especially at parties. "I don't even *hear* their names," she complained. Since her pattern of forgetting was so pervasive, it couldn't be attributed simply to her lack of interest or to her being overwhelmed by many new faces. His conclusion? She was so preoccupied with her own appearance and the kind of impression she was making that she was unable to concentrate on anything else.

It's natural to recall pleasure and forget pain. But sometimes forgetting goes beyond this simple formula and serves as an unconscious tool for avoiding unpleasant responsibilities. Thus: We forget dental appointments for fear of pain; we forget to take medicine because we won't admit we're sick; we forget to invite a friend to a party because we want him to feel slighted.

Memory improvement techniques alone cannot conquer chronic forgetfulness. The only true cure is to uncover the feelings that lie beneath the behavior—with one important exception. Dr. Bernstein points out that many of the really serious cases of forgetfulness he's encountered result from an organic dysfunction rather than an emotional disturbance. The aging process, for example, can take its toll on

> **Idiosyncracies have one thing in common: They enable us to minimize anxiety and achieve some sort of psychological balance.**

the brain's ability to remember. In these cases, patience coupled with an attempt to keep the elderly person physically and mentally active is the best policy.

Hypochondria

Feel that little lump on the thigh? Maybe it's cancer. What about that recurring headache? An incipient brain tumor, no doubt. Menstrual cramps got you down? Better stay home.

Although the hypochondriac really feels ill, and may even become ill as a result, persistent complaints and exaggeration of malaise do serve an emotional need. According to Dr. Bernstein, imaginary illnesses, like forgetfulness, not only exempt us from responsibilities we're afraid to face, but also elicit sympathy and protection instead of reprimands. However, most people find it extraordinarily difficult to deal with a hypochondriac. We don't want to appear unsympathetic (after all, even hypochondriacs get genuinely sick), but we never know what is a real illness and what isn't. Indeed, too much sympathy only encourages illnesses that are, in reality, no more than emotional escapes.

Severe hypochondriacs lead debilitated lives and they need psychological assistance if they are not to spend day after day in bed or at doctors' offices. Professional counseling can help them direct their energies away from their body parts and onto more constructive pursuits.

Withdrawal

When the great American author Henry David Thoreau went off to live at Walden Pond, he was indeed withdrawing—but not because of some inconquerable emotional upset. His excursion was merely the healthy activity of a man who enjoyed solitude. People like Thoreau, who enjoy reading, walking or just being by themselves, are certainly not mentally disturbed. But withdrawal that results from depression is quite another story.

Today, depression is the king of emotional disturbances, and withdrawal is one of its most serious manifestations. Although other symptoms include overeating, weeping, sluggishness and insomnia, withdrawal—especially when accompanied by drinking—sometimes precedes suicide.

Of course, there are exceptions to this rule. Deep personal losses—the death of a close relative or friend, for instance—are often accompanied by a natural mourning period. "But this kind of reaction should be self-limiting," says Dr. Bernstein. "We are low for a period of time, but soon our gloomy mood passes." Dr. Zitrin points out that depression and its accompanying symptoms, including withdrawal, are particularly common during critical life junctions—like adolescence, menopause and retirement.

What should we watch out for? Withdrawal that results not from a major external event (causing what psychologists call a *reactive* depression) but from feelings of worthlessness (endogenous depression, that is, coming from within). When someone is depressed for no apparent reason, he should not be left alone—and professional help should be encouraged.

What does it all mean? Simply that human beings are capable of bizarre patterns of behavior when they are under emotional strain. According to Dr. Zitrin, all these idiosyncracies have one thing in common: They enable us to minimize anxiety and achieve some sort of psychological equilibrium. However, the inevitable result is new disabilities and distresses. At some point—the dividing line is fine—the behavior quirks we've described begin to interfere so severely with normal functioning that psychotherapy of some kind is crucial.

Remember this: The truth really can set us free, even from the most deeply felt phobia. Whether it takes sharing the underlying problems with a friend or marriage partner or with a therapist, behavior can improve with self-knowledge, and old habits can be broken with effort and awareness.

THE TORTURE CURE

Winning criminal hearts and minds with drugs, scalpels, and sensory deprivation

Jessica Mitford

Jessica Mitford is the author of The Trial of Dr. Spock *and* The American Way of Death.

Philippe Weisbecker

RECOGNITION OF FAILURE dawns slowly in a bureaucracy but dawned it has in California prison treatment circles. Prison psychiatrists who are willing to level with reporters admit that they now spend 90 percent of their time on paperwork, writing up reports for the Adult Authority based on perfunctory annual interviews with prisoners, that "treatment" most often takes the form of heavy tranquilization of inmates labeled psychotic as well as those diagnosed as troublemakers. Group therapy, once hailed as an exciting new technique for transforming the "deviant personality," is withering on the vine. Nor have the treatment programs produced the anticipated docility in the convict population; work strikes, hunger strikes, and other forms of protest are now endemic throughout the California prisons.

Some disconcerting conclusions about the efficacy of treatment are set forth in a report to the State Assembly titled "The California Prison, Parole, and Probation System." It cites an exhaustive study conducted for the Department of Corrections in which the researchers observed gloomily, "Thousands of inmates and hundreds of staff members were participating in this program at a substantial cost to the Department of Corrections in time, effort, and money. Contrary to the expectations of the treatment theory, there were no significant differences in outcome for those in the various treatment programs or between the treatment groups and the control group." They further reported that group counseling did not lessen adherence to the inmate code, nor did it reduce the frequency of discipline problems.

James O. Robison, author of the report and longtime researcher for the Department of Corrections, traced the course of disillusionment. "The high mystique of treatment peaked at the end of the Fifties," he told me. "The idea took hold in Corrections that at last, through sophisticated techniques of psychotherapy, we have it in our power to transform the deviant and to predict with accuracy his future behavior. But in the early Sixties the high priests of Corrections began a sifting of the entrails. After that, disenchantment and embarrassment set in—the reason was the evident empirical failure of the treatment programs, as demonstrated by the recidivism rate remaining constant over the years.

3. METHODS

"The rationale for failure was always, 'We haven't carried treatment far enough, there isn't enough of it, it isn't professional enough'—in other words, we need more and better of same, in spite of the fact we've seen it doesn't work. Even this reasoning began to break down in the middle Sixties, when there was more attention paid to the fact nothing was happening and more talk of '*Why?*'

"What you are likely to see now is the end of the liberal treatment era—the notion that you can make convicts into converts of the dominant culture 'religion,' the missionary fervor—that's being replaced with 'behavior modification' experiments. The latest reasoning is that it's costly and inappropriate to go the psychotherapy route with these people, to pay high-priced psychiatrists to *talk* them into recognizing the truth of our 'religion'; instead, we'll focus on their deviant behavior and force them to shape up. Of course, this flies in the face of the earlier rhetoric. The Behaviorists say they are bad, not mad, and we can stop them being bad by utilizing new techniques. This fits in with the law-and-order, no-nonsense conservative viewpoint: henceforth the slogan will be, 'They must be *made* to behave.' "

This new trend in Corrections must be highly inspiriting for the behavioral scientists, who have long been eyeing the prisons as convenient reservoirs of human material on which to try out new theories. The shape of things to come was forecast a decade ago at a seminar of prison wardens and psychologists chaired by James V. Bennett, then director of the U.S. Bureau of Prisons. As described in *Corrective Psychiatry & Journal of Social Change*, Second Quarter, 1962, the seminar provided "provocative, fruitful interaction between social scientists and correctional administrators."

Addressing himself to the topic "Man Against Man: Brainwashing," Dr. Edgar H. Schein, associate professor of psychology at MIT, told the assembled wardens: "My basic argument is this: in order to produce marked change of behavior and/or attitude, it is necessary to weaken, undermine, or remove the supports to the old patterns of behavior and the old attitudes"; this can be done "either by removing the individual physically and preventing any communication with those whom he cares about, or by proving to him that those whom he respects are not worthy of it and, indeed, should be actively mistrusted."

Dr. Schein, who said he got most of his ideas from studying brainwashing techniques used by North Korean and Chinese Communists on GI prisoners of war, cautioned his audience not to be put off by this fact: "These same techniques in the service of different goals may be quite acceptable to us. . . . I would like to have you think of brainwashing not in terms of politics, ethics, and morals, but in terms of the deliberate changing of human behavior and attitudes by a group of men who have relatively complete control over the environment in which the captive population lives."

Some of the techniques which could usefully be applied in the U.S. prisons: "Social disorganization and the creation of mutual mistrust" achieved by "spying on the men and reporting back private material"; "tricking men into written statements" that are then shown to others, the objective being "to convince most men they could trust no one," "undermining ties to home by the systematic withholding of mail." The key factor is change of attitude: "Supports for old attitudes have to be undermined and destroyed if change is to take place. . . . Do we not feel it to be legitimate to destroy the emotional ties of one criminal to another, or of a criminal to a sick community?" How to bring about the desired change was explained by Dr. Schein: "If one wants to produce behavior inconsistent with the person's standards of conduct, first disorganize the group which supports those standards, then undermine his other emotional supports, then put him into a new and ambiguous situation for which the standards are unclear, and then put pressure on him. I leave it to you to judge whether there is any similarity between these events and those which occur in prisons when we teach prisoners 'to serve their own time' by moving them around and punishing clandestine group activity not sanctioned by the prison authorities."

The discussion, says the report, ranged from "specific, practical management issues such as 'How shall we manage the Muslims?' 'Whom should we isolate?' " to more basic questions, such as "the use and effectiveness of brainwashing and other means of persuasion." Dr. Bennett recalled that "during the war we struggled with the conscientious objectors —nonviolent coercionists—and believe me, that was really a problem . . . we were always trying to find some way in which we could change or manipulate their environment."

Much attention was focused on what to do about the Black Muslims: "not so much whether you take action against the Muslims as a group," as one speaker put it, "but how can you counteract the effects of the kinds of techniques they use to recruit members and cause general mischief in the prison system?" To which a Dr. Lowry responded, "We found that many of these Negro Muslims were highly intelligent . . . here again, we have to apply the techniques which we heard about in terms of appreciating what the goal of the Muslims is, or of any other group, and then doing some analytic study of the methods that they are using so that we can try to dissipate the forces that are going in the direction that we regard as destructive. "On ways of dealing with the unruly a panelist offered this: "To some extent where we formerly had isolation as a controlling technique, we now have drugs, so that drugs in a sense become a new kind of restraint. The restraint, therefore, is biochemical, but it is restraint nevertheless."

Summarizing the discussion, Dr. Bennett pointed out that the federal prison system, with some 24,000 men in it, presents "a tremendous opportunity to carry on some of the experimenting to which the various panelists have alluded." He added, "What I am hoping is that the audience here will believe that we here in Washington are anxious to have you undertake some of these things: do things perhaps on your own—undertake a little experiment of what you can do with the Muslims, what you can do with some of the sociopath individuals."

THAT DR. BENNETT'S counsel was taken to heart by his subordinates

24. The Torture Cure

in the federal prison system can be inferred from a report addressed to the United Nations Economic and Social Council, prepared and smuggled out of Marion Federal Penitentiary in July 1972, by the Federal Prisoners' Coalition, a group of convicts housed in the segregation unit for refusing to participate in the behavioral research programs. "In the latter part of 1968 some changes in the U.S. Department of Justice enabled the U.S. Bureau of Prisons to make a quiet beginning at implementing an experimental program at Marion Federal Prison to determine at first hand how effective a weapon brainwashing might be for the U.S. Department of Justice's future use," says the report. It describes how Dr. Martin Groder, prison psychiatrist, applies the proposals outlined in Dr. Schein's paper to "agitators," suspected militants, writ-writers, and other troublemakers. The first step, according to the report, is to sever the inmate's ties with his family by transferring him to some remote prison where they will be unable to visit him. There he is put in isolation, deprived of mail and other privileges, until he agrees to participate in Dr. Groder's Transactional Analysis program. If he succumbs, he will be moved to new living quarters where he will be surrounded by members of Dr. Groder's "prisoner thought-reform team," and subjected to intense group pressure. "His emotional, behavioral, and psychic characteristics are studied by the staff and demiprofessional prisoners to detect vulnerable points of entry to stage attack-sessions around. During these sessions, on a progressively intensified basis, he is shouted at, his fears played on, his sensitivities ridiculed, and concentrated efforts made to make him feel guilty for real or imagined characteristics or conduct.... Every effort is made to heighten his suggestibility and weaken his character structure so that his emotional responses and thought-flow will be brought under group and staff control as totally as possible.

"... It is also driven in to him that society, in the guise of its authorities, is looking out for his best interests and will help if he will only permit it to do so. Help him be 're-born' as a highly probable 'winner in the game of life,' is the way this comes across in the group's jargon." Once reborn as a winner, he will be moved into a plush living area equipped with stereo, tape recorders, typewriters, books. He is now ready to indoctrinate newcomers into the mysteries of the group "and like a good attack dog, he is graded and evaluated on his demonstrated capacity to go for the vulnerable points of any victim put before him." The entire program is made self-perpetuating and economically feasible by the participants doing the work themselves, says the report: "They are taught to police not only themselves but others, to inform on one another in acceptable fashion—as bringing out misconduct of another in a truth-session is not considered informing even if a staff member is present."

EVIDENTLY THESE TECHNIQUES are finding increasing favor with the federal prison administration. Scheduled to open early in 1974 near Butner, North Carolina, is a new federal institution, the Behavioral Research Center, built at a cost of $13.5 million, which, says a handout from the Bureau of Prisons, will be "a unique facility in the federal correctional system." Some of the unique features are spelled out in a confidential operations memorandum from the bureau to staff, dated October 25, 1972, on the subject of Project START, acronym for Special Treatment and Rehabilitative Training, already in operation in Springfield Federal Penitentiary. The goal, according to the memorandum, is "to develop behavioral attitudinal changes in offenders who have not adjusted satisfactorily to institutional settings" and to provide "care, custody, and correction of the long-term adult offender in a setting separated from his home institution." "Selection criteria" include: "will have shown repeated inability to adjust to regular institutional programs"; "will be transferred from the sending institution's segregation unit"; "generally, will have a minimum of two years remaining on his sentence"; "in terms of personality characteristics shall be aggressive, manipulative, resistive to authority, etc."

Dr. Martin Groder, who will direct the Butner operation, told Tom Wicker of the *New York Times* that he "believes in the possibility of rehabilitating prisoners" because he has done it, at Marion. He does not favor any large-scale return of incarcerated men to community programs; on the contrary, he prefers to keep them in his custody: "If we can get a top-notch rehabilitation program within the institution, a prisoner will be better off in it than wandering around the streets." Wicker reports that Dr. Groder is "not precise" about the rehabilitative methods he intends to apply, and that he is "cheerfully aware that the new federal center he will head is suspect in some circles —not least among federal prisoners, who are not anxious to be 'guinea pigs' in behavior research. He is nevertheless pressing ahead..."

A further elaboration on the brainwashing theme is furnished by James V. McConnell, professor of psychology at the University of Michigan, in an article in the May 1970 issue of *Psychology Today* titled "Criminals Can Be Brainwashed—Now." It reads like science fiction, the fantasy of a deranged scientist. Yet much of what Dr. McConnell proposes as appropriate therapy for tomorrow's lawbreaker is either already here or in the planning stages in many of the better financed prison systems.

Dr. McConnell, who spent many years successfully training flatworms to go in and out of mazes at his bidding by administering a series of painful electric shocks, now proposes to apply similar techniques to convicts: "I believe the day has come when we can combine sensory deprivation with drugs, hypnosis, and astute manipulation of reward and punishment to gain almost absolute control over an individual's behavior... We'd assume that a felony was clear evidence that the criminal had somehow acquired full-blown social neurosis and needed to be cured, not punished... We'd probably have to restructure his entire personality."

The exciting potential of sensory deprivation as a behavior modifier was revealed through an experiment in which students were paid $20 a day to live in tiny, solitary cubicles with nothing to do. The experiment was supposed to last at least six weeks, but none of the students could

3. METHODS

take it for more than a few days: "Many experienced vivid hallucinations—one student in particular insisted that a tiny spaceship had got into the chamber and was buzzing around shooting pellets at him." While they were in this condition, the experimenter fed the students propaganda messages: "No matter how poorly it was presented or how illogical it sounded, the propaganda had a marked effect on the students' attitudes—an effect that lasted for at least a year after they came out of the deprivation chambers."

Noting that "the legal and moral issues raised by such procedures are frighteningly complex," Dr. McConnell nevertheless handily disposes of them: "I don't believe the Constitution of the United States gives you the *right* to commit a crime if you want to; therefore, the Constitution does not guarantee you the right to maintain inviolable the personality forced on you in the first place—if and when the personality manifests strongly antisocial behavior."

The new behavioral control techniques, says Dr. McConnell, "make even the hydrogen bomb look like a child's toy, and, of course, they can be used for good or evil." But it will avail us nothing to "hide our collective heads in the sand and pretend that it can't happen here. Today's behavioral psychologists are the architects and engineers of the Brave New World."

For some convicts in California, those perceived as "dangerous," "revolutionary," or "uncooperative" by the authorities, it *has* happened here, and Dr. McConnell's Brave New World is their reality. Signposts in this bizarre terrain may need translation for the auslander:

Sensory Deprivation: Confinement (often for months or years) in the Adjustment Center, a prison-within-prison.

Stress Assessment: The prisoner lives in an open dormitory where it is expected he will suffer maximum irritation from the lack of privacy. He is assigned to the worst and most menial jobs. In compulsory group therapy sessions staff members deliberately bait the men and try to provoke conflicts among them. The idea is to see how much of this a person can stand without losing his temper.

Chemotherapy: The use of drugs (some still in the experimental stage) as "behavior modifiers," including antitestosterone hormones, which have the effect of chemically castrating the subject, and Prolixin, a form of tranquilizer with unpleasant and often dangerous side effects.

Aversion Therapy: The use of medical procedures that cause pain and fear to bring about the desired "behavior modification."

Neurosurgery: Cutting or burning out those portions of the brain believed to cause "aggressive behavior."

THE "BEHAVIOR MODIFICATION" programs are for the most part carried out in secret. They are not part of the guided tour for journalists and visitors, nor are outside physicians permitted to witness them. Occasionally word of these procedures leaks out, as in the autumn of 1970, when *Medical World News* ran an article titled "Scaring the Devil Out" about the use of the drug Anectine in "aversion therapy" in the California prisons.

Anectine, a derivative of the South American arrow-tip poison curare, is used medically in small doses as a muscle relaxant, but behavioral researchers discovered that when administered to unruly prisoners in massive amounts—from twenty to forty milligrams—it causes them to lose all control of voluntary muscles.

An unpublished account of the Anectine therapy program at Vacaville, California, by two of the staff researchers there, Arthur L. Mattocks, supervisor of the research unit, and Charles Jew, social research analyst, states that "the conceptual scheme was to develop a strong association between any violent or acting-out behavior and the drug Anectine and its frightful consequences," among which were "cessation of respiration for a period of approximately two minutes' duration." Of those selected to endure these consequences, "nearly all could be characterized as angry young men," say the authors. Some seem to have been made a good deal angrier by the experience, for the report notes that of sixty-four prisoners in the program "nine persons not only did not decrease but actually exhibited an increase in their overall number of disciplinary infractions."

According to Dr. Arthur Nugent, chief psychiatrist at Vacaville and an enthusiast for the drug, it induces "sensations of suffocation and drowning." The subject experiences feelings of deep horror and terror, "as though he were on the brink of death." While he is in this condition a therapist scolds him for his misdeeds and tells him to shape up or expect more of the same. Candidates for Anectine treatment were selected for a range of offenses: "frequent fights, verbal threatening, deviant sexual behavior, stealing, unresponsiveness to the group therapy programs." Dr. Nugent told the *San Francisco Chronicle*, "Even the toughest inmates have come to fear and hate the drug. I don't blame them, I wouldn't have one treatment myself for the world." Declaring he was anxious to continue the experiment, he added, "I'm at a loss as to why everybody's upset over this."

More upset was to follow a year later, when the press got wind of a letter from Director Raymond Procunier to the California Council on Criminal Justice requesting funding estimated at $48,000 for "neurosurgical treatment of violent inmates." The letter read, in part: "The problem of treating the aggressive, destructive inmate has long been a problem in all correctional systems. During recent years this problem has become particularly acute in the California Department of Corrections institutions . . . This letter of intent is to alert you to the development of a proposal to seek funding for a program involving a complex neurosurgical evaluation and treatment program for the violent inmate . . . surgical and diagnostic procedures would be performed to locate centers in the brain which may have been previously damaged and which could serve as the focus for episodes of violent behavior. If these areas were located and verified that they were indeed the source of aggressive behavior, neurosurgery would be performed . . ." Confronted by reporters with this letter, Laurence Bennett, head of the Department of Corrections Research Division, ex-

24. The Torture Cure

plained: "It is not a proposal, it's just an idea-concept." He added wistfully, "It's quite likely that we will not proceed with this, but if we had unlimited funds we would explore every opportunity to help anyone who wants such assistance."

Although the plan for psychosurgery was halted—at least temporarily—by the newspaper uproar that ensued, the authorities have other methods at hand for controlling the unruly, principal among which is forced drugging of prisoners. In widespread use throughout the nation's prisons is the drug Prolixin, a powerful tranquilizer derived from phenothiazine, which, if given in large doses, produces dangerous and often irreversible side effects. A petition addressed to the California Senate Committee on Penal Institutions by La Raza Unida, a Chicano organization of prisoners confined in the California Men's Colony, describes these: "The simple fact that a number of prisoners are walking the yard in this institution like somnambulists, robots, and vegetables as a result of this drug should be reason enough to make people apprehensive as to the effect it is having. That no prisoner feels safe because he never knows when he will become a candidate for said drug is another factor in producing tension in this institution."

According to its manufacturer, E. R. Squibb, Prolixin is "a highly potent behavior modifier with a markedly extended duration of effect." Possible adverse side effects listed by Squibb include: the induction of a "catatonic-like state," nausea, loss of appetite, headache, constipation, blurred vision, glaucoma, bladder paralysis, impotency, liver damage, hypotension severe enough to cause fatal cardiac arrest, and cerebral edema. Furthermore, Squibb cautions that "a persistent pseudo-parkinsonian [palsy-like] syndrome may develop . . . characterized by rhythmic, stereotyped dyskinetic involuntary movements . . . resembling the facial grimaces of encephalitis . . . The symptoms persist after drug withdrawal, and in some patients appear to be irreversible."

THE THEME OF PRISON as a happy hunting ground for the researcher is very big in current penological literature. In *I Chose Prison*, James V. Bennett poses the question, What will the prisons of 2000 A.D. be like? And answers it: "In my judgment the prison system will increasingly be valued, and used, as a laboratory and workshop of social change." Dr. Karl Menninger echoes this thought in *The Crime of Punishment*: "About all this [causes of crime], we need more information, more research, more experimental data. That research is the basis for scientific progress, no one any more disputes . . . Even our present prisons, bad as many of them are, could be extensively used as laboratories for the study of many of the unsolved problems."

Taking these injunctions to heart, researchers are descending in droves upon the prisons with their prediction tables, expectancy scales, data analysis charts. With all the new money available under federal crime control programs, and the ingenuity of grant-happy researchers, the scope of the investigations seems limitless. In California some $600,000 of the Department of Corrections budget is earmarked for research, but this is just the tip of the iceberg, for most of the work is done under lavish grants from universities, foundations, and government agencies.

Something of the quality of the research, and the bitter irony of the situation in which the convict-research subject finds himself, can be inferred from the stream of monographs, research reviews, and reports that flow out of the prisons. His captors having arranged life for the prisoner so that he becomes enraged, perhaps goes mad, and (no matter what his original sexual preferences) turns homosexual, they invite researchers to put him under their microscopes and study the result. A forty-eight-page monograph titled "Homosexuality in Prisons," published in February 1972 by the Law Enforcement Assistance Administration, reports, "in view of methodological difficulties, the following estimates of male homosexuality should be viewed with caution," and proceeds to give them, complete with footnotes referring the luckless reader to yet other publications on this subject. Estimates of the incidence of homosexuality given by experts vary, says the author, from 7 to 90 percent. He concludes, "There is above all a compelling need for a wide variety of comparative data," and proposes to fill the need by conducting "longitudinal or retrospective studies."

Among the offerings of the California Department of Corrections *Research Review* for 1971 is "The Self-Esteem Project," its aim "to obtain some picture of the effect of incarceration upon the perception of self-worth," in which the Modified Coopersmith Self-Esteem Scale is found to be "a useful instrument for measurement." Having subjected the inmate's self-esteem to the pulverizer of prison, the department proceeds to measure and tabulate what is left.

If the prisoner happens to be Chicano, he will be eligible for a study entitled "The Consequences of Familial Separation for Chicano Families," its purpose "to study the consequences of separation from family members for Chicano inmates and also for their families in terms of social, psychological, and economic needs and stresses." Thus the precise quantity and quality of suffering, anxiety, and impoverishment of families caused by locking up Chicanos can be tidily computed and catalogued for the edification of social scientists. By now the prisoner may well be ready for the Buss Rating Scale of Hostility or the Multiple Affect Adjective Checklist, "a standardized and reliable rating instrument that can be scored for anxiety, depression, and, most importantly, hostility."

Omitted from the 1971 *Research Review* is one of the more ambitious experimental projects of that year: establishment of a Maximum Psychiatric Diagnostic Unit (MPDU) designed to hold eighty-four convicts (a number possibly chosen in subconscious tribute to George Orwell) selected as research subjects from the 700 inmates of the state's Adjustment Centers. The goal of MPDU, as defined in the department's grant application to the California Council on Criminal Justice, is "to provide highly specialized diagnostic service for Adjustment Center inmates who are violently acting-out and management problem cases within the California prison system . . .

3. METHODS

and arriving at decisions as to the needed intervention and placement." The budget for this "service" would be approximately $500,000.

Who are the Adjustment Center inmates from whose ranks the eighty-four would be chosen? Robert E. Doran, who made a study of them under a grant from LEAA for the American Justice Institute, says they are "deviants within a society of deviants," or put another way, rebels who refuse to conform to prison life. They are younger and darker than the prison population as a whole: 61 percent are under thirty compared with 39 percent for the total prison population, 60 to 70 percent are black or Chicano compared with a nonwhite overall prison population of 45 percent. The majority are there for "disrespect for authority," disobeying some disciplinary rule—refusing to work, shave, attend group therapy; a growing number are there because they are suspected of harboring subversive beliefs.

IN 1972 TEN INMATES of Folson Prison filed a federal suit (unsuccessful), charging they had been kept in long-term solitary confinement because of their political views, and alleging that the practice is routinely used against prisoners who are outspoken about prison conditions or voice "militant" political views. Department spokesmen strenuously deny that they use lock-up in the Adjustment Center as punishment for political dissidents and leaders of ethnic groups. Philip Guthrie, press agent for the Department, told the *Sacramento Bee* on March 10, 1972: "We're very careful not to lock a guy up just because of his political views." But in their closed departmental meetings it is a different story. As reported in the confidential minutes of the wardens and superintendents meeting, October 11-12, 1972, under the topic "Inmate Alliances," Director Raymond Procunier "asked the problem be kept in perspective, comparing it to the Muslim situation ten years ago. The director suggested the leaders of the various groups be removed from the general population of the institutions and locked up."

Much has been written about the California Adjustment Centers, for it was in the exercise yard of "O-Wing," Soledad Adjustment Center, that three unarmed black convicts were shot to death by a guard in early 1970, triggering a series of events that culminated in the death of George Jackson, the trial of the surviving Soledad Brothers, and the trial of Angela Davis, all acquitted by juries. From three sources one can infer something about conditions of life in the Adjustment Centers, and the roots of violence therein.

Departmental memoranda to staff in charge of "O-Wing" contain these directives:

> *Yard Exercise: Two officers (one armed with a Gas Billy and one armed with Mace) will enter the tier to be released and, after subjecting each inmate to an unclothed body search, release him from his cell, by key, directing him to the yard.*
>
> *All inmates housed in "O-Wing" first tier, when escorted from the security section for any reason, are to be given an unclothed body search while still in their cells ... The inmate will be given a visual inspection of his body, to include his hair, ears, mouth, private parts and feet ... The inmate will be handcuffed behind his back and escorted from the section ...*
>
> *"O-Wing" Equipment: 1. Gas Billy (blast type). 2. Gas Billy Reload. 3. Triple Chaser Grenade. 4. Aerosol Mace (Mark IV Atomizer) ...*
>
> *Any inmate who self-mutilates or attempts to hang himself will be housed in the Hospital Annex cells only on the direction of the medical staff.*

Robert E. Doran describes what he learned about the guards' view of assignments to the Adjustment Center. "Those staff who have 'really been there,' experienced the trouble, used the gas, the batons, the weapons, and the muscle, and did so effectively, receive the highest status and deference from other custodial staff. . . . Staff battle ribbons and badges are won or lost within the A/C when trouble takes place. Actually the A/C, much like the general prison situation, has in terms of relative percentage of time, very little trouble. But it is the folklore, the beliefs and the history as passed from one generation of custodial personnel to the next that promulgates the idea that has grown up around the A/C which in effect says, 'This is the front line: here is where the battle is really won or lost for staff who wear the custodial uniform.'"

Testifying in San Francisco before a Congressional subcommittee, two lawyers related some exploits of these frontline heroes. Edwin T. Caldwell of San Francisco said, "I will testify for the record that I am a registered Republican from a conservative background. This is such a shocking thing for me I just can't believe it exists."

Caldwell told the committee his client in Soledad's "O-Wing" had been "viciously attacked" by guards on numerous occasions, and had suffered a fractured tooth, a broken jaw, and lacerations requiring six sutures. Fay Stender of Oakland handed the committee chairman a note signed by Lieutenant Flores, Adjustment Center guard, written in response to an inmate who was coughing blood and had asked for help. The note said: "Yell for help when the blood is an inch thick, all over the floor, and don't call before that."

DETAILS OF THE HIGHLY specialized services to be rendered the eighty-four chosen from this milieu, and the nature of the needed intervention, were discussed at a "think session" called in November 1971 at the University of California at Davis by Laurence Bennett, head of the Department of Corrections Research Division. Participants were some twenty-five representatives of the healing professions—medicine, psychology, psychiatry—many of them faculty members from nearby universities and medical schools.

The new unit, said Max May, program administrator, would be closely modeled after Patuxent Institution in Maryland, with four twenty-one-man cellblocks, "single five-by-seven-foot cells with bars, only we call them barriers." Construction costs would be kept to a minimum since the prisoners were to build their own cages, the work, according to the grant application, consisting "primarily of pouring two concrete floors, erecting wire screen partitions, also a gun tower."

24. The Torture Cure

The objective, said Bennett, is "to develop a basic knowledge of the causes of aggressive, violent behavior. Our aim is to learn how to identify small groups, how to deal with them more adequately. We hope through psychological management to learn how to lessen their violence potential."

Discussion from the floor, and at the pleasant luncheon gathering in the faculty club dining room, centered on methods by which this might be accomplished: "We need to find the stimulus to which the subject responds. We also need to find out how he thinks *covertly* and to change how he thinks." "We need to dope up many of these men in order to calm them down to the point that they are accessible to treatment." "Those who can't be controlled by drugs are candidates for the implantation of subcortical electrodes [electrodes plunged deep into the brain]."

Dr. Keith Brody of Stanford University, who said he runs a "unit for mood disorders," stressed the importance of "intensive data collection" via spinal taps and other tests: "These tests can lead to therapy decisions. We need to segregate out and dissect out these sub-groups." Other proposals for therapy were to burn out electrically those areas of the brain believed to be the "source of aggressive behavior"—one speaker said he reckoned about 10 percent of the inmates might be candidates for this treatment; the administration of antitestosterone hormones, which have the effect of emasculating the subject; the use of pneumo-encephalograms (injecting air into the brain cavities).

Asked whether the Anectine torture "therapy" would be resumed in the new unit, Bennett did not answer directly but declared with some exasperation, "If it could be shown empirically that hitting an inmate on the head with a hammer would cure him, I'd do it. You talk about his civil rights—civil rights for what? To continue to disrupt society?" Nor would he answer the further questions: "Does not the prison system itself, and particularly the Adjustment Center, generate violence?" and "Would the researchers be directing any part of their inquiry to violence by guards against prisoners?"

As for the compliant participation of the distinguished group of faculty members in this bizarre discussion, one possible explanation was suggested by the lone black psychiatrist present, Dr. Wendell Lipscomb, who had stormed out of the meeting halfway through, declaring he "couldn't take any more of this crap." Later, he told me, "What you were seeing at that meeting were the grant hunters, hungry for money, willing to eat any shit that's put before them."

MENTAL RETARDATION

Designed specifically for the course of study known as Exceptional Children or Mental Retardation. It is excellent for students and teachers who plan to work with the educable, moderate and severely retarded.

For more information about this book and other materials in special education, contact Joseph Logan, Editor, Special Learning Corporation.

Special Learning Corporation
42 Boston Post Rd. Guilford, Connecticut 06437   (203) 453-6525

Behavioral training strategies in sheltered workshops for the severely developmentally disabled

Paul Wehman
Adelle Renzaglia
Richard Schutz

This paper is a behavioral analysis of learning and behavior problems which may be expected of severely developmentally disabled persons in vocational settings. The behavioral analysis includes three major sections: (1) a categorization and description of primary problems encountered by a severely handicapped population, (2) a logically arranged hierarchy of behavioral procedures which can be used to treat different types of problems, and (3) a general set of management strategies. It is recommended that the hierarchy of behavioral procedures be empirically validated.

In recent years, applied behavior analysis is one training methodology which has been used successfully in the amelioration of emotional and learning handicaps found in several deviant populations (e.g., Haring & Brown, 1976). Behavioral training techniques have also been effective in training complex assembly skills in moderately, severely, and profoundly retarded adolescents and adults (Bellamy, Peterson, & Close, 1975; Crosson, 1969; Gold, 1972; Hunter & Bellamy, 1976).

Much of the vocational research and programs with the severely developmentally disabled has been directed toward instructional strategies to facilitate the acquisition of complex manual tasks. Basic tenets of discrimination learning (Gold & Scott, 1971; Zeaman & House, 1963) and task analytic skill sequencing have been used when difficult job skills are required (Crosson, 1969).

Although research completed on acquisition of complex tasks, such as assembling cable harnesses, drill presses, or bicycle brakes, has demonstrated that the severely handicapped can learn if material is presented in a logically arranged sequence, relatively few efforts have been directed toward developing innovative techniques and strategies for accelerating work performance. Typically, efforts at increasing production have included some manipulation of reinforcement contingencies (Brown & Pearce, 1970; Schroeder, 1972). However, other behavioral treatment practices have not received attention by researchers in vocational programming for the severely retarded. This paper provides a behavioral analysis of work problems which may be expected of severely developmentally disabled clients, and identifies and discusses a logically arranged sequence of behavioral procedures available to overcome specific vocational problems.

25. Behavioral Training

"On a pantry wall, there is a little slogan taped up, saying, 'How come you've never spoken before?' 'How come you've never asked?'"

* * *

In the pantry of the John Collier House on 16th Street, there is a little inspirational slogan taped up. It says:

"How come you've never spoken before?"
"How come you've never asked?"

* * *

Close eases the car off the McKenzie highway into the gravel parking lot where the group hike set out that July Sunday. A hundred feet behind is the bridge where John Collier died. The puzzle is why John perished and Jim survived. John Collier was the star performer of the group. From the first day he came to 16th Street, John Collier discovered that he wouldn't be allowed to curl up in front of a TV until he died. He became the tester of new programs, the pioneer of skills. "This guy had it all together," Close remembers. "He walked with a normal gait. He rode the bus alone. He was the first graduate of the travel training program. He walked to work by himself for seven months. He had the best verbal skills. He learned the tasks faster than anyone else." Of all the group, John Collier had the most experience with traffic; yet he apparently walked out into the middle of a busy highway.

The survivor, Jim Clay, was one of the slowest in the group, a man with virtually no language who would be unable to cross Eugene on his own.

Nearly everything between the moment of Jim's disappearance and the moment of his rescue is assumption, says Close. Some of those connected with the group home don't even think it is right to speculate on what happened in between or why. But the riddle teases the mind.

Close sees all behavior as a matter of cues. The job in teaching a skill is to break it down into its component cues. The last known cue the two men received that July was verbal. The group had hiked along the river trail and then cut back to the highway opposite the ranger station. Half the group had already crossed the road when a staff member became involved in untangling Barry's zipper. John and Jim were standing behind her when she said, "Go see Paulette. We're going home."

When she looked up, John and Jim were gone, and she assumed they had crossed over to where Paulette had parked the station wagon. Instead, the two had disappeared back down the trail they had just hiked.

Close is sure it was John Collier who led the way. "No one knows what he processed," says Close, but he believes that somehow John was convinced that he had fallen behind the hike and was trying to catch up. The logical way to go "home" is to go back the way you came. Whatever the cue, John covered the four miles back to the starting place at top speed. He was run down an hour and 20 minutes after he left the ranger station.

Retracing his steps was no small achievement. Close pulls an orange poncho over his head and plunges down the narrow track from the parking lot to the river trail. In the summer, the underbrush would have been heavier, says Close, and the trail even harder to follow. At the junction with the river trail stands a marker post. In the first sweep down the trail after John, Close himself had missed the turnoff and had walked 100 yards past it before realizing his mistake. But John Collier must have found it the first time in his rush to his fate.

Under the great canopy of the Douglas firs, the October rains stop. Close strips off the poncho and looks back down the river trail. For some reason, Jim did not follow John Collier. Probably he fell behind and after passing several inviting cross trails and side roads, Jim turned left on a rutted road and crossed the river where he encountered the boy. In his fright, Jim followed a power-line cut up a steep ridge and then picked up the ridge trail. That trail led to the cabin where he was found all those days later. Incredible luck or instinct?

Jim could not tell his rescuers how he survived. Close has a few good guesses and many blanks. For one thing, says Close, the July skies clouded over, reducing the risk of heat prostration. Then Jim probably has no clear concept of a personal death. For Jim, danger is an immediate and direct threat such as a verbal challenge from a strange boy. But once Jim ran off into the deep woods, he was blissfully unaware of his very real danger. Panic is the greatest danger in getting lost. Aside from the weight loss, Jim was in fine condition when he was found. His clothes were untorn and clean. He wasn't covered with scratches and bruises. He didn't look like a man who had been running about in a panicked frenzy. He looked like a man who had kept calm, found shelter, saved his energy and waited in one place for rescue. It was almost textbook survival technique.

Yet the blanks resist simple explanation. In teaching behavior at the group home, cues are made specific and uniform. Generalized or vague cues only confuse the folks. Close feels that is might have been the vagueness of the instruction "We're going home," and the lack of a clear physical prompt such as pointing that set John Collier off on his fatal walk.

In surviving, Jim performed skills he had never been directly taught. He selected a good path and then recognized shelter. He carried stream water back to the cabin in a jar. The water jar is a prime puzzler. Jim had filled plastic water jugs at the group home from a tap, but the connection between water from a running stream and water from a tap was his own discovery.

The river roars in the distance. Close starts back to the car. Up until the moment he lost John Collier on the trail, Jim's every waking moment had been programmed, the cues selected and presented in a uniform fashion. Then for seven days, Jim Clay ran his own life. "When he lost our cues, he found his own," says Close.

3. METHODS
PRESENTING PROBLEMS

Work behavior may be subdivided into learning a skill (acquisition), and then performing it accurately at a high enough rate (production) to meet competitive employment standards. These two processes can be analyzed more closely, however, through a specific description of the client's vocational behavior excesses or deficits.

Acquisition Problem—Discrimination Deficits

A problem typical of severely handicapped workshop clients is failure to attend to the salient cues (size, color, form) of a task. The person ignores relevant variables and instead may try to assemble or sort materials without watching what he or she does or while attending to the wrong cue in the task. As Gold (1973) notes, this is the main obstacle for the mentally retarded in acquiring complex manual skills. Gold (1972) has found that retarded people can master a difficult job at a rate similar to nonretarded peers when they attend to relevant dimensions.

Acquisition can also be impeded by a client's failure to attend to verbal cues of the supervisor. A common characteristic of severely handicapped adults is noncompliance behavior and inability or unwillingness to follow simple instructions. Even though a worker may attend to the learning task, his failure to follow instructions can interfere with acquisition rates, particularly if job requirements or materials vary slightly from day to day.

Acquisition Problem—Sensory-Motor Deficits

Many severely developmentally disabled persons receiving vocational programming services also display sensory-motor deficits. For instance, clients with cerebral palsy, loss of limb, and spasticity or athetosis may require prostheses or specially arranged environmental support.

Certain clients may be visually handicapped or hearing impaired, thus prohibiting the use of standard training procedures. The rare combination of both aural and visual handicaps in retarded workers is perhaps the most difficult disability to overcome for the acquisition of complex work skills. Yet some workers have found that such disabilities need not impede learning progress on difficult tasks such as bicycle brake assembly (Gold, 1976).

Low Production—Slow Motor Behavior

Once a vocational task is mastered, high rate performance becomes important. This is a serious problem with many severely and profoundly retarded workers, particularly those with a long history of institutionalization. Slow motor behavior is one characteristic of severely developmentally disabled workers who have not previously been required to meet a work criterion for success. Clients may be persistent and stay on task, but their actual motor movements are lethargic and at far too low a rate to be competitive (Hollis, 1967a, 1967b). Often such clients are unresponsive to the commonly used workshop incentives such as praise or money.

Without objectively established work criteria, it is difficult for workshop supervisors to determine which clients are performing competitively. Workers who stay on task and do not disrupt workshop routine are often viewed as performing adequately. This view is based on a popular vocational training model of "work activity" or "keep busy" rather than a developmental model which looks to expand the client's work skill repertoire.

Low Production—Interfering Behaviors

Equally problematic in accelerating production rates with the severely and profoundly retarded are interfering or competing behaviors, such as high levels of distractability and hyperactivity, out-of-seat behavior, excessive looking around, making bizarre noises, and playing with the task.

Similarly, the work performance of severely developmentally disabled clients may be highly susceptible to changes in the work environment. Fairly commonplace alterations in setting or routine, e.g., furniture rearrangement, can upset work behavior, thus making continuity of programming extremely difficult. A worker may display criterion-level work rates, but only for short periods of time. Interfering or competing behaviors interrupt the work level required for successful community placement.

SPECIFIC TRAINING TECHNIQUES FOR ALLEVIATING WORK PROBLEMS

To meet these various workshop problems with severely developmentally disabled clients, a logically arranged sequence of training and behavior management procedures is required. This section provides a hierarchy of techniques and guidelines for alleviating these workshop problems. Workshop staff members may draw on the techniques which are the most effective, the least time consuming, and the most economical. The sequence is affected by traditional methods of alleviating problems within the world of competitive employment. The less severe or more typical training and management procedures are listed as most desirable for use.

For example, giving a verbal reprimand would be preferred (Schutz, Wehman, Renzaglia, & Karan, in press) to using restraint if both procedures were equally effective in alleviating the problem. However, it may be necessary for a trainer to use his or her own discretion with each individual client in determining the most appropriate procedure. If a trainer has had previous experience with a particular client and has found that a verbal reprimand *increases* inappropriate behaviors (e.g., Madsen, Becker, Thomas, Koser, & Plager, 1970), it would be beneficial to begin with the next technique in the hierarchy to ensure success.

Table 1 contains a summary of the proposed hierarchy of training and behavior management procedures for ameliorating workshop problems. These are arranged for each problem area.

Acquisition Problem—Discrimination Deficits

The most frequently used training method in competitive employment is verbal instructions. Many times a new task will be presented with only a verbal explanation. Thus, this should logically be the initial method used to train a new task. If unsuccessful, a trainer must attempt to train a task through alternative methods.

Alternatives include verbal instructions paired with modeling of the correct movements (Bellamy et al., 1975; Clarke & Hermelin, 1955), priming the response, and physical guidance (Williams, 1967). Breaking a task down into small measurable components (task analysis) is also effective in aiding acquisition (Crosson, 1969; Gold, 1972), as is presenting learning material in an easy-to-hard sequence (Gold & Barclay, 1973; Irvin, 1976). For clients who fail to attend to relevant cues or task dimensions, cue redundancy, e.g., color-coded parts, facilitates acquisition (Gold, 1974).

Acquisition Problem—Sensory-Motor Deficits

In meeting the needs of clients with sensory-motor deficits, the trainer must first consider the clients' physical capacity. For clients with poor motor coordination due to cerebral palsy or loss of limb, the first four suggested strategies in the hierarchy do not differ from those used with clients whose acquisition problems are due to discrimination deficits. However, if the client's physical limitations are extensive, the arrangement of materials or the use of prosthetic devices such as specially designed jigs may be crucial in the acquisition of vocational skills (Hollis, 1967a). It may be necessary for a trainer to modify the task so that clients can complete a task with the least effort and most speed.

Low Production—Slow Motor Behavior

As clients become more proficient at performing a task, increasing the rate of production to competitive employment standards becomes a focal point. The severely developmentally disabled must produce at a competitive level to obtain and maintain community workshop employment. A verbal prompt to "work faster" appears to be the least time consuming and most efficient technique, providing that it is effective (Bellamy et al., 1975). Peer modeling (Brown & Pearce, 1970; Kazdin, 1973b; Kliebhahn, 1967) and trainer modeling have also increased production rate.

The manipulation of reinforcing events is another extensive area of possible techniques. Increasing reinforcer proximity, increasing the frequency or the amount of reinforcement, and increasing the number of redemptions of token reinforcers in a work period all are logical techniques for increasing production rates (e.g., Schroeder, 1972). Furthermore, our experience indicates that mixed schedules of reinforcement, such as continuous social reinforcement for each unit completed and penny or token reinforcement for every ten units completed, can be extremely effective in altering production rates with the severely handicapped (Wehman,

3. METHODS

Renzaglia, Schutz, & Karan, 1977). Intermittent schedules of reinforcement are a means of programming for response maintenance and approximating competitive employment work situations.

However, if the problem of low production rates still persists, it may be necessary to provide aversive consequences. Once a trainer has established a minimum criterion for production rate, the use of aversive consequences may be necessary. Implementing a verbal reprimand procedure and no reinforcement (Schutz, et al., in press), or a response cost procedure for low production, may be effective if used in conjunction with positive consequences for acceptable work rates. With an established minimum criterion for performance, an isolation-avoidance procedure may also be used successfully (Zimmerman, Overpeck, Eisenberg, & Garlick, 1969). (An isolation-avoidance procedure entails removing the client from the work area if a designated criterion is not met.)

Because low production is often a result of slow motor behavior, which is characteristic of the severely developmentally disabled, implementing a positive practice overcorrection procedure with the intent of teaching fast motor behavior is a feasible alternative (e.g., Rusch & Close, 1976). This procedure requires guiding the client through a task a number of times (so that it constitutes an extended duration) quickly, and therefore, teaching a client to move with speed. If positive practice is implemented, a trainer must take care to make the physical guidance sufficiently unpleasant that it is not socially reinforcing.

This procedure was recently applied to a profoundly handicapped adolescent who was performing at a very low production rate (Wehman, Schutz, Renzaglia, & Karan, 1977). When positive reinforcement for meeting criterion work levels was combined with positive practice, the trainee rapidly reached the target rate. In this situation, the client increased the rate of on-task behavior to avoid positive practice training.

Low Production—Interfering Behavior

Low production rate as a result of nonfunctional competing behavior poses a somewhat different problem. A trainer must not only increase a client's work rate, but also decrease or preferably eliminate the amount of time a client engages in the interfering behavior. Manipulating different parameters of reinforcement may also be effective here; unfortunately, little or no published research is available describing efforts to overcome excessive distractability by severely developmentally disabled clients in vocational settings.

To decrease many interfering behaviors, it may be necessary to implement aversive consequences. The use of response cost (Kazdin, 1973a), time-out (MacDonough & Forehand, 1973), restraint, and positive practice (Azrin, Gottlieb, Hughart, Wesolowski, & Rahn, 1975; Wehman, Schutz, Renzaglia, and Karan, 1977) procedures as immediate consequences for engaging in interfering behaviors may successfully decrease stereotypic behavior, aggression, out-of-seat behavior, and bizarre noises. These techniques have been effective with handicapped populations in different settings (Gardner, 1969), and should be seriously considered in workshops for the severely developmentally disabled.

GENERAL STRATEGIES FOR TREATMENT

To facilitate specific sequences of training and management techniques, a number of general strategies for treatment may be employed. The general intervention strategies discussed in this section include changing-criterion methodology, isolated treatment programs, and self-control strategies.

Changing-Criterion Design

A changing-criterion design may be used when work behaviors are gradually shaped to a competitive level (Axelrod, Hall, Weis, & Rohrer, 1974; Bates, Wehman, & Karan, 1977; Hartmann & Hall, 1976; Kazdin, 1975). Employing this design, a client must meet a minimum criterion or level for production rate to earn reinforcement. As a client's productivity consistently meets the criterion, the criterion is gradually increased or made more stringent. Thus, over time and with the use of effective behavior shaping methods, productivity may greatly increase from the initial criterion.

This design may be used with specific operant techniques to alleviate low production due to slow motor behavior or competing behaviors. In the case of low production behaviors, a changing time contingency may be introduced. This procedure requires setting a specific time limit for the completion of a task; it places the client under a time limit to receive reinforcement. A timing device, such as a kitchen timer or sports time-clock, may be used as a cue for the client and a subsequent indicator that a time limit was not met. As the client consistently meets the required time limit, the time allowed can be gradually decreased. This procedure has been successfully demonstrated and evaluated in a changing criterion design in a recent study performed with an institutionalized profoundly handicapped adult (Renzaglia, Wehman, Schutz, & Karan, 1977).

Isolated Treatment

Low production rates resulting from a client's excessive interfering behaviors poses a difficult remediation problem. Operant techniques employed within the work environment, such as manipulating different parameters of reinforcement, may not obtain successful results with particularly distractable or disruptive clients. With such clients, it may be advantageous to implement a treatment program in a relatively stimulus-free environment. Previously discussed training techniques may be enhanced by reducing the number of environmental cues to which a client might attend. As a client demonstrates increased on-task behavior, the treatment program may be gradually faded back into the work environment.

A general strategy of behavior control which may be used in an isolated treatment program is differential reinforcement of other behavior. With this approach, the trainee might be reinforced for instances of *not* being bad (Repp, Dietz, & Dietz, 1976; Wehman & Marchant, Note 1), for instances where he was performing only the appropriate behavior (Thomas, Becker, & Armstrong, 1968), or for low rates of responding (Dietz & Repp, 1973). Differential reinforcement is used in most training efforts when the trainee is taught fine discriminations and also in the reinforcement of high work rates. It is certainly not limited to an isolated treatment program. However, in an isolated, relatively stimulus-free environment, it may be easier to use differential reinforcement of the target behavior.

Self-Management Strategies

The operant techniques and procedures discussed thus far pertain to external control on the part of a significant change agent, such as a workshop supervisor. These techniques involve staff-administered contingencies; if relied on entirely, they present potential disadvantages to self-sufficient vocational behavior (Kazdin, 1973b).

One major problem is that an external control approach precludes the development of self-directed choice behaviors on the part of severely developmentally disabled clients. Many rehabilitation professionals recognize this deficit as a primary obstacle in the community transition process for these clients (Wehman, 1975). Secondly, an external control approach presents a number of inherent drawbacks. Since it is difficult to notice all instances of an appropriate response, a workshop supervisor or counselor usually misses many opportunities to reinforce a client. Furthermore, the change agent himself may become a cue for a behavior rather than a natural environmental stimulus (Redd & Birnbrauer, 1969). This drawback relates also to the problem of transfer of training and durability of program progress. Thus, whenever possible, external control must not be viewed as an end itself, but rather as a means to train a client to control his or her *own* behavior and achieve self-selected goals.

Self-control has been defined in reference to "those behaviors an individual deliberately undertakes to achieve self-selected outcomes" (Kazdin, 1975, p. 192). Self-control training procedures which are applicable to the severely developmentally disabled include self-observation, self-reinforcement, and stimulus control.

Self-observation has been successfully implemented with mentally retarded clients through the use of behavioral graphs (Jens & Shores, 1969) and daily feedback of work performance from a videotape (DeRoo & Haralson, 1971). With this procedure, a client is trained to become aware of his or her work performance through immediate external feedback and through a visual record of work behavior. Gradually a client's self-observation can be faded to pictures of improvement in work performance.

Self-reinforcement is another strategy which holds potential, particularly in

3. METHODS

workshops that use a token economy as a motivational system. Two concepts of self-reinforcement are self-administered reinforcement and self-determined reinforcement. An important requirement for both self-administered reinforcement and self-determined reinforcement is that the individual is free to reward himself at any time, whether or not he performs a particular response (Skinner, 1953).

Self-administered reinforcement refers to a client taking a reinforcer himself, but under an externally determined criterion. Once a client's self-administered reinforcement response is shaped, it is possible to move toward *self-determined reinforcement*. This broader concept of self-reinforcement allows clients to determine their own work criteria (e.g., Glynn, 1970). It may be possible for contingency contracts to be set up between clients and workshop supervisors. Within such a contract would be a set rate of work and social skills which a client agrees to perform. In return, he or she can self-select reinforcement preferences for performance of the contract.

How severely handicapped trainees can manage their own work behavior was illustrated recently (Wehman, Schutz, Bates, Renzaglia, & Karan, 1977). The workers' production rates were assessed under no reinforcement, externally administered reinforcement, and self-administered reinforcement, with pennies used as reinforcers. Treatment conditions were presented in a Latin Square sequence to control for order effects. Results indicated that through modeling and physical priming initially the trainee was able to reinforce himself and maintain a high level of production. Other research in workshop settings also supports the development of self-management skills in the severely handicapped (Helland, Paluck, & Klein, 1976; Nelson, Lipinski, & Black, in press).

Another self-control strategy which may be employed is stimulus control. *Stimulus control* refers to specific behaviors performed in the presence of specific stimuli which serve as cues and increase the probability that the behavior will be performed. For example, self-observation may function as a reinforcing consequence initially, but may also function as a discriminative stimulus for subsequent task-related behaviors.

Possible applications of the stimulus-control strategy, in workshops for the severely developmentally disabled, include altering stimuli which consistently lead to frustration-aggression situations, modifying cues that presumably contribute to task failure, or pairing positive stimuli with low preference tasks. Social behaviors such as eliciting social greetings, being on time, or appropriately using leisure time might also be developed through stimulus control.

CONCLUSION

This paper has attempted to provide direction in treatment strategies for workshop personnel who work with the severely developmentally disabled. It pointed out that a severely handicapped population presents a unique set of learning and behavior characteristics which can make traditional training and management techniques less applicable. It is strongly suggested that the hierarchy of strategies proposed for treatment be systematically examined with different learning/behavior problems to validate which methods are most effective with which workshop problems.

It should be apparent that the behavioral training and management procedures identified and sequenced in this paper can also be applied to behavior problems and deficits found in students or clients in other settings than workshops. It may be advantageous for parents, teachers, clinicians, and other practitioners to adopt a more planned approach to selection of behavior change procedures. Hopefully, the presentation in Table 1 takes one step toward a more systematic approach to ameliorating instructional and behavior problems in any setting.

25. Behavioral Training

STOP PUTTING UP WITH PUT-DOWNS

Tired of getting stepped on by other people? Sick of doing what others want instead of what you want? Perhaps you need a course in "assertive training."

Neal Ashby

To her great surprise, one day not long ago, Mary Ellen Flynn found herself confronting the man who supervises her work as a program specialist. At issue was the performance rating he had given her. Mary Ellen liked and respected her boss at the Office of Education, in the Department of Health, Education, and Welfare, in Washington, D.C., and it was only a question of two points on her rating. But she felt she deserved them.

"At one time," she says, her dark eyes sparkling, "I would have felt it picky to question him on it. Ungracious.

"But this time I just went to him and said, 'I'm not asking you to change this, but I'd like to discuss it with you.' I gave him my definition of the terms in the two categories that were involved. He gave his. I said another person might not agree with his interpretation, might see it differently."

Mary Ellen's supervisor seemed surprised by the confrontation. But he said she'd brought up some good points, and he'd think about it. "The next day," relates Mary Ellen, "the evaluation paper was back on my desk. The points had been changed in my favor."

Mary Ellen knew she was taking some risk in confronting her boss; he might have been angry with her, he could conceivably have fired her—but such drastic consequences among rational people are rare. Even if he *had* been angry, that's better than Mary Ellen's being angry with herself for not sticking up for what she thought was right. That line of thinking is the basis of a new form of behavior therapy called Assertive Training.

Assertive—also called Assertiveness or Assertion—Training is part of a larger therapeutic approach to problems in living, called Behavior Modification, which surfaced in psychological experiments some 30 years ago. "Behavior Mod" seeks to correct undesirable patterns of functioning in a pragmatic way, without attempting to get at any deep-seated psychological causes. In recent times, as its techniques have been refined and fairly widely employed, it has proved especially effective in dealing with problems of self-control, particularly in losing weight.

Accordingly, Assertive Training is based on the premise that inappropriate meekness is learned behavior. It can be unlearned, proponents say, by teaching its victims new skills for coping with intimidating situations.

The price of being meek is getting stuck with the unpleasant jobs, not getting paid what you deserve, being walked over by people (especially children and mates), being cut in front of in lines, being expected to do excessive favors for friends, doing what others want to do instead of what *you* want . . . the whole demeaning catalogue of "put-downs." The unassertive person also is likely to be slow to praise or to voice affection.

As far as assertiveness is concerned, "almost anyone could use a little more of it," believes Marsha Linehan, Ph.D., who directs the Assertive Training program at Washington D.C.'s Catholic University, where Mary Ellen Flynn trained. Women, especially, have been conditioned in our society to be docile, giving, submissive, to take a backseat to men—who at the same time have been programmed to be assertive and dominant, whether or not they have leadership qualities. (Indeed, a couple of husbands "wouldn't let" their wives attend the Catholic University sessions because the women would have been out at night.)

Still, there is enough of a spark left in many of the mild-mannered for them to reach out for help when it is offered. Some 350 women and men—ages 20-50, in a two-to-one-ratio—responded to Catholic University's announcement of 40 openings in its research-based program, one of the most advanced in the United States. There was a similar oversubscription to a companion program at the State University of New York at Stony Brook.

That same kind of broad-based response to training programs is occurring all across the nation. The training sessions are held in meeting halls, at medical centers and universities, or in the professionals' own offices, with fees ranging from gratis to $150.

"The reason there's so much interest in these programs is that people haven't known before that methods exist to *help* them," notes Marvin Goldfried, Ph.D., professor of psychology at Stony Brook and head of the program there. "They believed they were stuck with being naturally timid."

Mary Ellen Flynn proves the fallacy of that theory. "When push comes to shove," says the attractive young government worker, "I've never felt I have the right to assert myself with others, especially where it involves any evaluation of my performance. But since I participated in the training course, I've just felt freed."

Be persistent. Don't get upset about angry responses or hostility toward you—anger is the problem of the person feeling it, and that's not you.

That freedom extends to areas of her life other than work. There's a young fellow who, at this writing, appeals to her. But he's what she calls a dedicated "workaholic" who toils into the night at his own government job on Capitol Hill.

"For the first time," she says, "I stepped over the line. I drove over and walked into his office. I said, 'You're too much into work. How about our going out?' He said, 'Fine!' And I said, 'How about my calling now and then to see if we can do something?' He said 'Fine' to that.

"I'm not doing this to make a feminist point. I'm expressing a desire and need and watching how he responds. It's always been the male who risks rejection, so a girl has to be really together to do this kind of thing. I know I'm not going to be decimated if he says no."

That's really what Assertive Training is all about: working through the anxiety normally experienced at the thought of expressing wants and feelings boldly, and learning the corollary skills that enable one to speak out *effectively*.

Few people would argue with these aims, but there are opponents to Behavior Mod who say that the general theoretical approach fails to get at root causes and should never be employed in cases of serious mental disturbances or multiple neuroses. They say it may change behavior but at the same time mask significant symptoms and fail to make a troubled person truly feel better.

There is actually little in those fears to discourage Assertive Training proponents. In a recent issue of the *Health Science Review*, published by the University of Washington Health Sciences Center in Seattle, Charlotte Booth, an instructor in the center's Adult Development Program Assertiveness Training Laboratory, spoke to this point:

"The people who come to this lab," Ms. Booth said, "are students, not patients . . . here to learn, not be helped."

But Marilyn Kourilsky, Ph.D., professor of education at the University of California at Los Angeles, has further doubts.

"Behavior Mod, including rewards for certain types of behavior, does succeed in getting rid of unwanted behaviors but seems to take away some of the feeling that one is controlling one's own life. It seems to diminish initiative and creativity."

All this, of course, is a matter of professional opinion, and the majority of psychologists and psychiatrists acknowledge that behavior modification techniques often are the therapy-of-choice in strictly behavioral problems—such as the lack of assertiveness.

However individual programs are structured, the basic mechanics of Assertive Training are much the same from place to place. Part one calls for the subject to rethink his or her response to intimidating situations. Most find that they have been seeing threats where none exist, or at least exaggerating the dangers involved. Psychologists call such thinking "irrational self-statements," and they sound like this:

"The boss doesn't think much of me. If I go in and ask for a raise, he'll chew my head off. He might even fire me."

Or, "I can't tell my husband I don't want to go to his sister's house for dinner again this week; that I can't stand his sister or her husband and want to see as little of them as possible. He'll say I'm trying to keep him apart from his family. He'll be angry and won't be loving toward me."

Inside the unassertive person, images of these dire consequences create anxiety, dread, pain. Assertion is withheld, Dr. Goldfried notes, often creating negative feelings of anger and guilt. The person may now express his wants and feelings in annoying, unbecoming ways such as sulking, whining, weeping, or withdrawal.

But, the student learns, this emotional turmoil is actually unnecessary, precisely because the original fears—"He'll chew my head off," "He'll be angry"—were unrealistic. Everyone is entitled to state his wants and feelings. And most people, like Mary Ellen Flynn's boss, recognize that right. The compliant person's imaginings of consequences are usually exaggerated, too. In Assertive Training, he is made to consider: Would the boss really rant and rave? The husband reject the wife who spoke honestly? Probably not.

But—and this is perhaps the most crucial component—*even if they did, how awful could it be?* "We feel good about ourselves when we speak our minds," says Dr. Linehan. "Getting fired by an unreasonable boss might not be bad; you might get a much more agreeable job. And probably if you regularly speak honestly to your spouse, he'll accept it."

Being assertive, says Roberta Baer, psychology resident at Northwestern University in Evanston, Illinois, does mean "having to accept responsibility for your actions." Ms. Baer, who did her doctoral dissertation on the subject, goes on to say that, "if a person feels unprepared to cope with the consequences of a particular stance (i.e., losing her job), he or she may choose to say nothing. But knowing that you have a choice and can exercise it when you are ready is in itself a liberating experience."

"Most of all," stresses Dr. Linehan, "you'll still be a worthy person even if somebody does fire you or become angry."

Students are taught to be alert to the rise of anxiety and to recognize those mo-

3. METHODS

> Ironically, many who are submissive finally—after being frustrated repeatedly—explode into aggressiveness, and still their needs go unmet.

ments when fear might prevent them from acting in their own best interests. Sweating or "nervous stomach" may be indications. These are times to make an extra effort to relax, to be calm, and to think clearly.

OK. You acknowledge your rights, perceive the situation realistically, and suppress your anxiety. Now for part two—the specific skills of assertiveness. If you were actually in Assertive Training, you would now be taught to:

• *State directly what you want or don't want.* Assertive Training proponents believe that's more likely to lead to self-assurance and achieving of goals than are speeches about fairness and your hurt feelings. And don't be thrown off by the other person's rejection of your reason —that's his problem. As long as it makes sense to you, you've a right to take a stand. Christopher Storey, Ms. Booth's associate in Seattle, was most reassuring about this point in the *Health Science Review:* "What people don't realize," said Mr. Storey, "is that you don't always have to be rational, fair, or even know why you do something. You are your own judge and not wanting to do it is reason enough. So long as you are willing to pay the price and accept the responsibility for the consequences of what you choose to do or not to do, then you can control a situation."

• *Speak firmly and confidently.* Don't let a pleading, apologetic, or hesitant voice give the other person a chance to conclude that you don't really mean it. Nonverbal components of assertive behavior are also important in getting your message across, for example—tone of voice, body posture, or facial expressions.

Suzanne Bronheim, a therapist at Catholic University, tells of a woman client, one of many who presented problems involving their children. The woman says she now realizes that when she said "no" to her children, she was saying it in a way that told them, "I'm saying no, but if you whine enough, I'll give in." Says Ms. Bronheim, "A parent who is assertive not only does right by himself but also serves as a proper model for his child." But if at first you don't succeed . . .

• *Be persistent.* Repeat your statement. Don't get upset about angry responses or hostility toward you—anger is the problem of the person feeling it, and that's not you. Actor Tony Randall provides a good example of the hard line. "I don't let anyone smoke around me," he declares, "on the set, in the theater, anywhere. I think smoking is a killer, and I don't like the smell or anything about it. They think I'm a crank, but I just keep at it."

If persistence doesn't work, say something like, "You don't seem to be hearing me. I'm telling you . . ." to make sure the other person understands that you are in earnest and not likely to be brushed off. If that doesn't do it . . .

• *Spell out some consequences.* No vindictive threats, but perhaps, "Look, I feel that what I'm asking is reasonable, and I'm just not going to feel the same about you if you pay no attention." When it's a matter of basic rights, or imperative wants or needs, it may be in order to . . .

• *Demand what you want.* "I'm not going to argue; I insist that you . . ." Again, don't make overt threats, but do make it clear that you're very serious. Always keep in mind you should look the other person in the eye, stay relaxed, and don't fidget or wring your hands in distress.

So much for submissiveness. Now for the other extreme—aggressiveness. That's out. "Being aggressive gets us nowhere," says Dr. Linehan. "Others are turned off by that."

Ironically, many who are submissive finally—after being frustrated repeatedly—explode into aggressiveness, and still their needs go unmet. They overreact, scream, curse, and threaten, before receding back into meekness and further frustration. Dr. Goldfried relates an example. At a Broadway play recently, a man in the audience grew increasingly angry as another man, sitting in the row behind, continued to make audible comments about the action on stage. The offended patron said nothing—until intermission, when he suddenly rushed up to the talker in the crowded lobby and shouted:

"You've got a hell of a nerve disturbing all of us with that blabber!"

When the embarrassed talker defensively answered, "Why don't you mind your own business?" the objector pulled back his fist, and the two had to be separated by other patrons. The manager rushed over, glaring, and the objector's wife blurted:

"This is humiliating. We're going home!" A polite, whispered request for quiet in the beginning probably would have prevented the whole eruption.

One of therapist Bronheim's clients had the same kind of problem—at home. This woman's teenage son regularly stayed out late with the family car. "I was worried sick about it, and angry, too," she says. "But I'd think, 'If I say something, he'll think I'm horrible, and hate me.' Then after the seventh or eighth time, I'd explode in rage at him. *That* would make me feel worse.

"Now I'm able to say, 'Listen, I don't like this. It creates a lot of problems. Get in on time.' There's less tension in the house now. I feel better."

Logically enough, the assertive skills to counter aggressiveness include expressing views forthrightly, avoiding the antagonism, sarcasm, or coldness that will only incline the other person to dig in and fight back. Clenching fists, pounding tables, or otherwise signaling hostility are likewise ineffective maneuvers.

Perhaps the most important nonaggressive lesson taught is to avoid "shoulds." Don't rage inwardly because someone is not behaving the way he "should." Which of us can decree how another "should" perform? Instead, state the kind of treatment you expect: "I was here first; it's *my* turn"; "It's not fair for me always to be the one to pick up the tickets"; "I can't concentrate on my work with that music playing." The emphasis is on your expectations, not the other person's motives.

These principles are reinforced in several ways in training. One is the technique of role-playing, in which the therapist takes the part of the feared figure, perhaps an intimidating store clerk, and the trainee plays himself, trying to be properly assertive in saying boldly, "I find I don't like this sweater, and I want to return it and get my money back."

Other methods include those of feedback, in which the therapist evaluates the trainee's performance; and role reversal, which is much like role-playing, only in reverse: The trainee takes the part of, say, the hard-to-approach boss, and the therapist plays the employee asking for a raise. In this way, the trainee is able simultaneously to observe the correct assertive model for a particular situation and realistically gauge how the other person—in this case, the boss—would react. In another procedure, called modeling, the therapist may demonstrate how to respond to the recorded comments of a "difficult" person, which is especially helpful in situations where the client may not even recognize a put-down until it's too late.

Finally, there is practice. Lots of it. In class, with other clients, and in the outside world. It is important for the trainee to set simple goals for herself in the beginning, says Roberta Baer, so that she will meet with early successes. Confronting a co-worker, for example, or a supervisor from another division, rather than going directly to her boss, will enable her to practice the new behaviors with less initial anxiety and with less costly consequences should she fail at first.

In the Catholic University program, trainees are given five homework assignments each week. They must report back on how they fared in such real situations as:

• Asking for change for a $1 bill in a drugstore without buying anything.
• Asking a gas-station attendant to check the air in your tires without buying any gas. (One woman who did said, "He wasn't annoyed at all. I was kind of disappointed.")
• Requesting something that's not on the menu in a restaurant.
• Asking a co-worker to buy a newspaper for you while she's out to lunch.
• Disagreeing with someone's opinion.

One aspect of the training program at the Long Island Jewish Medical Center in New York is to encourage trainees to go back and try to correct situations in which they failed to be assertive. Go *back* to the store, or reopen the discussion.

Difficult as such assignments may seem to the uninitiated, there is evidence on all sides that Assertive Training does work. Roger Bartman, one of the therapists at Catholic University, reports that all eight of his clients say they're speaking up as never before.

One woman told Bartman that she used to dress in her finest to go shopping in a department store, in hopes the clerks would consider her someone of refinement and be nice to her. Now if they're not nice to her, she tells them they're being rude.

One of Ms. Bronheim's clients was irritated that her husband always planned the family's weekend activities. "One week," says the woman, "I said, 'Why don't we pack a lunch and go to the state park on Saturday?' My husband seemed surprised and said he'd already promised to take our son fishing. I kept at it, and the next couple of times he made excuses again. But last Wednesday after dinner he said, 'What do you think we should do this weekend?' "

Such victories may seem small, but in terms of the frustration and tension avoided and the endorsement of open communication, they add up, as the therapists themselves can testify. One of them, Gerry Paone of the Catholic University program, has been in a car pool with a friend who works with him at Spring Grove State Hospital, in Baltimore. On the friend's days to drive, he almost invariably was late to arrive, making Paone late to work.

"This is a friend, and I felt a lot of anxiety about talking to him about it," says Paone. "It's a 30-minute ride, and I was feeling a lot of turmoil. Here I was in an assertive situation myself. So I finally said to myself, 'What are the chances that he'll really get mad and not like me anymore?'

"So one day I told him, 'Gee, I'm really annoyed about your being late all the time. I hope you're not going to do it again.' He said, 'Yeah, I guess you're right. Sorry. I'll try to come earlier.' "

Dr. Linehan recently had a similarly assertive experience. A sister was in town for a visit, bought some clothes, decided she didn't really want them, and asked Dr. Linehan to return them to the store for her. Dr. Linehan started to comply, then thought, 'Why should *I*?' Her happy solution: "I'll come with you while you do it."

Naturally, all does not always go so smoothly in Assertive Training. Some clients "psych" themselves up nicely to speak out, then fall apart when they are met with back talk. Others can assert themselves in some situations, such as those involving strangers, but fail in confrontations with their husband or wife. The reverse is as frequently true. Some, in the beginning at least, insist that "I want to be nice, I would never say *that*." Or, "I'd feel silly." More often, nice gradually loses out to reasonable, and silly eventually becomes satisfied.

Still, Mary Ellen Flynn, whom we left feeling reasonable and satisfied in the beginning of this story, recently experienced a backfire. After she complained to her landlord about the constant loud noise in another apartment, the tenant in question stopped her on the street and proceeded to berate her loudly and embarrassingly.

"I stood there and took it," Mary Ellen said. "But I know I should have said, 'this is very unreasonable,' and walked away."

A setback? Maybe. But being able to view the situation objectively—even if belatedly—may be considered a victory in itself for the Assertive Training graduate. And one gets the distinct impression that the next time someone tries to embarrass Mary Ellen Flynn, it won't be so easy.

Autism: A Defeatable Horror

How Parents Can Treat Their Troubled Children

One theory of this rare but crushing condition blames parents, but the proof is thin. Here is a treatment—not a theory—that teaches parents to be effective therapists and lets them join the struggle to civilize their children, autistic or normal.

by Laura Schreibman and Robert L. Koegel

Laura Schreibman has been working with autistic children for eight years, six of them at the University of California, Los Angeles. She

earned her B.A., M.A. and Ph.D. in psychology from UCLA, and is currently assistant professor of psychology at Claremont Men's College. She has written numerous articles on childhood psychopathology, and serves as editorial consultant for several professional journals.

Robert L. Koegel also received his M.A. and Ph.D. in psychology from UCLA. Since 1971 he has been research psychologist at the Institute for Applied Behavioral Science and assistant professor of autism in the speech department at U.C., Santa Barbara.

The research reported in this article was funded by grants from the National Institute of Mental Health (awarded to Lovaas, Shreibman, and Koegel) and Title VI, B of Education for the Handicapped Act (awarded to the Santa Barbara County Schools).

BECAUSE IT STRIKES ONLY ONE CHILD out of 2,500, autism does not seem to be an alarming problem, at least statistically. But then, few children get hit by cars either. When autism does strike, the effects are dramatic and, until recently, tragically untreatable. In the past few years, however, we and other researchers have developed a successful new method of treating autistic children, using their own parents as therapists.

Without special training, parents of autistic children face a particularly depressing task (see "A Christmas Tree for Kristin," page 67). These children often throw violent, screaming tantrums. They may bite themselves or bang their heads against the furniture. Some must be physically restrained to prevent permanent injury. Autistic children may spend most of the day engaged in self-stimulatory behavior such as rocking back and forth, flapping their arms or waving their fingers in front of their eyes. Many are mute, and those who are not parrot meaninglessly whatever sounds they hear.

One characteristic of autistic children that depresses parents and puzzles therapists is their unresponsiveness to their social environment. They do not play with toys, or interact with other children. In fact they show no need for affection or any other form of contact with anybody. They don't even seem to know or care who their parents are. For a loving parent trying to help, this can be crushing. Even severely retarded children often give their parents the satisfaction of love and affection.

Life With a Wild Animal. Those who have never lived with an autistic child might blame parents who give up on them and decide to put them in institutions. But even the kindest, most loving and patient parent finds it difficult or impossible to live with what one has called "a wild animal, a living terror."

Many parents find themselves chained to their home, forced to adjust their lives to their children. They don't invite friends over because they fear embarrassment. When you enter some homes you are struck by the barrenness: no draperies, no delicate furniture, no plants, ashtrays or other throwable objects.

Taking an autistic child to any public place means gambling against the odds of disruption or embarrassment. At a restaurant, the child may start screaming for no reason, throwing food or spoons. At a friend's house, the child may rock incessantly back and forth against the seat cushion. Simply taking the child for a drive risks a dangerous tantrum. Getting away alone can also be difficult. Most baby sitters are incapable of looking after an autistic child; and those potentially able are usually reluctant to take on the responsibility.

To add to the parents' dilemma, few public schools offer much support. Autistic children cannot function in normal classrooms, not only because of their disruptive behavior, but also because of their serious behavioral limitations. They do not use language, understand instruction, pay attention, or interact with others. Few schools have personnel trained to deal with such problems. Even the staffs of schools for the mentally retarded, where many autistic children are placed, usually lack the training necessary for dealing with them.

Condemned for Life. Although a number of techniques for treating autistic children have been developed in recent years, they are not yet generally available. With no help from schools or specialists, and unable to handle their children them-

27. Autism

One must not reward an incorrect response because the child was "trying hard," or fail to reward a correct response because it is something every child "ought to know." The consequences must also be unambiguous.

Starting from the Beginning.
2 Sharon, a speech therapist, makes Johnny wait until she gives him proper instructions.
3 She demonstrates how to make the sound "mm."
4 Next she presses Johnny's lips together to help him make the sound himself.

When Johnny succeeds, he earns a hug from Sharon.

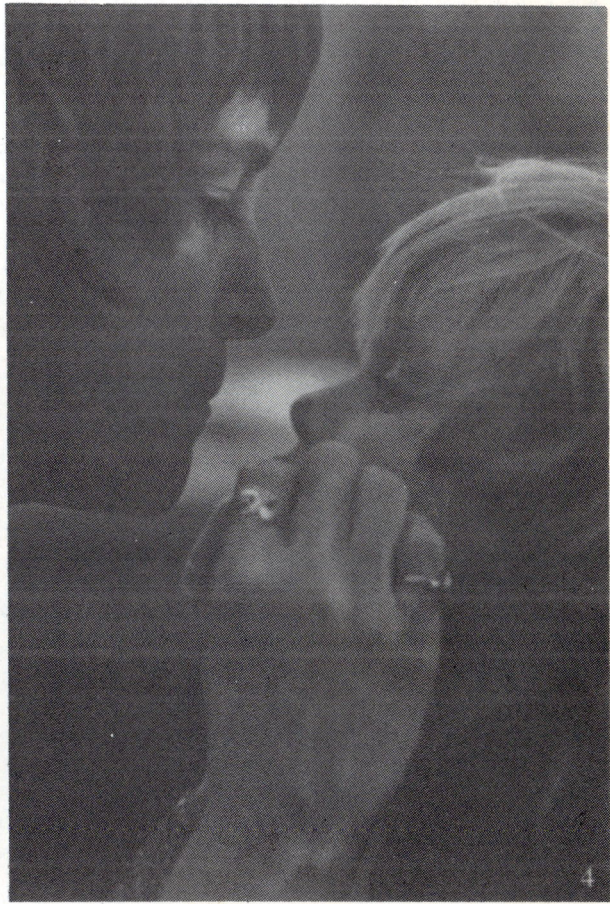

3. METHODS

selves, most parents do give up eventually. Their children end up in mental institutions, condemned for life because they have nowhere else to go.

The desperate decision on institutionalization usually comes after several unsuccessful trials with available programs, especially as the child grows older and harder to handle. One California child, for example, now 13 years old, has attended 16 schools and clinics so far. Eight rejected her because of her disruptive behavior; her parents withdrew her from the others because they saw no improvement. The father of another child who had bounced around various clinics and schools grew demoralized over the prospect of the boy's life in a mental hospital. One night he shot and killed his son while he slept.

Until recently, the most common theory of autism blamed it on the parents, suggesting that their own emotional problems somehow cause their children's tragic withdrawal. Therapists who adhere to this theory often counsel parents to seek psychotherapy themselves. No one has ever proven, however, that parents cause autism, or that treating the parents will help cure their children. In the absence of proof, blaming parents uselessly and cruelly reinforces the guilt they mistakenly feel, thus adding to their already heavy burden. One bit of evidence that complicates the parental-blame theory is the fact that autism strikes four times as many boys as girls.

A more current theory, also unproven, describes autism as an organic disorder, caused by some biochemical problem in the brain. This theory also offers little hope to parents. Since they can do nothing about an organic problem, they are simply told to learn to live with it.

But even if the disorder is organic in nature, should that discourage parents from seeking further treatment? If a child breaks his leg, we do not sentence him to life in a hospital. Why should we do so for an autistic child?

Parents As Therapists. The few professionals who treat autistic children generally exclude parents from the treatment process. But since parents are the most important agents of change in any child's life, excluding them wastes a valuable and necessary resource. In our research, we have proved not only that parents and teachers can learn to become effective therapists, but that their participation in the treatment process is essential.

By systematically rewarding appropriate behavior while ignoring or punishing inappropriate behavior, our parent and teacher therapists have produced dramatic improvement in previously untreatable autistic children. Using similar behavior-modification techniques, pioneers in the field such as Montrose Wolf, Todd Risley, Frank Hewett, and particularly Ivar Lovaas, have been able to control the disruptive behavior of these children, and teach them to talk, to play, and to deal with other people [see "A Conversation with Ivar Lovaas," PT, January 1974].

Compared to other methods of treating autism, the behavior-mod approach has several major advantages: it is based on principles of learning that can easily be taught to nonprofessionals; its effectiveness can be measured by objective data rather than subjective impressions; it does not blame the parents; and it does not require any knowledge about the cause of autism.

With this approach, autistic children could achieve considerable improvement in a clinical setting. But after leaving the clinic, those discharged to hospitals, foster homes, or parents who had not received training began to deteriorate rapidly, losing most of their treatment gains. In contrast, children discharged to parents who had received training maintained all of their treatment gains, and often continued to improve.

To test the importance of behavior-mod training, we asked a group of 26 untrained parents, teachers and college students to try to teach an autistic child some particular skill, such as tying shoes, or distinguishing colors. We provided each adult with a supply of food to use in rewarding the child.

In more than 50 15-minute teaching sessions, only one of the adults produced any measurable improvement in the child's response. In fact, in 28 sessions, the child made fewer correct responses at the end of the session than in the beginning. Many of the adults had great difficulty simply controlling the children, let alone teaching them. The children were confused and frustrated; they frequently screamed, threw objects, and attempted to kick or bite their teachers. Although they tried hard, the untrained adults were clearly ineffective therapists.

We next experimented with letting the parents and teachers watch a trained therapist teach a particular task, to see if that would improve their own approach. We found that such observation helped the adults in teaching the *same* task to their children, but only that particular one. For example, if a parent had observed a therapist teaching a child to tie his shoes the parent could then teach his own child how to tie his shoes, but not how to brush his teeth, or how to say "mama."

Five Essential Steps. Since autistic children have numerous behavioral problems, an effective training program must teach parents and teachers to deal with a large variety of behavior. In collaboration with our colleagues, Dennis Russo and Arnold Rincover, we therefore identified a set of five general procedures that apply to all situations:

1 Identifying The Target Behavior

Untrained parents and teachers tend to pick global goals, such as happiness or self-confidence. While there is nothing wrong with trying to make a child happy, a therapist can only achieve this goal if he first defines the particular behavior a child would need to learn to become happy. For example, if the therapist defines a happy child as one who laughs, talks, and plays with toys and other children, he can teach the child these specific behaviors and, it is to be hoped, end up with a happy child.

2 Presenting Proper Instructions

The therapist must first get the child's attention, and then make sure the child can easily understand the instructions. Our research has shown that autistic children often fail to respond correctly when presented with multiple instructions. For example, when teaching the child to discriminate colors, the untrained teacher might say: "Now we are going to work on colors. I'm going to teach you to touch a red square when I say 'red,' and to touch a green square when I say 'green.' But don't touch any of the other colors unless I say their name. Ok, now get ready to touch the red square, but don't touch any of the other colors. Ok, now do it." Such instructions don't work with autistic children.

In an efficient presentation, the therapist must first wait until any inattentive or disruptive behavior has stopped, then establish eye contact with the child. Then the teacher should present a simple instruction such as "touch red."

3 Prompting Correct Responses

Sometimes, even when the therapist presents an instruction correctly, the child will not respond because the response is simply not part of his repertoire. For example, if the therapist asks the child to say "b," a mute child might try, but his noise would in no way resemble the sound "b." Under such conditions the therapist can prompt or guide the child's response. He might hold the child's lip together to help form the sound. The prompt must work, however. It must produce the correct response. If not, no matter how good the intentions, or how many times it has worked, it should be abandoned for a better prompt. One should also minimize the number of extra cues.

4 Shaping and Chaining Behavior

Both of these procedures break the target behavior down into a sequence of very small steps. The therapist rewards successive approximations of the target behavior until the child finally responds correctly and completely. To earn a reward, each response must be at least as good an approximation as the previously rewarded response. In shaping, for example, if the therapist tries to get the child to say "ball," and the child's first two attempts come out "ba" and "baaal," then both responses should be rewarded because they represent progress. If, on the other hand, the child first says "ba," then "baaal" and then "ba" again, the last sound should not be rewarded because it is not as good as the previous response.

5 Providing Effective Consequences

After a child makes a correct response, the therapist should provide an appropriate consequence. The child must receive a reward when he responds correctly, and no reward when he does not. One must not reward an incorrect response because the child was "trying hard," or fail to reward a correct response because it is something every child "ought to know." The consequences must also be unambiguous. The therapist should not smile while saying "no," or frown while saying "good."

After explaining and demonstrating these five procedures to the adults in our program, we then observed while they practiced them on their own children. All of them reached an acceptable level of effectiveness, usually within one to five hours. This range possibly depends on such factors as their education, intelligence, and desire to succeed.

Once they had mastered the five-part technique, we asked the adults to teach their child some new behavior. This time, every one of them produced marked increases in the child's correct responses, regardless of what behavior they were working on. Their success seems espe-

The successful adults did not think of the children as "ill"; instead of pitying and excusing bizarre behavior, they concentrated on increasing normal behavior. They showed a willingness to commit a major personal effort to helping their child.

The Fruits of Therapy: **Learning to perform complex tasks, such as using a record player, represents great progress for an autistic child. Kristin's success liberates her so that she can entertain herself with the joy of music.**

3. METHODS

cially impressive to us in that although amateurs, they learned to become effective therapists in a matter of hours, in sharp contrast to the years of extensive training usually prescribed for professional therapists.

The Successful Parent-Therapist. Comparing the results of all the adults in the experiments, the more successful ones could be distinguished by certain general characteristics. They cared a great deal about succeeding, showing happiness when the children improved, and anger when the children disrupted the sessions. The successful adults did not think of the children as "ill"; instead of pitying and excusing bizarre behavior, they concentrated on increasing normal behavior. They showed a willingness to commit a major personal effort to helping their child, instead of relying on professional help.

Ideally, both parents and teachers should work together to produce lasting changes in the behavior of autistic children. Once properly trained, they can provide continuous treatment for the child throughout the day. Literally every activity at home and at school becomes a learning experience. The child learns to dress and feed himself, to go to the bathroom alone, to play with toys and other children. At school he learns not only reading, writing and speaking, but also how to play with groups of supervised and unsupervised children, and how to behave in a classroom.

It is difficult to say just how much progress the children will make under this treatment, since the school programs developed through our training studies are quite new. They are at the Pachappa School, in Riverside, California, the Orcutt Autistic Class in Orcutt, California, and the Princeton Child Development Institute in Princeton, New Jersey. We can say that the children's appropriate behavior is steadily increasing, and that both parents and teachers are extremely pleased.

We can make some systematic report on 16 children who participated in our first experimental classroom during the years 1971 to 1973. All of them had been diagnosed as autistic by agencies not associated with our research. All were severely psychotic. Six were completely mute, and the rest displayed minimal if any intelligible verbal behavior. All engaged in a great deal of self-stimulatory behavior. Most were too disruptive to be tested on standardized intelligence tests. Although their average age was seven, their average social development ranged from two to four years. All had been expelled from or denied admission to regular public schools or special education classes. Four had been placed unsuccessfully in programs for retarded children.

Using the behavior-mod procedures described above, one teacher, two aides, and two parttime speech therapists began to teach these children to respond to commands, to imitate, and to use an elementary vocabulary as well as some reading and arithmetic skills. Ten of the 16 children were discharged within 18 months, and went on to regular or special education classes in the public schools. The other six still attend special schools for autistic children, developed from our model. While their progress has been slow, we expect them to be able to attend regular classes one day.

We do not claim to be able to cure autism; and some autistic children may never be completely normal. But we have found that all can achieve significant progress. Regardless of the degree of difficulty, we have not yet seen an autistic child who could not improve enough to be educated in a school program if his parents and teachers receive proper training.

All of the parents who have received our behavior-mod training report that it helps them not only with their autistic children, but also with their other, normal children. This raises an interesting point: perhaps the rearing of children is too important to be left to intuition. Society has provided training programs for most other important professions, yet offers prospective parents nothing but Dr. Spock, mothers-in-law, and tradition. Instead of letting everyone simply bumble on with the traditional trial-and-error method, perhaps it is time for research-based programs for training parents.

AUTISM

The history of Autism is looked at along with a prospectus on the course and current methodology, research and diagnosis.

For more information about this book and other materials in special education, contact Joseph Logan, Editor, Special Learning Corporation.

Special Learning Corporation
42 Boston Post Rd. Guilford, Connecticut 06437   (203) 453-6525

HOW NEVER TO BE LATE AGAIN

This special plan puts an extra hour a day at your disposal and gets you to work (and everywhere else) on time.

James Hailey

There is no such thing as being on time. To be on time you have to be early.

To be early, you must set a time at least a half hour in advance of your actual arrival. This half hour can become the most important time of your day, thirty minutes that create a serenity in your life and leave you free from the burden of procrastination and failed projects.

You will find this half hour is a movable feast. Not every appointment will require the thirty-minute advance arrival since, by arriving early for the first date, you will begin and finish work in a better rhythm and condition, hitting an even stride which will actually give you spare time and help to lay the foundation of punctuality.

To begin with, you will need a spiral notebook and a pencil. You must write down—don't try to keep it in your mind—the time spans of your day's activities, beginning with the moment your alarm clock goes off (not the mo-

Inside your glove compartment, a list of time routes, a clean shirt and tie.

3. METHODS

ment you get out of bed). These time spans must be accurate, and must be narrowed to no more than five-minute segments. For example, no more than five minutes should elapse between the time the clock goes off and the time you are out of bed. Between bed and bathroom, less.

If you spend more than fifteen minutes in the bathroom in the morning (or at any other point in the day) penalize yourself by getting up ten minutes earlier for each extra minute spent in the bathroom. Clock time and body time are not equal early in the day. Your body and mind are functioning at a much slower rate than coolly efficient clock time which is not drugged by sleep, frightened by a potentially angry boss or squeamish about a cold floor.

You should have a clock (not electric) in the bathroom. Watch it instead of the mirror. Do not make more than one stop at any comfort station. Wash your face, shave it, paint it, pommel it, but do it all in one stop at the hand basin.

It is better to stop at the hand basin before you shower (quicker) or bathe (slower because you have to fill up the tub before immersing yourself and you tend to linger in the warm water). Washing your face first wakes you up and, on the other side, the steam from the shower dries out skin, making nicks easier in shaving.

Once you have your bathroom time down to fifteen minutes, try to whittle it even further by examining the three five-minute blocks you spend there. Anything you can push back to the night before is a plus. If you have a thin beard, shave before you go to bed. Women should try permanent false eyelashes instead of mascara to save time. Again, most people are functioning at a higher efficiency rate at night than they are first thing in the morning; but clock time should be the same.

Out of the bathroom, and now no more than twenty minutes from the time the alarm went off, you dress from clothes laid out the previous night. Morning is a bad time for decisions, no matter how trivial (five minutes for men, ten for women).

If you don't eat breakfast, consider the studies which have shown how efficiency (hence timeliness) is dulled by skipping this all-important meal. A glass of milk, a banana and a slice of whole wheat bread with butter take no more than five minutes, discourage mid-morning snacking, which is costly (most office vending machines make more money than the company itself), fattening and nonnutritious. The banana and bread can be eaten in the car; you will find yourself working faster and better during the morning hours, more likely to be on time the rest of the day.

In your car, keep a small notebook which records the times between house and office or office and fairly regular

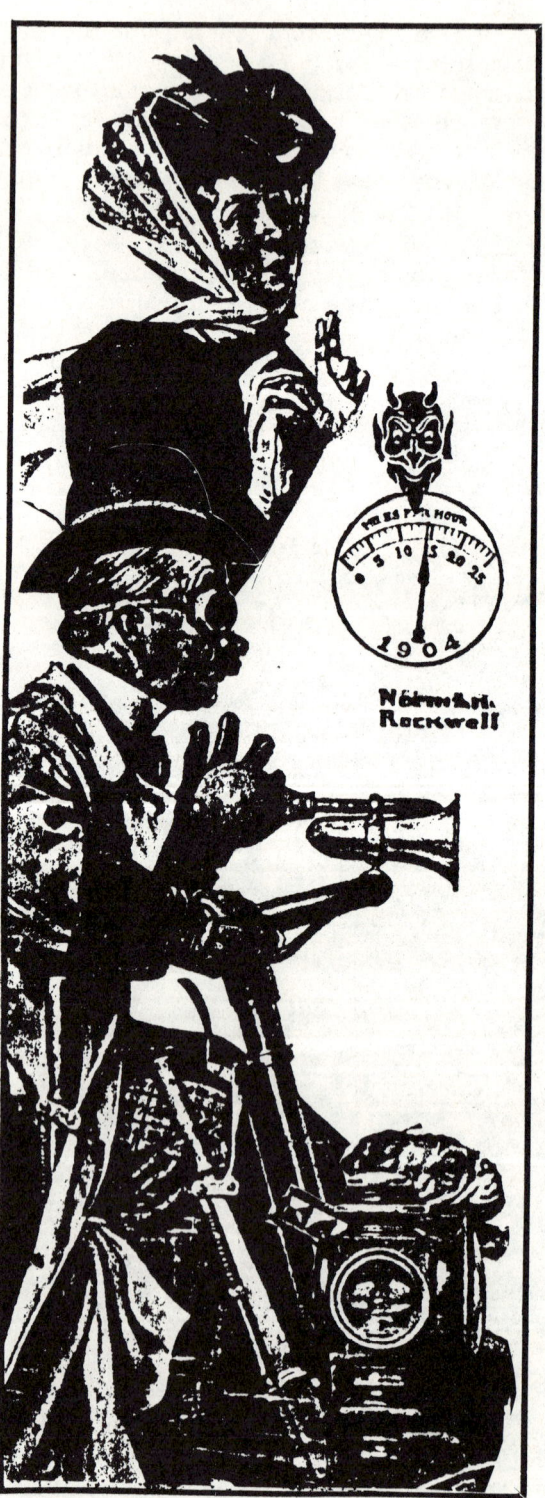

28. How Never to be Late

appointments including grocery store, school, or any other frequent stops. Vary your route. Make notes as to mileage and time, being certain you categorize as to hours of the day too, since some routes are more heavily traveled during certain times, causing slowdowns in traffic. You should be able to tell at an instant which way to go at any given time of the day.

Now trim your habits. What makes a person late may often be ingrained in his routines. Do you hang around after office hours to discuss the new girl? Do you lose fifteen minutes just getting out of the building? Do you regularly stop by a bar with the gang on the way home? Are you socializing only with co-workers? When people get too familiar, too used to each other, precise timing tends to become unimportant. When the gang's all together it doesn't matter that somebody's late. But being late—even for socializing—puts a person off the discipline and rhythm of punctuality; arriving late often has its roots in leaving late. If this sounds vaguely like prison, consider that punctuality builds free time, creates leisure, discourages procrastination, "the thief of time."

When you have mapped your time spans, you should also draw a line of your movements—between bed and car—car and office or appointment—to cut out unnecessary steps, especially during the critical morning time. Make a list of expendables too, a crash program which can be put into effect when there is a slipup in the schedule. For example, breakfast or bath can conceivably be eliminated. Make a quick plan for the space of time between departure and arrival, allot the essentials giving each at least five minutes more than you believe it will take, then give up lunch or the telephone call or speaking to someone who will not understand the schedule although you say you don't have much time. Time always works against you, never for you. You must never imagine that it will expand, or that the Peter principle (that everything that can go wrong will) does not apply.

Don't be afraid to run to appointments. You can pick up a minute or more by doubling your locomotion speed and the exercise is good for you.

All clocks should be advanced, then the fact forgotten. You can do this successfully if you advance them a quarter hour, or a half hour, then add seven or eight minutes—or eleven or twelve. The quarter-hour period may stick in your brain but the odd addition won't. Wear a wrist watch, one that keeps time and can be seen. Advance this also.

Practice being on time. When you go to the grocery store or the insurance agency or the drug store, set a time for arrival and one for departure. Concentrate on getting out of the store in the magic period of fifteen minutes.

Being late is a habit like any other and can be broken. First, you have to want to. Second, you must create a better habit to replace the old one. "Habits," according to Knight Dunlap in *Habits, Their Making and Unmaking*, "in their totality, make up the character of the individual; that is, they are the individual as he appears to other people." To most people, the ultimate compliment you can pay them is to be ready and waiting when they come for you, or to arrive at their meeting, party or office on time, i.e., early.

Now that you have put being on time in an important spot in your day, indicate in your notebook the five most important dates of the next twenty-four hours, engagements you would hate most to be late to. Then narrow it to one. It may be your job, your meeting with the boss, your appointment with your biggest customer.

Next, consider the most important date of the week. Of the month. Of the year. Of the rest of your life.

You begin to see the real value of being on time, and that being late for the most important date of your life may start with being late for the least.

Psychiatrists have said being late is an indication of your not really wanting to go someplace. There are books and books about managing your time and your life. They should be read, after you arrive at your destination on time. You will have an interval for reading when you are early and you always ought to carry a pocket book with you but you will find that other people will be early too when your reputation for punctuality becomes known.

Said Ben Franklin, "He that riseth late must trot all day." And "Do you love life? Then do not squander Time; for that's the stuff Life is made of." And "Lost time is never found again." And "Remember that time is money." And "Early to bed, early to rise makes a man healthy, wealthy and wise."

Employing negative reinforcement to establish and transfer control of a severely retarded and aggressive nineteen year old girl

Dennis E. Mithaug
David A. Hanawalt

Negative reinforcement in the form of experimenter-administered finger pressure on the inside upper bicept area of the subject's right arm was employed to increase task-initiated responding on a prevocational task, collating a booklet. Termination of the finger pressure was contingent upon the subject's touching the cover to open the booklet and begin to collate. When compared with two other conditions, tapping on the subject's hand to prompt her to begin work and repeating a verbal cue while ignoring aggressive responses, the finger pressure procedure not only increased response rates but also resulted in a decrease and elimination of self-biting and hitting the experimenter. When a teacher aide applied the procedure on the same task but at a different time in the day, the subject's response rates similarly increased and her self-biting and hitting remained at low levels.

Positive punishment and negative reinforcement procedures have been employed in a variety of settings to suppress undesirable behaviors and to increase appropriate ones. The application of an aversive stimulus contingent upon inappropriate behaviors has successfully decreased self-stimulation in autistic children (Lovaas, Schaeffer, & Simmons, 1965); reduced dangerous climbing in a severely deviant six year old girl (Risley, 1968); decreased self-destructive behavior in retarded children (Lovaas & Simmons, 1969); reduced self-injurious behavior in retarded adolescents (Corte, Wolf, & Lock, 1971); and decreased incorrect verbal responses in retarded children (Kircher, Pear, & Martin, 1971). The use of negative reinforcement procedures has produced increases in stuttering when termination of an electric shock was contingent upon stuttering (Flanagan, Goldiamond, & Azrin, 1958, 1959); increases in self-feeding in two psychiatric patients when termination of spilled food on the patients was contingent upon feeding themselves (Ayllon & Michael, 1959); increases in social responding in autistic children when termination of electric shock was contingent upon the child's physical contact with the experimenter (Lovaas et al., 1965); and increases in correct speech responses in a five year old brain-damaged child when termination of time-out from positive reinforcement was contingent upon appropriate verbalizations (McReynolds, 1969).

Risley's review of the literature on negative reinforcement suggested potential difficulties associated with such procedures:

> "... aversive stimuli may produce and maintain escape and avoidance behaviors which may be undesirable, such as leaving, avoiding, or removing the punishing situation, or the person dispensing the punishment. The literature on pain-elicited aggression (or "reflexive fighting") suggests that aversive stimuli may elicit aggression toward the person dispensing punishment and toward other organisms and objects as well" (Risley, 1968, p. 21).

Subsequent research on the use of aversive procedures has not supported these suggestions (Risley, 1968; Corte et al., 1971).

In the present study an aversive stimulus was employed to increase on-task behavior and, at the same time, decrease self-biting and aggressive hitting in a severely retarded and severely disruptive nineteen year old girl. After successfully employing a combination of procedures to establish control and increase on-task behavior, the experimenter attempted to evaluate the relative effects of the combined procedures by employing each in the absence of the others. The procedures included verbal praise and pats on the back for correct responses, physical prods in the form of hand taps on the hand and arm to elicit task responses, and finger pressure on the inside of the upper bicept area of the right arm to promote appropriate responding. Prior to the study the classroom managers had been unsuccessful in the use of primary reinforcers to increase correct responses and the use of extinction and time-out procedures to decrease disruptive responses.

METHOD

Upon enrollment in the Experimental Education Unit's prevocational training program, the subject was assigned to one manager who worked with her on several tasks for approximately two and one-half hours a day. The remaining two and one-half hours were divided equally between three other managers. The objectives were to establish procedures for controlling and motivating the subject's responses to one task and then to implement these procedures in programs administered by the other managers. A combination of procedures that proved effective during a collating task included aversive cues and positive consequences for on-task behavior. This experiment separated the procedures into different conditions to evaluate their relative effects for subsequent use with a different manager.

Subject

The subject, Sherry, was nineteen years old and severely retarded. She had no academic or preacademic skills and very limited self-help and fine and gross motor skills. Her receptive language was assessed at less than twelve months, and her expressive language was not functional, although she was able to imitate a few words. Sherry was on anticonvulsant medication for seizures which occurred approximately once every two weeks. The seizures consisted of blackouts for fifteen to twenty seconds, followed by a few minutes of drowsiness.

During a pre-enrollment assessment, Sherry's skills were evaluated on three prevocational tasks—collating, sorting by shape, and bagging three items. During this five-week assessment, there was minimal improvement in her performance of all tasks. During the collating task, which required that she insert four sheets into a booklet and stack the booklet, she was unable to open the book correctly. During the sorting-by-size task, Sherry was unable to sort two items of different shapes into two separate bins. During the bagging task, she could not pick up three square chips one at a time and place them on a template, pick up a bag, and then insert the items into the bag. For all tasks, she required continuous prompting and cueing to get her to participate in the step sequences. Usually her refusal to work was displayed by biting her hand, laughing and screaming loudly, hitting the manager, and throwing items across the room. Throughout the assessment period, her aggressive and disruptive behaviors increased while her time on task and progress in skill development remained at low levels.

Setting and Task Materials

The experiment was conducted in the prevocational training classroom where programs and services also were provided for five other severely and profoundly handicapped young adults. Sherry and the experimenter sat at one end of a 130 ×

3. METHODS

520 cm work table situated in the center of the room and shared by other clients working at the sides and the opposite end of the table.

The task consisted of collating four inserts between the first and second pages of a 48-page 8½ × 11 inch booklet. The materials included 10 booklets, 10 (8½ × 11 inch) blue brochures, 10 (8½ × 11 inch) blue brochures folded into thirds, 10 (8½ × 11 inch) pink brochures folded into thirds, and 10 (2 × 4 inch) envelopes. The stack of 10 booklets was located to the left of Sherry's midline at the corner of the table. The four stacks of insert materials were located to her right and approximately 4 cm from the front edge of the table. There were approximately 2 cm between stacks.

The task consisted of opening the booklet to the first page, taking one sheet from the first stack and placing it on the second page of the booklet, taking one folded sheet from the second stack, placing it in the booklet and on top of the first insert, taking one folded sheet from the third stack, placing it in the booklet on top of the second insert, taking one envelope from the fourth stack, placing it in the booklet and on top of the third insert, closing the booklet, picking up the collated booklet, and stacking it in the center of the table and to the left of the first stack. This sequence was repeated for each of the 10 booklets to complete one period lasting approximately 10 minutes.

Ethical Considerations

There are a number of issues one should address before considering a procedure involving any form of aversive stimulation, even though the procedure is harmless and can be safely applied without injury to the child. One of these, also considered elsewhere (Corte *et al.*, 1971) is the severity of the problem behavior. In the present study, Sherry's self-biting was intense and potentially damaging to her hand, although the resulting callouses limited some of the injury. Sherry's spontaneous throwing of objects across the room was dangerous and, on a few occasions, almost injured other clients. Sherry's hitting the managers, though not painful, resulted in avoidance by the teaching staff who were responsible for her training. The most serious problem, however, was Sherry's total noncompliance and unwillingness to work with any manager to learn the simplest tasks or the most basic skills. As a consequence of this uncontrollable behavior, school officials had decided that the public schools could not provide an appropriate educational program for Sherry. For similar reasons, her mother decided to place Sherry in a state institution for the severely and profoundly retarded. The long-range effects of failures to establish some form of behavioral and instructional control could be custodial care, in which Sherry's primary contact and attention from adults would be while receiving assistance for such basic needs as feeding, dressing, and toileting. Under these conditions, progress toward the long-range goal of independent functioning would be unrealistic.

A second issue of concern was the right of Sherry and her parents to determine the course of treatment most appropriate for her particular needs. Sherry's severe mental retardation left such decisions to her parents, who were consulted and advised of Sherry's problems and the possible solutions available. Sherry's parents had the right to approve or disapprove any procedure employed in her programs, to observe the implementation of all procedures to control her behavior, to review the data demonstrating the effects of those procedures and, ultimately, to decide whether to continue or discontinue the procedures at any time.

The third and final consideration was the process of selecting an aversive procedure rather than a more acceptable approach. This selection was a consequence of unsuccessful attempts using such procedures as verbal praise, physical contacts in the form of hand pats on the back for appropriate behavior, primary reinforcement, extinction, and timeout. In addition, information from Sherry's mother about the use of the aversive procedure by her father and a public school official indicated that finger pressure on the arm sometimes produced increased compliance. There were not data, however, demonstrating these effects or other, possibly undesirable, side effects.

Behavior Definitions

Three responses were monitored, a task-initiated response during which Sherry began the collating task by placing her hand on the booklet, a self-injurious response of biting her hand, and an aggressive response of hitting the manager.

29. Negative Reinforcement

Task-initiated response This response was defined by the interval of time between the experimenter's verbal cue to open the booklet plus his finger tap on the cover of the booklet and Sherry's left hand touching the cover of the booklet.

Hand-bite A hand-bite was defined by Sherry placing her left hand into her mouth and biting the area between the wrist and the thumb or forefinger.

Hit manager A hit occurred when Sherry's right arm and open hand made a hitting motion that made repeated contact (more than once) with any part of the experimenter's body.

Experimental Conditions

The three experimental conditions were finger pressure, hand tapping, and verbal only.

Finger-pressure During this condition the experimenter placed his left index finger and forefinger on the inside upper bicept area of Sherry's right arm and pressed firmly as he gave the verbal cue "open the booklet" and tapped the booklet with his right hand. He discontinued the pressure and released her arm immediately after Sherry's left hand touched the booklet. The pressure produced a moderately painful sensation which ceased immediately upon release of the arm.

Hand tapping During this condition the experimenter commenced tapping Sherry's left hand after cueing her to open the booklet, i.e., with a verbal instruction, "open the booklet," and a finger-tap on the booklet. The experimenter's taps alternated between the subject's hand or forearm and the booklet. The experimenter provided verbal praise for touching the booklet. All inappropriate responses were ignored.

Verbal-only During this condition the experimenter cued Sherry to open the booklet by tapping on the booklet with his right hand and repeating the verbal cue, "open the booklet." He ignored inappropriate responses (except to defend himself) and did not look at Sherry or make eye contact. When Sherry's left hand touched the booklet, the experimenter delivered verbal praise for good work.

During all conditions the experimenter deviated somewhat from completely ignoring hits as the sessions progressed. He warded off hits by blocking Sherry's striking right arm with his left forearm and then grasping her right hand and placing it in her lap. This was executed without making eye contact. After every third, sixth, and ninth booklet was collated and stacked, the experimenter placed a fruit loop on the table in front of Sherry. She was given approximately five to ten seconds to pick up and eat the fruit loop. If she delayed picking up the fruit loop or played with it instead of eating it, the experimenter took it back and commenced the next trial.

General Task Procedures

Although the dependent variable for study was the first step of the task (touching the booklet), Sherry was required to complete all subsequent steps before being presented with the next booklet to collate. Taking her through these steps required a combination of cues, prompts, and physical guides, each designed to lead her to task completion. The entire sequence began with the experimenter's cues to open the booklet. His right hand tapped the booklet and then directed Sherry's head so that she faced the stack of booklets. He repeated the head-directing procedure with his right hand each time she turned her head away from the stack. Immediately after Sherry's left hand touched the booklet, the experimenter placed his left hand on the top of her head to continue the head-directing when necessary. With his right hand, the experimenter pressed on the cover top until Sherry had separated the cover sheet from the rest of the booklet. Then he assisted her as she opened the cover page. Next, with his right hand, he pulled one insert sheet partially off the first stack to cue Sherry which sheet to pick up with her left hand. If she touched the incorrect stack or used her right hand, the experimenter corrected her by placing her left hand on the appropriate insert. After Sherry picked up and placed the insert in the booklet, the experimenter directed her head to the next stack with his left hand and repeated the cueing sequence again with his right hand. This was repeated until Sherry properly placed all inserts in the booklet. Next, he cued Sherry to close, pick up, and stack the booklet by pushing the open booklet toward her and slightly off the table. If

3. METHODS

she did not close or pick up the booklet, he physically guided her through the sequence. Once the collated booklet was stacked in the left center area of the table, the experimenter began the sequence again with the next booklet on the stack.

Experimental Design

The experiment's two phases were the establishment and transfer of manager control. The first phase evaluated three conditions: the verbal cue, hand tapping, and finger pressure. The second phase evaluated the effects of transferring control from the experimenter to a teacher aide who employed the procedures at a different time in the day.

Establishing Control

The daily sessions were divided into four periods lasting approximately 10 minutes each. After each period, Sherry was allowed to leave her stool and sit in the free-time area to listen to records for one to two minutes. Periods I and II were ABA and ABAB condition sequences, and periods III and IV were AB sequences. Periods I and II compared finger-pressure and hand-tapping procedures, and periods III and IV compared finger-pressure and verbal-only procedures.

Period I This period was the first 10 minutes of each daily session. During her first four days the experimenter applied finger pressure to initiate each collating task. During the second four days he used hand tapping, and during the remaining 18 days he applied finger pressure again.

Period II This period was the second 10 minutes of each session and consisted of hand-tapping for the first 13 days, followed by finger pressure for the remaining 13 days.

Period III During the third 10 minutes of each session, the conditions alternated between verbal-only and finger pressure. The first four days of verbal-only were followed by four days of finger pressure, three days of verbal-only, and a final 15 days of finger pressure.

Period IV During the last 10 minutes of each daily session, verbal-only was in effect for the first 15 days, followed by finger pressure for the remaining 11 days.

Transferring Control

During this phase of the study the teacher aide was trained in the use of the finger-pressure procedure. His background included a high school education and experience in the prevocational classroom, but no formal training in behavior management. His transfer training consisted of a period of observing videotaped sessions of the experimenter using the finger pressure procedure to increase Sherry's task-initiated responses. Following this introduction, he applied the procedures on the experimenter, who played Sherry's role. He practiced with the experimenter on 10 booklets, cueing the experimenter to begin while applying finger pressure, releasing the arm when the experimenter's left hand touched the booklet, and then providing the necessary physical prompts to open the booklet, pick up the inserts one at a time, place them into the booklet, close the booklet, and then stack the booklet.

This phase consisted of two morning sessions with the experimenter and two afternoon sessions with the teacher aide. During the morning sessions, the experimenter employed the procedures of previous sessions. The two periods were approximately 10 minutes each, with a one- or two-minute break between sessions. During the first four days of the first period the experimenter administered finger pressure on the second, fourth, sixth, eighth, and tenth collating tasks. During the remaining 10 days he administered the procedure when Sherry failed to respond within five seconds. During the second period he administered finger pressure after five-second delays on all 10-booklet trials.

In the afternoon sessions, periods III and IV, the teacher aide administered the collating task. Sherry's work during period IV began on the sixth day of the phase. The aide administered finger pressure on all booklet trials for both periods. He employed the task-completion procedures, which involved guiding Sherry's head and cueing her which inserts to pick up and place in the booklet.

Measurement and Reliability Procedures

The experimenter recorded Sherry's reaction times during each collating task by starting a stopwatch as he touched the booklet and verbally cued her to open the booklet. He stopped the watch when Sherry's left hand touched the booklet cover. These times were accumulated through 10 collating tasks or until a total time of 10 minutes had elapsed, whichever occurred first. The response data plotted for each 10-minute session were calculated by dividing the number of touch booklet responses by the accumulated times required to begin each task by touching the booklet cover.

All sessions were videotaped to permit observations of Sherry's biting and hitting responses. The experimenter recorded the percent of time that Sherry bit her hand or hit the manager by making a mark for any bite that occurred during each 10-second interval and another tally mark for any hit that occurred during the same interval. These data were recorded during the reaction time intervals which began with the experimenter's cues to open the booklet and which ended with Sherry's response of touching the booklet with her left hand. The percent-of-time measure was calculated by dividing the number of 10-second intervals during which a response (a hit or a bite) occurred by the total number of 10-second intervals in the accumulated reaction times for a 10-booklet period.

Reliability checks were taken for a different period each day. The two independent observers were graduate students in special education and teachers in the prevocational classroom. Their training consisted of learning the response definitions and recording data from three videotapes of sessions that preceded the experiment. Reliability checks for the four different periods were equally distributed throughout the 44-day experiment. The percent agreements for the number of booklets collated, the reaction times, and the proportions of time biting hand and hitting the manager were calculated by dividing the number of agreements by the total number of agreements and disagreements multiplied by 100. The percent agreements for the four variables (booklets, reaction times, bites, and hits) were respectively: .99, .93, .95, and .86.

RESULTS

Figure 1 presents Sherry's response rates for the four periods. The data were consistent for all periods. Sherry's rates of touching the booklet were at near-zero levels during both tapping and verbal-only conditions and increased dramatically during the finger-pressure conditions.

Figure 2 data on Sherry's hits present similarly consistent results. During both hand tapping and verbal-only, hits increased, and during finger pressure the percent levels decreased and were eliminated entirely during the final conditions.

The data for hand bites presented in Figure 3 show a similar inverse relation with the finger-pressure condition. However, the first finger-pressure condition of period III and the first three days of the final finger-pressure conditions of periods II and III show increases rather than decreases. These levels did not maintain when finger pressure was in effect for four or more sessions. During the last condition of all periods, hand bites decreased.

Figure 4 presents maintenance data during the experimenter's contingent use of finger pressure and transfer data during the teacher aide's continuous use of finger pressure. Although there were gradual decreases in response rates as the experimenter applied finger pressure for delayed responding, the levels stabilized at a mean of 37/minute for the last four days of period I and a mean of 37/minute for the last four days of period II. During the delayed responding conditions, the experimenter used finger pressure during sessions 6, 8, 10, and 12 of period I and sessions 8, 11, 12, and 15 of period II. In all but session 12 of period I, finger pressure was applied on only one trial. During session 12 the experimenter applied pressure for two booklet trials.

The teacher aide's success was evident in the increased response rates over the 15 sessions ending with a mean rate of 41/minute during the last four sessions of period III and 73/minute during the last four days of period IV. This success was matched by low levels of bites and hits through all sessions. The aide encountered problems in getting Sherry to stack the collated booklets during session 12. The experimenter intervened at that time by directing him verbally and through demonstrations on the procedures necessary to cue Sherry to close and stack the booklet. This was sufficient, and he had no further difficulty.

3. METHODS

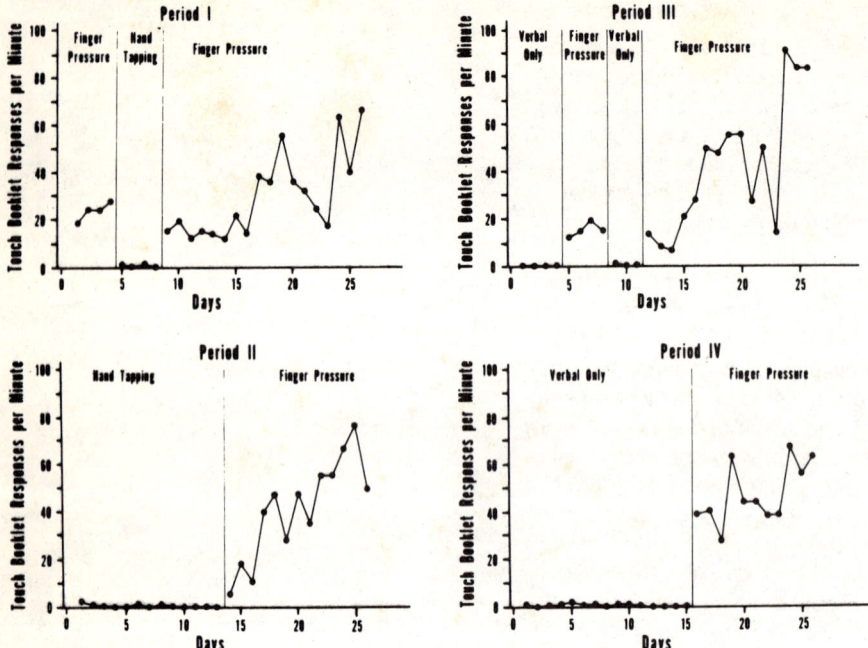

Figure 1. The number of touch-booklet responses per minute for each daily session, during the first period, upper left graph; the second period, lower left graph; the third period, upper right graph; and the fourth period, lower right graph.

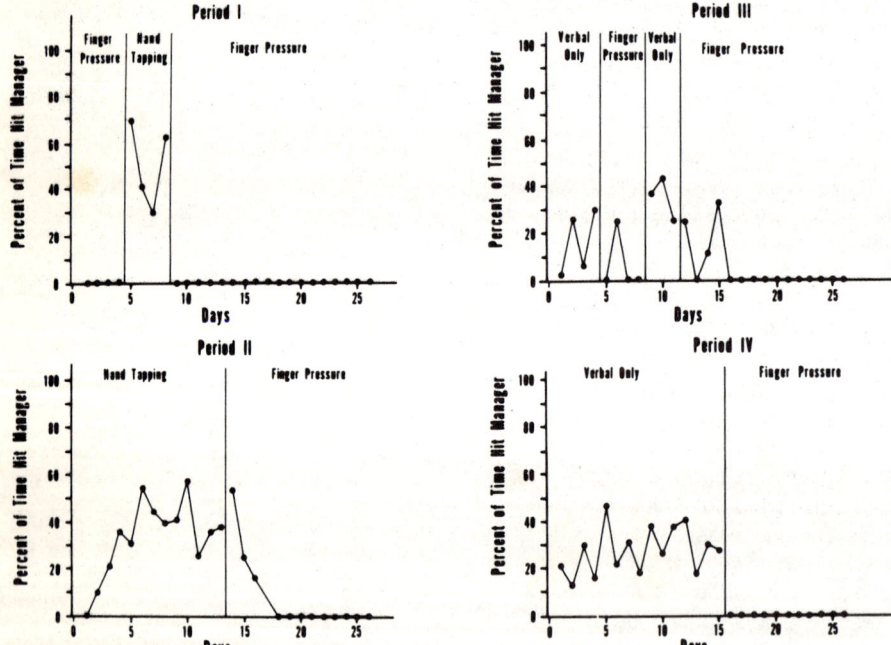

Figure 2. The percent of 10-second intervals during which a hit was recorded for the accumulated reaction time intervals for each daily session, of the first period, upper left graph; the second period, lower left graph; the third period, upper right graph; and the fourth period, lower right graph.

DISCUSSION

This study demonstrated the use of negative reinforcement to increase task-initiated responses and decrease self-biting and aggressive hitting in a nineteen year old severely retarded girl. Previous research has demonstrated the effects of using negative reinforcement procedures to increase behavior (Flanagan, et al., 1958, 1959; Ayllon et al., 1959; Lovaas et al., 1965; McReynolds, 1969), but few studies have employed negative reinforcement to decrease undesirable or inappropriate responses as well. This procedure is related to DRO methods that have been

29. Negative Reinforcement

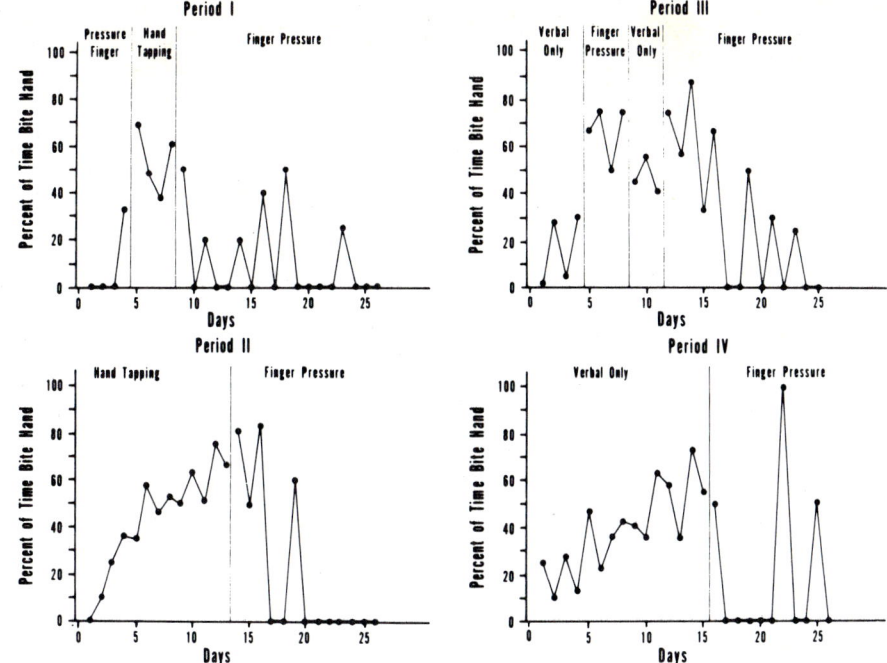

Figure 3. *The percent of 10-second intervals during which a bite was recorded for the accumulated reaction time intervals for each daily session, of the first period, upper left graph; the second period, lower left graph; the third period, upper right graph; and the fourth period, lower right graph.*

employed to increase incompatible responses in order to decrease inappropriate responding (Lovaas, *et al.*, 1965; Peterson & Peterson, 1968). Ayllon & Roberts (1974) reported a variation of the DRO procedure involving the use of positive reinforcement to increase *task* responses which in turn resulted in decreases in undesirable behavior. In the present study, task responses also were increased but through the use of negative reinforcement rather than positive reinforcement. Termination of finger pressure contingent upon Sherry's touching the booklet increased the rate of touching the booklet, which was incompatible with biting her hand and hitting the manager. Task initiated responding increased and biting and hitting decreased.

These findings are at variance with suggestions Risley found in the literature indicating that "aversive stimuli may elicit aggression toward the person dispensing the punishment" (Risley, 1968, p. 21). Only when finger pressure was in effect for a period of three days (i.e., the second and fourth conditions of period III and the last condition of period II) was there an increase in self-biting. These levels decreased dramatically over the subsequent sessions of the last conditions, indicating the importance of allowing sufficient time for the conditions to have an effect. Whether the same stimulus delivered as a punisher would produce different results is not known. For example, finger pressure delivered contingent upon a hand bite or a hit may or may not decrease hand bites. The effects of employing the same stimulus in negative reinforcement and punishment situations should be investigated further, e.g., McReynolds (1969).

One interesting finding was the apparent ease in transferring stimulus control to the teacher aide, who employed the procedure at a different time in the day. This may have been facilitated by the avoidance pattern learned for this task during the sessions with the experimenter. The experimenter's hand on Sherry's right arm may have functioned as a conditioned stimulus to elicit the avoidance response of opening the booklet. Like other avoidance responses that are resistant to extinction, this on-task response may have generalized to the teacher aide's touch. These effects are interesting in comparison with effects obtained when punishers are contingent upon undesirable behaviors. Other investigators have noted, for example, that the effects of punishment are specific to the setting in which punishment occurs as well as the person delivering the punishment (Risley, 1968; Birnbrauer,

3. METHODS

1968; Lovaas & Simmons, 1969; Corte et al., 1971).

While the study was in progress, the two other managers worked with Sherry for the remaining program periods and continued to have difficulties getting her to work and controlling her disruptive and aggressive behaviors. Following completion of the study, they agreed to employ the finger-pressure procedure on other tasks. During the subsequent 8 weeks, Sherry's hand bites decreased from an average of 86.8/day for the week preceding the procedure to a mean of 23.8/day for the 8th week of treatment. During that same period, hits were eliminated almost entirely. It is interesting to note, however, that not all managers obtained the same results. During tasks administered by the experimenter and teacher aide, Sherry's bites were at near-zero levels throughout the eight-week period. One explanation is that Sherry's discriminations between managers were partly a function of the stimulus properties of the tasks as well as the manager's task-related cues, prompts, and physical guides. On the collating task Sherry usually worked to complete a booklet once she started, provided the experimenter gave the necessary cues, prompts, and guides. In fact, during the study when the teacher aide failed to provide these cues, Sherry's disruptive behaviors increased. After brief retraining, the manager was able to continue the program successfully. A comparable detailed cueing system was not as well established for the tasks administered by the other managers. This may account, in part, for the slower progress in establishing and maintaining instructional control on other tasks. The negative reinforcement procedure, to be maximally effective, may require a system of cues and prompts to maintain the work momentum once it is started.

Finally, we should note the relative success of fading the use of negative reinforcement and employing it only for lags in reaction times. Although the transfer data reported in the study indicated a decrease in response rates, the levels stabilized and stimulus control was maintained with low levels of inappropriate responding. Several months after the completion of the study the teacher aide was similarly successful in employing the procedure as a consequence for response lags.

REFERENCES

Ayllon, T., & Michael, J. The psychiatric nurse as a behavioral engineer. *Journal of Experimental Analysis of Behavior*, 1959, 2, 323–334.

Ayllon, T., & Roberts, M. D. Eliminating discipline problems by strengthening academic performance. *Journal of Applied Behavior Analysis*, 1974, 7, 71–76.

Birnbrauer, J. S. Generalization of punishment effects—a case study. *Journal of Applied Behavior Analysis*, 1968, 1, 201–211.

Corte, H. E., Wolf, M. M., & Locke, B. J. A comparison of procedures for eliminating self-injurious behavior in retarded adolescents. *Journal of Applied Behavior Analysis*, 1971, 4, 201–213.

Flanagan, B., Goldiamond, L., & Azrin, N. H. Operant stuttering: The control of stuttering behavior through response-contingent consequences. *Journal of Experimental Analysis of Behavior*, 1958, 1, 173–177.

Flanagan, B., Goldiamond, L., & Azrin, N. H. Instatement of stuttering in normally fluent individuals through operant procedures. *Science*, 1959, 130, 979, 981.

Kircher, A. S., Pear, J. J., & Martin, G. L. Shock as punishment in a picture-naming task with retarded children. *Journal of Applied Behavior Analysis*, 1971, 4, 227–234.

Lovaas, O. I., Freitag, G., Gold, V. J., & Kassorla, I. C. Experimental studies in childhood schizophrenia: Analysis of self-destructive behavior. *Journal of Experimental Child Psychology*, 1965, 2, 67–84.

Lovaas, O. I., Schaeffer, B., & Simmons, J. Q. Experimental studies in childhood schizophrenia: Building social behavior in autistic children by use of electric shock. *Journal of Experimental Research Personnel*, 1965, 1, 99–109.

Lovaas, O. I., & Simmons, J. Q. Manipulation of self-destruction in three retarded children. *Journal of Applied Behavior Analysis*, 1969, 2, 143–157.

McReynolds, L. V. Application of timeout from positive reinforcement for increasing the efficiency of speech training. *Journal of Applied Behavior Analysis*, 1969, 2, 199–205.

Peterson, R., F., & Peterson, L. R. The use of positive reinforcement in the control of self-destructive behavior in a retarded boy. *Journal of Experimental Child Psychology*, 1968, 6, 351–360.

Risley, T. R. The effects and side effects of punishing the autistic behaviors of a deviant child. *Journal of Applied Behavior Analysis*, 1968, 1, 21–34.

The Fear Of Open Space

Being afraid to leave home to go shopping is something most of us, fortunately, have not had to cope with. But the fear of public and open places (known as agoraphobia) does restrict the lives of a number of people.

Unfortunately, agoraphobic patients usually have shown only limited improvement with behavioral therapy, and their progress stops entirely when treatment is discontinued. But now a British group at Oxford has developed a home-based treatment program that they believe will let patients overcome their fears primarily on their own.

Self-Help Plan. The program, designed by Andrew Mathews, John Teasdale, Mary Munby, Derek Johnston and Phyllis Shaw, is set up to be managed by the patients themselves with help from their spouses. Thus, the amount of time spent with a therapist is small and progress does not depend on the therapist, as it can with other types of treatment.

The method may prove very helpful if results from a trial with 12 married agoraphobic women are an indication of its effectiveness. All but one of them improved during the initial treatment that lasted four weeks and nine of them continued to improve during a followup period.

To begin, the patients and their husbands were each given detailed written instructions describing the treatment program. Treatment involved daily "practice sessions" in which the patient faced increasingly difficult situations that she feared, such as taking a bus to town or visiting a social club. Each couple was responsible for deciding, with the advice of the therapist, what situations would be encountered during practice. The therapists urged the patients to set aside an hour each day for practice, but the actual average practice time didn't amount to all that much.

Diminishing Advice. A therapist visited each couple three times during the first week, twice during both the second and third weeks and once during the fourth week, discussing progress and giving advice on how to overcome specific problems. Followup visits were made two weeks, six weeks and three months after the end of the four-week session. Couples were expected to continue the treatment program on their own, and records of the patients' time out of the house indicate that they did.

Behavioral tests, psychiatric assessments and self-evaluations indicated that 11 of the women had improved after four weeks of treatment and nine of them made further progress during the next six months when there was little contact with therapists. Overall, the patients' progress was the same as or better than the progress of patients in other treatment programs that call for spending more time with a therapist. About a third of the improvement was made during the followup period when no improvement was made by patients in other programs studied previously. Although they would like to see the study replicated under stricter conditions, Mathews, et al., say the findings do "suggest that the home program was successful in providing an ongoing alternative within the patients' own environment to the instructions and reinforcement normally provided by the therapist."

Ethical Issues in Behavior Modification

The most important ethical problem within behaviorism is a most subtle one . . . the fact that abuse has effected its effectiveness. Freudian psychology has been recognized to be more a mythology than a technology. Early theories are now thought to be somewhat laughable, and over-zealous use of them led people to go beyond what the original science told them.

"Politics" in decision-making have dictated what "kinds" of behavior are acceptable to "society", to a school setting, and what "kind" is a "deviant" or "misfit" behavior. As a result, behaviorists hide behind neutrality, which they are in fact far from any form of neutrality, because they can shape almost any behavior according to the amount the person is willing to pay to have his behavior modified.

Accepting the fact that we can modify behavior, we face the question of what behaviors should be controlled? Diversity in human beings should be planned and not accidental. So too, with the workings of Behavior Modification. We must keep in mind that this is a theory-based means of achieving goals of positive principle, as opposed to humanistic theories of the opposite viewpoint. In the end however, they both end up being very humanistic in form, as the tools of science, including behavior modification, allow the formation and achievement of **humanistic goals**. In this manner self-control brings the individual the gain of self-direction, thus bringing humanistic concepts into human responsive action.

Maslow has supplied us with the most basic definition of humanistic psychology and education thus far: "The first and over-reaching big problem is to make a good person." The emphasis is on action-orientation and what the individual does both internally and externally with their skills of action toward self-actualization.

On the other side of the coin, behaviorist theory is a vast conglomeration of techniques, assumptive principles and therapies which are catagorized as conventional, radical, or cognitive-oriented in their nature.

The end result is a concern with helping a person experience life and living in a more positive vein. Humanistic concerns must be translated into human responses as a means of truly effectual scientific inquiry. In this way self-controlling actions are made possible through self-observation and individual and environmental structures of planning. With this factual knowledge, we can begin to help one actually realize self-actualization of behavior. Also in this manner, we can wipe out previous misinformation and misunderstanding among behavioral educators, scientists, and humanistic scholars over ethical considerations which may have previously prevented badly needed scientific studies into self-control techniques.

Is the Pigeon Always Right?

Edgar Z. Friedenberg

"Behavior mod evades as far as possible questions of guilt, sin, intent, or moral judgment. It makes no appeals to conscience and shows no punitive intent. . . . Thus a school in which children are strapped or drugged is about as far from behavior mod as it can get."

The use of psychotechnical procedures and devices to modify human behavior has become commonplace. Schools, prisons, mental hospitals, and increasingly—as the appalling disclosures of Amnesty International reveal—the national state itself, rely on such means to socialize and control those subject to them. Many of us feel both alarmed and confused by the extensive array of practices now used. The technical manipulation of human behavior and attitudes has become institutionalized in so many different ways that it is hard to be sure just what is taking place. And not all the objectionable practices are objectionable for the same reasons.

For example, people who object to the use of behavior modification programs in schools often go on to complain of the widespread use of mood-altering drugs like Ritalin to control the behavior of children teachers find disruptive, using the pretext that they are "hyperkinetic." The two practices thus tend to become linked. But the use of drugs to control disruptive behavior is utterly inconsistent with the doctrines of behavior mod, which would regard this as a very gross and not really psychological way of controlling human behavior, having nothing in common with operant conditioning. This does not, of course, mean that school personnel who are pragmatic and insensitive may not use both, but their effect on the person subjected to them, and the reason for condemning their use, is quite different.

Drugs are used, sometimes with fiendish cruelty, in aversive therapy, of which the most familiar example is the treatment portrayed in *A Clockwork Orange*. Aversive therapy is a form of behavior modification and an abhorrent one—and its use seems to be spreading. One proposed program which was to have been introduced into a prison in North Carolina last year was aborted by the courts on constitutional grounds; but others making use of forms of negative reinforcement that sound equally cruel are continually being developed.

Orthodox proponents of behavior mod, however, usually don't think too much of aversive therapy. The doctrine holds, on the basis of a great deal of evidence from animal experimentation, that positive reinforcement is a much more effective form of operant conditioning than negative reinforcement which if severe is likely to so disturb or antagonize the subject that he or she won't learn anything from it. Strict behaviorists prefer to "extinguish" behavior they regard as undesirable by ignoring it or isolating its practitioner, while rewarding each successive approximation of the behavior they are trying to foster.

This similarity to accepted social practice leads most behaviorists to insist that behavior modification is really nothing new; it's something all of us do every day in the course of ordinary social interaction. But this is false. Families, schools, prisons, and society itself do, of course, make use of rewards and punishments more or less systematically to train people to do what the authorities want; and they

31. The Pigeon

> "You can train a pigeon to execute a complicated dance perfectly by the pure application of behavior modification; indeed, there is probably no other way to do it. But such a pigeon cannot be said to have developed an interest in ballet."

always have. But there are fundamental differences between the use of rewards and punishments in socialization and the use of positive and negative reinforcement in behavior modification.

[THE POWER TO WILL]

The most important difference has to do with the function of the will, which is basic to the western concept of morality. Our moral system holds that both good and evil must be willed; one cannot sin inadvertently, and there can be no crime without criminal intent. Traditional moralists therefore think of themselves not as encouraging desirable behavior and discouraging undesirable behavior, but as "teaching children the difference between right and wrong." The most authoritarian moralists, steeped in the doctrine of original sin, often used to speak of the need to "break the will of the child," forcing the child through guilt or fear to repress impulses they deemed evil, which included most spontaneous and natural behavior.

Nobody does anything like this to a laboratory rat or a pigeon; and so far the behaviorists would seem to occupy the higher moral ground. And they certainly have the easier technical problems. The Victorians, if I may use that term loosely and none-too-accurately to identify older-fashioned moralists, could make very little use of positive reinforcement, since they were trying to establish norms at the same time that they were trying to influence behavior: that is, they were trying to teach people what they ought to enjoy at the same time they were trying to get them to do it. But to serve as positive reinforcement the reward offered, however trivial, must be genuinely prized already—the pigeon, as behaviorists sometimes say, is always right. Victorian moralism at its worst sought to use the same occasions both to offer rewards and to define those rewards as desirable—a technical error no Skinnerian would be likely to make. Good little boys won prizes that could hardly have given them much satisfaction: edifying books that no one could read with pleasure; minor posts in school or church that cost them more status among their peers than they gained among adults. The phrase "brownie points" for status so earned still conveys the position exactly.

This is clearly one reason for the emphasis on competitive sports in British public-school life, both as a means of socialization and of selecting future leaders. For of course success on the playing fields did confer status in the peer group as well as among adults, and was ardently desired. It could be won, moreover, only by displaying a mixture of guile and brutality that established clearly that the sanctimonious lessons of official morality had not been so thoroughly internalized as to disqualify the student for future public service. England's battles were won on the playing fields of Eton in the sense that these provided a crucial testing ground for identifying those young members of the ruling class who could combine the most essential ingredients of a viceregal presence: sanctimonious adherence to an honorable creed; and the ability and disposition to kick the shit out of an adversary, especially one beyond the pale, literally or figuratively. By weighing points won on the playing field more heavily than brownie points, pre-World War I society insured itself against awarding actual positions of leadership to people who conformed too daintily to moral precepts.

Much of what we sense as freedom in western bourgeois life stems, however, from precisely this moralistic, inconsistent, and thoroughly Skinnerian use of reward and punishment—not to modify behavior, but to "build character." For this traditional use carries within itself the seeds of rebellion that have permitted Western Civilization to redeem itself from time to time. The essence of the traditional approach is that socialization requires that morality be internalized; that the child or the prisoner or the revolutionary be ultimately led to accept and endorse the creed of his subjectors—to agree with them about the difference between right and wrong. Thereafter, his conscience or his superego, however one wished to view it, is at the disposal of society; he has become his own narc. Crime and sin, conversely, can thereafter be defined as, necessarily, willful acts and their perpetrators as guilty.

When this sort of socialization fails, it may fail absolutely, as with members of the counterculture who, having come to despise the promised rewards of affluence, can no longer be threatened by poverty; though as they grow older they may find their exclusion from a meaningful role in society less supportable than their austere standard of living. These are the children who were socialized primarily by offering them rewards they were expected to learn to enjoy, whether they wanted them or not, in order to make their place in the middle class. When they were punished, they were punished by withholding these same rewards whose denial was ambiguous in its effects. This applies even to withholding affection—the standard middle-class punishment—which can be devastating to an infant or even to an older child before adjusting to it. But our recollections of our mothers must remind us that there comes a time when almost any child of six or older may feel about her threat to take her leave of him much as Hamlet did about Polonius's similar threat. Punishment affords many middle-class children about the only privacy they ever get.

Socialization that seeks to use conventional rewards as positive reinforcement before it has established that they are, in fact, rewards, is likely to come unstuck, strewing society with rebels, hippies, and other protagonists of free-

4. ETHICAL ISSUES

dom. Even when it does not come unstuck as completely as that, the fact that our normal socialization attempts to mold the will—rather than simply elicit desirable behavior—leaves the will dormant but intact and ready, if sufficiently provoked, to pit itself against society. As Lawrence Kohlberg has shown in his fundamental work on the development of moral awareness in human beings, those few who reach the highest levels of moral awareness become enemies of society through the very effectiveness of their socialization: they are people who have actually internalized the values of the society rather than its rules. These include of course, the nobler leaders of the peace and civil rights movements, who had been so well socialized into the western tradition that they accepted and acted upon the fact that sin must be willful and includes, especially, willful obedience to evil law. At this point, self-awareness and moral insight converge with a blinding flash and sometimes explosive violence, illuminating the institutions of a corrupt and unjust society and shaking them to—and sometimes from—their foundations.

[BEYOND FREEDOM]

All this could be avoided by the widespread use of behavior modification, which does not seek to mold or develop the will, but to avoid probate. Behavior mod evades as far as possible questions of guilt, sin, intent, or moral judgment. It makes no appeals to conscience and shows no punitive intent. This is why the scientists to whom Alex is delivered in *A Clockwork Orange* seem so much nicer than the jailers do. But in fact they are much crueler, not because they wish to punish him more severely, but because they do not care about him at all except as the object of their psychotechnology. He can neither seduce them, nor arouse their pity or their rage. Where the prison officials represent as best they can a lower-middle-class vision of the wrath and occasionally the pity of God, exacting from Alex in return an unbearable semblance of piety, the scientists at the institute exemplify His absence, a severer form of Hell. They cannot be placated, obeyed, or disobeyed; and they are not trying to teach Alex anything about the difference between right and wrong. They are simply trying to condition him so that he can no longer respond violently in any situation, whatever its moral context.

But this is aversive therapy which, though a form of operant conditioning, is not representative of most programs of behavior modification. What distinguishes behavior mod is not the use of bizarre techniques to inflict pain. It is rather the attempt to evoke the behavior sought through "reinforcing" it and "extinguishing" undesired alternatives while deliberately avoiding the moral confrontation involved. The outcome sought is conformity without conflict and without the need or perhaps even the capacity for moral judgment. One could even, of course, develop an apparent "non-conformity" in this way by responding favorably to a child's attempts to argue and "answer back" and to go off and "do his own thing" while ignoring his

"Behavior modification provides some highly effective techniques for reducing the occurrence of undesirable behavior. But it offers itself as an inauthentic substitute for love and will, and hence is essentially frivolous about existence. It leaves its practitioners in the moral predicament of using a tool on people they should have responded to as total beings."

efforts to be cooperative and join the group. One could encourage a child's—or an adult's—propensities for artistic or musical expression while cooling out his or her interests in and abilities in sport; or, of course, vice-versa.

Isn't this, then, precisely what goes on for better or for worse in the process of normal socialization? Isn't this how little boys learn not to cook and sew and little girls learn not to play football? Isn't this the way liberal Jewish parents raise radical Jewish children? I would say no, not by a damned sight. For in all these cases, the emotional and moral influences that mold the child are authentically and spontaneously present, for better or for worse, in the family and the culture as it is encountered; and the spontaneity and authenticity contribute to growth and mediate constraint; they are lively irritants. Every culture establishes certain roles and encourages those aspects of development that suit individuals to fill them, while discouraging others. But a culture is not a conspiracy; and the boy whose parents are trying to reinforce his limited interests in football may well have a brother who is a disappointment to his family—but not to himself—because he is a poet; a sister who is a policewoman, and an uncle who, as *chef de cuisine* at *Le Parvenu,* has the highest status in the family.

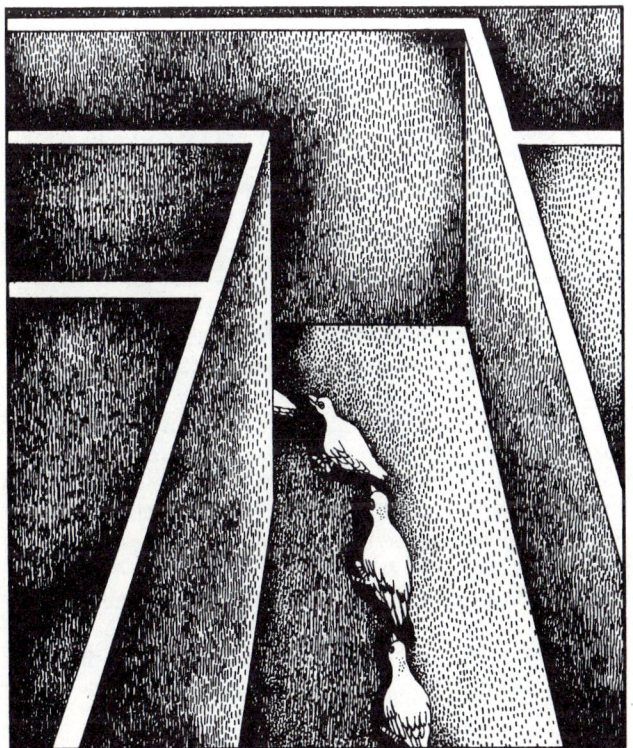

Even today, the world is a lot less ordered than a psychological laboratory, or a school in which children are given candy tokens for promptness or achievement and ignored if they are late or dilatory. Furthermore, there are errant and rebellious teachers just as there are students. Jim Herndon still teaches in Daly City, and manages to survive in his native land even though things ain't the way they're supposed to be. When Tierra Firma Junior High converts to behavior mod, they won't be able to keep him any more; and students who don't want their behavior modified will have no more place to hide.

Since the world is rife with oppression, conflict, and injustice, neither the school nor the family is likely to be free of them; and a child who had been so singularly fortunate as never to have encountered them there would probably find adult life astonishingly uncomfortable. Nevertheless, even at their worst, the school and the family, like the Austrian bureaucracy under the later Hapsburgs, are usually redeemed by their inefficiency and inconsistency, which make it possible to learn to be a human being there as elsewhere in the world. In a school that deals with pupils according to principles of behavior modification this would be far less likely; since how the teachers, and so far as possible, schoolmates, respond to a child is programed in advance with the intent of encouraging behavior defined by the school as socially desirable and starving out that which is less desirable. His experience of how other people respond to him becomes very limited: he may never learn, for example, how angry he makes them if his teachers have decided that displays of anger reinforce offensive behavior by providing recognition, and prescribe a good, hard ignoring instead.

Behavior modification is planned to mold desirable behavior directly, without rooting it in character or ethical purpose. It seeks to operate at Kohlberg's lowest level of moral judgment: behavior is good because it is rewarded. This is a serious denial of the humanity of the person subjected to it. But I think, to be fair, one must also state that this is the worst that can be said of it. As I have indicated, orthodox practitioners of behavior modification are less likely to be punitive than ordinary teachers or parents, because they have found negative reinforcement is an inefficient and unreliable way of extinguishing undesired behavior. This is not as satisfactory a reason for avoiding it as respect for the dignity of the victim; but it does mean that a school in which children are strapped or drugged in order to control their behavior is about as far from behavior mod as it can get.

There are other objections, however. Behavior modification programs by their very nature rely heavily on ex-

4. ETHICAL ISSUES

trinsic rewards; and these rewards, unlike school grades, are not even supposed to be granted in recognition of excellent performance but simply as pleasurable reinforcement for behavior desired by someone else. You can, indeed, train a pigeon to execute a complicated dance perfectly by the pure application of behavior modification techniques; indeed, there is probably no other way to do it. But such a pigeon cannot be said to have developed an interest in ballet. Everybody knows the old statistical saw about how 20 chimpanzees locked up in a room with 20 typewriters and an inexhaustible supply of paper would eventually write, among other things, *War and Peace.* If the primate lab were run according to the principles of behavior mod, and each primate reinforced for every phrase that resembled one of Tolstoi's, the task might be accomplished in 50 years. It would not leave the monkeys in a frame of mind, however, to go ahead and tackle *Anna Karenina* on their own.

Children educated by the techniques of behavior modification may not even know what ordinary people mean by being interested in something they do well. It must be conceded, however, that school grades which, in any case, are as extrinsic as the tokens or bits of candy that successful participants in behavior mod programs usually get, have also come to have almost as little to do with achievement and interests, as academic standards are adapted to meet the strains imposed by demographic and cultural change. An 'A' in a New York City high school today has about as much meaning as the free rum drink most Caribbean hotels give arriving guests to make them feel at home and avert culture shock.

[PUSHBUTTON MORALITY]

Much more serious ethical questions arise, however, with reference to aversive therapy. Although aversive therapy always involves negative reinforcement by doing something disagreeable and often agonizing or terrifying to the client on whom it is being practiced, it is totally different in its intent and psychological function from torture, and should be clearly distinguished from it. I think it is worse, though the choice of the lesser of two such evils is hardly worth making.

The painful stimuli used in aversive therapy are usually much less severe than those used in torture—though not always; both have made use of certain drugs that arrest respiration and arouse the feeling of impending death by suffocation, which is probably the ultimate in terror. But the torturer at least respects his victim to the extent of attributing to him a will to be broken; though with modern techniques which disorient the victim as they torment him, he hasn't much chance to resist in the long run. Torturers, moreover, do not usually want to alter their victim's mode of behavior in general, but have very specific ends. They want to extract a confession or information, and the less the victim is altered in the process the more plausible the confession will be. Torture is nearly always clandestine; and its revelation is an embarrassment to its practitioners. Its prevalence in the present era is, I should judge, essentially evidence of the dignity constitutional democracy once pos-

sessed, as well as of its decline. It flourishes in situations in which people still suppose themselves to possess certain rights that have in fact vanished, but have never been taken off the books. To achieve a final and conclusive victory, the torturer finds it most helpful if he can bring his victim into open court to deny that he has been tortured.

Aversive therapy differs from torture in almost all these respects. It is not clandestine, though the actual details may be played down for PR purposes. The existence of the program, however, is not denied; in fact it is usually reported as a sign of technical progress in therapy or criminology. Those who accept aversive therapy usually are called volunteers, though in fact they offer themselves under extreme social coercion—usually under the threat of becoming a social outcast. And it is used only under one set of circumstances.

Aversive therapy can be applied only to mess up and spoil something that gives the client or patient great pleasure, but that gets him into enough trouble that he is willing to allow that pleasure to be spoiled by being mixed with other sensations sufficiently disagreeable to overwhelm it, and possibly him as well. It differs from the use of ordinary criminal sanctions in that, like other forms of behavior modification, aversive therapy seeks to evade rather than to develop the will. The person whose behavior has been successfully modified by aversive therapy does not restrain himself from committing punishable actions that still entice him through rational or irrational fear of punishment; but because the pleasure they give him has been spoiled by being repeatedly and consistently mixed with nausea, anxiety, humiliation, pain, or any combination of these, and by his own at least tacit consent. The alcoholic accepts an injection of apomorphine in a gruesome mock-up of a bar, drinks, and throws up; or allows his body to be injected with chemicals which insure that drink will make him deathly ill. Men who have raped children or fear that they might, and even homosexuals, permit psychologists to wire them up and give them electric shocks as they are shown pictures that arouse them sexually. The effect of such programs with adults is likely to be transitory; since they are taking part in them precisely because they are already well-aware that alcohol or heroin, whatever damage they may ultimately cause, do not make them feel acutely ill; nor do they experience pain when they touch a child or a person of the same sex, as the case may be. What is likely to endure is a sense of permanent humiliation at having allowed one's body, and its precious capacity for diverse satisfaction, to be violated in the interests of confirming a social norm; instead of having used one's essential strength both to assert and to contain one's actual proclivities. Nothing saps the will, including the will to socially-defined misconduct, like self-betrayal.

There is one experience that is familiar enough to many adults—especially males, since girls are less frequently subjected to it in most families—to give them some idea of the psychological processes involved in aversive therapy, if childhood amnesia has not screened away the memory of the feelings involved. Spanking is a true, though pre-scientific, means of aversive therapy. This seems obvious where the victim's offense was masturbation or some other form of sex-play, since the effect is to abruptly replace pleasurable erotic sensations with others even more intense that are accompanied by enough humiliation and loss of autonomy to ruin the culprit's satisfaction. Whatever he gets spanked for, the child has to deal with the humiliation of being "turned on" by his assailant in a degradation ceremony in which pain, though nearly lost in the welter of sensations being aroused in him, is the only one that is socially validated; the others are extinguished. To show any awareness of lustful pleasure would be to compound his offense with impertinence and risk being really hurt; as well as exquisitely inappropriate to an occasion formally defined as dolorous. Spanking works by invoking sexuality only to invalidate and mock it; the message is that the victim has gotten too big for his britches, which are removed to facilitate the operation. It also hurts, but not much; only enough to underline insult with token injury.

But the wellsprings of his pleasure are defiled, and with his consent. Children must submit to spanking, if only under threat of more severe and protracted punishment; and are expected to feel that it has done them good.

Aversive therapy can only be used in conjunction with pleasure to be spoiled. The merely coercive use of pain or the threat of pain may or may not alter behavior, but it isn't aversive therapy. In this respect spanking is closely analogous to the use of nausea to spoil the pleasure of problem drinkers and hence eliminate their misbehavior; because paddling—indeed, like drinking—is also an old-fashioned *rite de passage* in our culture, and one which the victim is expected to recognize and accept as sportive, if not entirely playful, and certainly as more friendly than punitive, even though it is much more severe than spanking. It has been the commonest means of initiation into groups of young males and even of marking the passage of birthdays. Its function, in fact, is just the opposite of disciplinary spanking, as social drinking is the precise contrary of aversive therapy for alcoholics.

Though, like alcohol, it takes a while to learn to enjoy it, paddling helps make the initiation a Dionysian revel. It validated the initiate's sexual maturity. The active, slightly elder brothers, vigorously asserting their *droight de seigneur,* provided him with an unmistakable sense of his own potency and a powerful prophylaxis against the cold showers his parents and teachers were still recommending to reduce his new sexual urgency. In this way, the erogenous zones were declared officially open for business or pleasure, though some confusion might later arise about object-choice; sexuality's inconvenient links with violence, domination, and submission were unduly and unfortunately emphasized, along with the initiate's tendencies to become, like his brothers, a male chauvinist pig. They, of course, called this making a man of him.

Most of this is now happily behind us, as social taboos have shifted from the area of sex, the family has lost its authority and even some of its authoritarianism, colleges have begun declaring for open enrollment, and fraternities have given up the ghost even where they have retained the charter. Spanking, though children are still subject to it, has now become one of many techniques sex manuals recommend as possible ways for men and women get to know one another better. I have used this example despite its welcome obsolescence because it seems to me likely to be accessible to more readers—themselves I presume, largely reared and educated in an earlier era—and effective in making it clear why I think aversive therapy is fundamentally mean-spirited and hostile to life, however imposingly scientific it may appear and however unpleasant the behavior it seeks to modify may be.

Meanwhile, our conflicts have moved into other areas. Are there now schools in which teachers are positively reinforcing friendly contacts between white children and black, while programmatically ignoring or mildly discouraging the development of intra-ethnic friendships? I have not seen such a program described; but I wish I thought it more unlikely. Has anybody applied for a LEAA grant for a program in which policemen would shoot at effigies of black adolescents in apparent flight with a handgun designed to give them a nasty shock each time they pulled the trigger? I hope not. The brotherhood of man may be—probably is—a hopelessly unattainable vision; but it should be made of sterner stuff than a conditioned response.

Behavior modification provides some highly effective techniques for reducing the occurrence of undesirable behavior; and there is certainly plenty of it to be reduced. But it offers itself as an inauthentic substitute for love and will, and hence is essentially frivolous about existence. It may be, in some instances, a useful tool; but it leaves its practitioners in the moral predicament of having used a tool on people they should have responded to as total beings. That just isn't what we need more of.

Humanism vs. Behaviorism

"A silly squabble," says Madeline Hunter. "How to handle it?"

EDUCATORS have allowed themselves to be lured into the silliest "You fight him" squabble of the century. Intelligent people are lined up on opposite sides ready for battle, waving clichés as banners and armed with inadequate knowledge and massive misconceptions. Bearers of each banner predict dire results from their opponents' philosophy and methodology while claiming miraculous educational healing powers for their own.

Unfortunately, both theoretical camps—the humanistic on one side, the behavioristic on the other—suffer from hardening of the categories and seemingly cannot look beyond their own biases. In their name-calling contest, humanists label behaviorists "manipulators," "controllers of human beings," "inhumane mechanistic technicians," "cold scientists." Behaviorists retort that humanists are "mushy thinkers," "oblivious of research," "unrealistic zealots who allow students nonproductive license," who may produce "selfish, nonsocialized illiterates."

Teachers, as practitioners, should be too concerned with successful learning to stoop to uninformed name-calling and cliché throwing, and should look at what each orientation has to offer. Teachers can then bring off in reality what both "camps" are striving to achieve in theory—a student with a positive and valid self-concept and productive interpersonal relations who pursues his/her own interests *as well as those interests and skills (s)he would never have discovered* without expert teaching.

Let's consider what each of these seemingly divergent orientations means to you.

Humanism is an *end*. Humanism focuses on a *goal* in education. That goal is based on fundamental respect for the worth of the individual, the right to be in charge of his/her own fate: to be a decision maker; to be proactive rather than merely reactive to the environment; to be a productive member of a group of choice; and to accept responsibility, beyond parochial interest, for the welfare of other humans.

There must be many *means* to achieve humanistic ends. Our most humane, self-actualized productive members of society have had different family, school, and environmental backgrounds. Undoubtedly, there are some invariant characteristics of their education, but it is highly unlikely that *one* educational method or organizational scheme was the critical factor.

Behaviorism is not a goal but refers to a theory-based means for achieving whatever goal the educational designer is attempting to achieve. It comes as a shock to some to realize that "behaviorism" is one of the most humanistic theories, for it *stresses the positive* and sounds warnings about use of negative reinforcers or punishment. Behaviorism is not a way of conducting schooling, but refers to the application of learning principles yielded by validated research which can operate in the most *open* or the most *closed* structure. The educator cannot *choose* to use behavioristic principles, she *is using* them! Those principles, like breathing, are ever present in any human interaction. The only choice the educator has is whether to use those principles deliberately to achieve humanistic results, or by default, to take the chance that those principles will be used in a haphazard or incorrect way to produce unintended or undesirable results.

While they are not the only important principles of learning, understanding four basic principles of reinforcement (positive reinforcement, negative reinforcement, extinction, and schedule of reinforcement) enables a teacher to assist in the acceleration of student growth in either the most humanistic or the most Hitlerian direction. Not understanding and being able to thoughtfully apply those principles handicaps a teacher (and consequently students) in the achievement of *any* goal.

There are those naïve few who contend that the power derived from knowledge of principles of reinforcement should not be placed in the hands of every teacher. That power is there *already* and we can no more remove it than we can remove nutritional power from the hands of a mother who is feeding her children. Best that both teachers and mothers know what they are doing and why, so they can add the propulsion from that knowledge to achieve humanistic results.

The unfortunate "coattail" associations of behaviorism grow from the "M & M's" methodology that originated with pathology and then was incorrectly extrapolated to normal classrooms. Because students in neuropsychiatric clinics needed food or other tangible reinforcers to strengthen their learning, some normal students are subjected to a bribery system of token economies so they can "buy" toys and other materialistic rewards for learning. Materialistic rewards are to behaviorism what opening a can of beans

32. Humanism vs. Behaviorism

is to culinary art—the lowest possible form!

How can teachers achieve the goals of the humanists using some scientific means, one of which is the methodology of the behaviorists, while leaving to the "angels-on-the-head-of-a-pin-zealots," the silly squabble which maintains the fantasy that the two orientations are antithetical?

First of all, teachers can scrutinize their programs to see that their goals and objectives are directly related to the humanistic goals of student self-direction, decision making, productive relationships with others, responsible freedom with escalating skills in the tool subjects of learning.

Next, teachers must validate that student *behaviors* (if you will pardon that word in a paragraph about humanistic goals) are perceivable, nonimpeachable evidence that students are growing in humanistic directions. Teachers must validate that students really are pursuing interests, not just talking about them; are increasingly in charge of themselves, not just responding to whatever stimuli impinge on them; are productively responsive to their own and others' rights and responsibilities, not oblivious of the consequences of their own acts; are competent in the 3Rs, not happy illiterates; are developing a repertoire of alternative strategies for learning so they have a full armamentarium to attack life's future learning challenges.

Finally, teachers should use the results emanating from research in learning, including but not limited to behavioristic principles, in order to achieve the goals of humanism.

In the same way that the architect can use his architectural theory and his artistry to design a Taj Mahal or a prison, so can the educator use behavioristic theory to create an educational life space that frees students to achieve humanistic goals or restricts students to noncreative limits.

The uninformed think of science as outside of and antithetical to humanistic concerns. But the goals of humanism cannot be achieved without the tools of science. Let's abandon this silly squabble between the philosophic stance of humanistic goals and the scientific stance of methodology. Top theoreticians in developmental theory and learning theory are moving closer together. Shouldn't we, as the implementors in the real world of schooling, combine the best philosophic ends with the most powerful scientific means to achieve a better educational world?

WE WELCOME YOUR COMMENTS

Only through this communication can we produce high quality materials in the Special Education field.

Special Learning Corporation
42 Boston Post Rd. Guilford, Connecticut 06437

Behavioral Technology: A NEGATIVE STAND

JAMES F. DAY

Professor of Educational Psychology and Guidance, University of Texas at El Paso

BEHAVIORISM and its accompanying educational technology constitute a growing movement in American education. This movement largely stems from the behaviorist B. F. Skinner, his followers, the industrial ideology of scientific management, and dissatisfaction with teacher education programs and the public schools. Many terms are being used to label the movement: Skinnerism, behavioral technology, shaping, operant conditioning, behavior modification, behavior training, contingency management, programmed instruction, accountability, performance-based education, performance-based teacher training, competency-based education, and competency/performance-based education. These have tended to camouflage the phenomenon. What the next euphemism for Skinnerism will be, no one knows. Regardless of the label used, the strategies for controlling behavior remain constant, and thus make the variance in nomenclature of no importance. Always the strategy aims to control, manipulate, or shape behavior from outside the individual. No provision is made for feelings, attitudes, mind, or inner phenomenological choice. Thus, to many, the Skinner doctrine makes man into an "empty organism" whose only right is to respond to the rewards administered by the controller or shaper.

Today, many teachers are talking about the control and regulation of classroom learning through reinforcement. In a behavioristic way, performance contracting and accountability are shifting learning responsibility from student to teacher. Some educational centers, state departments of education, and schools of education have gone overboard in accepting Skinner's behavioristic-industrial model. Teaching machines, computers, modules, and various other gadgets and hardware are being introduced in the name of efficiency. According to some, the competency-based certification approach is to be a vehicle for promoting change within the educational establishment. Five states (Florida, New York, Minnesota, Texas, and Washington) are now working toward the implementation of competency-based teacher education. Many other states and their departments of education are beginning to show a similar interest. The U.S. Office of Education's money grants have done much to stimulate the orthodoxy of behaviorism.

Many individuals and groups are reacting negatively to the trend of behavioral technology. They contend that teachers and professors do not need more controls and pressures. More time is required to be free and flexible in order to work properly with children and students. They maintain that students will be suffocated with the paraphernalia of technological gimmickry, behavioral objectives, behavioral modification, and the like. Statements are being made that the behavioristic-industrial model is a narrow, rigid, non-bookish, skill-centered curriculum which consists of trivial activities. Many other reasons are being offered for rejecting behavioral technology as the basis for education and teacher training. A rationale for a negative stand is given below.

For school learning, Skinner's theory is far too narrow. It emphasizes the one principle of external reinforcement to the ridiculous. When used in the classroom, it makes teachers into trainers, mechanics, and technicians, rather than professional guides of learning. For a learning theory to be adequate, it must take into account developmental processes, the effect of earlier learning on later learning, and the interrelationships of learning conditions and their applications to the acquisition of knowledge and understanding. Cognitive processes must not be ignored, as is done in operant conditioning. The behaviorists should realize that considerable research supports the position that the only subjects who are conditioned are those who are aware of the response-reinforcement contingency. Such research supports a cognitive theory and not the behaviorist contention that the effects of reinforcement operate automatically. Much more must be known about learning before American education should be dominated by operant conditioning with its one unproven law of reinforcement.

Teachers of all people should know better than to swallow a simple learning theory and a factory model of input-output efficiency. Tanner aptly states that, in performance contracting and accountability, "pecuniary values are attached mechanically to education so that the processes of learning are regarded as machine processes, and the outcomes are regarded as industrial products." Since the 1920's, many attempts have been made to solve the problems of education by using the

33. A Negative Stand

factory model of scientific management, but these efforts have always failed.

Skinnerism as a social philosophy is not in harmony with our republican democracy. It goes against the American concept of human freedom and individual opportunity. Left to the behaviorists, our traditional democratic concepts of the individual disappear. If there is one thing which can crush individuality in children, it is excessive control. Our salvation lies in maximizing freedom of choice. To exchange an individual's freedom for Skinnerian control would be to dehumanize individuals, institutions, and the schools.

Behaviorism, and especially Skinner's system, is externalistic. Individual choice is lost, since power flows from the one or ones in control. This does not result in individualized instruction as some have claimed. Actually, it is controlled or, at best, regulated instruction. We must not train students in our schools as animals are trained in the circus.

At best, competency-based education is a questionable doctrine; at worst, it is destructive to American education and our society. It rests on control and power, not freedom. The competency-based doctrine is now being forced by administrative decrees upon public school teachers and university professors. This is an abuse of power, and it is questionable that the legal capacity to make demands of this scope is possessed by state agencies of education. Also, questions of Federal constitutionality can be raised. University professors are expressing concern and negativism toward the several varieties of competency-based teacher education through their associations. The National Council of Teachers of English passed a resolution urging caution in the use of behavioral objectives. In 1972, the American Historical Association went on record as opposing any attempt by any individual, agency, or center to control the content of academic history courses by requirements to conform to performance-based objectives or behavioral objectives. The Texas chapter of the American Association of University Professors expressed concern regarding the Competency/Performance Based Education Program of the Texas Education Agency. College professors are stating that a competency-based behaviorism would impose a straitjacket upon teaching and imperil the future of higher education and the country. Mowrer calls Skinner's system a "political dictatorship." Others call it a straightforward form of fascism. Many are saying that teachers do not need more controls and pressures. They need freedom to be flexible so that they can develop their own unique teaching styles. Increasingly, the tables are being turned—teachers are now saying that the behaviorists who talk of teacher accountability are the ones who should be held accountable for the effects their demands are having, and will have, upon education.

Behavioral technology will not lead the way to quality education, but will lead to narrowness and triviality. In behavioral-based education, the student studies the module and possibly other instructional packages and then is evaluated. If his score is adequate, he goes to the next unit or module. Both learning and assessment are a step-by-step controlled progression through discrete and often non-bookish units. Such education would be dominated by objectives that are readily quantifiable. Under such domination, education would be skill training, and professional teacher education would become apprenticeship training. The consequences would be disastrous.

One consequence would be a narrowness which ignores important objectives. An assessment which only considers the degree to which performance objectives are realized will be an inadequate evaluation. Many of the effects of education can not be stated in measurable objectives. In education—and especially in professional teacher training—the important objectives are not subject to measurement because they are complex, broad, and, in many respects, unique to each person. Performance assessment would ignore such important matters as understanding, patience, flexibility, ego development, attitudes, and character.

Another consequence would be to turn education into an industrial factory. The emphasis would be on bureaucratic efficiency and the end product. Education, one hopes, is concerned with what goes on within the school and not with just what is produced. Pace says: "A college or university is a habitat, a society, a community, an environment, an ecosystem. It should be judged by the quality of life that it fosters, the opportunities and exploration it provides, the concerns for growth, for enrichment, and for culture that it exemplifies. The question is not just 'what does your machine produce?,' but also 'how does your garden grow?'"

A growing number of clinicians and counselors are rejecting Skinnerism from the standpoint of mental health. They contend that behavior modification techniques based on reinforcement hinder the development of mental health. Such techniques show utter neglect of the deep-seated origins of symptoms and disrespect for the meaning of symptoms from the individual's point of view. Some school children and students are greatly upset, and need help in the way of psychotherapy. The school should help in the treatment of these individuals by creating settings which convey acceptance, understanding, and respect for the emotional needs of students. For young people, humanistic thinking and planning is required, not behavioral tinkering and shaping which is devoid of feeling.

Both development and humanistic psychology supplement each other in making suggestions to education. Both are 180 degrees from behaviorism.

Developmental psychology is having a great influence on British schools, especially the infant schools. It is making for more informal, open education. The teacher is not concerned with controlling learning, but rather with being aware of each child's level of development, style of learning, and problems. There are no fixed seating arrangements. The teacher is a helper, a guide, a facilitator of learning of the child and of the group. Fortunately, mechanistic behaviorism has had little effect in England. Also, English school administrators are master teachers and give teachers freedom to be professionals in the classroom. The result is a humanizing atmosphere of teaching and not a rigid, skills-centered,

4. ETHICAL ISSUES

controlled behavioristic form of instruction.

Humanistic psychology takes the position that, in order to understand behavior, we must take into account a great web of variables. Each person is unique and functions as a whole. Thus, he should be taught and studied as a whole, since his parts are closely interrelated. The teacher must accept, understand, and focus on the whole child. The humanistic attitude is basic to education and educators. It is an opposite and preferred orientation to the analytic and atomistic approach of behaviorism. Many would agree with Maslow's statement: "I have become more and more inclined to think that the atomistic way of thinking is a form of mild psychopathology, or is at least one aspect of the syndrome of cognitive immaturity."

Teachers must satisfy student basic needs by putting more humaneness into our classrooms. A controlled behaviorist school and its many gimmicks such as performance contracting, voucher systems, and accountability should all be put out to a rocky pasture. Already, enough fragmentation of learning in the form of academic disciplines, subjects, and assignments exists in the traditional school. This artificial fragmentation will be a hundred times worse if the behaviorists take control. Educators should have enough sense to realize that important learnings and real growth are dynamic and complex and can not be accomplished with a prepackaged curriculum and by proceeding from skill to skill or from module to module. This is not education. Education comes through thought probing, exploring, and experimenting. American education needs the influence of developmental and humanistic scholars such as John Dewey, William James, Jean Piaget, Carl Rogers, Adolf Meyer, and the late Abraham Maslow, but not that of B. F. Skinner.

The history of America upholds professional teachers and traditional education. Certainly, our society does not support gimmickry without substance. Education can not afford to change in such wrong directions as behavioral technology. Should behaviorism continue to penetrate American education and professional teacher training, there soon will be no quality education—there will be factories concerned with skill training. Our people and culture will exist in a dehumanized desert with no learning, no understanding, and no freedom. Traditional education has changed gradually in attempting to meet student needs and social demands. Such education has survival value, while behavioral technology is untested.

At present, educational research has not provided results showing what works best in education. Research from a recent study conducted by a nonprofit research organization for the Office of Economic Opportunity (OEO) shows that the new experimental technology used in performance contracting proved to be no more successful than traditional classroom methods in school learning. This OEO research places reinforcement theory and its hardware of gimmicks on the chopping block. If we stay with traditional education, all can agree that professional teachers are needed. Such teachers—with a sound understanding of theory, knowledge, and instructional procedures—can gradually lead the way to improvement. This will not result in the educational confusion and high levels of anxiety which have accompanied the sudden introduction of behaviorism and its accompanying educational technology to American education.

Many hopeful signs are on the horizon. The Board of Directors of the National Education Association recently resolved to fight simplistic approaches to accountability in our schools. The NEA contends that our schools are in an "accountability crisis," and places much of the blame for this crisis on the faulty belief that schools can be run like industry. Robert Bhaerman, Director of Educational Research, American Federation of Teachers, has taken a negative stand on accountability.

Journals increasingly are containing articles which are opposed to Skinnerism. Teachers and university professors are joining ranks to stop behaviorism from dominating American education. One now can be somewhat optimistic that Skinnerism and educational technology will be contained and soon will be a thing of the past. American education then will be able once again to make sense and move toward quality.

After the containment of behavioral technology, American education must turn in proper directions. Changes toward improvements and quality education must be gradual and not upsetting. Research, sound thinking, and the experience of professional teachers can provide cues to guide the way toward quality education which satisfies student needs and social demands. It can be expected that Piaget's developmental psychology, humanistic psychology, and other points of view will have their influence. Perhaps even a few elements from behavioral technology will be retained and assimilated into education in the future.

B. J. MASON

BRAIN SURGERY TO CONTROL BEHAVIOR

Controversial operations are coming back as violence curbs

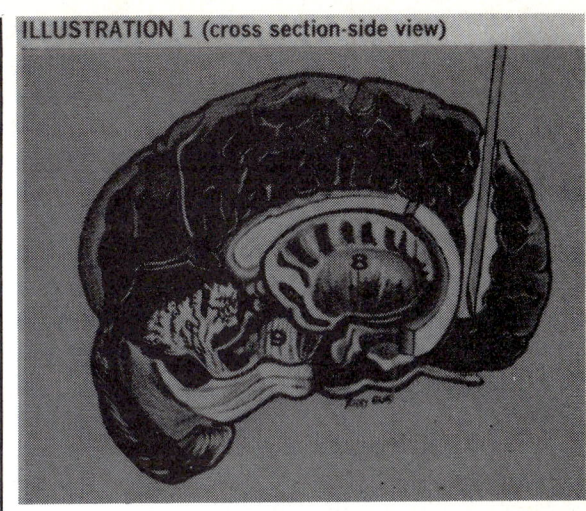

ILLUSTRATION 1
7. The frontal lobe is center of highest intelligence; operating here controls patients' level of awareness.
8. The hypothalamus contains cells that control hunger, thirst, sex drives; also source of anger and fear.
9. The midbrain area has centers that govern body movements. System helps keep brain alert.

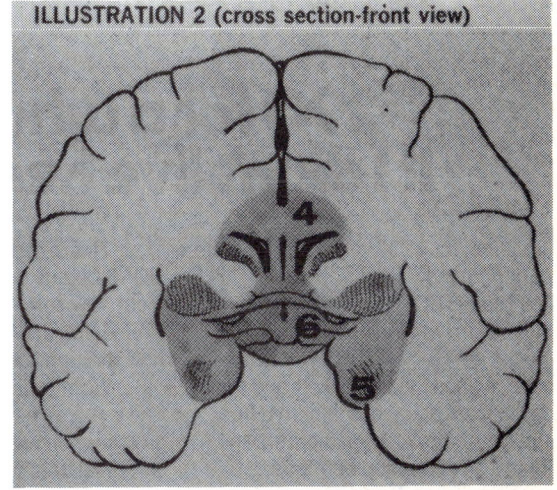

ILLUSTRATION 2
4. The cingulum bundle contains connections between parts of brain. Surgery here can make patient docile.
5. The Amygdala is nerve center on inner side of temporal lobe; moderates emotions. Removal alters behavior.
6. The thalamus is mass which functions as brain's switchboard; analyzes sensations. Surgery makes patient manageable.

An intelligent boy of nine is considered a pest by his mother. She takes him to a doctor who describes him as "hyperactive, aggressive, combative, explosive, destructive and sadistic." To make him more obedient and to control his behavior, the doctor slices the child's scalp open, drills holes through his skull and plants a few electrodes in his brain. Nine months later, the operation is repeated and the doctor reports that the boy's behavior is "markedly improved" and he is able to return to school. A year passes and his symptoms reappear. The doctor performs a third operation, after which he observes "impaired memory for recent events"—grounds for a fourth operation, following which all of the boy's original symptoms disappear. Satisfied, the doctor halts surgery but concludes: "Intellectually, however, the patient is deteriorating."

THIS bizarre scene is being replayed in dozens of hospitals across the country. Known as psychosurgery in medical circles, this form of brain surgery is widely used by neurosurgeons to control violent or otherwise "unacceptable" behavior in patients. Critics of this technique charge that it is no more than a new form of lobotomy, a type of brain operation performed during the '40s to make patients more manageable. Described as "swishing an ice pick around behind the eyeballs to destroy portions of the brain's frontal lobes," the lobotomy was superseded by drug therapy and electroshock in the late 1950s. Its opponents warn, however, that is now being revived—at the rate of 600 operations a year. Targets are supposed to be depressed women, hyperactive children, drug addicts, alcoholics, epileptics, neurotics, psychotics, convicts. Targets are often blacks.

Psychosurgery is the term used to describe the removal of brain tissue to modify or alter behavior without treating a known brain disease. Typical patients include those who display what psychosurgeons refer to as "symptoms of abnormal behavior," such as emotional tension, anxiety, aggressiveness, destructiveness, agitation, distractability, suicidal tendencies, nervousness, mood changes, rage, stealing and explosive emotions. It appears that two aspirins and a few minutes' rest will no longer do the trick. And since every human being exhibits at least one of these traits presumably all one has to do to qualify for such an operation is to rub society the wrong way.

Indeed, the Senate Appropriations Committee recently instructed the

4. ETHICAL ISSUES

National Institute of Mental Health (NIMH) to award a $500,000 grant to Dr. William Sweet, Chief of Neurosurgery at the Massachusetts General Hospital, to determine if there is any connection between violent behavior and brain disease. More specifically, he was asked to develop a way to identify and control persons who commit "senseless" violence, as well as those "who are constantly at odds with the law for minor crimes, assaults and constantly in and out of jail." This perked the interest of the Justice Department's Law Enforcement Assistance Administration (LEAA), which invested $108,930 in further brain research by two of Dr. Sweet's colleagues, Dr. Frank Ervin, a psychiatrist, and Dr. Vernon Mark, Chief of Neurosurgery at the nearby Boston City Hosiptal.

It didn't matter that the Kerner Commission had already concluded that white racism was at the root of civil violence. The Justice Department ordered the grantees to "determine the incidence of brain disorders in a state penitentiary for men; to establish their presence" in a civilian population; and to "improve, develop and test the usefulness" of electrodes and brain surgery "for the detection of such disorders in routine examination." Judging from the language of this directive, the Justice Department is interested in devising an early-warning system for riot control.

So are Drs. Sweet, Mark and Ervin, it seems. In a letter to the Journal of the American Medical Association titled, "Role of Brain Disease in Riots and Urban Violence," they wrote:

". . . if slum conditions alone determined and initiated riots, why are the vast majority of slum dwellers able to resist the temptations of unrestrained violence? Is there something peculiar about the violent slum dweller that differentiates him from his peaceful neighbor? . . . It would be of more than passing interest to find what percentage of the attempted and completed murders committed during the recent wave of riots were done without a motive . . . We need intensive research and clinical studies of the individuals committing the violence. The goal of such studies would be to pinpoint, diagnose and treat these people with low violence thresholds before they contribute to further tragedies."

Aside from its racist overtones, the letter clearly advocates a national screening program for the identification of blacks who *might* commit violence, not to mention that it set the stage for the NIMH grant to Dr. Sweet's Neuro-Research Foundation.

For some time now, Dr. Sweet and Dr. Mark have been performing psychosurgery on epileptics and people with emotional problems at Boston City Hospital. The part of the brain which controls their "strange" behavior is called the amygdala—an almond-shaped nerve center located on the inner side of the brain's temporal lobe. Since they believe it moderates emotions and drives, brain specialists agree that removing the amygdala curbs aggressive behavior and makes the patient docile. Dr. Peter Breggin, a Washington, D. C. psychiatrist and vocal opponent of psychosurgery, adds that "the only way this kind of operation can work is by blunting the emotions of the patient. To the extent that it blunts, it will also destroy some of the capacity for violence."

Dr. Mark denies that he and Dr. Sweet have been tampering with their patient's behavior. "Of course not," he says. "People who've had amygdalotomies don't change. If they're psychotic beforehand, this doesn't change their behavior." He stresses that he only operates on patients with temporal lobe epilepsy and feels that "brain surgery should never be done on individuals with a normally functioning brain to control their behavior—if they don't have brain disease."

However, Dr. Mark's psychiatric associate, Dr. Lawrence Razavi, contradicts him in a recent outline of their research objectives, which states that the purpose of the brain studies is to validate a battery of tests on "1) normals 2) epileptics without violent behavior 3) violent epileptics 4) violent individuals *without* apparent epileptic disease." The paper then goes on to state that brain surgery, "particularly where the amygdalus is entirely normal, may be construed as behavioral manipulation."

"No one," says Dr. Breggin, "could pretend to be on the side of the individual whom he is screening for the purposes of social control. The absurdity of saying that they are trying to 'help' their clients is pointed out by the fact that their brain studies are funded by the Justice Department." Dr. Alvin Poussaint, associate professor of psychiatry at Harvard University Medical School, puts it more bluntly. "The study is racist," he says. "It assumes that black people are genetically damaged —that they're so animal and so savage that whites have to carve on their brains to make them into human beings. The whole concept is vicious. When all these institutes around the country decide to study violence, who do they go look at? The *black* man. But who's committing all the violence? The *white* man, white society, white policemen. They don't consider that something's wrong with *their* brains."

"But we're talking about *senseless* violence," says Dr. Sweet, who is one of the original lobotomists. "Senseless violence is more likely to be associated with organic brain disease than violence with an ascertainable motive. The individuals who have this ultra-low threshold to violent assault and behavior would be utterly wanton and bring discredit on their movement by excesses of one sort or another. For example, when an individual opens fire on total strangers. A normal individual just doesn't do this." Dr. Mark adds: "What we were looking at were people who behave inappropriately in a riot."

Persons more in tune with the indignities suffered by blacks would argue that there is no such thing as "senseless" violence—that individuals who commit brutal acts in a riot always have reasons, whether whites consider them apparent and valid or not. They would further suggest that ghetto violence is not a symptom of brain disease, but a reaction to the pressures of white racism. One wonders if Drs. Sweet and Mark realize that ghetto *conditions*—not ghetto residents—are abnormal; or if they know that black rage follows no script. As for their concern about the black movement being discredited, there is the nagging suspicion that what is described as "senseless" is in reality that which white society cannot accept.

"Naturally, whites consider black violence senseless," says Dr. Poussaint. "It's their way of not looking at the system and seeing how it produces criminals. Instead of saying that blacks commit crimes because they're out of work or out of a thousand other things, they say it's because of brain damage. It's a spin-off from the old genetic theory, which held that blacks commit crime because of inferior intelligence. The difference is that Sweet and Mark carry it one step farther: not only are blacks retarded and dumb, but they also have something actively out of whack. They forget that everybody is capable of at least one act of violence. For them to try to find an organic reason for that one act is weird—and you can bet that this study will be more directed at black males to make them more docile—even if they only test whites."

Case History #2: A black male, 28, unemployed. Married. Wife supports him with meager earnings as clerk. Insecure, suspicious,

4. ETHICAL ISSUES

moody, explosive, he frequently accuses his wife of extra-marital relations, then strikes her about the face and arms. Doctor describes his condition as "uncontrollable rage." Following later brain surgery, patient loses memory of recent events and shows marked decline in simple awareness. Doctor notes: "aggressiveness no longer present."

DR. O. J. ANDY, neurosurgeon at the University of Mississippi Medical Center, has been performing thalamotomies on neurotic adults and aggressive adolescents—as well as hyperactive children as young as age six, some of whom are black. The thalamus is a pair of egg-shaped masses which function as a switchboard in the brain. It analyzes sensations and governs subjective feelings. Partial destruction of it makes patients more manageable.

According to a letter written by Dr. Andy's assistant, Dr. Marion Jurko, "The older children and adolescents have often run afoul of the law." He says that these children "could function in society if it were

Dr. Peter Breggin, Psychiatrist, Faculty Member, Washington School of Psychiatry: "These brain studies are not oriented toward liberation of the patient. They're oriented toward law and order and control—toward protecting society against the so-called radical individual."

not for their explosive, impulsive and unpredictable behavior." Apparently, we no longer have to worry about such shocking personality traits because Dr. Jurko tells us that "lesions . . . have reduced the tension level to a degree compatible with society." Describing the results of the operations, he says, "These individuals will not be contributors to society, but at least they will be tolerated." Frightening? But there is more: "The adults are average to above-average in intelligence. Many have low frustration tolerance. . . . most of them will tell you that they are tense, nervous, anxious, depressed . . ."

Dr. Andy himself has no doubts about the effect that psychosurgery has on behavior. "There's no question that it can be controlled," he says. "We have performed surgery on patients in which it has been very effective in controlling behavior or resulting in behavior being altered so that it conformed more with a normal human being in contrast to one that's at the extremes of behavior. You can say that his explosive emotional response has not only been blunted—it's no longer present." Although Dr. Andy claims that most of his patients are persons with some evidence of brain damage, he believes that people who are involved in any type of uprising—such as Watts and Detroit—"could have abnormal pathologic brains" and "should undergo tests with whatever capacity we have now."

34. Brain Surgery

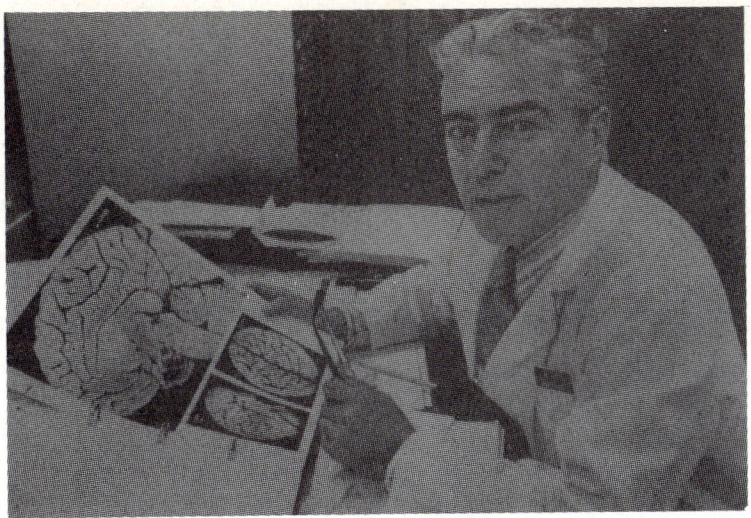

Dr. O. J. Andy, Neurosurgeon, University of Mississippi Medical Center: "Criminal aggressive behavior out on the streets? Yes. I think those who are involved in any uprising such as Watts or Detroit could have abnormal brains. Those people should undergo tests with whatever capacity we now have."

People who are unstable and explosive should then be operated on because "society demands correction or appropriate control."

The citizens of Philadelphia beam with pride when one mentions Hahneman Hospital. They point out that some of the world's best surgeons practice there and that its medical services rank second to none. Part of their praise is reserved for Dr. Jewell Osterholm and his associate, Dr. David Matthews, both neurosurgeons who have been performing cingulotomies on drug addicts, alcoholics and neurotics during the past two years. The cingulum contains connections between various parts of the brain. "A cingulotomy is nothing more than the newest version of lobotomy," says Dr. Breggin, former consultant for the National Institute of Mental Health. "It can turn a person into a zombie. It makes the patient docile, subdued and easy to manage. In order to be effective, it must pacify the person's personality. If it doesn't, it must be repeated and more and more of the patient's brain is removed until he's eventually subdued."

"It is very unrealistic for psychiatrists to think of psychosurgery as a threat," says Dr. Matthews. "The cingulum doesn't control behavior." But disputing his contention is Dr. M. Hunter Brown, senior neurosurgeon at Santa Monica Hospital. Dr. Brown is know as "Father Cingular" because he invented the operation in 1947. "Clinical observation has shown a high degree of successful control," he writes, "in cases of anxiety, phobias, depressions and obsessions. Since 1965 our major thrust has been directed to control or cure hard-core schizophrenic aggression."

Dr. Osterholm believes that persons who kill or beat others without any apparent motive are suffering from undisclosed seizure disorders. When asked about the difference between military killers and trigger-happy policemen on the one hand, and violent slum residents on the other, he says: "Oh, that's a different kind of thing. That's a training kind of thing. That's an *expected* behavior."

One of Dr. Osterholm's patients was a black man who had a pain disorder, a gunshot wound in his leg. "Everything had been done for that boy," Dr. Osterholm says, puffing on his pipe. The

4. ETHICAL ISSUES

Dr. Alvin Poussaint, Associate Prof. of Psychiatry, Harvard University Medical School: "These brain studies are racist. They say that black people are so animal and savage that whites have to carve on their brains to make them human beings. The whites are committing all the violence, but they don't consider that something's wrong with *their* brains. Ask them why not."

doctor operated on his brain for a gunshot wound in his leg, although one understands that the 'boy' was a drug addict. There were others, one of whom allegedly committed suicide. "No comment," says Dr. Osterholm: "Psychosurgery is only designed to relieve suffering, to make people feel better—not control their behavior." *And when suffering is relieved, do they act better?* "Yes," he says, "they're better people."

Case History #3: Female. Young. Psychiatric history incomplete. Brought in for surgery on emotional part of brain. Electrode implanted, but patient later becomes worse. A second operation is performed, after which she becomes enraged at both psychiatrist and neurosurgeon and refuses to talk. Electrodes removed. Rage dismissed as "paranoid." Patient's mood improves and she is allowed out of hospital to shop. Patient rushes to phone booth, calls her mother to say "goodbye," then poisons herself.

PRISONERS seem to be fair game for the psychosurgeon's knife. Three convicts recently underwent brain operations at the California Medical Facility at Vacaville. Reportedly designed to make them more manageable, the operations were performed in the prison surgery ward. It is likely that these medical maneuvers would have remained secret had the facts not been accidentally leaked to the public in a letter from Corrections Director R. K. Procunier to the California Council on Criminal Justice, requesting more funds for experiments on "violent inmates." Unfavorable press comment and a barrage of protests from the Berkeley Medical Committee for Human Rights caused prison authorities to temporarily shelve the project.

Prison officials claim that these operations are performed only when or if voluntary consent is obtained from selected inmates, but critics of the program argue that there is no such thing as "freedom of consent" in a penal institution since prisoner "cooperation" is invariably achieved under the threat of sanctions.

"What parole board wouldn't listen," asks Dr. Poussaint, "if an

34. Brain Surgery

Dr. Vernon Mark (r.), Chief of Neurosurgery, Boston City Hospital, talks with psychiatrists Dr. David Allen (l.) and Dr. Dietrich Blumer about his views on psychosurgery: "People who are sick deserve to be treated, and anyone who interferes with proper surgical treatment is unethical." Dr. Mark is recipient of Justice Dept.'s brain research grant.

unscrupulous doctor says that a prisoner has a lesion 'associated' with violence? If a convict submits to an operation in order to gain his freedom, he has to pay for it with a piece of his brain. If he *refuses* to submit, he has to risk having more time tacked on his sentence." Perhaps Dr. Poussaint recalls the British judge who ordered a chronic gambler to either agree to a brain operation or serve time in jail.

There is another concern.

The opponents of psychosurgery contend that confused or illiterate patients cannot give informed consent; hence, they can easily be duped into permitting an operation. Indeed, in many cases when a patient is judged incompetent, authorities rely upon the advice of the psychosurgeon who, with the consent of the patient's unsuspecting relatives or guardians, is usually eager to practice his trade.

"At best," says Dr. Breggin, "the choice is a sham. Once you've been labeled a mental patient, you become vulnerable to the worst things society has to offer: massive drug dosing, electroshock and lobotomy." Dr. Breggin once worked as an intern at the Massachusetts Mental Health Center, where he saw the vacant stares of lobotomy victims. Adds Dr. Poussaint: "Mental hospitals have been known to use electroshock in threatening or punitive ways. It's like, 'shape up or get zapped!'"

The advocates of psychosurgery respond that this argument is irrelevant if applied to patients who have been "suffering from continuous depression and anxiety which could not be relieved by any other treatment." Furthermore, they argue, people who are being "offered" the chance of undergoing psychosurgery, after which they *might* be able to lead a life within the law, are referred by a committee of medical consultants who would presumably eliminate coercion.

But Dr. Breggin is skeptical of watch-dog boards, "because control of them is almost never in the hands of the consumer. Besides, the psychiatrists with whom such boards will deal will not present an honest picture of the damaging effects of psychosurgery."

4. ETHICAL ISSUES

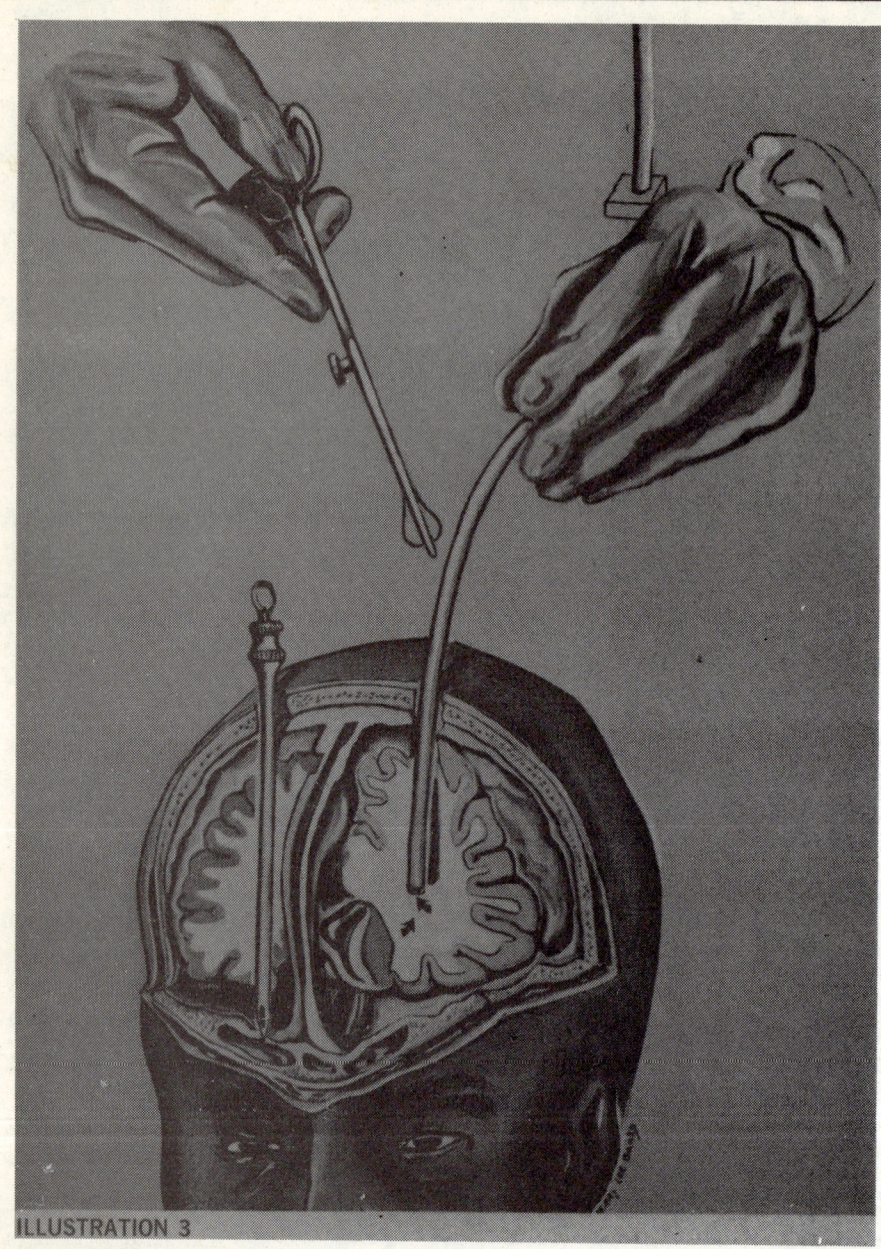

ILLUSTRATION 3
During the '40s and '50s lobotomy patients were turned into human vegetables after surgeons severed brain nerves. Although technique was outlawed, critics claim lobotomies are back as psychosurgery, the removal of brain tissue to curb unacceptable behavior without treating a known brain disease. Current brain studies are being funded by National Institute of Mental Health and Justice Dept. to determine connection between violence and brain disorders in convicts, children and rioters.

Finally, there is concern about the *effects* of psychosurgery. It is said to produce bad side-effects, such as loss of memory, dreams and daydreams, intellectual emptiness, lack of awareness, shallow religious feelings, lack of creativeness and loss of the ability to get angry. Thus, the crux of the argument against psychosurgery seems to be that *it evokes suffering instead of relief, and that other treatment at less risk is available.* Dr. Charles King, president of the American Ortho-Psychiatric Association, puts it this way: "If such experiments result in a nation of zombies, we might ask if the next step would be mass execution of 'undesirables.'" At present, there are no reliable controls.

Several Congressmen have withdrawn their support of a second research grant for brain studies, totaling $1 million. Among them are Sen. Cornelius Gallagher (D-N.J.); Sens. Edward Brooke (R-Mass.) and Ted Kennedy (D-Mass.). The list of opponents grows daily. They have brain surgery on their minds.

The Compleat Behavior Modifier: Confessions of an Overzealous Operant Conditioner

Roger MacNamara

ROGER MACNAMARA, M.Ed., Superintendent, Mansfield Training School, Mansfield Depot, CT 06251.

American society attaches great premium to excellence in all endeavors: athletic, technologic and philanthropic. It should therefore not surprise us that extraordinary triumphs in human services are similarly applauded by attendant professionals. Americans have always coveted their heroes and continue to enthusiastically elevate individuals possessing special talents or highly developed skills. Perhaps we have conditioned ourselves, into a dependency on the presence of paragons in our daily lives, whose records inspire us. Why should modern behaviorists be any different? Why shouldn't they have standards of excellence by which to recognize their superior members?

Beth Sulzer has created a hierarchy of classifications for behavior modifiers. She suggests four levels of skilled practitioners: (a) Behavior Co-Technician (carries out day-to-day operations of projects and program activities); (b) The Behavior Technologist Engineer (a designer of programs and implementor of same), (c) The Behavior Technology Coordinator (supervisor and trainer of technologists and technicians), (d) The Behavior Analyst (conceptualizer, supervisor and evaluator). She supports the system with hard, behavioral data, providing us with a useful taxonomy for organizing the efforts of clinicians; however, her system fails to provide universally clear signposts by which it is possible to instantly recognize the relative skills of behavior modifiers. A nomenclature that is empirically-based and unconfusing is suggested.

Level 1: The person who has never heard of behavior modification, nor wants to.

Level 2: The person who has seen and appreciated the movie, "Clockwork Orange."

Level 3: The person who has read one of Skinner's popular novels before it was listed on the best seller list.

Level 4: The person who has received 15 hours of in-service training or completed 6 hours of graduate study in learning theory.

Level 5: The person who has taught 15 hours of in-service training or 6 hours of graduate study in learning theory who may or may not have achieved Levels 1 through 4.

Level 6: The person who has developed into "the Compleat Behavior Modifier," the quintessence of modern behaviorism, a 6-gold medalist, a triple crown winner—the Compleat Behavior Modifier whose exploits in the arena of training and treating disabled and disturbed populations are legendary.

Because of the sacrifices required to accumulate the vast store of knowledge essential to the machinery of inductive reasoning, few practitioners attain the level of Compleat Behavior Modifier. The Compleat Behavior Modifier has fashioned a lifestyle based on learning theory, and he never weakens his methodology by investing anything less than his total effort in all of his activities. You will not find his office ostentatiously decorated with successful graphs from past projects; nor will you see the books of prominent authors strategically scattered on tables or stacked on his desk. Unlike his struggling counterparts, there are no posters on his walls exclaiming, "Give a desperate friend an M & M," "Catch a kid being good today," or "Where are your data tonight?" His is a serious mission, and it permeates every aspect of his life; he is frequently misunderstood and maligned for his dedication.

The following are true stories; only the names have been changed.

Instrumentation has always been a sign of status: the physician's stethoscope conspicuously dangling from the pocket of his long white coat; the accountant's pocket calculator; the teacher's grade book, and the administrator's Air Craft Carrier top desk. Consulting with an institution of self-injurious behavior, I wished to underline the need for cottage staff to gather specific data on the frequency of the behavior and any existing environmental relationships to it. I advised the staff that I would be extracting time samples from the topographies of the self-injurious behavior of the residents and not to allow my observations to interfere with their daily routines. They merely shrugged their shoulders and said that it wouldn't really matter to them. Recognizing that I had dual tasks of collecting the information I needed to form generalizations about the residents' self-abuse and establishing credibility with the employees, I always announced my arrival at the building cheerfully and joined the staff in coffee, while I reset my stop-watches, checked the batteries of my intervalometer, returned the digital counters mounted on my clip board to zero and inserted a fresh piece of interval spoilage chart paper. They regarded me with curiosity. I explained the nature of and the reasons for my equipment, and elucidated the myriad statistical benefits of objective behavior analysis. After 3 weeks of observation, I had retrieved a respectable supply of data, but it was anything but in-

4. ETHICAL ISSUES

ternally consistent due to the sharp fluctuations in the residents' behavior and the inconsistencies of their environment. I settled into the building for a lengthy observation session with my full array of equipment, forms and sharpened pencils. I stationed myself at a vantage point from which I could visually track the movements of targeted residents. Overly engrossed in my concentration, I paid little attention to a short but squarely built resident who had wandered over to me and was staring at me as I clicked, checked, timed and rustled my papers. I glanced at her briefly, threw her a quick smile and continued uninterrupted with my charting – sensing my auto-reinforcement of the discipline that allowed me to concentrate on my objective, despite all the distractions of the day hall. I closed out the fifth 30-second frame when the resident now by my side casually punched me in the groin. The searing pain expelled air from my lungs with an audible ooooff, and fighting the compelling urge to double over, I walked painfully by staff who smiled and wished me and my data well.

A large institution had asked me to offer inservice education for their aide personnel, a request I was happy to fulfill. During a coffee break of an ensuing class, I wandered into the kitchen of the building for a glass of water. I discretely observed a working resident washing dishes and utensils. She smiled pleasantly at me but continued with her tasks diligently. She was an attractive woman, well-groomed and appropriately dressed. I immediately began to wonder why she lived at the institution – probably another misplaced individual, when her head suddenly dropped at a 45 degree angle toward the floor in a crane-like motion. I drank another glass of water and continued to watch her obliquely. As she became aware of my attention, the response accelerated noticeably. I took a quick tabulation of the behavior and confirmed that this behavior was in fact significant. This tic could and should be removed by behavior analysis. Not thinking about the possible interpretation, I scribbled on a piece of paper the name of the building, a description of the resident and the target phrase "necking" behavior. After class I visited the Residential Program Director and questioned him about the resident and her tic. He confirmed my observation, explaining that she had been doing it for years and that there was nothing the physicians could recommend for it. I asked him if he had ever heard of reactive inhibition and he said, "*gesundheit.*" I corrected his misimpression by instructing him that reactive inhibition was the tendency of a neuron that has been over-excited to resist transmission of the electrical chemical energy of the brain. He said, "You have had some wonderful ideas that have been very helpful, but perhaps you should go back to your class and discuss other matters with them." "Look," I said, "the concept is unimportant, the point is that negative practice could possibly eliminate this necking behavior." He said that never helped him in college. He looked at me skeptically. I persisted, "Have you ever attempted to practice a word that was particularly difficult for you to pronounce and suddenly discover that you could not articulate it at all?" "This," I declared, "was the reverberatory inhibition that could have the identical effect on necking behavior. By reinforcing each response, and then gradually switching to an intermittent or variable ratio schedule of reinforcement, we could accelerate the necking behavior to such a high rate that when the reinforcement contingency was withdrawn, the inappropriate behavior would sharply decline in frequency." "And what if it reinforced the behavior and maintained it at a high level," he asked. Weakly, I said, "Well, we could always ignore it."

While a consultant, I visited an institution to assist with a few of their many problematic residents. In one building I found the staff engaged in their daily activities but carefully observing a young female resident who was sitting on a chair talking to a mop. She was discussing her mother with the mop, insisting that she should be going home for a visit that day. After an interval of approximately 30 seconds, a staff member approached the resident and gave her an M & M and told her that was "good talking." After watching the scene for 10 minutes, I wandered down to the office and asked the person in charge about the resident. She explained that the "girl" had recently been transferred to the facility from a mental hospital, and was described as verbal, and incapable of all self-help skills, but after a few days of silence, the staff had called the Psychology Department to request professional advice. The psychologist who answered was very understanding and recognized a familiar problem of poor reality orientation and suggested that the staff reinforce partial verbalizations with sweet foods. He was, at the time, busy graphing data from last year's toilet training program; otherwise he would have observed the resident himself. Besides, he said that he had perfect confidence in the building staff. "Give her an M & M every 30 seconds of verbal behavior and call me in the morning if the condition doesn't change." As far as I know, the resident and the mop are still good friends.

Discussion

Behavior modification is practiced in one form or another, correctly and incorrectly, and under several euphemisms in large and small agencies across the country. When an agency executive boasts, "Yes, we have behavior modification programs," what does that statement imply: that the agency ascribes to a specific program ethic or that it dabbles in the very popular approach? The sophistication to casually drop a theoretical term or articulate cahins of behavioral rhetoric only indicates that staff have expanded their vocabularies because conversance in behavioral methodology is not synonymous with competence in program development.

Behavior modification has been criticized as a poor descriptor for applied learning theory because of the possible connotation that all behavior can or should be altered. Call it behavior engineering, humanistic behaviorism, operant conditioning, reinforcement theory, behavior shaping or social engineering, behavior modification has survived *Playboy's* description of it in "Zap, you're cured," and *Psychology Today's* treatment of it in "Big brother and psychotechnology." But the most ominous threat to modern behaviorism is that we shall institutionalize it without preparing a proper place for it in our programs. It must have a context – a valid posture in relationship to the goals and objectives of our agencies. If behavioral methods are legitimate devices that have benefited the special populations we serve, then it is time to incorporate these techniques more logically and consistently into our systems, because if we fail to relate to behavior modification in terms of its intrinsic value to the programs we offer, we may isolate it and create possibilities that its value will be lost to us or that it will be abused by persons without scruples. Creating a proper and balanced position for behavior modification in organizations implies change, perhaps fundamental reforms to services. This casts the behaviorist in the role of agent for change, a delicate and frequently volatile position, which he will soon learn has highly personal dimensions. The reformer who believes that change is not an extremely personal process had better content himself with activities in pure research or curriculum development. "They call it business. Okay. But it's personal. . . You know where I learned that from? The Don. My old man. The Godfather. If a bolt of lightning hit a friend of his, the old man would take it personal." (Puzo, 1969).

The advocates of behavior modification wish to see the principles of human learning translated into the daily activities of institutional staff. To achieve this goal, they must develop a variety of strategies for promoting organizational change. These plans should embrace several practical axioms, including the notion that "change begins at the top." Superintendents of institutions and school systems may not exercise implacable control over their organizations, but their authority defines acceptable and unacceptable staff behaviors. It would be naive for behaviorists to believe that they can improve agency services without administrative endorsements. Even with this authority they may fail. Witness the number of progressive administrators who have been frustrated in their attempts to improve their own programs. Behavior modification, as a system, portends additional staff training, improved methods of communication, more intelligent supervision and continuous, objective self-evaluation. Without administrative understanding and sanctions, change will be limited and fractional. The administrator must personally feel the need for change, and this conversion, if it is one, is accomplished through a persuasive, logical and well-documented "sell" of new ideas. Today's administrators are numbed by criticisms, proposals and new systems. As a result, they may be jaundiced toward new inventions and proselytizing staff members. Modern administrators who believe in the participation of staff in the planning process and attempt to equalize the pressures of bureaucracies and constituents deserve more than programmatic pablum before they issue licenses to change their agencies. Managers must acquire confidence in change agents, a trust that they will act responsibly and sensibly. Administrators have had unfortunate experiences with change agents who have created chaotic situations and then run to the executive for solutions to the conflicts and frustrations they precipitated. Institutions have been the burial ground for good intentions and the careers of administrators. The conservativism of executives has been naturally acquired from experience but is amenable to thoughtful proposals carefully designed to produce maximum results with minimum repercussions.

Conclusion

We really do not need Compleat Behavior Modifiers to solve all the problems of the world. That which we do need are sensible, tenacious professionals who are unafraid to take calculated risks to obtain improved services for exceptional children and adults. The following points are suggested regarding the past and future impacts of behavior modification on programs.

1. No single approach to the problems and opportunities of behaviorally disorganized persons should be taken too seriously lest it be corrupted by over-application.

2. Behavior modification is not a theory; it is a compendium of methods and techniques, and we should be more interested in that which succeeds in the fulfillment of our objectives rather than that which commands our attention merely because of its esoteric sounds.

3. Line staff need to be thoroughly taught the process for successfully implementing and critically evaluating behavioral methods.

4. The organizational structures of our agencies, including the patterns of administration and supervision, need modernization to provide a compatible climate and meaningful context for behavior modification.

In 1966 when one of the first operant conditioning programs in an Eastern state was established our private school administration used it as an excuse to raise the tuitions of clients. I consulted with a program in another state in which the staff subsequently twisted the methods into cruel and unusual punishments. In yet another "progressive" state, I visited programs of behavior modification and discovered that they hadn't a share of evidence for the claims they had printed in their news letters. Is this the fate of behavior modification: to be overused or underused or misapplied? Where is the balance? Is behavior modification an important development in human services as the literature of the last 10 years has indicated? If it is, then it is time to disabuse it, eliminating suspicion and malpractice from it. We must thoroughly teach our staff its methods and its accountabilities and supervise their activities objectively and constructively. Behavior modification must be administered to directly as a manifest element in our programs for the developmentally disabled or be relegated to a minor issue, a fad that once captured the imaginations of a few zealots during a brief period of our professional history.

Self Behavior Modification Techniques

Shyness, extreme jealousy, insecurity, perpetual tardiness, all of these might be considered adverse behaviors. At the time that an individual finds it important to alter these behaviors it is quite possible, that through the implementation of behavior modification techniques, a self-change procedure can take place. By employing a carefully planned system of reinforcement the average person may make alterations of their own behavior in a wide variety of areas. Essential to the effectiveness of this process is an indepth inner search on the part of the individual for those factors which might be considered positive reinforcers and those which would be considered negative. This involves a true soul-searching activity, during which the person discovers exactly what they find satisfying, so as to serve as an aversive stimuli or punishment. Perhaps the businessman chronically late for work finds that daily he looks forward to his favorite cocktail on his return to home. This naturally can now serve as a positive reinforcer for him as he attempts to extinguish his tardiness.

Israel Goldiamond, an important researcher in the field of behavior modification, suggests the revision of the Greek maxim, "Know thyself" to "know thy behaviors, know thy environment, and know the functional relationship between the two . . . "

Goldiamond stresses the concept that if you want a specified behavior from yourself, it is essential that you first set up the conditions which you know will control it. Among the most common self-control projects that have met with success have been those to control smoking, being overweight, and getting organized.

A Road to Self-Control

Behavior modification stirs fears of authoritarian manipulation. Not likely, says a behavior therapist, in a course of treatment that allows the client, not the doctor, to pick the goals of therapy. Here is what has become of B.F. Skinner's baby.

by G. Terence Wilson
and Gerald C. Davison

FINGERNAILS BITTEN TO THE QUICK, eyes puffy from lack of sleep, Mrs. S. told the behavior therapist of a life dominated by anxiety and spells of nervous depression. Waves of acute fear and deep feelings of worthlessness would sweep over her, uncontrollable and unpredictable. Tension headaches, often precipitated by insomnia, brought almost daily stress and pain.

Mrs. S., aged 29, worked part-time in a college library, where the strain of her personal problems was beginning to show. Neither reassurance from friends nor Librium from her physician had helped. After her husband had accused her of being mentally disturbed and threatened to divorce her, she decided to seek professional help.

Traditional psychotherapists, of course, are confronted almost daily with such complex clinical problems. It is not generally known, however, that behavior therapists—who are sometimes said to deal only with single-symptom phobias—have been wrestling with the same kinds of challenges.

To help Mrs. S., the behavior therapist, like any professionally trained therapist, spent the first session establishing rapport. Regardless of the methods ultimately used, the patient's trust and cooperation are essential for success.

As the therapist gained her confidence, he began to make a behavioral assessment of the case, a searching analysis of the biological, psychological and sociological factors that were responsible for her distress. He then divided her problems into those resulting from behavioral excesses (such as frequent rages) and those resulting from behavioral deficits (such as underassertiveness). To learn more about her problems, he asked Mrs. S. about her social skills, her personal strengths, her sex life. He identified the specific conditions under which her problem behaviors occurred and charted Mrs. S.'s thoughts about her problems, noting how competent she felt as a wife and whether her personal standards were unrealistically stringent.

The Uptight Mrs. S. Specificity is the hallmark of behavior therapy. The therapist must find clear instances of behavior that exemplify the client's often vague, subjective impressions. Mrs. S., like most clients, tended to describe her problems in terms too general for a behavioral analysis: "I guess I'm just an uptight person." So the therapist asked her to keep a daily diary in which she was to record important events and her reactions to them. In addition to helping the therapist assess her behavior, this self-monitoring helped Mrs. S. develop her own awareness of the things that were causing her suffering.

After a half-dozen sessions, the behavioral assessment revealed a picture of a woman who had always been underassertive and often anxious in her relations with other people. Mrs. S.'s inability to express her feelings led to her exploitation by others, which in turn bred resentment, hidden anger, intense guilt over her anger, and low self-esteem. Her depression appeared to be tied closely to her negative picture of herself. The therapist also learned that Mrs. S. had never experienced an orgasm. She had tried to hide this fact from her husband, but felt that her lack of response was depriving him of a satisfying sexual relationship and might lead him to extramarital affairs. Such thoughts appeared to exacerbate her anxiety and her low opinion of herself. Since this problem and most of her other problems centered on her marital relationship, Mrs. S. agreed to the therapist's suggestion that they include her husband in the therapy.

While making the behavioral assessment, the therapist was also deciding tentatively on which therapeutic techniques to employ. Unlike many traditional psychotherapists who use an all-purpose treatment, behavior therapists can choose from a variety of methods within a theoretically consistent framework, tailoring the technique to the client rather than fitting the client's problems into a preordained therapeutic regimen. For Mrs. S., as for most complex cases, the therapist forged a multifaceted treatment program.

Early on, Mrs. S. began a program of relaxation training to curb her anxiety. This training shows the client how to tighten and then relax groups of muscles systematically so as to become more aware of the build-up of tension and to acquire the ability to relax at will. This training greatly reduced the severity of Mrs. S.'s insomnia and headaches in addition to damping down her anxiety.

Strategies for Assertiveness. In these same early sessions, the therapist started a program of assertion training. He had Mrs. S. rehearse more expressive ways of responding in situations in which she had always been submissive. He modeled appropriate behavior for her and made constructive comments on her efforts to emulate him. After helping her husband adopt a more supportive attitude toward her, the therapist instructed the couple in ways to use assertion strategies at home. In this way Mrs. S. learned to be

Humanists attack behavior therapy as a mechanistic, totalitarian form of control. But it's the client who has the major say about the goals of treatment.

assertive outside the therapist's office.

The third major facet of treatment was a Masters and Johnson-type program aimed at overcoming Mrs. S.'s lack of orgasm. Bolstered by the cooperation and understanding of her husband, Mrs. S. responded well and, after three weeks of treatment, began to have orgasms. This success, coupled with the assertion training, greatly enhanced the quality of their relationship.

Nevertheless, Mrs. S. still became depressed on occasion and continued to doubt her adequacy as a wife. These reactions appeared to stem from her unnecessarily low opinion of her own abilities, and the excessively negative interpretation she placed on different life situations. For example, rather than viewing as merely unfortunate her failure to meet her husband's train on time one day, she tended to see it as a catastrophe. Accordingly, the therapist used rational-emotive techniques originated by Albert Ellis [see "The No Cop-Out Therapy," pt, July 1973]. He encouraged Mrs. S. to think up and repeat constructive statements about herself that were incompatible with her feelings of worthlessness. After some initial struggling, she gradually acquired better control over her neurotic thought patterns than she had ever had.

Approximately four months after getting in touch with the therapist, Mrs. S. reported a dramatic reduction in anxiety and depression. Moreover, as part of her newfound emotional freedom and self-confidence, she had decided to return to school to work toward an advanced degree.

The Origins of Be Mod. The historical roots of behavior therapy go back to the beginning of this century, but it was not until the 1950s that behavior therapy emerged as an alternative to the prevailing psychodynamic or Freudian approach. One of the most influential pioneer investigators was Joseph Wolpe, whose book *Psychotherapy by Reciprocal Inhibition* appeared in 1958 [see "For Phobia: A Hair of the Hound," pt, June 1969]. In it, he introduced the anxiety-relieving technique of systematic desensitization, drawing on the earlier clinical work of Andrew Salter, and based on classical conditioning principles as developed by the Russian behaviorist Ivan Pavlov and the American behaviorist Clark Hull.

In systematic desensitization, an anxious or fearful client learns to relax completely. Then, while in a relaxed state, he is confronted with or is asked to imagine the situations or objects he fears, beginning with the least stressful and progressing to more and more difficult images. After several repetitions, this relaxed confrontation leads to a reduction in anxiety.

Wolpe's clinical studies in South Africa, as well as the innovative broad-spectrum approach of Arnold Lazarus, laid the groundwork for the contemporary practice of behavior therapy. At Maudsley Hospital in London, Hans J. Eysenck and his students gave important impetus to a scientific treatment of abnormal behavior based on learning theory. In the United States, the influence of B. F. Skinner and the development of operant conditioning helped establish observable behavior as worthy of study in its own right, rather than as a symptom of some underlying pathological illness [see "Beyond Freedom and Dignity," pt, August 1971]. The operant approach, with its emphasis on encouraging desirable behavior, was soon extended to the modification of a whole range of psychiatric disorders, particularly those of children and institutionalized adults.

The most sophisticated view of behavior therapy to date is the social-learning framework proposed by Albert Bandura of Stanford University. This approach focuses not only on changing behavior by using the techniques of operant and classical conditioning, but also on the role of thought in developing and maintaining the change. Bandura stresses the importance of vicarious learning, in which one watches another person model appropriate behavior. In contrast to a strict operant viewpoint, in which man is often seen as a passive reactor to external forces, Bandura has emphasized people's capacity for self-directed behavior change. The development of self-control procedures that promise people greater mastery over their own lives represents perhaps the most significant feature of contemporary behavior research and therapy.

Several misconceptions surround the practice of behavior therapy. It is often alleged, for example, that behavior therapy ignores the client's mind. While this allegation may be true of some radicals in the field, therapists who adhere to social-learning theory believe that what goes on inside a person is both a legitimate and necessary target for therapy.

Another misconception is that behavior therapy modifies only symptoms, whereas psychodynamic therapies deal with the real underlying causes of behavior disorders. Actually, the differences stem from different ideas about "underlying causes." Traditional therapists favor the past and the unconscious as determining a person's behavior, while behavior therapists emphasize current factors, such as rewards and punishments that follow behavior, as well as other sources of social influence on that behavior. An inadequate assessment of a client's behavior doubtless will lead to an incomplete treatment program and might well result in rapid relapse or apparent "symptom substitution." But this would be bad behavior therapy. In the case of Mrs. S., for example, simply using relaxation and assertion training would have left important causes of her distress untouched.

The burgeoning evidence from well-controlled clinical research suggests that behavior therapy has been successful in treating the entire spectrum of psychiatric disorders and is clearly the therapy of choice in many areas. It has been especially successful in the treatment of childhood disorders. Bed-wetting, for example, can be rapidly eliminated and, far from resulting in symptom substitution, its elimination produces generalized improvement in the child's functioning, both at home and at school. The treatment of autistic children by Ivar Lovaas and his colleagues has produced substantial, often dramatic therapeutic gains [see "A Conversation With Ivar Lovaas," pt, January 1974]. Other clinicians have made comparable advances with severely retarded children. Studies also have shown the efficacy of behavioral treatment for such problems as social withdrawal, delinquent acts, phobias, aggression, and social disruption.

Systematic desensitization is the most thoroughly researched technique used with adults. In 1969, after reviewing the evidence, Gordon L. Paul concluded that "for the first time in the history of psychological treatments, a specific technique has reliably produced measurable benefits for clients

5. SELF MODIFICATION

The End of Playboy Therapy
Homosexuality: No Target For Behavior Modification

A gap between behavior theory and behavior therapy is apparent in the matter of homosexuality. Theory, on the one hand, states that homosexual behavior is not intrinsically abnormal, that it develops and continues in the same way as heterosexual behavior. It is labeled abnormal only because of society's prejudice. Therapy, on the other hand, has worked hard to "heal" people's homosexual orientations.

Gay liberationists, concerned less with theory than with practice, have protested for years against such use of behavioral techniques. Therapists generally responded that they used the techniques only with clients who freely asked for them. The gays countered that, given society's prejudice, free choice was impossible. But only slowly have behavior therapists begun to recognize the discrepancy between their theory and their practice.

Gerald C. Davison, who developed and popularized a change technique called orgasmic reorientation, or "Playboy therapy," met the challenge head on last year in his presidential address to the Association for Advancement of Behavior Therapy.

"How can we honestly speak of nonprejudice," he asked his fellow therapists, "when we participate in therapy regimens that by their very existence . . . condone the current societal prejudice and perhaps also impede social change? . . .

"What is the real range of free choice available to homosexually oriented people who are racked with guilt, self-hate, and embarrassment, and who must endure the burden of societal prejudice and discrimination? What of the anxieties arising from this discrimination—how have we helped them with *these* problems?"

Davison went further. He called on behavior therapists to "stop engaging in voluntary therapy programs aimed at altering the choice of adult partners." Among the techniques he suggested dropping was his own Playboy therapy.

Indications are that many behavior therapists agree with Davison's point of view. Davison reports that he recently conducted a survey of attitudes among behavior therapists in the United States and England and found that "the vast majority of behavior therapists would indeed help their homosexual clients adjust more satisfactorily to a permanent homosexual identity."

—Kenneth Goodall

> *By emphasizing clear-cut goals chosen by the client, behavior therapists try to avoid the covert manipulations and subtle persuasions of less-structured therapies.*

across a broad range of distressing problems in which anxiety was of fundamental importance."

More recently developed methods such as "flooding," in which the client's avoidance reactions are directly modified in the real world, appear to be even more effective than desensitization. Masters and Johnson's successful, rapid-treatment program for sexual dysfunction uses many procedures that have been a standard part of the behavior therapist's repertoire since Wolpe's and Lazarus' pioneering contributions. Behavior therapy appears to be the preferred treatment for obesity, and progress has also been made in the treatment of smoking and alcoholism.

Although agreement certainly is not unanimous about the overall efficacy of behavior therapy, it is noteworthy that a special task force of the American Psychiatric Association concluded in 1973 that behavior therapy has "reached a stage of development where [it] unquestionably [has] much to offer informed clinicians in the service of modern clinical and social psychiatry."

Goals and Values. Opponents of behavior therapy, especially the followers of humanistic psychology, have attacked it as a mechanistic, totalitarian form of control that is imposed arbitrarily upon clients. Behavior therapy really is a collection of principles and techniques about *how* to change behavior; it says nothing about *who* should modify *what* behavior, or *why* or *when*. It is the client who has the major say in deciding on therapy goals. Selecting effective techniques with which to change behavior is an empirical question in which the therapist is presumably an expert; choosing therapeutic objectives is a matter of value judgments. The therapist's contribution to the latter lies in generating alternative strategies for the client to follow and in analyzing the likely consequences of pursuing different courses of action.

Selecting therapeutic goals is particularly difficult with clients who are in prisons or mental hospitals or who are too young or too mentally impaired to participate in determining the objectives of therapy. In these instances goals should be approved by an independent review committee created to safeguard the individual's civil rights and general well-being. In this connection, a special commission of the American Psychological Association is developing detailed guidelines for the ethical and legal practice of behavior therapy with different kinds of people.

Recent court decisions have argued that residents in correctional and psychiatric institutions possess a set of inalienable rights, and these rulings affect the practice of behavior therapy. For instance, some behavior therapists have offered inmates and patients the amenities of life as reinforcement for constructive changes in behavior. This practice has meant that these amenities were denied inmates at early stages of the program and then restored as the treatment progressed. In keeping with recent court rulings, such programs, predicated as they are upon the initial withholding of rights, seem no longer acceptable. As a result, behavior therapists will have to use increasing ingenuity in their efforts to find meaningful incentives for behavior change.

In a related area, behavior therapists have helped develop incentive systems to increase the productivity of inmates in prison industries and to encourage patients to help maintain hospital wards. The objectives of such systems are to provide rehabilitative experiences and to offer some distraction from the monotony of institutional life. Recent court rulings indicate that the servitude implicit in these programs must be replaced by compensation at or above the Federal minimum wage, and that participation must be voluntary. This ruling may work to the disadvantage of patients. Institutional directors, interested in maximum efficiency, may call upon outside employees to perform the essential jobs within institutions, thereby denying patients opportunities to acquire skills that could make them able to support themselves upon discharge.

The Politics of Be Mod. It is now widely acknowledged that all forms of therapy involve social influence. By explicitly recognizing this influence process and by emphasizing clear-cut, client-defined goals, behavior therapy attempts to avoid the covert manipulations and subtle persuasions inherent in less structured therapies. This approach, in which the sources of behavior control are openly identified and publicly disseminated, is a necessary deterrent to totalitarian control. As representatives of the Association for Advancement of Behavior Therapy argued at a recent conference of the American Civil Liberties Union, to allow these forces to remain beyond public scrutiny is to increase the possibility that the few who are skilled in these techniques will manipulate people for potentially antisocial ends.

Behavior therapy is far from being inconsistent with a humanistic philosophy. On the contrary, it is probably the most effective means of promoting personal freedom and individualism because it enhances the individual's freedom of choice. Mrs. S. had been a depressed, dependent woman, unable to express her genuine feelings or assert her right to be treated with respect. Freeing her from her crippling inhibitions and teaching her to be appropriately assertive gave her a sense of human dignity and expanded the courses of action open to her. She was able to assert herself with her husband without experiencing guilt, to obtain sexual fulfillment without embarrassment, and to return to college to pursue her studies. Behavior therapy need not limit creativity or produce conformity; rather, as Mrs. S.'s case illustrates, it can foster diversity, expand personal horizons and facilitate self-fulfillment.

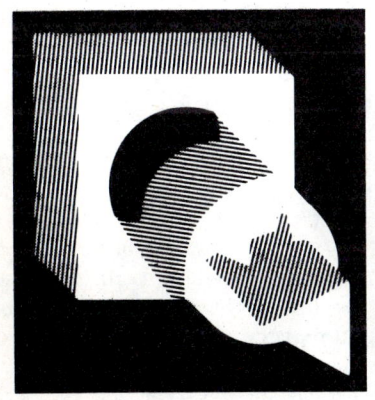

Diagnosis and Placement

Current trends in diagnostic procedures, along with a detailed look at medical assessment of exceptional children are discussed. The controversy of mainstreaming versus placement in self-contained special education classes is also featured.

For further information about this book and other special education materials, contact:

Joseph Logan, Editor
Special Learning Corporation

Special Learning Corporation
42 Boston Post Rd. Guilford, Connecticut 06437 (203) 453-6525

"WE'RE GONNA TEAR YOU DOWN AND PUT YOU BACK TOGETHER"

Thousands of educated citizens in New York, San Francisco and other cities buy $250 tickets for the latest pop-psych trip, Erhard Seminars Training, or est. Most come out inexpressibly pleased, eager to convert friends. A stubborn journalist reports his experience with est and with the supersalesman who invented it out of psychotechniques, Eastern and Western.

Mark Brewer

LOOSE AND COOL IN A BLACK SILK SHIRT and doeskin jacket, Werner Erhard sauntered down the center aisle of San Francisco's Civic Auditorium to thunderous applause. His smooth, handsome, male-model features bore the confident smile of a man who had packed a large auditorium at three dollars a head without a lick of advertising, and the 7,000 bright and well-dressed people who received him exuded the equally rare satisfaction of those who are about to be reminded they are perfect.

The fact is, however, that Werner could have told them almost anything, because the crowd that night was made up totally of est graduates—a fast-growing brand of person who has "gotten it" through an experience called Erhard Seminars Training, of which Werner is founding genius and guiding light. What they had all gotten in the "Training" was a "new dimension" that has, according to thousands from New York to California, changed their lives.

Est is no ordinary California cult. It is a multimillion dollar corporation that has doubled in size each year and operates nationwide with the efficiency of a crack brigade. It boasts a President who taught at Harvard Business School and left the position of General Manager of Coca-Cola Bottling Company of California to join Werner; it has been endorsed and even joined by prominent lawyers, doctors and psychologists; it has trained California schoolchildren under a Federal grant; and its Advisory Board is chaired by a former chancellor of the University of California Medical School, San Francisco.

That night as Werner took the stage in his easy, practiced, TV-emcee style, I was probably the only doubter in the house. His intimate, slightly nasal voice commanded a rapt attention as he addressed a subject dear to his heart: What It Is.

"It," he intoned, with a variety of examples, is "the awareness that you are"; which gradually led to the equally simple revelation that "the only way to be happy is to do what you're doing."

"SO WUT" Those words may be too facile for the uninitiated, but to the est people who sat spellbound by them, they were virtual gospel. The 90-minute performance concluded with a neat explanation of how everyone's life was turning out perfectly every instant, and then Werner thanked them humbly and disappeared through a rear exit to his waiting Mercedes 450 SEL and whooshed away into the night, his personalized license plates demanding, "SO WUT" So he has a pretty nice little deal going, that's wut.

All this started back in 1971, but the origins of est are not a favored topic of discussion with the staff, and neither is the paltry matter of who owns est. Mild-mannered corporate President Don Cox gave the following rather stiff explanation:

"Technically, est is owned by a trust which operates est for the benefit of the public, to whom est ultimately belongs. I'm not at liberty to divulge the name of the trust."

In a later conversation, however, when I brought up the subject again, it amused Cox to invoke the punch line of an old Hindu proverb, saying "it's like 'on what the elephant is standing no one knows.'" Est people are like that. On the same matter, Werner quipped, "Don't wanna know and there won't be any mystery."

Whoever owns the thing, est is a company whose primary business is the sale of a "standard training" which currently goes for $250 a head and lasts from 15 to 18 hours each Saturday and Sunday for two consecutive weekends. It is a training that "doesn't teach anything," according to Werner; "what it does is give people the space to learn from themselves."

More accurately, est has sold this space to over 35,000 people, there are some 8,000 more waiting in line for it, and est has

37. Back Together

To talk to an est graduate is like talking about LSD when you've never tripped.

probably grossed over six million dollars by now. This has all been accomplished by a national staff of fewer than 100 people, but who are considerably augmented by a small army of unpaid volunteers. In 1974 more than 3,500 volunteers contributed anywhere from a few hours to more than 40 hours a week to further the cause, and it is the est volunteer even more than the paid staff who makes est what it is. Stuffers of envelopes, reconcilers of records, answerers of phones, the est volunteers (who are typically middle class and in their late 20s) keep the office lights burning literally all hours. They are known to non-est people chiefly for their zombielike attention to duty, for their unfailing adulation of Werner and loyalty to the cause, and for a searching smile that one Berkeley psychologist, even *after* she took the "Training," described as ghoulish. Recently, Don Cox has had to impose a curfew to keep est workers from hanging around the office toiling all the time.

Free Vitamins but Few Bucks. The busy three-story office building that est leases on Union Street in San Francisco (and has already outgrown) is indeed an unusual place. It hums with an efficiency that is rather astounding, inspired by the guiding precept "to serve Werner and make est work." To this end, they work like ants for low pay, or none at all and, as Cox happily attests, never get sick. They do get free medical examinations and insurance, free vitamins, free chiropractic maintenance, and as an occasional bonus for exemplary service, they can get Rolfed, a process of twisting and pummeling the body that is reputed to be therapeutic [see "Sing the Body Electric," PT, October 1970]. "The result," Cox concluded, "is that this organization produces miracles."

Cox represents a miracle of sorts in himself. Formerly Vice President and Director of Planning with Coca-Cola, USA and then General Manager of Coca-Cola Bottling Co. of California, Cox took a hefty cut in salary to become est's chief executive.

"What you're seeing," Werner snapped one afternoon, "is people who know how to make the world work. People who know how to make life work!"

The "Training" is the common bond that holds it all together, and to talk to an est graduate about what it all means without having "gotten it" yourself is a lot like talking about LSD when you've never tripped. Moreover, it is a crucial and well respected tenet of est that graduates will

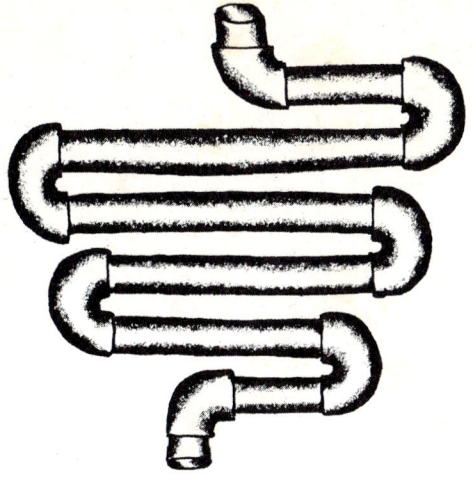

not discuss the content of the training with the uninitiated.

This rule stems from the est maxim that the training cannot be explained or understood, but only experienced. It is a convenient line of the sales pitch, but there is also a good deal of truth to it. What the training is more than anything else—and far more than any wide-eyed description that est graduates or staff give—is a brave new application of classic techniques in indoctrination and mental conditioning worthy of Pavlov himself. Nevertheless, it is difficult to condemn offhand anything that produces as high a degree of satisfaction and as strong a sense of new personal worth as est usually does.

No Advertising. The fact is, though, that almost none of the trainees know what they're getting in for when they arrive for the first long day of training. Ever since a small hand-picked group took Werner's initial est training in a borrowed apartment, the organization has eschewed advertising in favor of strong personal endorsements by new graduates. The glowing but suitably vague testimonials of a friend or relative bring potential recruits to guest seminars held in swanky hotel banquet rooms and led by est volunteers who have been rigorously drilled through a series of special "postgraduate" trainings on the tactics of getting people signed up for the trip.

"The purpose of the training," says Werner officially, "is to transform your ability to experience living so that the situations you have been trying to change or have been putting up with, clear up just in the process of life itself." And the guest seminar leaders cleverly come no closer than that to telling their audience what it is they're being urged to buy. They are inevitably asked, if it is encounter, Zen, meditation, positive thinking. It is all those things and none of them, they smile. It is also Transactional Analysis, the Bible, Gestalt and Taoism—and a good seminar leader can name several more. It is the latest model with all the options, a sort of short course in all those things you've heard about but never had time to get into. And there always seem to be only a few spaces left in that next training, but if you sign up that night you can make it.

My own training began at San Francisco's plush old St. Francis Hotel, where the new customers were processed on the mezzanine by est-folk who checked application forms, cheerfully verified or forthwith collected everyone's payment, then fitted each one with a tag that blared their first name and led them down to the spacious California Room.

No Talking. The recruits were told to take one of the 250 straight-backed chairs arranged in three neat groups before a low dais. Such a sense of rigid order, such a condescending mental-ward tone to the brisk instructions of the enigmatic est assistants prevailed that only the vague promise of a new life seemed to keep most of the newcomers present. Then when a tall, bespectacled automaton named Ron suddenly took the stage to bark like a drill sergeant that there would be NO TALKING, only the prepaid 200 bucks kept them.

As people began to look around carefully out of the corners of their eyes, Ron droned on: During the training, no one would move, talk, smoke, eat, or take notes, and no one would leave the room at any time for any reason unless a formal break (of which there would be a maximum of two each 16-hour day) was announced. Nor, during the nine-day period of the training, would anyone partake of alcohol, narcotics, or prescription drugs, although medicine required under doctor's orders could qualify for exemption. These, Ron impressed again and again, were "agreements"—not rules—and the trainees were instructed to register their accord by sitting still. Ron added finally that no general comments from the group would be "appropriate," but that if anyone cared to "share" something he was personally experiencing, he could simply raise a hand and, if recognized by the trainer, one of the young volunteers would speedily provide a microphone. Ron spent the next five minutes showing us precisely how to hold the mike, and the tone of the training was effectively set.

5. SELF MODIFICATION

"We're gonna throw away your belief system, tear you down and put you back together."

Napoleon in a Sport Coat. So in swept Tony Freedley, one of Erhard's original est disciples and the senior trainer who would harangue and cajole the recruits through the first half of their training. A dapper, diminutive fellow—who like all est men dresses exactly like Werner in sport coat, open collar, slacks and sleek shoes—he strode to the fore like Napoleon preparing to exhort indolent troops on the eve of a hopeless battle. Military training was apparent in his carriage and in the slightly pigeon-toed gait, and in fact, after receiving a degree in English literature from Harvard, Tony did three tours in Vietnam as a SEAL (Sea, Air and Land) commando for the Navy, running over 80 missions behind enemy lines. He has a round, almost soft face, but there is something tough and smart about it and he is one of the sharpest and most perceptive men you might ever meet.

He goes for the throat. They were present, he roared in command voice, because their lives did not work. Their lives were *shit*. Hopeless. They did not know what they were doing, did not know how to experience life, were struggling, desperate, confused. They were ASSHOLES! Tony savored the word a moment, used it again, and thenceforth, as is a matter of course in the training, the recruits were always referred to as assholes...until they "got it."

He began to describe all the pain and stress and discomfort and anxiety they were going to feel in the long hours ahead. Like an interrogator assuring a captive that he will inevitably crack, Tony took pleasure in predicting the sheer desperation with which each trainee, hours and hours hence, would desire merely to talk, stand up, leave the room, smoke a cigarette, go home, take a shit, anything. How they would feel hatred, boredom, ripped off..."until finally you begin to get," he shouted, "that you will do anything to keep from experiencing what is actually happening to you."

Werner's Razor. That line is essentially Werner's razor: your mind is so confused with beliefs and reasons about what is or could or should be wrong with you, or the world or everyone else, that you are incapable of even experiencing life, much less enjoying it. Therefore, yelled Tony, "We're gonna throw away your whole belief system.... We're gonna tear you down and put you back together."

Such efforts, of course, are commonly known as brainwashing, which is pre-

cisely what the est experience is, and the result is usually a classic conversion.

So on a Saturday morning in the St. Francis Hotel, Tony Freedley and his est assistants were starting off on another edition of the timeless endeavor to make the new man. By distorting the fundamental stimulus-response mechanisms of eating, moving, sleeping, smoking a cigarette or going to the john, while Tony bombarded them hour after hour about how their lives and their thinking were all fucked up, the training would shake, confuse and finally, in a great majority of cases, dislodge the old ideas and behavior patterns. And then in would go the desired est perceptions, and ultimately the notion that you are perfect the way you are.

When I asked Werner the difference between est and mass mind control, he brushed my query aside as not being "a representational question." At a subsequent interview, however, he offered a rather characteristic reply. "It's exactly the opposite of that," he explained. "When you do the opposite of something though, there will be several people who'll say that you're really doing whatever that something is."

Even some members of the est Advisory Board, whose duty it is to evaluate the techniques and results of the est training, are not much clearer about what's going on. The chairman of the Board is Philip Lee, M.D., Chancellor of the University of California Medical School from 1969 to 1972 and now a professor of social medicine and health policy there. It was the training, along with "getting to know Werner," that led Lee (who also sits on the boards of the Carnegie Corporation and Mayo Foundation) to join the Advisory Board, which he views as a sort of public service activity, adding that "as a faculty member, it's one of the things we're expected to do."

"We want to find out what it [the training] does, and second, then why," said Lee, explaining one of the roles of the Advisory Board. "We don't know either one yet."

Commonsense Psychology. It takes nearly 70 hours to get most or all of the trainees converted, and that time is filled with a variety of techniques and processes designed to alternately confuse and enlighten the subjects, to develop the authority of the trainer and build his suggestive power over the hapless "assholes." There is also, to be sure, a good double dose of commonsense psychology from which almost anyone could profit. And no matter what Erhard and his disciples teach or how they teach it, the training is a masterful amalgam of consciousness-altering techniques. And its effects upon the innocent is a rare thing to witness.

After several hours on the initial premise that the trainees are worthless, Tony produced on the blackboard, like Mephistopheles revealing the sign of the microcosm, the est chart of thought. It was a table of mental processes delineating all conceivable mental functions, divided into realms of experience and nonexperience. Belief, reason, logic and understanding were shown to be nonexperiential, and these secondhand mental exercises had to be abandoned to get at the meat of life.

In other words, as Werner methodically instructed me one morning, while we sat before the marble fireplace that warms his Victorian office, "Anything you're stuck in, you're the effect of. Man can't reason, he can only *have* reason. Most people can't feel, they can only have feelings that get pulled out by certain stimuli. That's the way man reasons—on a stimulus-response basis. When you transcend reason, then you are able to reason. Like, instance, Einstein transcended reason when he developed the theory of relativity. So he was able to reason."

For hours on end, however, out of boredom or real doubt, the trainees poured their resistance to this unthink into the microphones, and each time Tony was on them like a SEAL commando.

"But don't you *have* to believe in something to...."

37. Back Together

Lying on the floor, writhing amid a din of whimpers, sobs, retching and groaning.

"Don't give me your goddamn belief system, you dumb motherfucker!" he roared at one guy, charging off the dais. "That doesn't work! That's why your whole life doesn't work. Get rid of all that shit!"

The afternoon dragged past and Tony's assault on belief continued. Endlessly he seemed to recognize hands; dull-faced assistants hustled down the aisles with mikes, and one trainee after another shared disbelief, skepticism, pain or antagonism. Tony cursed or kidded each into seeing that it was all just another belief. And after each "sharing" Tony thanked the offerer and the other 249 "assholes" applauded briskly, as previously instructed, and the sharer generally sat down in confusion. Which was all right, Tony assured them all, because confusion was the first step toward "natural knowing," the very pinnacle of est-think.

It's Your Own Fault. Gradually, Tony moved on to another mainstay in the est body of knowledge, the idea of "taking responsibility for your life." It is basically the perception that your problems aren't caused by sicknesses or fate or other people, they are caused by you, and until you accept that, you'll never solve any of them. Not surprisingly, almost everyone in the room had an example of some exception in his own case, but Tony would have none of it. He wouldn't have cared if you'd been gang-raped or born with a brain defect, it was no goddamn excuse. Hours passed, Tony pounded away.

In our culture, however, six hours of deprivation is like seven years of locusts, and when aching backs, filling bladders, and desperately wandering minds finally neared the point of open rebellion, Tony showed them est's curative process. Concentrate on the pain, he taught them, until you can see its shape, its color, its texture, its very volume, and then it will disappear. And lo, one after another testified that indeed—no really!—it was gone. Tony smiled down serenely and sipped from a stainless steel beaker of tea.

The remainder of that first session, which lasted until about midnight, presented the preliminary forms of the est "process." The processes are crucial to the est experience, and they are officially referred to as "directed meditation," used according to Werner "to help people learn to create their own experience," but there are other names and explanations.

It began with Tony telling the trainees that they were going to enter a medita-

tional state and transport themselves to an idyllic beach. As a respite from hours of harangue, the prospect was received like water on the desert, and with all bodies properly positioned in the chairs and all eyes shut, Tony began to direct their minds. In the droning repetitive monotone of a language record, he bid them," . . . Create a space in your left foot. . . . Good. . . . Create a space in your left foot . . . Thank you. . . . Create a space in your left foot. . . . Good."

"The Poem." Always repeating the direction three times, he moved them from one foot to the other, step by step up each leg and through each area of the body, relaxing the group with incantations reminiscent of some theatrical mass hypnotist. Then, when the state of reverie was apparently reached, but before they were led to the promised beach, Tony read them a long creed that est refers to as "the poem." No copies of it may be had, even by est graduates. About as poetic as the Pledge of Allegiance, the lines are a long repetitive series of first-person affirmations about expanding awareness and heightening powers.

Tony led the group through three long processes that night, beginning each one with the same hypnotic direction (". . . Create a space in your head. . . .") and then the rambling creed, impressing their minds with positive attitudes and reinforcing his suggestive power. After each one, the trainees emerged blinking and slack-jawed, as if from a trance, and finally, near midnight, Tony sent them home rather tired and confused. But before they left, he promised them the big Truth Process the next day.

The Truth Process was indeed the high point of the second day, and it was approached over eight arduous hours like the peak of some mountain. What the trainees finally experienced, however, lying all over the floor of a banquet room in the Jack Tar Hotel, and prefaced of course by "directed meditation," was very similar to the Freudian process of abreaction.

We were told to choose one big problem that we wanted to solve and were then coached for hours on how, under the trancelike "directed meditation," to dredge up from memory all the actions and emotions associated with the things until we ultimately reached the cause of it, whereupon, like the pains of the day before, the afflictions would miraculously disappear.

Sobbing on the Floor. To varying degrees, the same technique is used in Gestalt therapies, Primal therapy and the "auditing" of Scientology, but in the est training it was done by almost 250 of us, lying on the floor, writhing and gesticulating amid a din of whimpers, sobs, retching and orgasmic groaning. At the end of it, the majority of the "assholes" were convinced that they had undergone a mysterious and deeply cleansing ordeal.

William Sargant, a British psychiatrist who made a study of very similar techniques of indoctrination and conversion in *Battle for the Mind* (1957), has described abreaction as "a time-worn physiological trick which has been used, for better or worse, by generations of preachers and demagogues to soften up their listeners' minds and help them take on desired patterns of belief and behavior." Werner staunchly maintains that the training is not intended to be psychotherapeutic. But his truth, it seems, shall make you free of symptoms.

One est graduate who relates having a "fairly dramatic" experience during the Truth Process is Philip Lee of the Advisory Board, and yet even he is a bit doubtful. Lee recalls "having had backaches on and off for, oh, 18 years, symptoms that would be fairly typical of a disc," and he "was having pain at the time of the training.

"I traced that back, went back to where it began, and during this process I realized that that pain wasn't a disc, but it was related to my relationship with my father. It wasn't clear to me what the factor was that was causing the pain, but after that I didn't have the pain. . . . Well, that was enough to convince me that there was

5. SELF MODIFICATION

About one a.m. they poured onto the streets, cocky as marines on leave after boot camp.

something to this."

Yet when I asked Lee how he thought the process worked, he seemed less sure of its value: "Well, I don't know. You know, I had that experience. But I'm a very uhh ... you know, I think it's easy to be conned. I think we're very gullible. I'm skeptical constantly about whether it had all these profound effects."

After dinner that second night, the trainees were put through what seemed like a bizarre induction to the est corps. The seats had been rearranged into long rows, the assistants seemed even stricter and more vigilant than usual, and a squad of fire-eyed est volunteers sat in a separate phalanx of chairs at the rear.

Row by row, we were commanded to line up on the stage, standing straight with our toes flush against a long white line, to be searchingly examined by our peers in the training, and it would be difficult for you to imagine the tension and fear that Tony and his assistants were able to whip up over this objectively ridiculous exercise.

Quiet and Afraid. While the assistants sternly patrolled the ranks of seated "assholes" to make sure they were quiet and attentive and suitably fearful of their own turn on the line, Tony strutted back and forth shouting in his best voice that this was it—none of that "bullshit" they always used to get along in life could help them now; they were going to be seen as they really were!

"Wipe that smile off," Tony snarled at one young man; "We don't think you're funny; we think you're pathetic." To another: "Stop trying to look so cool. They can see right through that. And there's NOTHING behind it!"

After each row had been on the line for a few minutes, the cadre of inspectors at the rear rose together, split into two groups and marched up either side of the room like stormtroopers. Reaching the front, they moved down the line, stopping suddenly before some unlucky trainee to stare feverishly into his eyes, nose to nose, for several minutes before returning to their seats as suddenly as they had come.

The tension and harassment, along with the trauma many of them suffered at standing openly before a large crowd, produced a number of breakdowns. In each row of 30 or 40 persons who took the stage, there were usually four or five who sobbed piteously or even swooned, completely overcome. Tony usually snapped, "That's just another act." One man hung his head

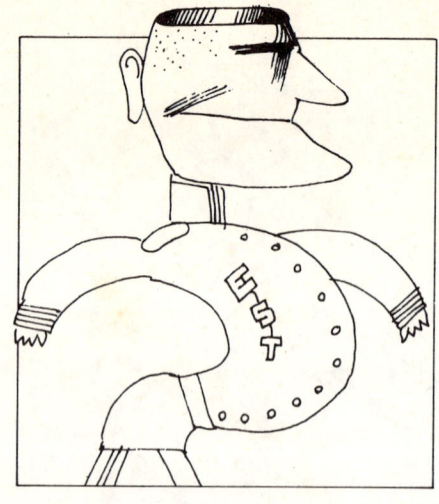

and bawled like a soul in hell. Another vomited.

"The Sunday Night Massacre." In the larger context of the est experience this ordeal is a key step in the process of conversion. "The Sunday night massacre," as one timid little man termed it, epitomized the aim of the first weekend. As in any serious training, the overriding effort is to hound and confuse the subjects until they crack under the pressure, and, in the helplessness of that moment, embrace the system.

Finally the trainees were ordered to stack their chairs and hit the deck again, whereupon Tony led them through another noisy and emotional process. At the end of it, he told them, by God, go out there and give 'em hell all week, and at about one a.m. the "assholes" poured onto abandoned streets, halfway through their training and as cocky as marines on the first leave after boot camp.

The intervening week, however, according to the trainees' testimonials at a mid-training seminar, was full of strange effects. There were those of course who expressed dismay at feeling no different from before. "Just stick with it," they were encouraged, "you'll get it." Several proclaimed a sort of early conversion, relating exciting states of happiness, increased energy and a great sense of well-being, while others, typical of people who have had their mental constructs juggled, reported strong and erratic emotions, such as crying for no apparent reason or breaking up in laughter at something no one else thought funny. Several others simply said that they felt pretty weird, at which the seminar leader would grin fiendishly as he led the group in a round of applause.

Still, regardless of their reactions to the course, virtually all of the "assholes" re-

mained true to the instruction not to try to figure out what was happening to them. Indeed, they seemed content to be told it was all done "because Werner found that it works."

When I tried to discover the paths through which Werner had acquired this wisdom, it was not easy. Est is a closed and defensive organization apparently believing with some justification that anyone, especially a journalist, who has not completed the training is an unknown entity and potentially a detractor. It was difficult to get much information out of them. But I persevered in wondering where Erhard came from, and the est office finally gave me a brisk two-page item headed "Werner Erhard: Professional Activities."

Aside from mentioning that he was born in Pennsylvania in 1935 and was graduated from high school in 1952, which was the extent of his formal education, it says only that "From 1963 to 1971 he was associated with *Parents Magazine*'s Cultural Institute and from 1967 to 1971 he served as its vice president." Now Parents Cultural Institute ceased to exist in 1969, so they must have made a mistake on the dates, but perhaps that's just as well, because from 1969 to 1971 Werner had other associations that might easily be misinterpreted.

A Change of Name. Long before, however, he was born near Philadelphia as Jack Rosenberg, son of a small-restaurant operator. After finishing high school he worked at several jobs, eventually becoming a sort of supervisor for a construction outfit. A few years later, about 1960, "to avoid the responsibilities I had," he took off for parts unknown. Those responsibilities amounted to a wife and four kids, and he avoided them all the way to St. Louis in the company of a woman named Ellen who is now his second wife. At about the same time, he changed his name to Werner Hans Erhard.

In St. Louis, Erhard worked as a representative for a school that taught operation of construction equipment and sold used cars. After a while he headed further west and began working for a correspondence school. He called on people who had indicated interest in the courses and, like good est volunteers today, talked them into buying some. Later he did a stint up in Spokane selling the Great Books and undergoing and studying hypnosis.

In 1963 Erhard joined the Parents Cultural Institute, a subsidiary of *Parents Magazine*. The Institute's sole business

37. Back Together

"You can't be anything but what you are. And that's a machine."

was publication of a set of encyclopedias to sell door to door. Werner excelled and did indeed become a vice president. He likes to recall that his duties were to "develop personnel, train executives," and run "a sort of development course," but the personnel department at *Parents* recalls that "his actual duties were as sales manager" and that he hired, trained and supervised door-to-door salesmen.

When PCI folded in 1969 Werner moved onto the fast track of the door-to-door circuit, Grolier Society, Inc. That corporation, which is presently inactive, was one of numerous Grolier Inc. subsidiaries, and its business was selling encyclopedias door to door. Here again, Werner recalls his job with Grolier as that of executive for development, but an old hand at Grolier remembers that he was a division manager who trained and supervised a stable of salespeople.

Werner stayed with Grolier until 1971, or roughly until est started, but this tenure somehow does not find its way into the résumé. The Grolier Society was at that time the target of several legal actions for fraudulent and deceptive sales techniques. The State of California filed two suits against Grolier Society, Inc. in 1970, charging that along with outright lies, the Grolier sales pitch used a variety of deceptive routines to trick people into buying encyclopedias. The State sought permanent injunctions against these practices and was successful in both cases.

On to Scientology. While with Grolier, Werner took up Scientology and distinguished himself by having been "expelled from the church," according to one spokesman. In fact, Scientologists get a sort of glint in their eyes when Werner is mentioned, and a public information officer maintains "we feel he took a lot of data from us and called it his."

After Scientology, Werner took the Mind Dynamics trip, which was a highly successful course that taught people how to control their minds and make them more efficient, largely through self-hypnosis. Werner thought it was great stuff and soon became an enthusiastic MD instructor. But Werner does not include Mind Dynamics among his professional activities either. MD, which has gone out of business, is being sued by the State of California for fraudulent claims and practicing medicine without a license. Publicity about Werner's MD days would also dull his claim that he is solely responsible for the techniques used in est,

for much of est is patterned after Mind Dynamics. Some of the processes are almost perfect copies.

In late 1971 Werner branched off and started his own training so that he could "do what I think everybody wants to do, which is to serve people." And as usual, serving the people has proved to be good work if you can get it. As founder and Chairman of the Board, Werner claims to receive only $30,000 a year from est (which incidentally showed a small loss in 1973 and is said to be designed only to break even), but in addition to his $14,000 Mercedes, he lives in a home worth at least $100,000, high in the hills of Marin County, works in a magnificently furnished Victorian mansion on Pacific Heights in San Francisco that serves as his office and *pied-à-terre*, has a personal staff including valet, a leased plane, literally thousands of people who work for Erhard Seminars Training, Inc., without pay, and thousands more who would walk to Bogotá if he suggested it.

It is interesting to note that Werner wrote a brief article entitled "Service" for the Mind Dynamics house organ a few years back. To enhance their appreciation of MD, he wrote, the graduates should "serve" others by getting them to take the course: "Choose five people that you are going to be responsible for having in Mind Dynamics. Be especially alive and in tune with these people . . . discover and carry out whatever service is necessary so that these people are able to overcome their obstacles and actually be in the course." Naturally, he did not mention that he would be pocketing a substantial portion of each $200 that these new recruits would fork over when they signed up for his class.

So perhaps it's best that not many of the trainees checked up on Werner. They might have gotten the idea that Werner has *almost* always been in the business of training people and psyching them up to sell something for him.

"You don't know anything yet," Ted Long hollered at us the next Saturday morning. "You've got a long way to go."

Long is a thirtyish-looking man with rather thin, severe features and prematurely gray hair, who was an attorney and vice-mayor of a small town near San Francisco before he saw the light and became an est trainer. Like virtually all est-men, Ted Long dresses, talks and acts like Werner.

The first session that Saturday lasted eight hours without a break, and the subject matter—after another dose of you're an asshole, your life is miserable, the training cannot not work—was a harangue on the nature of reality. The point came in a sudden switch, where nonreality (defined as that which is based solely on personal experience) suddenly became reality, and that which had been referred to for several hours as reality (the objective physical world) became unreal.

"You're a Machine." Sunday's instruction tackled no less a subject than the human mind and how it works. In a sealed ballroom of the Sheraton-Palace, the trainees sat in their chairs for an exhausting 10 straight hours, while Ted broke the mind into five nifty functions, which he rammed down their throats, as much by virtue of his own tenacity and the hopelessness of arguing as by the relative plausibility of it all, or the already well-conditioned receptiveness of the audience. In the end he had a beautifully interlocking model of the mind as a stimulus-response machine. It showed that, since your mind has no choice about the stimuli it records or the responses it produces, you have absolutely no choice about what you are or what you do. "That's *it*, folks," Ted crowed triumphantly. "You're a machine. *A machine!* Nothing but a goddamn machine! That's it," he repeated in a cruel, mocking tone. "You can't be anything but what you are. And that's a machine."

All those hours of training, all those processes and indoctrinations, had solidly established the authority of the trainer, and many at that moment must have felt as if the age-old questions of free will and determinism had been settled for all time.

5. SELF MODIFICATION

And since the vast majority of the trainees had been long ago persuaded that they were leading worthless lives, the effect of this thumping conclusion was shattering. The power that the training had achieved over their minds was never more impressive than at this point. It plunged the crowd into a profound depression. To pay 200 bucks, be convinced you're an "asshole," then told there was nothing you could do about it was too much. In the dead, dull silence it was as if the veil of hope were rent and a helpless damnation revealed. It blew their minds.

The Miracle. Then came the miracle. If you accept the nature of your mind, Ted explained with a rising optimism in his voice, and take responsibility for having created all the stimulus-response mechanisms it comprises, then in effect you have freely chosen to do everything you have ever done and to be precisely what you are. In that instant, you become exactly what you always wanted to be!

The validity of this explanation faded in and out of mental focus like a line of poetry not quite remembered, but in that dramatic moment of the training, the tired yet painstakingly conditioned trainees grasped it almost desperately, and it was implanted in their minds.

They were—no!—they *had been* "assholes" only because they did not realize that whatever they were, warts and all, it was exactly what they wanted to be.

The light dawned slowly, with Ted chirping, "See? See?," and then one and another and another acknowledged eagerly that, yes, they got it, and gradually a swell of exultant revelation swept the place. It was amazing to behold. They were perfect exactly the way they were.

There were those who didn't catch on, or who didn't think much of the revelation, or who were even hopping mad about being sold a bill of goods. But as usual about 200 people, roughly four fifths of the crowd, proclaimed their conversion, and the mood changed as if lepers had been cleansed. At this juncture they were allowed to go to the bathroom.

The initial rushes of the est conversion are, of course, hard for non-est people to swallow, since they appear absurdly simple or idiotic or both; and a lot of friendships and marriages have busted up soon after the training. Later on, though, when things have settled, some graduates simply have a feeling of okayness and self-confidence, while others, consumed by the notion that their mind is not only a machine but a perfect machine, act like robots. They are trained human beings, and they love it.

Est Ecstasy. Afloat on the new surge of confidence and lightheartedness, the majority of trainees returned from dinner that night eager for the next and final stage of instruction. They were greeted by a bubbly little number who was nearly ecstatic as she told them how clearly she knew that the main thing on their minds right then was wondering how to tell their family and friends about the amazing est experience. And boy, oh, boy, she giggled, nothing would enhance their experience like telling someone else about it. But, she warned, they had to be careful; they certainly didn't want to go trying to describe everything and ruin their friends' chances to have their own experience, now did they? Of course not. The thing to do, she instructed them, was to bring their friends to one of the guest seminars so that people who have been specially trained in these matters can handle them. And guess what? Their first chance to turn someone else on would be at their own post-training seminar the very next Wednesday night. Then she coached them for a few minutes more on how not to say too much, but just enough to indicate that this is something really far out.

The next Wednesday night, about a third of the new grads brought someone with them, and the new faces were quickly separated for special "guest seminar" treatment, while the grads themselves received another dose of est salesmanship.

Sitting again in the familiar chair formations with a trainer before them on the dais, they were introduced to the graduate seminar series, without which, it was clearly suggested, their experience would be incomplete. These seminars are conducted by various est trainers on subjects like "Be Here Now," or "What's So" or "About Sex," and they are held for several hours one night each week for about 200 graduates over 10 or 12 weeks, usually at the bargain price of $25 a head.

Below each of their chairs, the new graduates were conveniently provided a pencil and a sign-up card for the seminars, and when the trainer instructed them to go ahead and fill out the cards—even if they didn't think they wanted to take one of the seminars—the group complied automatically.

The Big Pitch. "I didn't like the way they pushed those seminars on us," said one of the graduates who manages a door-to-door-sales organization and is familiar with the tactics of coaxing a purchase. "He was taking advantage of the control he had over everyone, and I could see exactly what he was doing, but he was giving them the pitch so beautifully I couldn't say anything. Like this chick next to me said she wasn't going to take one, but then sure enough, when she started filling out the card she signed up."

The pitch, a steady barrage of mailings, and occasional telephone blitzes, has put about 80 percent of est graduates in the seminar program. But as Werner and Don Cox are quick to point out, they charge such a low price for the seminars that they actually lose money on all of them.

So why do they push them? To serve the graduates, of course, and as Werner says, "to the degree I'm serving people, I am being served." In other words, besides keeping the body of faithful intact, the seminar series provides a constant corps of proselytizers who are receiving a weekly re-infusion of the word, along with subtle and not so subtle encouragements to spread the light by selling the training to their friends, neighbors and family. This may be what they really mean when they say that est "makes your life work."

Many est graduates eschew the evangelical role and resent the insidious salesmanship. But they are a minority, and the much larger result is a sort of legally clean pyramid sales routine that has, in each year est has operated, doubled the number of graduates.

So est makes people happy and efficient, and perhaps such training is the wave of the future. In fact, it is Werner's hope that est will find its way into our social institutions. The recent, Federally funded est training of school children is a step in that direction.

Any citizen is free to spend money experiencing himself as a mechanical anus, and therefore discovering himself to be perfect. To each his own. However, I personally distrust any organization that transforms and uplifts thousands through the nihilism of a belief system that denies all other beliefs as bullshit. The use of brainwashing techniques, ostensibly to enhance peoples' lives, becomes bizarre when the outcome is to create unpaid salesmen. Smiling, they march out each week to share their brainwashed joys with friends, neighbors and co-workers, and they know that many will want to be sold. A friend of mine, an enthusiastic est graduate who considered becoming a guest seminar leader until it all began to seem insidious, wistfully recalled the power of the training. "They could've told me anything."

The Discovery of Middle Age

by WILLIAM BRIDGES

We are beginning to pay more attention to that long stretch between youth and old age. It turns out to have some significant features, and if we read them right, the finish can be even more rewarding than the beginning.

William Bridges is a writer and lecturer on human development. As the director of Passage-Ways in Santa Rosa, California, he does counseling and consulting, particularly in the area of midlife transitions.

1932—*Life Begins at Forty* by Walter Pitkin
1954—*The Revolt of the Middle-Aged Man* by Edmund Bergler
1967—*The Middle-Age Crisis* by Barbara Fried
       Men in Middle Life edited by Kenneth Soddy and Mary C. Kidson
1968—*Middle Age and Aging* edited by Bernice L. Neugarten
1973—*The Wonderful Crisis of Middle Age* by Eda LeShan
1975—*Prime Time* by Bernice and Morton Hunt
       The Male Climacteric by Helmut Ruebsaat and Raymond Hull
       Four Stages of Life by Marjorie F. Lowenthal, et al.
1976—*Passages* by Gail Sheehy
       Making It from Forty to Fifty by Joel Robert Davitz
       The Ulyssean Adult by John McLeish
       The Inner World of the Middle-Aged Man by Peter Chew
       The Angry Middle-Aged Man by Pat Watters

Illustrations by George Zebot

5. SELF MODIFICATION

> What if one's so-called problem is really the turmoil that naturally accompanies a new beginning—a breakthrough rather than a breakdown?

And by the time this appears in print, there will be others—other books on the middle years of adult life and the unexpected difficulties and opportunities that cluster at key times during those years. Nor do the books themselves tell the whole story. On TV there are "Phyllis" and "Maude," those menopause mentors who may be more influential than all the books put together. At the other end of the cultural spectrum, there are a flock of new psychology texts in "life-span" development (i.e., development that does not end at 25). In the past year there have also been whole magazine issues devoted to adulthood by *Daedalus, The Counseling Psychologist* and *The Nursing Journal*. God only knows the number of different articles that have come out and the number of dissertations begun on midlife this year!

It is tempting to chalk all of this activity up to the success of Gail Sheehy's bestselling *Passages*, and it is undeniable that that book is having the impact on the market that big new books in previously untilled fields have. But a glance at the list of books at the head of this article will show that Sheehy's book is itself a part of a larger and already-existing current. This becomes even clearer when we consider that she and her fellow writers draw heavily on research by Gould, Levinson and Jacques that began to be published in scholarly journals in the mid-'60s. Behind them is the work of such seminal investigators as Carl Jung and Charlotte Buhler, both of whom published important work in the '30s, and Erik Erikson, whose influential eight-stage scheme of human development appeared in 1950. And then there is the work, begun in the '40s under the Committee on Human Development at the University of Chicago, and the Kansas City Studies ... and ...

The point is that the mighty current has been abuilding for a long time *and* that it has rather suddenly emerged into full view in a flood of books and articles. While there is something very "trendy" about the sudden appearance of the pop versions of developmental psychology, there is also something significant about the slower and larger growth of interest in adult development and the idea of a midlife transition. This interest cuts far deeper than (but is still related to) the appearance of middle-aged heroines on TV. It has to do with what can only be called "The Discovery of Middle Age."

As with most great discoveries, this is a rediscovery in many ways. But it is nonetheless significant for that. Every epoch sees its own image in some arc of the life cycle and comes thereby to understand both that life phase and itself differently. The Romantics discovered childhood and saw their own hopefulness and naturalness embodied in the child. At the end of the 19th century, in the tired disillusionment the French called the *fin de siècle* spirit, gerontology and the systematic study of old age were born.

Today, as we try to turn away from an age of carelessness and chauvinism, wondering whether the future will bring decline and deterioration or some new phase of cultural development, we find ourselves studying the "midlife transition." I believe, in fact, that the bicentennial of America—an event that never quite found its own significance—was best understood as a Midlife Crisis of a whole society, just as the 200-year-old event in Philadelphia was essentially a Coming of Age.

To argue thus the timeliness of midlife issues is not to suggest that the midlife experience is new. There are plentiful records of men and women finding things going stale or falling apart sometime between 35 and 50. As many of the current midlife books note, Dante was 37 when he was banished from Florence and began to write his great *Divine Comedy*. That poem opens with the lines,

> Midway in life's journey I was made aware
> That I had strayed into a dark forest,
> And the right path appeared not anywhere.

Montaigne, Lincoln, Longfellow—one can extend the list of men who could have endorsed Dante's lines. And women, too. St. Theresa was 39 and a nun for more than half those years when her whole life was reoriented and renewed by a vision. The great Danish writer Karen Blixen ("Isak Dinesen") broke out of a time of difficulty and despair in her mid-40s to write the stories that finally brought her fame.

Some other cultures have had an image of the lifetime that incorporated this midpoint transition as we do the difficult stage or stages between childhood and adulthood. The ancient Hindu life cycle had four phases—apprentice, householder, forest dweller and pilgrim—with the first two devoted to the world's business and the second two spent on spiritual development and reattunement to the universe. Speaking of that time of turning at life's halfway point, Huston Smith has written:

> The time has come for the individual to begin his true adult education, to discover who he is and what life is about. What is the secret of the 'I' with which he has been on such intimate terms all these years, yet which remains a stranger, full of inexplicable quirks, baffling surds, irrational impulses? What lurks behind the world's facade, animating it, ordering it—to what end?

Our own culture lacks any such idea of midpoint turning, although the recent books may begin to change this. (Things move fast in these matters: *New West* magazine has already had an article on the "midlife crisis of two Southern California restaurants"! Oh,

38. Middle Age

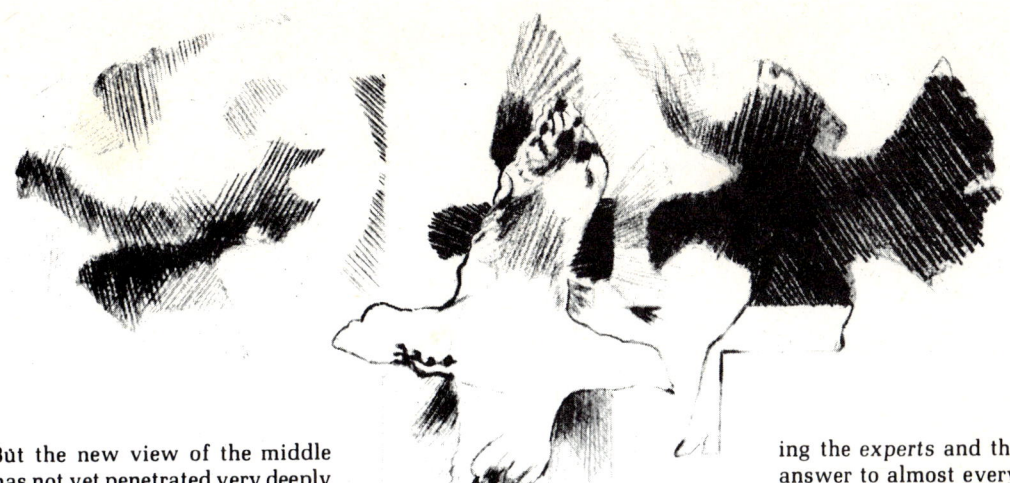

my!) But the new view of the middle years has not yet penetrated very deeply into the culture's fiber or the individual's consciousness. We still tend to think of adulthood as "life" itself—not as a time or times of different kinds of experience and choice and action, but simply as "living." Before 25, we know about the intellectual, emotional and physical development; after 65, we know about the physical deterioration and the adjustments that one must make to that. But in between—well, the image of those years is that of "functioning" rather than of growing. And on this functional plateau between 25 and 65, we have tended to think that "problems" are either externally caused or else a holdover from the world of childhood.

In the case of external problems, we look for traditional kinds of help and turn to the physician, the social worker, the minister or the lawyer. In cases where the problem suggests unfinished business from childhood, we turn to the psychotherapist or the analyst.

But what shall we do if the difficulty is neither extrinsic nor the result of childhood trauma? What shall we do if the difficulty is discovered to be a sign of one of life's transition times? What shall we do if the so-called problem is really the turmoil that naturally accompanies a new beginning—a breakthrough rather than a breakdown? Where shall we turn for help then? Who are the midwives of rebirth?

It is into this void that today's books on midlife flow. They vary enormously in approach and depth. Some, like *Passages*, sketch out a general scheme of the adult years and the "predictable crises" that are encountered by many people after 30. Others, like Watters's *The Angry Middle-Aged Man*, are personal chronicles of self-discovery. Still others, like LeShan's *Wonderful Crisis of Middle Age* and the Hunts' *Prime Time*, are primers for self-help in a difficult time.

Many of the current books are written by journalists or professional popularizers, and this has both good and ill effects. On the good side, there is the lack of dogmatism that the good reporter provides—something that many scholars, with their commitment to a particular point of view or a type of research, lack. And there is also the reporter's real concern to stick to things that have clear relevance to most readers and to leave the esoterica to others.

But there is a negative side, too. Imperceptibly the subject begins to shift from the topic itself to the process and the experience of pursuing the topic. In Chew's *Inner World*, for instance, we get the constant reminder of the reporter, notebook in hand, interviewing the experts and the subjects:

One brisk morning late in the month, we [William Henry Donaldson and Chew] sipped hot coffee and talked in the cheerful, high-ceilinged porch of his Kalorama house while sunshine streamed through the windows. He was not what my mind's eye had pictured. The former Wall Street tycoon and Undersecretary of State was wearing Topsiders with the marks of summer upon them; a T-shirt, sweater, and weathered slacks. "Boyish" isn't exactly the word, but it won't go away.

While Sheehy's book never reaches this personal level, there is the same reportorial stance—the same sense that an interview (or two or a hundred) is the way to get to the heart of the matter. People often attack the media for popularizing things and simplifying them, but popularization is a valid and important function. What the journalists of the press and the air *do* do, though, is to work on the principle that interviewing the *experts* and the *victims* is the answer to almost every situation. One imagines such possibilities as:

"When did you first notice, Mrs. Median, that the world was actually coming to an end?"

She pushed her blonde hair back out of her eyes with the back of her hand and said slowly, "Let's see, I think that it must have been about 3:15. I was just leaving the house to pick the twins up at school, and . . ."

—or—

Scholars differ on whether or not the white-robed figure that is currently "judging the quick and the dead" actually *is* the risen Christ or not. When I talked to Dr. Harrison Brown in his book-lined office at Union Theological Seminary, he puffed pensively on his pipe and said . . .

The quotes come thick and fast in this kind of writing. On one page it is Dr. So-and-so, and on the next it is "an old friend" or "a prominent attorney" or "several people that I talked to." Scholarly articles and cocktail chitchat jostle one another on the pages, and the result is not so much *writing* as a verbal collage that is much more sophisticated than, but otherwise not so different from, those old papers about China that we all wrote in the seventh grade.

That is one factor to note about many of these books, a shortcoming that is not so much theirs as it is a limitation of this culture's whole approach to important issues. Another problem has more to do with this particular subject, and it is that *Passages* and its fellow travelers are really concerned only with the first half of life. Sheehy subtitles her book *The Predictable Crises of Adult Life*, but she has almost nothing to say about life after 50. She inherits this problem from her sources, Roger Gould and Daniel Levinson. There is nothing wrong with limiting one's study to the years between 30 and 50, and these are certainly decades that have long been

191

5. SELF MODIFICATION

> The importance of attending to life's second half is that no part of a life makes complete sense without the whole life cycle being meaningful.

neglected by psychology. But a real survey of "adult development" must do more.

This is one reason why John McLeish's *The Ulyssean Adult* is an interesting book. Subtitled *Creativity in the Middle and Later Years*, it challenges the "declining years" image with dozens of examples of people, well-known and previously unknown, who continued or began to live creatively and do important projects after midlife. If Sheehy's book is journalistic, McLeish's is informal in an old-fashioned way. He cites the case of his own aunt and those of several friends, besides those of famous artists, statespersons and writers. He reviews both the conventional material on aging and the current criticisms of that material. He is sometimes a little overwhelming in his positive thinking, and the book is uneven. But *The Ulyssean Adult* nonetheless provides us with a useful supplement to most of the adult development books, which don't really cover the adult years as a whole.

The importance of attending to the second half of adult life is not simply that we need maps for that portion of the journey, too. It is that no part of the life cycle makes complete sense without the whole cycle being meaningful. Jung knew this, and he insisted that life's second half is an essential complement to the first. Erikson has always made the same point and has said that "a civilization can be measured by the meaning which it gives to the full cycle of life, for such meaning, or the lack of it, cannot fail to reach into the beginnings of the next generation."

The lack of such a holistic life view distorts the current research on adult development. When the interviewers go out with their notebooks, they are talking to people who are living their lives without benefit of such a life view. When they talk to researchers, they are talking to men and women who study people who lack any such view. What the interviewers discover is important —that there *are* patterns in adult life. We need to hear that, because for so long we have said that those patterns were limited to childhood. But child development has been the study of people growing toward something, toward adulthood. To say that the significant changes do not stop—that they continue through midlife (Sheehy) and into old age (McLeish)—is not the same as saying that "development" continues. Development presumes some larger pattern within which change is found to be significant. The task of integrating current research with some larger pattern of development remains to be done.

In the meantime, it is good that we have these books. The works of Neugarten, LeShan, Lowenthal, Sheehy and McLeish are crucial reminders that the pursuit of happiness is a life-long one. They remind us that most of our age norms ("Act your age!") are self-imposed. More importantly, they remind us that age stereotypes serve as self-fulfilling prophecies. To expect life to grow sad and thin after 60, to expect no new consuming interests after 50, to expect one's sexuality to become less and less important and gratifying after 40 is usually to be proven right. Because in nothing is expectation so powerful as it is in the matter of growing older—a journey in which we paradoxically both need our guidebooks and need to put them aside.

One of the seldom-noted phenomena in the world of psychology today is that much of the most exciting work is being done on topics that relate to the points of passage in the life cycle. I refer to both the work in natural childbirth and death and dying. I refer to the work on midlife transition and the coming of old age. I refer to the work on youth and language acquisition and right-left brain distinction. I refer to the interest in the androgynous aspects to life's second half, preretirement education, parent training and divorce counseling.

This is such a mixed bag that it is no wonder that we do not always see the connection among its contents, but the connection is a crucial one. On a very wide front, we are moving into new attitudes toward different times of life, different kinds of life transitions, different ways of beginning life and ending it. And out of this activity will come a different image of the life cycle.

The field of adult development and of midlife change in particular will be a part of this larger pattern and will gain from it the larger context it now lacks. For one thing, I believe that we will discover that the real significance of the midlife crisis depends as much on what comes after it as on what came before. The midlife transition is more than another time of reassessment; it is a turning time between life's two halves, a time of reorientation from the tasks of the first half to those of the second. Most of the writers on midlife today have no real sense of life's second half— except that it needn't be bad.

That's okay for now. And so are Phyllis and Maude, and their younger siblings, Mary Tyler Moore and Rhoda. (Why are all the new heroes heroines? That'll take another essay.) Through them and the journalists and the scholars and the precursors, the current flows, and imperceptibly the channel begins to change. We see that those problems we've had are not unique and that, in fact, they may even make sense. We begin to see that "unusual" lives— career changers, late starters, lifestyle changers—may not be so unusual after all. We may even discover, in fact, that "aging" isn't so bad and that, like Balzac's character who was delighted to find that he'd been talking prose all his life, we've been "developing" for all these years.

How to Overcome Shyness

Philip G. Zimbardo

Ever arrive at a party to discover the only person you know is the hostess—and she's not in sight? "Who are you?" someone asks, and only invisible butterflies come out of your mouth. Or have you stood in an elevator right next to the president of the company—your heart pounding, your palms dripping and your voice barely capable of squeaking a faint "Hello"? If you've experienced these or similar traumas, you've experienced the agony of shyness. Shyness can vary from occasional feelings of awkwardness in the presence of certain people, to torturous episodes of anxiety that totally disrupt a person's life.

In a survey of more than 4,000 people, more than 3,200 (80 percent) reported that they were shy at some point in their lives, and of these, 1,280 (40 percent) now considered themselves shy. Thus four out of every 10 people you meet, or 84 million Americans, are shy. The majority of these people are only shy in certain situations with certain types of people. They never learned the basic social skills and how to use them. Thus they have trouble meeting people, can't speak up in a group and get nervous at parties.

At one time, psychologists concentrated on tracing the problems of the shy to deep-seated pathological-emotional-motivational states. But today, instead of analyzing the oedipal complex of someone who is afraid to go on a job interview, for instance, some psychologists concentrate on giving that person the specific skills to have a successful interview. And the specific skills to overcome shyness are what this article will reveal.

Most advice to rid you of shyness comes under the heading of assertiveness training. Whenever I talk about assertion techniques at the Shyness Clinic at Stanford University invariably a voice is heard complaining that there already are too many aggressive bodies pushing their weight around. But to be assertive is not to be selfish, pushy or insensitive. Assertive people get a fair share of what life has to offer by communicating their needs, relating to the needs of others and choosing a lifestyle.

Before listing specific techniques, there are some general rules basic to combating shyness and making you more effectively assertive.

The first is the need for *action*. The drive isn't always there because anxiety, boredom and passivity generate more fatigue than the heaviest labors. But you will discover untapped sources of energy when you are doing what you want and reaping rewards for your actions.

The second is the importance of *role playing*. Given a part to play, shy people can step out of their timid selves by pretending to be someone else. You are not vulnerable because the "real" you is not being evaluated. Often shy people are too concerned that their actions do not reflect their real selves. But once having played the role, it is part of you. Research has shown that enacting a role different from your usual one results in corresponding changes in attitudes and values.

"I found that my shyness and embarrassment vanished when I assumed a role in a play," said a 50-year-old shy woman. "It was not me on the stage, it was someone else—and a chance to shed the uncomfortable me. This saved the shy me from serious emotional trouble and provided me with personal rewards and feelings of significance and achievement."

When role playing, you probably will find it useful to base your act on a script prepared in advance. Visualize the specific assertive actions you will engage in. In front of the mirror, rehearse specific lines, gestures and movements. Remember to speak so you'll be heard. Later on, when "stagefright" disappears, you can try more spontaneous, improvised performances.

Also, when it's time to put on your performance, *look as good as you can*, even better than you usually do. Get a haircut that is good for you—not just the latest style. If you don't use makeup, you might try using a little to highlight facial assets. Figure out which clothes look the best on you; if you don't know, ask your friends. Make sure what you're wearing is clean and neat. When you dress assertively (and comfortably), you will start *feeling* more assertive—and it will be even easier to pursue the following techniques to overcome shyness.

MAKE A CONTRACT WITH YOURSELF

To impose demands on yourself for an improved lifestyle, write out an explicit contract specifying:

1) The changes you want to make.

Decide on realistic changes. Talking to a group of 400 is not a realistic goal for someone who is afraid to meet one person. You might want to divide your goal into smaller, more manageable parts. For instance, if you'd like to make more friends, perhaps the first step would be to say hello to four new people this week.

2) How you will monitor yourself.

Keep a chart or a journal to note your progress. Or ask friends to monitor you.

3) How you will reward yourself as you fulfill each part of the contract.

"Every time I say hello to someone new, I will feel good inside and reward myself with a bath or a long walk or a movie." Be ready, willing and able to reinforce any and all behavior that meets (or exceeds) your desired standards of performance. It is especially crucial not to be stingy when it comes to dispensing rewards to yourself. Praise yourself profusely: "That was a good thing I did," "I'm pleased by the way I went about that."

5. SELF MODIFICATION

4) How you will know when you've completed the contract.

Set a deadline: "At the end of next week I will have said hello to four people and be ready for the next step in making friends."

5) What you will do if you fail to meet the contract.

Choose a punishment and make it stick. Cleaning the basement, raking leaves and straightening out the silverware drawer all qualify.

You can base a contract on any or all of the activities

listed below. These activities are designed to increase your stock of social skills so you can relate more effectively to the people in your life. Take the ones that are most important to you and design a program to accomplish each one. With concentration and practice, these skills will become second nature.

If you have a hard time talking to *anyone*, try some of these exercises:

PHONE CONVERSATIONS

- Call information and ask for the telephone numbers of people you want to call. Besides getting practice in talking to strangers you'll know you have the correct number. Also, thank the operator and note his or her reaction.
- Call a department store and check on the price of something advertised.
- Call a radio talk show to say you like the programming and ask a question.
- Call a local movie theater and ask for show times.
- Call the sports desk at the local newspaper and ask for the scores of a basketball, baseball or football game.
- Call the library and ask for some information you'd like to have.

You can use the phone to get yourself talking to someone while still remaining anonymous. Gradually, you can transfer this experience to calling people you want to contact and to greeting people on the street, as in the next exercise.

SAYING "HELLO"

For the next week, greet every person you pass on the street, in your office or at school. Smile and say, "Hello, nice day," or some other short greeting. Since most of us aren't used to being greeted on the street, you may find that some people do not respond, but in most cases you'll get an equally pleasant response.

ANONYMOUS CONVERSATIONS

A good way to practice your conversational skills is to strike up a conversation with strangers in such public places as grocery store lines, theater lines, a political rally, the doctor's waiting room, a sports event, the bank, the PTA, church, the library.

You can start the conversation with the *common experience* you are sharing: "This line is so long, it *must* be a good movie," or "I had a horrible time parking around here, do you know a good place?" or "Is that a good book (good buy, etc.). I've never read it (tried it)?"

GIVING AND ACCEPTING COMPLIMENTS

An easy way to start conversations and to help others as well as yourself feel good is to give compliments. You can compliment someone's appearance ("I like your suit," "Your hair looks great"), skills ("You are an excellent gardener"), personality traits ("I love your laugh, it's infectious"), or possessions ("What a terrific car"). To get into a conversation, simply add a question: "What a terrific car. How long have you had it?" or "You're an excellent gardener. What do you do about bugs?"

Learn to enjoy the compliments made to you. If someone says, "I like your suit," don't say, "Oh, this old thing. I should throw it away." This makes the other person feel foolish. At the very least, say, "Thank you." The best reply would be to add some positive feelings of your own. "Thanks. I like it, too," or "That's nice of you to say."

For the next two weeks, try to give at least three compliments a day—and keep track of the compliments made to you. Let yourself feel good about them, and show the person who compliments you that you really appreciate it.

You might also try complimenting people who you admire but who probably don't get many direct compliments because of their position of authority or power. As an example, try complimenting a teacher on a good lecture, your parents on a good deed, your boss on some action taken.

MEETING PEOPLE

Try to meet people. At first it's quantity that's important, not quality. Go to places where you feel the most comfortable: the supermarket, a book store, the library, a museum. Strike up at least one conversation wherever you go. Then branch out and try places that interest you but that aren't as "safe" as your comfortable spots: a coffeehouse, a writer's workshop, a hiking group, a woman's study group, a "Save the whales" group. Start at least one conversation using your mutual interests. If you feel uneasy, take a friend at first.

When you go to parties or other events, get your friends to introduce you to *their* friends. Be alert for others who will welcome your approach.

Plan to go somewhere at least three times a week for the next month. Decide week by week where you will go and who you will go with. If you plan to invite friends, get them to agree in advance. After each experience, write down where you went, what happened and how you felt. Figure out what made your experiences positive or negative and work to improve them.

HAVE SOMETHING TO TALK ABOUT

To get into good conversations, you must have something to say. Keep yourself informed. Read newspapers and/or newsmagazines. Know what the political situation is nationally and/or in your city and state. Read movie and book reviews; then go to movies and read books. Be knowledgeable on political, cultural or scientific topics. Take notes if you wish.

Come up with four or five interesting or exciting things that have happened to you recently. Turn them into brief stories by practicing in front of a mirror or with a tape recorder. Practice telling interesting stories that others have told you.

Jot down jokes if you feel comfortable telling them; but remember the punch lines or don't tell jokes!

See how many different stories you can tell other people in the next week. Gradually expand the number of stories you can tell. Always evaluate the appropriateness of your material.

STARTING A CONVERSATION

So there you are at the library, adult education course or dinner party. How do you start a conversation?

First, choose someone who looks approachable. He or she may be smiling at you or sitting alone or wandering around. Don't approach someone who's obviously busy doing something else.

When choosing a way to start a conversation, select the one that is most appropriate to your situation and that is most comfortable for you. Practice in front of a mirror or with a tape recorder. Then go out and try the following conversation starters to see which ones work best—and why.

1. Hello, my name is.... Introduce yourself and then exchange information on where you live, what you do, your family, etc. This is best for gatherings where everyone is a stranger.

2. Compliments followed by a question: "This is a great drink. How do you make a tequila sunrise?"

3. Requesting help. Make it obvious that you need help and that the other person can provide it. "Can you show me that dance step?"

4. Self disclosure. You'll find that when you make an obviously personal statement, it will elicit a positive, sympathetic response. "I'm not sure what I'm

39. Shyness

doing here, I'm really quite shy," or "I just got a divorce and feel a little shaky."
5. **Normal social graces** can start a conversation. "May I light your cigarette?" or, "Looks like you need a fresh drink. Can I get you one?"
6. **If you're at a total loss**, you can always fall back on some trite, but workable openers: "How do you like this weather?" or "Do you have a match?"

KEEPING THE CONVERSATION FLOWING

Once you've started a conversation you can use any of several techniques to keep it going.
1. Ask a question that is either *factual*, "How did the Dodgers do yesterday?" or *personal*, "Do you think Cyrus Vance will be a better secretary of state than Henry Kissinger?"
2. Offer one of the personal stories or opinions you've practiced telling.
3. Get the other person talking about himself or herself. "Where did you grow up? Do you like your work?"
4. Express interest in the other person's expertise. "How does a book get published?" or, "How do you start a day care center?"
5. Most important, share your reactions to what is taking place at that moment. What are you thinking and feeling about what the other person has said or done?

ACTIVE LISTENING

Become an *active* listener by paying attention to what people say. You can pick up lots of information and personality clues by listening carefully to conversations or discussions. Remember to:
• Give clear clues that you are paying attention—verbal ones: "Yes," "Uh, huh," "I see," "That's interesting," "Incredible," "Really?" and nonverbal ones: lean forward, sit up, stand closer, nod appropriately, etc.
• Do not make assumptions about motives and the person's inner states without checking them out: "It seems to me that you are really feeling hurt by not being invited to the party. Is that so?"
• Active listening also involves identifying with the other person's situation whenever possible. Or recasting what you've heard into an experience you can relate to: "I've never been in the army, but I can relate to following petty orders that are meaningless. When I worked as a camp counselor . . ."
• When you're in a conversation, don't hesitate to ask for clarification if you don't understand something. People often enjoy explaining things to others.

"SO LONG, IT'S BEEN GOOD TO KNOW YOU"

The rhetoric of leave-taking is a complicated ritual that has considerable significance for interpersonal relations. How you part from another person, and the manner in which you bring a conversation to an end, can either help your next encounter or undo all your efforts.

When you are finished saying all you have to, or when your allotted time is up, you must signify that you are about to go. However you do this, three messages must be conveyed: you will be leaving soon, you have gotten pleasure or benefitted in some way from the talk, and you hope there will be further contact in the future. There are several ways you can do this:

Reinforcement—short words signifying your agreement to the last thing the person said: "Sure," "Okay," "Right," etc.
Appreciation—a statement of pleasure: "I really enjoyed talking to you."
Completion sentence—"That's about it."
Nonverbal actions—Breaking eye contact, moving legs or feet toward the exit, leaning forward, smiling, nodding, handshaking—all say you are ready to leave.

Watch how your friends, acquaintances and people with whom you interact end *their conversations*. Right after you take your leave, write down all you recall saying or doing in the last minutes. Decide which leave-taking signals are clearest, feel most comfortable to you and seem to leave the other person feeling positive about the conversation with you. Work them into your personal rhetoric of goodbye.

BECOMING A SOCIAL ANIMAL

Here are a number of exercises that will help you get used to socializing. Choose several of these to accomplish in the next week. Start with the easiest and progress to those that are more difficult for you. Record your reactions to each of these exercises as well as the reactions you've elicited.

1. Introduce yourself to a new person in your office building, the grocery store or in a class.
2. Invite someone who is going your way to walk with you.
3. Ask to join the bull session you see in progress. If you're in an office, join a coffee-break talk group.
4. Ask someone you don't know if you can borrow ten cents for a phone call. Arrange to pay them back!
5. Find out the name of someone (opposite sex) in your office or class or social club. Call him or her on the phone and ask about the latest work issue, class assignment or upcoming event.
6. Stand in a line at a grocery store, bank or movie. Strike up a conversation about the line with whoever is near you.
7. Converse with the gas station attendant as he is filling the gas tank and checking the oil.
8. Sit down beside a person of the opposite sex in a bus, class, movie theater, etc. Make some sort of opening commentary.
9. Ask three people for directions. Talk with one of them for a minute or two about something other than the directions.
10. Go to a jogging track, beach or swimming pool. Converse with two or three strangers.
11. Notice someone who needs assistance in your neighborhood, class or office. Offer to help.
12. Carry a copy of a controversial book with you for one day. Count how many people you can get to start a conversation over it.
13. Throw a small party (three–five people). Invite at least one person you don't know well.
14. The next time you have a problem, find someone in your office or neighborhood who is not close to you, and ask his or her advice.
15. Invite someone out to lunch—someone you have not eaten with before.
16. Say "Hi" to five new people today who you would not usually greet. Try to provoke a smile and a return "Hi" from them.

FRIENDS FROM ACQUAINTANCES

Of the people you know only casually, which ones would you like to be closer to—to have as friends? Decide on several whom you will make a serious effort to get to know better. Write down everything you think you know about each person, and what you have in common. Decide on possible conversation topics and natural openers. Prepare for and make a brief initial contact by phone call or face-to-face. Be sure to identify yourself and announce that you want to chat for only a short time to get some advice, to check something out, to share something that he or she might be interested in. End with a positive expression of feeling.

During the week, follow up with an invitation to join you in some casual activity—a coffee break, a pizza, a local event or a walk. If you feel like it, express warmth toward the person by your attentiveness, support, encouragement and self-disclosure—and by saying so. Expand your circle of friends by using this "getting to know you" approach a number of times.

HANDLING INTERPERSONAL CONFLICT

Sharon and Gordon Bower, in their book *Asserting Yourself*, present a unique technique for handling most interpersonal conflicts—from the car repairman who is "ripping" you off to your husband who criticizes you in front of other people. The technique is called "DESC Scripts." (Describe, Express, Specify and Consequences).

DESCRIBE: Begin your script by de-

5. SELF MODIFICATION

scribing specifically and objectively the behavior that is bothersome to you: "You said these car repairs would cost $35 and now you're charging me $110." Or "The last three times we have been with other people you have criticized me in front of them."

EXPRESS: Say what you feel and think about this behavior. To the mechanic: "This makes me angry because I feel I'm being ripped off." To the husband: "This makes me feel humiliated and hurt."

SPECIFY: Ask for a different, specific behavior: "I would like you to readjust my bill to the original estimate unless you can clearly justify these extra charges." Or "I would like you to quit criticizing me and I will signal you every time you start to do it."

CONSEQUENCES: Spell out concretely and simply what your reward will be for changing the behavior: "If you do this, I will tell all my friends that I have gotten good service at Bob's repair shop." Or, "If you quit criticizing me I'll feel a lot better and bake you your favorite apple pie."

The best way to make these scripts effective is to write them out ahead of time and practice them in front of a mirror. Eventually, you'll be able to make up a script on the spot and deliver it effectively.

COPING WITH STRESS

Here are several techniques to help you cope with stress and/or anxiety. You can use these when you're anxious about going to a party, calling for a date, making a speech, etc. Sometimes one or two techniques will work. Sometimes you may need to use them all.

1. Be as prepared as possible. If necessary, practice beforehand.
2. If you can, relax or meditate for 20 minutes.
3. Lie down and imagine the entire scene in your head, detail by detail. Don't stop at any point, but keep moving through your scene.
4. Think of your comfort zone. This is a place where you feel the most comfortable. It might be on a beach or in the bathtub or walking through a field. When you're feeling anxious think about this experience in detail—the feelings, the smells, etc.
5. Say over and over in your head, "I know I can do this. I'm going to be good at it. I'm going to enjoy it."

All of the practice exercises discussed can help facilitate growth toward becoming a more effective, assertive social being. They must be practiced just as you would practice any other new set of skills. Initially, they may seem too artificial, planned or manipulative. But with practice and positive results, you will be able to adapt them into a personal style —your own style. Then they will no longer be externally imposed strategies for self-improvement, but self-initiated plans for enjoying a more satisfying life with other people.

LEARNING DISABILITIES

Specifically designed to follow an introductory course in learning disabilities, this book provides a comprehensive overview.

For further information about this book and other special education materials, contact:

Joseph Logan
Editor
Special Learning Corporation

Special Learning Corporation
42 Boston Post Rd. Guilford, Connecticut 06437   (203) 453-6525

The liberated grandmother

She treasures and uses her well-earned freedom, refusing subservient role offered by burdensome "grandmother myth."

Dorothy C. Finkelhor, Ph.D.

Do you think you're a successful grandmother because you do most of the things a typical grandmother is supposed to do? Or do you think you're an unsuccessful grandmother because you do it your way rather than play the typical grandmother role?

In view of the research I've conducted over the last five years, you may be in for a big surprise. The typical grandmother is usually a guilt-ridden failure. The grandmother with the gumption to break the typical grandmother mold is usually a success. She's the liberated grandmother.

Here's the difference between the typical grandmother and the liberated grandmother.

If you're a typical grandmother, you are:

A servant on call 24 hours a day without pay. A one-woman baby-sitting service who never says no. The family banker who seldom gets paid back. A teacher, counselor and guide whom no one listens to.

The cement that always tries to hold the family together especially on Thanksgiving and Christmas, but often with heartbreaking results. A woman who devotes her life to her grandchildren, who rejects her right to be her own true self and who seldom receives a thank you in return.

And, most of all, you're a woman who feels a compulsion to demonstrate your love by ceaseless attention to your grandchildren over and above your limit of endurance.

Talk to most grandmothers and once they get past the point of bragging about their grandchildren, they admit that "loving grandchildren as we think a typical grandmother should love them" is a bone-wearying job. Almost without exception, these women told me, "I'm happy to see my grandchildren come, and I'm happy to see them go. I haven't the energy for them over a long period of time."

Guilt feelings arise from assuming responsibilities far beyond her abilities and her strength. But why should a grandmother take on such nerve-wracking responsibilities?

"Because," answers the liberated grandmother, "most grandmothers are the victims of the grandmother myth. It's a pattern of emotional, physical and financial burdens forced on her by a male-oriented society. It's this myth that turns a normal, mature woman into a typical grandmother with heavy duties she can't possibly cope with."

The liberated grandmother will have no part of this myth. She refuses to let it trap her into subservience to her grandchildren and their parents for the rest of her life. By the time she reaches grandmotherhood, her maternal duties are done, her natural responsibilities to her family except to her husband are over. It is part of nature's plan to permit her to lead a full life according to her own needs and interests. It's natural for a grandmother to be free and liberated.

If you're a liberated grandmother:

You break the shackles of typical grandmother bondage. You guard your freedom zealously, because you know it's the most precious gift nature has to offer you. You have the right to your own life. You have the right to make come true the long-deferred dreams that you wistfully put

5. SELF MODIFICATION

aside while your children were growing up. You have the right to create a new you out of all the potentials locked up during the long years of maternal responsibility.

And, most of all, you have the right to love your grandchildren freely, sincerely, and as a special individual like no other in the world. You can see why a liberated grandmother is free from guilt. You can understand why a liberated grandmother is a successful grandmother.

Here's a fast way to find out if you are a successful grandmother:

RATE YOURSELF AS A GRANDMOTHER
A one-minute test

                                                                            YES NO

1. Do you feel it's your duty to pass on all your experiences in child-rearing to your children? ___ ___

2. Do you try to impose your ideas on your children because "Grandma knows best"? ___ ___

3. When you see your children doing something wrong for your grandchildren, do you step in to set things right? ___ ___

4. Do you attempt to bring up your grandchildren by telling them to "do things that are best for them"? ___ ___

5. Do you consider it your job as a grandmother to teach your grandchildren the graces? ___ ___

6. If it's a question of your approval or their parents', should it be your approval your grandchildren should look for? ___ ___

7. Since you're a good mother, does that mean you're a good grandmother? ___ ___

8. Do you spend endless amounts of time selecting toys, books and phonograph records for your grandchildren? ___ ___

9. Do you feel it's your duty to give money gifts to your grandchildren? ___ ___

                                                                            YES NO

10. When your children ask you to do something for your grandchildren, do you always do it? ___ ___

11. Do you feel you should express your love for your grandchildren as intensely as you did for your children? ___ ___

12. Do you believe you must live near your children so you can be helpful? ___ ___

13. Do you regard yourself as the perfect babysitter who is always available? ___ ___

14. Do you feel obliged to let your grandchildren visit you at any time, and stay as long as their parents let them? ___ ___

15. Do you feel it's your duty to play with your grandchildren? ___ ___

16. When you take care of your grandchildren, do you assume full responsibility for them? ___ ___

17. Do you believe holidays are happy times and that all the grandchildren should come to Grandma's? ___ ___

18. Is it your opinion that once a grandchild is born, it's only natural that your husband should take second place? ___ ___

19. Do you believe that your sex life is over once you become a grandmother? ___ ___

20. Do you enjoy being called Grandma by strangers and relatives other than your grandchildren? ___ ___

How to rate yourself:

If you answered any of the questions Yes, your Grandmother Rating is unsuccessful. The more Yes answers you checked off, the more unsuccessful you are as a grandmother. If you answered none of these questions Yes, you're a successful grandmother.

Any Yes answer characterizes you as trying to live up to the typical grandmother image, and that makes you a victim of the grandmother myth. The liberated grandmother answers No to all of these questions. Learning how to say No to the grandmother myth, and stop being a typical grandmother, is the key to your success as a grandmother, and as a fulfilled human being.

To become a liberated grandmother is far easier than you think. All you have to do is live your life guided by:

THE LIBERATED GRANDMOTHER'S BILL OF RIGHTS

1. You have the right to turn the job of grandmothering into a freelance activity.

Do work at being a grandmother your own way. You're the boss. Think out and feel out problems. Make your brain and your emotions work for you to come up with the happiest solutions.

Do avoid getting into typical grandmother routines. They're mechanical and thoughtless, and prevent you from being yourself.

2. You have the right to help your grandchildren, but only within the limits of your physical, emotional and financial strengths.

Do know your physical limitations in relation to your grandchildren, and never exceed them.

Do know just how much childhood imagination and activity you can take. When you've had enough, call it quits.

Do be realistic about giving money to your grandchildren. Your big income years may be in the past. You may need the cash more than the grandchildren. But don't be a skinflint either.

3. You have the right to teach your grandchildren, but only when the parents are willing and the grandchildren are ready to listen.

Do be sure you have the parents' approval before you teach your grandchildren anything.

Do wait until your grandchild is ready to listen to you before you begin to teach. Be patient and understanding and you'll know when the right time has arrived.

Do teach only those things that

40. Liberated Grandmother

only you can. For example, family history, good relations, and how to lead a productive and happy life.

Do read aloud. Your grandchildren will learn about the pleasures of reading cuddled warmly in your arms. You'll open their minds to the great world of books.

Do communicate with your grandchildren emotionally. Make your words and gestures carry your feelings. It's your right to teach your grandchildren the many ways of expressing affection and love.

To be a *real* "Supergrandmother," a woman must first be her own person.

Do overlook the routines of brushing teeth, shining shoes, and arriving home on time for dinner. Those are outside a grandmother's curriculum.

4. You have the right to baby-sit or not as you choose.

Do baby-sit only when you feel up to it, when you feel you'd like to, and when you're not overly inconvenienced doing so.

Do baby-sit in your own home, not your children's. In your children's home, your grandchild is likely to think, "My mother doesn't do it the way you're doing it, Grandma," and the child will often rebel. In your own home, there's no question about who's the boss.

5. You have the right to go anywhere in the world you please and stay as long as you like.

Do use your freedom from child-rearing to travel whenever the fancy strikes you, and live wherever you like. And don't watch the clock or the calendar. One of the great joys of your later years is not having to cut short a fun time by hurrying back to family cares.

6. You have the right to love your grandchildren as a grandmother, not as a mother.

Do get over the notion that you ought to love your grandchildren equally. That's a mother's duty, not a grandmother's. Make up your mind to this guilt-erasing fact: It's impossible for a grandmother to love all her grandchildren with the same fervor.

Do give more of yourself to those grandchildren who need love most.

7. You have the right to be made happy by your grandchildren and their parents.

Do get used to the idea that love is a two-way street: You should be getting as much as you're giving. Without pussyfooting, come right out and say to your children, "Here are some of the things you and the kids can do to make me happy. . . ." Then tell them exactly what they are. Most grandmothers I've interviewed will settle for three simple things.

"Telephone." Grandmothers love to hear the details of their grandchildren's lives.

"Ask me what I do all day long." Grandmothers want their children to understand and appreciate their activities, especially when they're new activities made possible by increased leisure time. I have never met a grandmother who didn't need the approval of her children. Most grandmothers feel that when the children approve, the grandchildren will follow suit.

"Send me letters." Without exception, grandmothers told me that one of the most dismal sights in their day-to-day existence is the empty mailbox. The newsy letters from their children and from their grandchildren are, as one grandmother put it, "like greeting cards all year."

8. You have the right to be your own person.

Do realize that you are a special kind of individual like no other in the world.

9. You have the right to self-esteem.

Do rid yourself of the notion that you can only get a feeling of self-esteem by acting like a typical grandmother. The more you do, the more unsuccessful you'll be as a grandmother.

Remember, you don't automatically become a typical grandmother the moment your first grandchild is born. You don't automatically decide to devote the rest of your life to your grandchildren. You remain yourself with the same needs, prejudices and feelings as before. If you want to develop that self along your own lines, go to it! For the first time in your life, nature has handed you your chance. Let me explain:

Consider your life as a pie. When you're a baby, the whole pie of life belongs to you; you have no responsibilities to anybody. When you're four years old, you're sent to nursery school. You now have responsibilities to the school, and a slice of life's pie is lost to you.

When you enter regular school, you lose another slice of the pie. With each brother and sister born into the family, more and more slices of the pie are cut away from you. Higher education, your worklife, your marriage scoop out all but one of the remaining slices. And that slice disappears when you become a typical grandmother. You could be left with not even a crumb of life's pie.

But when you don't become a typical grandmother, one last slice of life's pie remains. It's the slice nature has reserved for you alone. It can be the best slice. When you start to enjoy it, you start to build your new life. And you're free to make of that life anything you desire.

That's what being a liberated grandmother is all about.

199

Psychotherapy After Forty

Resources are available to help people adjust to problems in the second half of life, but the aged and their families must seek them out.

by T. L. BRINK, Ph.D.

41. After Forty

Can't cope with life? Learn how! Be happy—for a price! All across America the mental health business is booming. Fifty years ago it was thought that only *crazy* people should be handed over to a psychiatrist. Now it is realized that many persons, even without severe mental or emotional problems, can benefit from psychotherapy. Many normal, basically healthy persons experience some difficulty adjusting to the problems of the second half of life. Unfortunately, many of those who could benefit from psychotherapy are ashamed to seek it, or do not know where to look for it. Worse yet, some individuals are wasting hundreds and even thousands of dollars on treatment which for them is inappropriate, useless, and even harmful.

Psychotherapy is treatment for mental and emotional disorders. It involves a patient (often referred to as the client) and a therapist with whom the patient talks over his problems. The therapist assists the client to better understand himself or herself and to become a happier, better adjusted person who is capable of coping with his or her life situation. It is this aspect that distinguishes psychotherapy from other ways of treating persons with mental problems.

Other methods include psychosurgery (removing part of the brain), psychopharmacology (controlling behavior through drugs), and conditioning (which applies the same principles used in training rats to run mazes.) Only psychotherapy seeks to remove emotional disorders by increasing the patient's self-understanding. There are many kinds of people who practice psychotherapy: psychologists, psychiatrists, psychoanalysts, social workers and even clergymen. Also, there are many different schools of thought about how psychotherapy should be conducted.

Dr. Brink has served as a psychological consultant to a chain of convalescent hospitals and has written articles for Modern Maturity, the Journal of Individual Psychology, and the International Journal of Aging and Human Development.

Understanding differences in therapy, particularly as related to the concerns of those over 40, may be achieved most effectively by examining three case studies.

Edgar was a crotchety septuagenarian. He lost his wife when he was 60 and was forcibly retired from his job 5 years later. Although enjoying his work, he looked forward to the leisure time brought by retirement. Edgar's little home had a basement equipped with a shop, where he could spend days on end working.

At first, retirement went well for him. The only thing he really lacked was someone to share and appreciate his interests. Unfortunately, the Chicago suburb in which Edgar lived was planning to construct a new civic center, and his property was condemned. Edgar's children had all moved out of state. Rather than join them, he decided to return to the Chicago neighborhood of his youth. There, he was able to find a converted retirement hotel. On the face of it, this appeared to be an ideal arrangement; however, Edgar somehow ceased to enjoy life. The old neighborhood had changed. Worse yet, he was thoroughly bored, with nothing better to do than sit around and complain all day long. Some of the other residents of the hotel, especially the ladies, began to take offense at some of Edgar's language.

Edgar realized that he was not happy. But he was willing and interested enough to try to reverse his situation. This is generally the first step toward getting help. Edgar heard from a young worker at the hotel about a psychotherapist who was supposed to be good and became a client. Since he could not afford individual treatment, Edgar signed up for group therapy.

When he showed up for his first session, Edgar discovered that he was the oldest person present. He began to wonder if the other members of the group, or even the therapist, would be able to understand his specific problems. After two sessions, Edgar decided that he was not getting anything out of the group.

Edgar's experience is not rare. Unfortunately, just about anyone can set himself up and offer to solve people's emotional problems by doing something with them, to them, or for them. The line between psychotherapist and guru is often very fine. If you want to make sure that you are not patronizing a quack, demand to see the psychotherapist's credentials. Be cautious if the *psychotherapist* can only produce a certificate or diploma from some special institute that you never heard of. Such *credentials* are no substitute for university training. Most reputable psychotherapists do attend such institutes, but only after they have earned a doctoral degree at a university. Edgar's psychotherapist, it turned out, had been a high school dropout. He was smooth and charming, but lacked any qualification for this kind of work.

Fortunately for Edgar, he stopped by his neighborhood mental health center. There, he was able to see a social worker knowledgeable in the problems of the aged. She listened carefully as he talked about his problems. She invited Edgar to a senior citizens social center not far from his residence. When he came over, she showed him around the center and casually mentioned the need for some repairs. He eagerly volunteered his services, which gave him a chance to feel useful and important again. He had felt that way on his job, and also in his basement workshop, but not in his retirement hotel room.

The social worker also put Edgar in touch with some other centers who could use his skills. The change in Edgar's personality was dramatic, from crotchety to constructive. He was still very talkative around the retirement hotel, but now instead of complaints, his conversation revolved around all of his projects. He even found two other men who wanted to work with him.

Wanda was a widow in her late fifties who had taken her husband's death very hard. She seemed horribly depressed and burdened by guilt feelings. Coming to America as a young child, she held to the Old Country belief that a woman's duty in life was to serve her husband and family. It was in her role as wife that Wanda had

5. SELF MODIFICATION

sought fulfillment in life, but widowhood had now taken away that opportunity. Even so, that had not been the beginning of the problem, since the last dozen years of her marriage had been stormy ones.

Her son accurately perceived that Wanda was suffering from a heavy load of unreasonable guilt. He had taken a course in psychology in college. He remembered that Sigmund Freud and his school of psychoanalysis were greatly concerned with the dynamics of guilt complexes. At her son's encouragement, Wanda became a patient of a renowned psychoanalyst but was not very impressed with the first few sessions. The psychoanalyst was not too interested in Wanda talking about her present problems. He was more interested in her dreams and her relationship to her own father. After 6 months of these $60-an-hour sessions, there was no visible improvement, and Wanda's son agreed to call it quits.

Wanda's experience with psychoanalysis is not unusual. It is a basic tenet of Freud's doctrine that all adult emotional difficulties are due to a childhood sexual attraction to the parent of the opposite sex. Psychoanalytic psychotherapy tries to take the patient back to these experiences in the hopes that, by reliving and understanding them, a cure can be effected. Psychoanalysts are specially trained psychiatrists, and this accounts for their high hourly fees. This type of psychotherapy is usually quite extended, often lasting several years. Unfortunately, it is not appropriate to the problems of most older people, although it may be for others. Freud himself advised against the use of psychoanalysis on person over forty.

Wanda finally experienced relief from her guilt-laden depression, not through the intervention of a psychoanalyst, but through pastoral counseling given by her priest. Father Bauer, like many younger clergymen, had taken extensive training in psychotherapy. Though he was not as well trained in Freudian theory as was the psychoanalyst, the priest did enjoy two advantages.

First, he was better versed in the specific problems of the aging. Second, he could talk to Wanda in terms she could understand: sin and atonement. Wanda had lingering doubts about whether she had been a good wife. She really blamed herself for the problems in her marriage. Though her husband had died of natural causes, she thought that she might have been the cause of his death, that maybe God had punished her in this way for being a bad wife. For this type of problem, a theological approach often proves more fruitful than a psychoanalytic one.

Anna was nearly 80 and living with a married daughter. For the last 5 years Anna had experienced a progressive loss of memory. At first, she just forgot a few insignificant things, such as where she had placed her reading glasses. Gradually, the problem got more serious until she sometimes could not maintain a conversation: she forgot what she had just been told and asked the same question again. At times she would get lost or would even lose her way inside her daughter's house. Anna became more and more of a burden. The advice of Anna's doctor was to have her placed in a home for the aged.

Anna's experience is all too common. Many older persons suffer from some sort of short-term memory impairment: they forget what just happened but can tell you the details of an incident that occurred half a century ago. All sorts of medical theories have tried to explain this phenomenon of senility. The one taught in most medical schools is that such mental deterioration is caused by physical changes in the brain . . . and is irreversible. Therefore, most physicians and medically trained psychiatrists tend to give up too easily on an older person with a failing memory.

Fortunately for Anna, her daughter did not take the advice of the first doctor. They saw another physician, who referred Anna to a psychotherapist specializing in geriatric practice. In less than 2 months, Anna's deteriorating mental condition was reversed. This psychotherapy was not cheap. However, it was less expensive than psychoanalysis and certainly a bargain compared to the cost of keeping Anna in a home for the aged.

The cases of Edgar, Wanda and Anna illustrate some of the problems faced by persons in the second half of life. Crises such as retirement, widowhood, and physical decline must be faced without the hope that life will give us a fresh start. Many older persons who were able to maintain their mental health all through their lives find that they need help in their later years. However, unlike the child, adolescent, or young adult, older persons have a proven track-record of coping effectively with life's problems. With a little psychotherapy from someone who truly understands the stresses of aging, many of them can find satisfaction and fulfillment in their lives.

The three cases discussed show how to avoid some of the pitfalls in psychotherapy. Edgar, Wanda and Anna found successful psychotherapeutic intervention when they were referred to someone knowledgeable in the problems of the aging. These case studies also illustrate three places to find reliable help.

First, a public mental health agency has trained personnel, at manageable levels of cost. If such an agency cannot provide you with the help you need, it is in touch with specialized professionals in private practice. Second, your clergyman is a good place to start. Many priests, ministers, and rabbis have had training in pastoral counseling and can perform psychotherapy effectively. Likewise, if they cannot, they are good references for competent professional help. Third, your family doctor can be a good reference. He has access to professionals in related fields.

All of these people can help an aged person in his or her attempt to cope with problems. However, these mental health resources do not go out looking for people to help. It is the responsibility of the aged and their families to seek help.

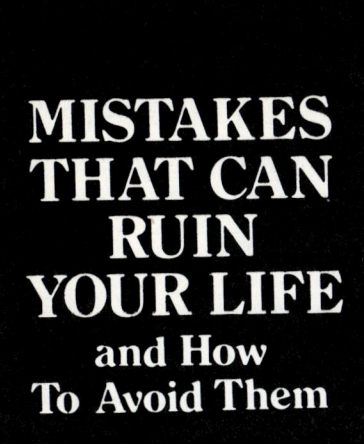

MISTAKES THAT CAN RUIN YOUR LIFE
and How To Avoid Them

Two noted doctors tell how you may be causing your own emotional problems and what you can do to find inner peace

ARNOLD LAZARUS, Ph.D., AND ALLEN FAY, M.D.

Two behavorial experts, Dr. Arnold Lazarus and Dr. Allen Fay, have found that most of us grow up believing things that simply are not true. By the time we are adults, we are locked into these beliefs which cause us nothing but misery and emotional pain. In this excerpt from their new book, the two doctors list the most common of these mistaken beliefs, explain them fully and give step by step instructions on how to rethink and change so that you will avoid making, or continue making, these mistakes that can ruin your life.

Mistake #1
Don't make mistakes

A junior business executive had many creative ideas that she repeatedly failed to mention at staff meetings because she was afraid she might be wrong and thus not be promoted. When the time came for evaluations, her employers regarded her as unimaginative and did not promote her.

She believed: (1) People will think less of me if I make mistakes. (2) I appear stupid or foolish if I make mistakes. (3) If I make a mistake, try to cover it up. DO YOU BELIEVE ANY OF THIS?

How To Change

A. Rethinking
1. Consider the idea that to make mistakes can be desirable.
2. One of the major ways of learning is through mistakes. They provide clues for further growth.
3. Being right all the time leads to the constant need to be on guard. It leaves one tense and defensive.
4. People who observe your mistakes will be relieved to see that you are human, and a closer relationship will thus be possible. If someone puts you down, such criticism probably arises from the other person's insecurity.

B. Corrective Behavior
1. Draw attention to some of the mistakes you make instead of covering them up. (We recognize that in certain situations it is necessary to cover up mistakes, but such situations are few and far between.)
2. You might even deliberately go out of your way to make some minor mistakes.
3. In a pocket notebook, make a check mark every time you catch yourself covering up a mistake, or when you fail to take action for fear of making a mistake. Tally the total at the end of each week. (We ask you to keep a record of events because by becoming aware of your actions you automatically gain greater control over them.)

Mistake #2
Try to be good at everything, or pretend that you know everything

A gifted writer had won prizes for his short stories and for two plays. He had also invented several industrial appliances. Yet he was extremely frustrated over the fact that poor coordination prevented him from excelling in sports.

He believed: (1) Being beaten by others, and being no good at certain things or in certain situations, is a sign of my stupidity and incompetence. (2) If I try hard enough I can excel at anything and everything. (3) To show that I cannot do something, is to display my basic inferiority. DO YOU BELIEVE ANY OF THIS?

How To Change

A. Rethinking
1. Consider the reality that everyone has major limitations. If you are a good musician, carpenter or typist, why get upset if you have no talent at painting, playing bridge, solving math problems, or whatever!
2. Most people aren't exceptionally good at anything. At best they do certain things well. In a complex and highly specialized society such as ours, it is impossible to have more than a vague working knowledge in most areas.
3. The idea that you can master anything if you really put your mind to it is damaging, because many people waste their time and energy trying to prove the impossible to themselves and to others.
4. Saying "I don't know" is more likely to earn respect for your integrity rather than disdain for your ignorance.

B. Corrective Behavior
1. Observe the settings and situations in which you hesitate to say "I don't know," and where you actually pretend to be well informed on a subject about which you know little. A common example is when someone mentions a book that you have not read, and you nod your head knowingly as if you've read it.
2. If there are times or places where you act like a know-it-all,

5. SELF MODIFICATION

try admitting your failings and see whether the results are generally in your favor. (We predict that people will tend to like and trust you more.)
3. If you engage in social pastimes such as tennis or golf, do you behave as though a million dollars were at stake on every stroke? If so, deliberately tell yourself "it's only a game" and enjoy the mastery of trying to do *your* best (instead of *the* best) so that you genuinely enjoy yourself—win or lose.

Mistake #3
The less you disclose about yourself the better off you will be

A young woman sought therapy because she felt depressed, lonely, and also suffered from feelings of "unreality." Her family had taught her to keep all her opinions to herself and to reveal as little as possible to other people.

She believed: (1) If other people know what I am really like, they will automatically think less of me. (2) Familiarity breeds contempt, so try to remain mysterious. (3) The strong, silent type of person is a good model of mental health. DO YOU BELIEVE ANY OF THIS?

How To Change

A. Rethinking
1. Consider very carefully the fact that close and meaningful friendships are impossible without mutual trust, confidences and personal revelations.
2. While it can be wise to keep your opinions to yourself in certain work-related situations (for example, it may not be prudent to tell your employer what you really think about him), it is damaging to carry this guarded attitude into your personal encounters.
3. Familiarity breeds contempt only among the contemptible! To avoid shared feelings and intimacies with significant others is to guarantee a lonely and detached existence.
4. The very few people who may try to use personal information against you could never be "friends" and are best dropped from your social circle.
5. If you pretend to be what you think others want you to be, you will never know what it is like to be loved for what you really are.

B. Corrective Behavior
1. Make a list of anything you have ever done, felt, or thought about, which you have never disclosed to anyone. Then try to decrease the items on this list by confiding them to trusted others.
2. Take the risk of being a more open and self-disclosing person. Then see whether you find that your dealings with other people become closer, more comfortable and much deeper.

NOTE: We are not asking you to give up being tactful or discreet while correcting all the mistakes listed here. Don't go overboard and "spill your guts" to all and sundry. We hope you will extract and apply the balanced perspectives that we intend to convey.

Mistake #4
Other people are happy

A woman of 26 who had very little social life was quite depressed. On a spring day while glancing out the window she commented: "Look at all those happy couples. Why am I so lonely and miserable? Why me?"

She believed: (1) Most other people are happy, they may have problems "but not like mine." (2) People who have extrinsic marks of success (wealth, fame, good looks) are happy, or happier than people who don't. (3) "I wish I were somebody else." DO YOU BELIEVE ANY OF THIS?

How To Change

A. Rethinking
1. In most instances it is not true that other people are happy. You simply assume that they are.
2. Everyone has problems and virtually everyone in this world has at some time been depressed and even had suicidal thoughts.
3. Tens of millions of people live under conditions of incredible hardship—poverty, starvation, illness and deformities of all kinds.

B. Corrective Behavior
1. When walking in the street, using public transportation, or while at work or at school, look at other people's expressions. Have your observations been correct about how happy other people *look*?
2. Ask people you know very well if they are happy. If they say yes, ask what makes it that way for them. If not, ask what is missing.
3. Look for problems, limitations, hang-ups and suffering in those you think are happy in order to get a balanced perspective.

Mistake #5
Make sure that you please other people and that they like and approve of you

A young woman who went out of her way to please everybody to win affection found herself in a difficult position when several intimate friends would make conflicting demands. Of course, her own needs were never expressed, and she began to experience anxiety and panic.

She believed: (1) It is better to please other people than to please myself. (2) If I constantly go out of my way to please other people, they will like and respect me. (3) Putting other people's needs before my own will permit me to count on them when I need them. DO YOU BELIEVE ANY OF THIS?

How To Change

A. Rethinking
1. People who try to please everybody tend to end up being nothing to themselves. When you are nothing to yourself, how can you be something to anyone else?
2. People who do not act in their own interest do not seem "real," and others tend to be very uncomfortable around them.
3. Even if you could please everyone, you would be in a vulnerable position. As soon as someone showed displeasure you would be completely thrown because you would not have acquired appropriate ways of responding to even the mildest criticism. Learning how to risk others' displeasure and how to deal with it when it does occur is a necessary part of growth.

B. Corrective Behavior
1. Practice doing more things to please yourself, even when this sometimes runs counter to the needs of others.
2. In every situation where decisions are made, try to think: "What would be best for me?"

Mistake #6

You must earn happiness

A middle-aged woman's puritanical background led her to believe that she was not entitled to happiness unless she first did something worthwhile. Whenever she felt spontaneous feelings of pleasure or contentment (which was not too often!) she immediately became guilty and anxious, unless she was able to justify her good feelings.

She believed: (1) The purpose of life is to be productive—not happy. (2) Those who value happiness are self-indulgent pleasure-seekers who will never get ahead. (3) Beware of pleasure and happiness, for it is always followed by pain and misery. DO YOU BELIEVE ANY OF THIS?

How To Change

A. Rethinking
1. Consider the proposition that happiness is a birthright. You are alive, therefore you are entitled to happiness.
2. Remember that too many people who faithfully follow the prescription to work hard, sacrifice and get ahead either "crack up" or find an emotional vacuum at the end of it all.

B. Corrective Behavior
1. Spend at least one hour per day doing something for "pure pleasure." (Take care here that your pleasure-activities do not conflict with another goal. For example, if you wish to lose weight, do not choose an hour's worth of eating for your "pure pleasure.")
2. Make a list of those things that have been fun for you, or could be fun. Systematically try to inject more and more of these "fun things" into your daily activities. For example, if you enjoy concerts, dances, swimming, painting, bowling, reading, etc., increase doing whatever turns you on.

Mistake #7

Play it safe. Don't take risks

A 48-year-old druggist who worked in a hospital dispensary was distressed over the fact that he had missed the opportunity to open a drugstore with one of his friends. "I didn't want to take any chances. My friend then asked someone else to join him in the venture, and one year later they opened up two new branches."

He believed: (1) It is vital to check and recheck everything and to be careful before I leap. (2) Play it close to home and I won't get hurt. (3) Security is more important than happiness.

DO YOU BELIEVE ANY OF THIS?

How To Change

A. Rethinking

1. Very often, when you keep "looking before you leap" you end up "missing the boat." It is wise to give careful consideration to certain matters, but sometimese when you "leap before you look," you may "hit the jackpot."

2. Life itself entails a series of risks.

3. The old philosophy—nothing ventured, nothing gained—underscores the fact that people who avoid risk-taking gain nothing but loneliness and frustration. Many people who feel alone in this world do not venture out of their ruts but keep hoping that by some stroke of fortune, good things will just happen to come their way.

4. Do you know *anyone* who leads a happy and fulfilling life who does not take risks?

B. Corrective Behavior

1. Ask yourself: "What can I start doing that I have avoided doing?" Then take the risk of doing some of these specific things: for example, asking for a raise, asking for a date, inviting someone over, revealing an intimate feeling, or expressing a different point of view.

2. Take at least one psychological risk each day. (Example: "I spoke back to my uncle." "I refused to work overtime." "I asked a friend to pay back the money he owed me.") At the end of a week, if you have taken seven or more risks, you will probably have more self-confidence and feel more in control of your destiny.

Mistake #8

Try to become totally independent and self-sufficient

A young man who boasted that he "did not need anyone for anything" also stated that he could see no value, no purpose, and no meaning to life.

He believed: (1) To need someone's help or assistance automatically places me in a vulnerable position. (2) I am either a self-reliant and independent person or a weak and immature underling. (3) Turning to someone else for advice or assistance is to admit your own limitations. DO YOU BELIEVE ANY OF THIS?

How To Change

A. Rethinking
1. There is a world of difference between "healthy" and "parasitic" dependency. In our complex society, we are all dependent on others to a greater or lesser extent. Most people do not grow their own food, repair their own TV sets, etc.
2. The Annie-get-your-gun philosophy ("I can do anything you can do ͵ better!") runs counter to basic psychology. Whereas a cooperative attitude ("There must be certain things you know and can do that I don't know and can't do!") can create union and trust.
3. When people pool their resources they are mutually strengthened. Successful marriages, for instance, are predicated upon mutual sharing, whereas competition between spouses is generally corrosive.

B. Corrective Behavior
1. Practice asking small favors of others. It will be difficult at first but will become much easier.
2. Practice accepting compliments and saying "thank you" instead of dismissing them or putting yourself down.
3. Remember that it pays to achieve a balance between dependent and independent behaviors.

INDEX

abortion, 22, 86
accident proneness, 24
achievement, 48
Achievement Place, 174
adaptive environment, 45
adolescence, 48
adrenalin, 10
adulthood, 48
adult interventions, 44
adverse reactions, 99
affective needs, 51-54
aggression, 20, 204
Al-Anon, 118, 119
Alcohol, 105, 110-114
alcoholics, 110-114, 118-120, 180, 187, 204
Alcoholics Anonymous, 111, 113
alternative schools, 74
American Medical Association, 163
American Psychiatric Association, 13
analysis of self-control, 142
analysis of social relationships, 142
angry child, 53, 85
anti-social behavior, 23, 174
anxiety, 16, 26, 83, 84, 116
apprehensive child, 82
appropriate learning environment, 121
arterial plaque, 10
artificial flavors, 97-101, 105-106
artificial food color, 97-101, 105-106, 204
art therapy, 168-170
aspirin compounds, 98
assertive training, 81
assessment and intervention, 53
attention, 38
attention span, 49
attitude, 84
autism, 36, 64-67, 169
aversive therapy, 183, 185

behavior deficits, 143
behavior therapy, 141
behavioral analysis model, 141
behavioral assets, 143
behavioral dimensions, 36
behavioral disorders, 36-37
  placement, 80, 205
behavioral excesses, 143
behavioral models, 19
behavior modification, 38, 47, 60-63, 171-173, 183-188, 194
behavior rating scales, 36
behaviorists, 183
birth control, 86
bizarre behavior patterns, 59
bizarre techniques, 185
blood pressure, 10
boredom, 39
brain damage, 97
brain waves, 181
brutality, 19
Bureau of Child Guidance (BGG), 203

Calderone, Mary S., 24
case history,
  hyperkinesis, 95
  educable mentally retarded, 61
castration anxiety, 47
chaining responses, 60
change, 6
child development, 15
childhood psychic pain, 179
child management, 57
child mental health service training, 197-203
child observation, 52
Child Study Association of America, 19
Children's Centers Program (CCP) of the Los Angeles Unified School District, 51
cholesterol, 8
chronic misbehavers, 135
chronic traumatic neurosis, 28
classroom behavior, 168
CNS dysfunction, 134
cocaine, 115-117
cocaine anesthesia, 116
cognitive performance, 17
Committee on Drugs of the American Academy of Pediatrics, 104
community involvement, 174
competition, 8
  competitiveness, 9
confusion, 26
Connor's Rating Scale, 99
contact lenses, 106
constant motion, 92
consultant teacher approaches, 73
continuation schools, 71
coronary artery disease, 8
counseling techniques, 38
criminal behavior, 153, 205
  causes, 154
  to support drug habits, 158
criminology, 152-156
crisis-teacher resource room, 71
criticism, 54
cruelty, 19
curriculum materials, 50

dance therapy, 168-170
deaf children, 58
death, 5, 27
delinquency, 123-126
delusions, 13
Department of Health, Education and Welfare, 99
dependency needs, 16
depressed child, 53
depression, 36
deprivation, 154
desirable behavior, 184
desperation, 18, 26
destructive encounters, 49
developmental analysis, 142
developmental model, 43
diabetes, 8

Direct Analysis, 13
discipline problems, 38
  non punitive approaches, 38
discrimination, 46
disorientation, 31
disruptive behavior, 122
disruptive outbursts, 45
disruptive youth, 121-122, 174
distress, 32
disturbance, 43
divorce, 16-18
doctors,
  as pushers, 157
dreams, 33
dropouts, 69
drug abuse, 134
drug induced violence, 117
Drug Enforcement Administration, 157, 159
drugs, 157-164, 168, 180
  amphetamines, 161
  barbituates, 161
  behavior modifying drugs, 97, 100
  demerol, 159
  eskatrol, 160
  heroin, 158
  and hyperactivity, 103-104
  tranquilizers, 157
drug store thefts, 158

ecological approaches, 43
educable mentally retarded, 69, 134
educational diagnosis, 135
educational environment, 45
  programming, 70
efficacy studies, 72
Eisenhower Violence Commission, 156
electrified drinking therapy, 112
electroconvulsive therapy, 14
emotional attachments, 18
emotional disorder, 29, 168
emotionally disturbed youth, 131
empathy, 86
environment, 4
Environmental Health and Light Research Institute, 102, 106
EST, 182
etiology, 13
exhaustion, 5
extension of self, 28

fantasy, 13, 15, 20, 43, 84
fears, 47, 50
feedback system, 174
feminism, 25
fluorescent lights, 102-106
food additives, 204
food reinforcers, 192
Food Research Institute, 99
forged prescriptions, 158
free schools, 72
freedom schools, 72
Freud, Sigmund, 23, 179

gang affiliation, 143
    behavioral analysis of, 145
    problem behavior, 145
gas stove, 205
General Adaptation Syndrome, (G.A.S.), 5
goal setting, 50, 106
group community meetings, 124
group experiences, 52
group support, 6
group therapy, 13
guilt, 6, 16, 22-25, 27, 47

hallucinations, 13, 14
happiness, 18
Hari Krishna, 182
"head-down" procedure, 79
hippies, 184
homosexuals, 188
hopelessness, 26
hormone systems, 5
hostile feelings, 9
human behavior, 37, 152
humanism, 192-193
hyperactive child, 53, 94-95, 204
hyperactivity, 55, 79, 102-106
hyperkinesis, 92-93, 94-96, 97-101, 183
hypertension, 10, 180
hypochondria, 26

immediate feedback, 175
impulsive child, 82, 92, 94
inadequacy, 47
inappropriate behavior, 143, 144
inappropriate social behaviors, 77
incarceration, 147
Incas, 117
individualized instructor, 60
individuation, 43
inservice training, 37
intervention programs, 36
intervention strategies, 48
intra-ethnic friendships, 188

juvenile courts, 126, 127, 130, 131, 144
juvenile delinquents, 130-136

Kaiser-Permanente (K-P) Diet, 97-101

lead foil shields, 102, 106
learning centers, 72
learning disabilities, 38, 97, 102-106, 201
    problems, 95
lecture system, 175
lengthy pretrial detention, 129
loner, 54
loss of control, 47

marijuana, 41, 115
masturbation, 24, 188
McVey Diagnostic Impact Center, 171
medical hazards of drugs, 116
medication, 95
meditation, 16
megavitamin therapy, 205
mental disorders, 26, 179
mental health, 36
mental health intervention, 197
Mental Health Service Program, 52
mental retardation, 36

mild behavioral disorders, 36
    moderate, 36
misplaced flight response, 5
Moonies, 182
moral standards, 30, 40
morale, 30
mother-operated intervention, 55-59
motility, 43
Motion Picture Association of America, 19
motivation, 60
motivational analysis, 142
multi-cultural schools, 72
music therapy, 168-170

National Alternative School Program, 72
National Institute of Education, 99
National Society for Autistic Children, 64, 70
negative behavior, 18
negativistic child, 81
negative reinforcement, 186
nervous gestures, 6
neurologic damage, 100
neurophysiological theories, 180
New Focus Arts and Corrections, 148-151
nonalcoholic solutions, 112
non punitive approaches, 38, 39
nor adrenalin, 10

on-task behaviors, 79
open schools, 71
operant conditioning, 60, 176, 194
order, 46
orderly exploration, 47
overconcern, 6

painful stimuli, 187
paranoid delusions, 116
parent-teacher mistrust, 202
parental expectations, 45
parental rules, 45
passive-dependent child, 81
Pavlov, Ivan, 111
pediatric clinic, 198
pediatric medicine, 52
peer reinforcement techniques, 62
perception, 43
perfumes, 98
permisiveness, 45
phobia, 26, 47, 176
physical drug addiction, 96
physical fitness, 6
physical immaturity, 94
Piaget, Jean, 196
positive behavior, 38
positive feedback, 78
positive reinforcement, 184
post traumatic neurosis, 26
praise, 38, 55
pre-delinquent children, 71
preservice training, 37
President's Commission on Law Enforcement and the Administration of Justice, 130
President's Task Force Report on Juvenile Delinquency, 130
The Primal Institute, 181

Primal religion, 181
Primal Therapy, 178-182
problem solving, 61, 201-203
programmed, 175
psychiatrists, 26
psychological counseling, 126
psychological factors, 9
psychopathic tendencies, 19
psycho-sexual adjustment, 134
psychosis, 65
psychotherapy, 147
psychotic behavior, 116
Public Law-89-164, 131
punch card, 172
punishment, 38, 190
puppet making, 169
put downs, 201

quinine, 116

Radiation Control Act of 1968, 106
radiation from television sets, 106
radiation stress, 103
rape, 137-140
    psychological damage, 139
    public attitudes toward, 138
reactions to stimuli, 49
reality, 43
recreation therapist, 170
reinforcement procedures, 13, 195
resentment, 24
residential setting, 70
Revised Beta, 132
Rikers Island, 70
Ritalin, 96, 100, 183
role playing, 60-63
role reversal, 61
runaway girls, 126

schizophrenia, 12-14, 36, 169
    etiology of, 13
    treatment, 13
schools-within-schools, 72
schools without walls, 71
security, 28
self-concept, 77
self-contained classroom, 69
self-defeating pattern, 200
self-education, 182
self-esteem, 16
self-image, 189
self-punishment, 23
Selye, Hans, 5
senility, 5
separation, 53
severe behavioral disorders, 37
severely disturbed, 45
sex crimes, 21, 137
sex education, 84
Sex Information and Education Council of the United States, 24
sex-play, 188
sex-role typing, 17
sexual activity, 84
sexual discrimination, 40
sexual disorders, 179

sexual dysfunction, 120
sexual intercourse, 18
   premarital, 85
sexualization of female crime, 127-129
sexual stereotype, 128
shaping, 194
sheltered workshop, 64
shock treatment, 111
short attention span, 94
skill training, 61, 196
Skinner, B.F., 60, 174, 194
Skinnerian Theory, 184
social behaviors, 48
social development, 17
   stage, 48
   immaturity, 95
social disorganization, 30
social drinkers, 112, 113, 114
social pressures, 111
Social Security Administration, 164
Social Service Profile, 52
Spansules, 100
special classes, 39
special education, 130-136
Special Services for Groups, Inc., 124
speech, 43

speech and hearing disorders, 134
speech impairment, 200
stealing, 121
split brains, 180
stelazine, 100
stress, 4-7, 8-11
student behavior, 121
student misbehavior, 38-39
stuttering, 180
suicide, 24
suspension, 38
Sydney Ministrey of Health, 99

teacher attention, 38
teacher perceptions, 36
   mild, 36
   moderate, 36
teacher responses, 47
teaching machines, 175, 194
temperamental characteristics, 49
time-out, 79
Toffler, Alvin, 6
tofranil, 100
token-economy cultures, 13, 174
tokens, 187
trainable mentally retarded, 134
trauma, 29

triggering behaviors, 43
trust and response stage, 44

underachievement, 81
United States Children's Bureau, 129
United States Department of Justice, 124
United States Food and Drug Administration, 104
University of Southern California School of Social Work, 124
unwed fathers, 40
unwed mothers, 40

veneral disease, 86
verbal feedback, 78
verbal psychotherapy, 170
violence, 20, 137, 205
vistril, 100
vocational materials, 70
vocational programming, 69

withdrawal, 49
work-study program, 39, 73

Youth Service Bureau, 124

STAFF

Publisher	John Quirk
Editor	Joseph Logan
Director of Production	Maureen Luiszer
Director of Design	Donald Burns
Photographer	Richard Pawlikowski
Research Asst.	Rod Mulock
Staff Consultant	Dona Chiappe
Editoral Asst.	Helen Flynn

Cover Design — Li Bailey of Enoch and Eisenman Inc. New York City.

Appendix: Agencies and Services for Exceptional Children

Alexander Graham Bell Association for the Deaf, Inc.
Volta Bureau for the Deaf
3417 Volta Place, NW
Washington, D.C. 20007

American Academy of Pediatrics
1801 Hinman Avenue
Evanston, Illinois 60204

American Association for Gifted Children
15 Gramercy Park
New York, N.Y. 10003

American Association on Mental Deficiency
5201 Connecticut Avenue, NW
Washington, D.C. 20015

American Association of Psychiatric Clinics for Children
250 West 57th Street
New York, N.Y.

American Bar Association
Commission on the Mentally Disabled
1800 M Street, NW
Washington, D.C. 20036

American College of Obstetricians and Gynecologists
79 W. Monroe Street
Chicago, Illinois 60603

ACLU Juvenile Rights Project
22 East 40th Street
New York, N.Y. 10016

American Diabetes Association
18 E. 48th Street
New York, N.Y. 10017

American Foundation for the Blind
15 W. 16th Street
New York, N.Y. 10011

American Medical Association
535 N. Dearborn Street
Chicago, Illinois 60610

American Orthopsychiatric Association
1790 Broadway
New York, N.Y.

American Psychological Association
1200 Seventeenth Street, NW
Washington, D.C. 20036

American Speech and Hearing Association
9030 Old Georgetown Road
Washington, D.C. 20014

Association for the Aid of Crippled Children
345 E. 46th Street
New York, N.Y. 10017

Association for Children with Learning Disabilities
2200 Brownsville Road
Pittsburgh, Pennsylvania 15210

Association for the Aid of Crippled Children
345 E. 46th Street
New York, N.Y. 10017

Association for Education of the Visually Handicapped
1604 Spruce Street
Philadelphia, Pennsylvania 19103

Association for the Help of Retarded Children
200 Park Avenue, South
New York, N.Y.

Association for the Visually Handicapped
1839 Frankfort Avenue
Louisville, Kentucky 40206

Boy Scouts of America
North Brunswick, New Jersey 08902
(Scouting information for boys with handicaps)

Camp Fire Girls, Inc.
1740 Broadway
New York, N.Y. 10019

Career Service, Rehabilitation/World
20 West 40 Street
New York, N.Y. 10018

Center on Human Policy
Division of Special Education and Rehabilitation
Syracuse University
Syracuse, New York 13210

Center for Sickle Cell Anemia
College of Medicine
Howard University
520 "W" Street NW
Washington, D.C. 20001

Child Fund
275 Windsor Street
Hartford, Connecticut 06120

Children's Defense Fund
1520 New Hampshire Avenue NW
Washington, D.C. 20036

Civil Rights Division
United States Department of Justice

Closer Look
National Information Center for the Handicapped
1201 Sixteenth Street NW
Washington, D.C. 20036

Clifford W. Beers Guidance Clinic
432 Temple Street
New Haven, Connecticut 06510

Committee to Combat Huntington's Disease
200 W. 57th Street
New York, N.Y. 10019

Child Study Center
Yale University
333 Cedar Street
New Haven, Connecticut 06520

Child Welfare League of America, Inc.
44 East 23rd Street
New York, N.Y. 10010

Children's Bureau
United States Department of Health, Education and Welfare
Washington, D.C.

Children's Center
1400 Whitney Avenue
Hamden, Connecticut 06514

Council for Exceptional Children
1411 Jefferson Davis Highway
Arlington, Virginia 22202

Epilepsy Foundation of America
1828 "L" Street NW
Washington, D.C. 20036

ERIC Document Reproduction Services (EDRS)
P.O. Box 190
Arlington, Virginia 22202

Gifted Child Society, Inc.
59 Glen Gray Road
Oakland, New Jersey 07436

Herner and Company
Clearinghouse on Programs and Research in Child Abuse and Neglect
2100 M Street NW
Suite 316
Washington, D.C. 20037

Highland Heights
651 Prospect Street
New Haven, Connecticut 06511

Institute for the Study of Mental Retardation and Related Disabilities
130 South First
University of Michigan
Ann Arbor, Michigan 48108

International Association for the Scientific Study of Mental Deficiency
Ellen Horn, AAMD
5201 Connecticut Avenue NW
Washington, D.C. 20015

International League of Societies for the Mentally Handicapped
Rue Forestiere 12
Brussels, Belgium

Joseph P. Kennedy, Jr. Foundation
1701 K Street NW
Washington, D.C. 20006

League for Emotionally Disturbed Children
171 Madison Avenue
New York, N.Y.

Little People of America, Inc.
P.O. Box 126
Owatonna, Minnesota 55060

CUSTOM PUBLISHING

CUSTOM-PUBLISHED BOOKS FOR YOUR COURSE OF STUDY

TEXTS DESIGNED FOR YOUR COURSE

Special Learning Corporation publishes books that are particularly tailored for a specific course and that fit a professor's specific needs. Special Learning Corporation will compile a book of required readings based on a bibliography selected by the professor teaching the course. These selected academic readings serve as the required course of readings and in some cases the major book for the course. It also benefits other small enrollment areas at various other colleges. Originally designed to serve small course areas in special education, e.g. *Readings for Teachers of Minimally Brain Damaged Children*, the idea spread to larger course enrollments in Special Education, Psychology, and Education.

HOW DOES CUSTOM PUBLISHING WORK?

- A professor selects a list of articles relevant to his course from a bibliography. These articles usually come from scholarly journals, magazines. The professor can also suggest other articles, unpublished papers, and articles he has written.
- Special Learning Corporation does all editoral work, clears permissions and produces the book--using the facsimile reproduction of the articles.
- The book is then used in the professor's course of study.

Pages: 192 to 224 or about 50 to 70 articles.
Price: $5.95 to $6.95 (Hardback available to libraries for $12.00).

For more information please contact:

Joseph Logan
Editor
Custom Publishing Division,
Special Learning Corporation

Special Learning Corporation
42 Boston Post Rd. Guilford, Connecticut 06437

College Catalog
SPECIAL LEARNING CORPORATION

The Special Learning Corporation has developed a series of readers designed for the college student in preparation for teaching exceptional children. Each reader in this high quality series closely follows a college course of study in the special education field. Sending for our free college catalog will provide you with a complete listing of this series, along with a selection of instructional materials and media appropriate for use in special education.

For further information please Contact:
Joseph Logan
Editor

College Catalog Division
Special Learning Corporation
(203) 453-6525

SPECIAL LEARNING CORPORATION
42 Boston Post Rd. Guilford, Conn. 06437

1978 Catalog
SPECIAL LEARNING CORPORATION

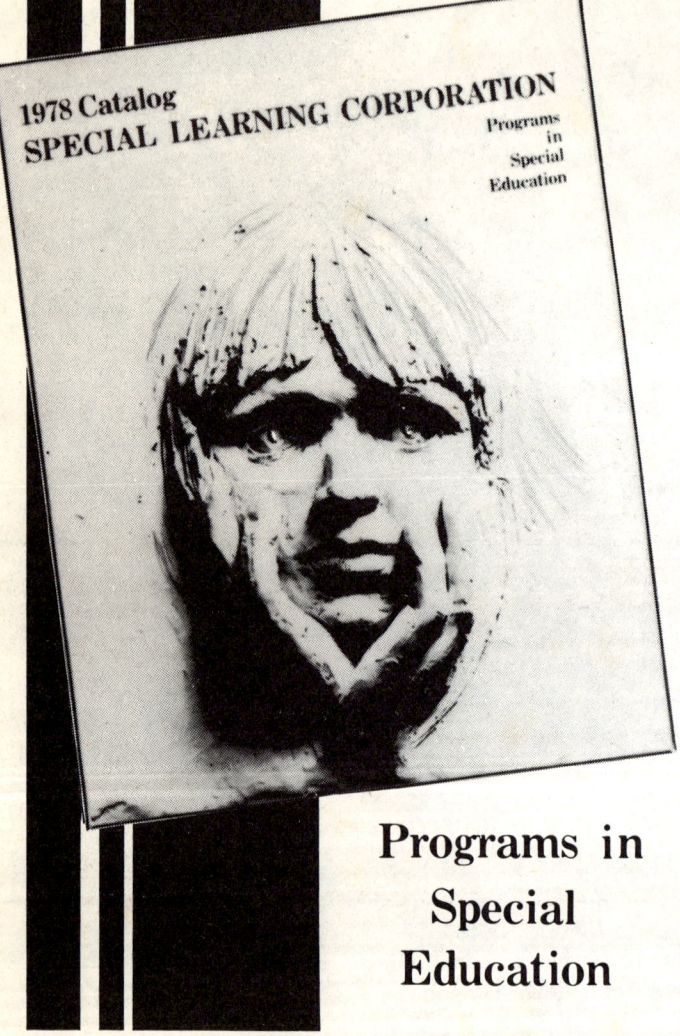

Programs in Special Education

Table of Contents

Basic Skills

I. Language Arts

II. Self-instructional Special Education Math

III. Mathematics

IV. Special Education Materials

V. Early Childhood Education

VI. Bi-lingual Programs-L.A. and Math

VII. College and Professional Books

VIII. Media-cassettes, films filmstrips

IX. Social Learning

X. Science

XI. Testing Materials

XII. Mainstreaming Library

- special education ● learning disabilities ● mental retardation
- autism ● behavior modification ● mainstreaming ● gifted and talented
- physically handicapped ● deaf education ● speech and hearing
- emotional and behavioral disorders ● visually handicapped
- diagnosis and placement ● psychology of exceptional children

Special Learning Corporation
42 Boston Post Rd. Guilford, Connecticut 06437 (203) 453-6212

COMMENTS PLEASE:

SPECIAL LEARNING CORPORATION
42 Boston Post Rd.
Guilford, Conn. 06437

SPECIAL LEARNING CORPORATION

COMMENTS PLEASE:

Does this book fit your course of study?

Why? (Why not?)

Is this book useable for other courses of study? Please list.

What other areas would you like us to publish in using this format?

What type of exceptional child are you interested in learning more about?

Would you use this as a basic text?

How many students are enrolled in these course areas?
_____ Special Education _____ Mental Retardation _____ Psychology _____ Emotional Disorders
_____ Exceptional Children _____ Learning Disabilities _____ Other _____

Do you want to be sent a copy of our elementary student materials catalog?

Do you want a copy of our college catalog?

Would you like a copy of our next edition? ☐ yes ☐ no

Are you a ☐ student or an ☐ instructor?

Your name _____ school _____

Term used _____ Date _____

address _____

city _____ state _____ zip _____

telephone number _____

CUT HERE • SEAL AND MAIL

B/M